Indian Philosophy

Indian Philosophy

An Introduction to Hindu and Buddhist Thought

Richard King

Georgetown University Press

Georgetown University Press
Washington, D.C. 20007

Typeset in Times
by Norman Tilley Graphics, and
printed and bound in Great Britain
by MPG Books Ltd, Bodmin

ISBN 0-87840-756-1

Library of Congress Cataloging-in-Publication Data

King, Richard, 1966-
Indian philosophy : an introduction to Hindu and Buddhist thought / Richard King.
p. cm.
Includes bibliographical references.
ISBN 0-87840-758-1 (paper)
1. Philosophy, Indic. I. Title.
B131.K49 1999
181'.4—dc21 99-25986
CIP

There are times in life when the question of knowing if one can think differently than one thinks, and perceive differently than one sees, is absolutely necessary if one is to go on looking and reflecting at all. People will say, perhaps, that these games with oneself would be better left backstage; or, at best, that they might properly form part of those preliminary exercises that are forgotten once they have served their purpose. But then, what is philosophy today – philosophical activity, I mean – if it is not the critical work that thought brings to bear on itself? In what does it consist, if not in the endeavor to know how and to what extent it might be possible to think differently, instead of legitimating what is already known?

Michel Foucault (1992), *The Use of Pleasure. The History of Sexuality*, vol. 2, London: Penguin, pp. 8–9

Contents

Acknowledgements

Most of this work was written during a sabbatical leave period from January to August 1998, but represents reflections based upon a course on Indian philosophy that I have taught a number of times over the past nine years. I would like to thank the students involved in such courses for their enthusiasm, interest and willingness 'to think differently'. I would also like to thank Jane Feore, for initially approaching me with the idea of writing a new introduction to Indian philosophy, and Helen Galassini and the rest of the team at Edinburgh University Press for the efficiency and care they have taken in all stages in the production of this work. Mention should also be made of my colleagues in the Department of Religious Studies at the University of Stirling, for taking on my administrative and teaching responsibilities during that time.

I would like to express my indebtedness to Dr Daniel Mariau of the University of Hull for first introducing me to the profundities of Indian philosophical thought as an undergraduate and for encouraging me to pursue my interests further. Particular mention should be made of my friend and colleague Jeremy Carrette for his encouragement and ongoing support of my work. Perhaps now this book is finished we can finally have that debate about Foucault and Nāgārjuna! Most of all I would like to thank Juli for tolerating the long periods of time when I was busy (far too busy) in 'deep *samādhi*' whilst completing this book in Spring and early Summer 1998. As always, Juli is a constant reminder to me of the importance of grounding philosophical insights in practical and lived reality.

Richard King
July 1998

Abbreviations

BS	Brahma Sūtra of Bādarāyaṇa
BS Bh	Brahma Sūtra Bhāṣya of Śaṅkarācārya
Bṛ Up	Bṛhadāraṇyaka Upaniṣad
Ch Up	Chāndogya Upaniṣad
MMK	Mūla Madhyamaka Kārikā of Nāgārjuna
NS	Nyāya Sūtra of Gotama
NB	Nyāya Bhāṣya of Vātsyāyana
NV	Nyāya Vārttika of Uddyotakara
PDS	Padārtha Dharma Saṃgraha of Praśastapāda
PS	Pramāṇa Samuccaya of Dignāga
PV	Pramāṇa Vārttika of Dharmakīrti
SK	Sāṃkhya Kārikā of Īśvarakṛṣṇa
VS	Vaiśeṣika Sūtra of Kaṇāda
VV	Vigrahavyāvartanī of Nāgārjuna
YS	Yoga Sūtra of Patañjali
YS Bh	Yoga Sūtra Bhāṣya of Vyāsa

Introduction

> Indian philosophy will become contemporarily relevant only when it is conceived as philosophy proper.
>
> Daya Krishna, 1991: 15

What is 'Indian philosophy'? Why has India generally been excluded from the history of philosophy? This book is primarily intended as an introduction to Indian philosophy and examines the main trends of thought in both the Hindu and Buddhist traditions of ancient India. In a post-colonial context, however, one can hardly write an introduction to such material, particularly when it is aimed primarily at a western audience, without taking account of the reception and location of Indian philosophical ideas within a wider cultural and political dynamic. Consequently, I have approached the material at hand paying close attention to the question of the status of 'Indian philosophy' as a type of 'philosophy'. The main motivation behind this work then is to challenge the parochialism of 'western philosophy' and to contribute to the growth of a relatively new, and much-maligned, field known as 'comparative philosophy'. In this respect, this work represents the first step in an attempt to think through the implications of a post-colonial approach for the study and practice of philosophy as a cross-cultural phenomenon.

Most university courses on Indian philosophy, particularly in Britain, are offered in departments of Religion and not Philosophy. Why is this the case? Some might argue that the study of Indian thought requires a thorough grounding in the language and culture of India and should be left to the professional Indologist. Since most western philosophers do not read Sanskrit, Indian philosophical materials remain beyond their purview. This argument, however, is not applied consistently. Most western philosophers display no such anxiety when it comes to discussing and interpreting the works of Plato and Aristotle, even if their only medium is that of a modern translation from the ancient Greek. Moreover, the idea that ancient Greece represents the roots of western civilisation and is thereby more understandable to the westerner than Indian culture is as problematic as it is overstated (Bernal, 1987; see also Chapters 1 and 2). We are no longer in a position, therefore, to dismiss 'Indian philosophy' on the grounds of its linguistic and cultural 'otherness'. The time has come then for a repudiation of the simplistic separation of 'us' from 'them' and the Orientalist tropes associated with the construction of 'East' and 'West' (Said, 1978; King, 1999).

I have deliberately avoided dividing chapters into separate accounts of the different schools of thought (*darśana*), as I wanted to present the history of Indian philosophy as a history of real debates. Philosophies are developed through debate and interaction with other points of view. Introductions to Indian philosophy have sometimes given the impression that the *darśanas* are static and self-contained world-views that do not live, breathe or develop over time. Such an approach tends to represent Indian philosophical ideas as well-established dogmas rather than as theories contested in inter-scholastic debates. Consequently, I have chosen to organise the material around specific themes and philosophical questions rather than providing separate chapters on each school. I hope that most of these themes will be familiar to the western reader and will provide an map for exploring the varieties of ancient Indian philosophy.

The thematic approach, of course, has its own limitations. All schools of Indian philosophy have something to say about all of the issues discussed within this book (and much more besides). To include each school's view on every issue, however, would undermine my broader aim which is to provide an introduction to these schools in terms of their primary interests and orientations. I have endeavoured to refer to the wider context of opinion wherever possible but beg the reader's forgiveness for the inevitable omissions.

Most notable amongst these omissions is the role played by Jainism and so-called sectarian movements such as the Śaiva philosophical schools in the history of Indian philosophy. This is a major drawback but became unavoidable due to limitations of space. I have also made no attempt to provide an account of the views of contemporary Indian philosophers. Again, this was not due to some misguided belief that Indian philosophy is something that 'happened in the past'. My concern throughout has been to provide a useful introductory primer to the 'classical' traditions of Indian thought. With that aim in mind I have spent considerable time discussing the various schools of Buddhist philosophy in India. Sometimes the mistaken assumption is made that 'Indian' equates with 'Hindu', thereby silencing or marginalising the very real contribution that Buddhist thinkers made to Indian philosophical debate for well over a millennium.

The contemporary Indian philosopher Daya Krishna has criticised accounts of Indian philosophical schools which characterise them as homogeneous and inflexible approaches to reality.

> They are treated as something finished and final. No distinction, therefore, is ever made between the thought of an individual thinker and the thought of a school. A school is, in an important sense, an abstraction. It is a logical construction springing out of the writings of a number of thinkers who share a certain similarity of outlook in tackling certain problems ... All that Śaṅkara has written is not strictly Advaita Vedānta. Nor is all that Īśvarakṛṣṇa has written, Sāṃkhya. Unless this is realized, writings on Indian philosophy will continuously do injustice either to the complexity of thought of the individual thinker concerned, or to the uniqueness of the style of thought they are writing about.
>
> Daya Krishna, 1991: 14

In my own humble way, I have attempted to write an account of Indian philosophical ideas that is sensitive to the innovativeness of individual thinkers as well as to the broader scholastic (*darśana*) and traditional (*saṃpradāya*) allegiances which serve as the platform for their speculations. The astute reader will notice, for instance, the distinctions made between the philosophy of Śaṅkara (eighth century CE) and the interpretations of his thought by the subsequent Advaita Vedānta tradition (Chapter 9). Following in the spirit of Daya Krishna's work, I have also refrained from the tendency to define 'classical Sāṃkhya' as the philosophy of Īśvarakṛṣṇa (Chapter 8). In general, I believe that greater emphasis should be placed upon the contestatory nature of philosophy in ancient India, not just between schools but within them as well. There were no doubt rival strands of Advaita philosophy during Śaṅkara's time, though we are only really aware today of examples such as the linguistic-monism of Bhartṛhari (fifth century CE), the Śaiva traditions of Kashmir and of disputes between Maṇḍana Miśra (seventh to eighth century CE) and Śaṅkara. Similarly, Īśvarakṛṣṇa's version of Sāṃkhya represents one, albeit historically influential, strand of Sāṃkhya thought, but was by no stretch of the imagination the only strand in existence at that time.

Although philosophy is often understood to be a form of highly abstract theorising, it remains a specific (some might say peculiar) type of practice. I have tried to emphasise the contextual nature of the *practice* of Indian philosophy by focusing upon the development of the *vāda* rules of debate (see Chapter 6). In so doing I hope to have demonstrated not only that the history of Indian philosophy is, contrary to the view of Anthony Flew (1971), a history of argumentation and debate, but also the role played by the *pramāṇa-vāda* framework in the interactive development of Indian philosophical ideas. Moreover, by drawing attention to the development of philosophical world-views in terms of the formalised practice of debate, I wish to 'breathe some life' into contemporary western understandings of the history of Indian philosophy. Although this book is a brief introduction to some very ancient world-views, I wish to reinvigorate our engagement with them by emphasising the way in which philosophical world-views are developed, that is, in the lively 'to-ing and fro-ing' of a debate between historical human beings. Indian philosophical texts may appear as dry and arid as some of their western counterparts at times but we should not lose sight of the history of debate and experimentation which underlies them.

CHAPTER 1

India and the History of Philosophy

– DEFINING THE SUBJECT-MATTER –

What is 'Indian philosophy' and what is particularly distinctive about it? These are the sorts of questions one would usually expect to ask when introducing the topic of this book. My initial response to such questions, however, is to respond with a set of my own: What do we mean by 'philosophy'? When one talks of 'Indian philosophy' is one implying that there is a singular way of thinking that is peculiar to Indian culture and the Indian people? Indeed, how useful is it even to talk of 'Indian philosophy' as if it were a homogeneous and unified phenomenon? Should we not talk instead of a variety of Indian philosophies?

Clearly, there is no such thing as 'Indian philosophy' if by that one means a particular way of looking at the world that is peculiar to and universally accepted by the people of India. Nor indeed is there really something called 'western philosophy' in the sense of a homogeneous and specifically western way of looking at the world. This, of course, is not all that surprising if one ponders the rich diversity of human experiences that make up the various cultures of the world. Categories such as 'western', 'eastern', or even 'Indian' simply cannot capture the heterogeneities that they are meant to represent. Nevertheless, European and Indian cultures have, until the advent of colonialism, developed in relative (though not absolute) isolation from each other. One would expect, therefore, to find particular traditions of intellectual thought within both that are culturally specific and a number of broad cultural assumptions within both that differentiate their respective approaches.

What, though, do we mean by philosophy? There are a number of ways in which the term 'philosophy' is used in the modern English language. One can use the term in a purely descriptive or doxographical manner to refer to the world-view or ideological position of a particular person or community.

In this sense one can talk of the philosophy of the United Nations, the philosophy of corporate management or the philosophy of my late grandfather ('never turn down a free drink'). Philosophy, however, is often used to denote a specific type of intellectual activity – something like 'the exercise of systematic reflection'. One can buy books, sign up for evening classes, do university degrees and even pursue an academic career as a lecturer in 'philosophy', so presumably the word must stand for something.

In this more specific sense 'philosophy' denotes a particular type of mental activity – a form of practice, often described as something like 'the systematic and rigorous exercise of rationality'. In the modern era the term also refers to the discipline of professional philosophy, that is to a substantive academic discipline sanctioned by the institution of the modern university and practised by a group of professional academics who call themselves philosophers. Professional philosophers sometimes conflate their own academic discipline with the broader set of practices that might be deemed as the practice of 'philosophy' by claiming that to engage in rigorous and rational discourse, of a highly technical and increasingly specialised nature, requires one to have undertaken some professional (i.e. academic) training in the subject. In the narrowest sense of the term this is no doubt the case since there is a loosely defined canon of respected thinkers who are described as philosophers (the canon differs somewhat according to the tradition of philosophy) with a preponderance, one might note, of deceased, white men. To study philosophy then is to be introduced to these figures and their writings and to learn a specific craft – the art of 'doing philosophy'. Often, the Greek etymological roots are appealed to – *philosophia* – 'love of wisdom', in an attempt to define philosophy as the search for wisdom *par excellence*. In this sense we should note that

> The discipline of philosophy emerged at a certain moment in history. It was not born like a natural organism. Rather, it was an artificial construct that had to be invented and legitimized as a new and unique cultural practice. This took place in Athens in the fourth century BCE, when Plato appropriated the term 'philosophy' for a new and specialized discipline – a discipline that was constructed in opposition to the many varieties of *sophia* or 'wisdom' recognized by Plato's predecessors and contemporaries.
>
> Nightingale, 1995: 14

Western philosophers tend to agree that 'philosophy' originated in ancient Greece. One should note, however, that there is no such unanimity about what philosophy actually is amongst those people who have described themselves as philosophers. It is equally clear that conceptions of philosophy are not only diverse in the contemporary context but have undergone a number of significant shifts throughout the centuries. Before the social, political and intellectual revolution known as the Enlightenment occurred in eighteenth century Europe, the natural sciences were known as 'natural philosophy' – that is, the systematic investigation of the natural world. The broad subject-matter of 'philosophy' at this time seems to have been questions of ontology (i.e. questions about the nature of existence). However, with the rise of the natural sciences (especially physics) as a distinctive intellectual discipline, philosophers tended to shift their attention towards what one might call the 'metaphysical'. The distinction between physics and metaphysics, of course, is based upon Christian and Platonic dualism which sharply distinguishes between the material and the spiritual realms – the former being the domain of physics and the natural sciences and the latter that of metaphysics. However, with the growth of secularism in Northern Europe during the Enlightenment, philosophy increasingly divorced itself from theology which was more obviously concerned with the realm of the spiritual.[1]

An excellent example of this trend can be seen in the work of the philosopher Immanuel Kant. Kant's *Critique of Pure Reason* represents perhaps the first systematic attempt by a European thinker to define the limits of rational enquiry. His work offered something of an assault upon the viability of metaphysical speculation. For Kant the world of noumena (things in themselves) cannot be directly experienced. Human beings, by virtue of the nature of their cognitive faculties, can only perceive phenomena (things as they appear). Thus, one of Kant's projects was appropriately entitled *Religion within the Limits of Reason Alone*. With the decline of ecclesiastical religion in intellectual circles and the spectacular successes of the natural sciences, metaphysics has become of less and less interest to the contemporary philosopher.

Having lost the 'physical' domain to the sciences and the 'metaphysical' to theology, philosophy in the modern era has tended to focus increasingly upon the mental realm. Thus, philosophers, in turning their attention away from questions of ontology, began to spend more time discussing epistemology, i.e. the nature of knowledge itself. This move, however, was fairly short-lived before it was under renewed attack from the new field of psychology, which soon became a specialised and autonomous discipline in its own right. The increasing complexity of capitalist societies has led to a diversification of labour amongst intellectuals and the development of more and more specialised and autonomous intellectual and professional disciplines. With the advent of psychology, philosophy has taken what has sometimes been called 'the linguistic turn', that is, it has turned its attention to the workings of language as a means of defining itself as a substantive discipline. Thus, one finds twentieth-century philosophers such as Rudolf

Carnap (1891–1970) arguing that the old metaphysical questions of philosophy are really "pseudo-problems" which require reformulation in terms of a logical analysis of the most appropriate ways to use language. Thus, there has been a renewed interest in the link between semantics, logic and language aligned with an ongoing investigation of epistemological issues (such as discussions about the nature of perception) which remain on the fringes of psychological discourse.

From the mid- to the late nineteenth century the notion of philosophy as the 'queen of the disciplines' developed and modern professionalised philosophy was born. This view was supported by the claim that the differentiation of the natural sciences and other cognitive disciplines over the centuries has been at the expense of philosophy. However, it is clear that when one talks of philosophy in ancient Greece, medieval Europe, or the post-Enlightenment west, one is not talking about an homogeneous, cognitive discipline unaffected by the vagaries and discursive processes of history. Indeed if one argues, as I shall in this chapter, that one of the predominant features of post-Enlightenment western thought has been the tendency to conceive of rationality in opposition to tradition in general and religion in particular, it becomes apparent that the modern claim that Philosophy is the 'queen of the disciplines' amounts to little more than an attempt to locate the subject as the secular successor to Theology, which of course held the primary position of authority in European universities before its usurpation during the Enlightenment.

In the modern era many philosophers have continued to express the view that Philosophy is something of a meta-discipline which can be applied to other intellectual disciplines (for example, theology, sociology, the natural sciences etc.), and indeed to any branch of human activity in general. This view is often accompanied by the belief that philosophical thinking involves abstract reflection and the exercise of the faculty of reason in some kind of decontextualised and neutral regard, that is, 'pure argumentation' detached from particular concerns and agendas. However, modern western academic philosophy has taken on these forms as a result of its differentiation from other cognitive disciplines. The process whereby such disciplines arise, of course, is never purely intellectual and involves a number of non-discursive factors – most notably the shifts in power relations between the professional classes within European and American societies. The authority of 'Theology' in European universities was undermined by intellectuals who were unhappy not only with the metaphysical concerns of the subject but also with the power of ecclesiastical authority within society. To deny that intellectual disputes relate to questions of power relations within communities is to ignore the social, cultural and political fabric of academic life. However, 'Theology' and the Church no longer constitute an influential factor in the politics of the modern university. Despite this, many contemporary philosophers retain an air of anti-religious secularism that informs both their awareness of the nature of the discipline in which they are trained and their understanding of its variegated history.

> This secularization of the history of philosophy ... makes possible the characteristically Enlightenment distinction between religion and philosophy that is appealed to starting at the end of the eighteenth century in order to denigrate as 'merely religious' those contributions that non-Greeks may have made to the intellectual traditions out of which modern philosophy is said to have developed. Simultaneously, the secularization of philosophy makes possible claims on behalf of philosophy to an independent place in the new kind of university then being created in places like Göttingen and Berlin for the purposes of training young men for careers in civil administration in service to a state that is to become a centre of power distinct from the church.
>
> Howard, 1996: 47

Contemporary western notions of the nature of philosophy are also generally dependent upon the distinction of the discipline from the 'natural sciences' and the empirical investigation of the material world on the one hand, and theology with its discursive examination of the 'spiritual' on the other. In such a context philosophy has tended to be conceived of as an abstract and solely mental activity, to be sharply distinguished from the physical and the spiritual realms. In a modern cultural environment where secular presuppositions remain at the forefront and the natural sciences have proven spectacularly successful in their manipulation and control of the natural world, philosophy has tended to align itself more closely with the methods and findings of science than with those of theology. It is important to bear this in mind and the historical reasons informing such moves when considering the question of the existence of 'philosophy' within non-western cultures.

It is also fair to say that the practice of philosophy has generally been associated in the west with highly abstract and reflective thought. Because of the intellectual skills and training usually required to pursue abstract and systematic reflection in a rigorous manner, philosophical works tend to be the product of the educated intelligentsia of any given community. 'Philosophy' as such is an activity of 'high culture'. This reflects the generally elitist nature of similar practices in other cultures.[2] Walter Ong in fact has suggested that philosophy along with the sciences and the arts are analytic procedures which

> depend for their existence on writing, which is to say they are produced not by the unaided human mind but by the mind making use of a technology that has

> been deeply interiorized, incorporated into mental processes themselves. ... Philosophy, it seems, should be reflectively aware of itself as a technological product – which is to say a special kind of very human product. Logic emerges from the technology of writing.
>
> Ong, 1982: 172

However, if philosophy is dependent upon the development of literary skills, as Ong suggests, then this would seem to negate the possibility of philosophical speculation occurring within primarily oral cultures. 'Philosophy', as usually understood, is an elitist occupation not just in the sense that it requires some training and time to pursue, but also because of the tendency for it to be associated with a systematic expression of rational reflection. Such an association, of course, immediately distinguishes philosophy from its other – the non-rational or the irrational. This is an important point since philosophy requires a demarcated area of non-philosophy in order to define itself (Deleuze and Guattari, 1994: 217–18). Indeed, as Andrea Nightingale argues in her discussion of the invention of philosophy by Plato,

> In order to create his specialized discipline of philosophy, Plato had to distinguish what he was doing from all other discursive practices that laid claim to wisdom. It is for this reason that, dialogue after dialogue, Plato deliberately set out to define and defend a new and quite peculiar mode of living and of thinking ... Indeed it was precisely by designating certain modes of discourse and spheres of activity as anti-philosophical that Plato was able to create a separate identity for 'philosophy'.
>
> Nightingale, 1995: 10–11

Attempts to define 'philosophy' in terms of the exercise of rationality have also tended to become implicated in a broader colonialist agenda. The main targets of exclusion for Plato were the sophists – represented by him as merchants (*emporos*, for example, *Sophist* 222e–224) or intellectual mercenaries, selling ideas to the highest bidder. The sophists, it should be noted, were foreigners in ancient Athenian society and were deemed suspect not only because of their 'outsider status' but also because they tended to travel from place to place unencumbered by the responsibilities of family or state. Their threat lay in their claim to offer wisdom to Athenian citizens at a price but without offering any allegiance (or taxes) to the Athenian state (Nightingale, 1995: 22–5). Similarly, Andrea Nye in her feminist reading of the history of (western) logic notes that the examples used by Aristotle in his *Prior Analytics* – a handbook for the refinement of argumentation – assume 'a specific Athenian institution of elaborate, often artificial debate in which farmers, laborers, or workers were not involved' (Nye, 1990: 42). It was also an institution and a practice that excluded women, slaves and foreigners –

all deemed irrational by Aristotle – 'the barbarian and the slave are the same by nature, making it fitting and right that the Greeks rule over them' (*Politics* I, 1: 252b5–10). As Nye notes,

> In Aristotle's *Politics*, the rationality of those who are natural rulers is continually defined in opposition to other unacceptable speech: the emotional expressions of women, the subrational words of slaves, the primitive political views of barbarians, the tainted opinions of anyone who does manual labor. ... Once rationality is defined as what is not emotional and emotionality established as the characteristic of women, once rationality is seen as a characteristic of mind, not body, and a slave is understood as what is only a body, there could be no discussion of the institutions of slavery or sexism.
>
> Nye, 1990: 50

In considering the possible existence of something resembling 'philosophy' in non-western cultures, it is important therefore to bear in mind the nature of philosophy as a form of (so-called) 'high culture' in the west. The early western orientalists tended to equate Indian culture with the Sanskritic culture of the Hindu Brahmins, thereby ignoring both the diversity of Indian culture and the possibility of alternative (or even subaltern) perspectives. It is important to realise from the outset that an introduction to Indian philosophy is not an account of the philosophical beliefs of Hindus or Buddhists in general. Such a claim would be as preposterous (if not more so given the wide gulf traditionally between the educated elite and the non-literate masses in India), as it would be to suggest that the works of Augustine or Thomas Aquinas represent the beliefs and practices of Christians, or that the Cambridge Platonists, the British Idealists or the Logical Positivists are representative of the changing philosophical opinions of the British people from the seventeenth to the early twentieth century. Nevertheless, philosophical movements and trends are representative of wider prevailing trends within cultures as a whole.

There has been a tendency within modern western philosophy to revere innovation and individual creativity at the expense of continuity and tradition. This is rooted in European Romanticism and the myth of the autonomous and creative genius. Standard histories of philosophy tend to focus upon individual thinkers as initiators of cultural change rather than as manifestations or representatives of those changes themselves. Such elitist historiography has been further enhanced by modern individualism which not only underplays the role of tradition and community in all creative and critical thought, but also perpetuates what might be called "the trickle down theory of knowledge". The Romanticist notion of the autonomous literary author is connected to another modern theme – that of the isolated reader:

> Unseating the ideology of reading as essentially and only a solitary activity challenges the hegemony of an associated model of how culture works, a conception that I call the 'trickle down' model of cultural dissemination. It holds that innovative ideas and values originate with transcendent high cultural figures and are delivered by abstracted processes – and in diluted form – to the lower (and in this model, relatively passive) levels of the socio-cultural hierarchy.
>
> Long, 1992: 205

The 'trickle down theory of knowledge' presupposes that social, historical and cultural transformations occur as the result of the inspired interventions of a small minority of cultural leaders and initiators. This approach (with its implicit distinction between the elite patricians and the plebeian masses) ignores the complexity of historical processes and the agency of the 'subaltern' in initiating new eras and ways of thinking. The 'trickle down' approach to history can be seen, for instance, in histories of philosophy which focus upon key figures and neglect the broader context in which the creative insights and actions of individuals occur. Such an approach supports the claim that philosophy is an activity of abstract reflection that is free from socio-cultural conditioning (and thus immune to sociological and cultural analysis). Such an approach also promotes a model of intellectual history which places philosophers on a pedestal as important intellectual leaders within society. This emphasis upon the autonomy and creativity of individual thinkers ignores the roles played by tradition and community in the creative expression of such intellectual 'free-thinkers'.

– HISTORIES OF WESTERN PHILOSOPHY –

Phrases like 'Indian philosophy' or 'western philosophy' are useful at a rudimentary level, but become misleading once one wishes to examine these diverse traditions with any degree of depth. Just as there is no uniform or monolithic entity known as 'western philosophy' or 'western culture', it is also the case that there is no identifiable essence or entity referred to by the term 'Indian philosophy'. This point needs reiterating since there is a tendency for the myth of cultural homogeneity to present itself in both western and Indian accounts of themselves and each other. This trait is manifested, for instance, in the tendency to provide a linear and evolutionary account of the history of western culture. Note, for instance, the frequent claim found throughout western philosophical literature that 'philosophy began with Thales'. The impression is given that there is a thread of common philosophical concern running through the works of such diverse thinkers as Plato, Aristotle, Aquinas, Hume, Kant, Wittgenstein, Heidegger, Habermas, and perhaps even Gadamer and Derrida (depending upon one's philosophical canon). This is certainly a disparate group!

One of the major problems with historical accounts of western philosophy lies in the exclusion of certain figures and movements from anything but the most cursory analysis. Of course, one has to draw the line somewhere when writing such histories, but it remains interesting to see the priorities employed in such works.[3] Attempts to construct a smooth and linear history of (western) philosophy are misleading because they portray the development of western intellectual thought in a manner which 'papers over the cracks' and avoids the ruptures, heterogeneities and discontinuities of western cultural history. Thus, Richard Rorty argues that

> We should stop trying to write books called *A History of Philosophy* which begin with Thales and end with, say, Wittgenstein. Such books are interspersed with desperately factitious excuses for not discussing e.g. Plotinus, Comte, or Kierkegaard. They gallantly attempt to find a few 'continuing concerns' which run through all the great philosophers who do get included. But they are constantly embarrassed by the failure of even the most silent and unskippable figures to discuss some of the concerns, and by those vast arid stretches in which one or other concern seems to have escaped everybody's mind.
>
> Rorty, 1984: 65

Rorty's position is that it makes no real sense to talk about 'western philosophy' since it remains a heterogeneous and unfinished project (Rorty, 1992a: 4). African philosopher Tsenay Serequeberhan, however, argues that the one shared premise that unites the modern tradition of western philosophy has been the acceptance of the cultural superiority of the west. Philosophy has tended to function as the handmaiden of European colonial dominance. Underlying modern accounts of the nature of (western) philosophy, he suggests, is

> the *singular* grounding metaphysical belief that European humanity is properly speaking isomorphic with the humanity of humans *as such*. ... Philosophy, furthermore, is the privileged discourse singularly rooted in European/human existence *as such* which articulates and discloses the *essence* of the *real*. Thus, European cultural–historical prejudgements are passed off as transcendent wisdom!
>
> Serequeberhan, 1991: 7

The classical humanist tradition in the west has tended to locate its origins in ancient Greece, attributing this region and era with the invention of logic and the establishment of a set of principles for the exercise of 'pure rationality'. Although this conception is enshrined in standard historical accounts of western philosophy it remains representative of much broader cultural perceptions about the roots of Euro-American culture. Modern academic philosophers, however, have displayed a particular tendency to locate the origins of modern western 'civilisation' in the Greek differentiation between *mythos* and *logos* – often seen as the seminal act in the invention of 'philosophy'. Indeed, one consequence of this distinction in the western context has been the tendency to draw a sharp line between mythology (denoting the sacred stories that give meaning to particular communities) and history (what actually happens in an objective sense).

The ancient Greek distinction between *mythos* and *logos* functions in a modern context to exclude a great deal from the category of 'philosophy' both within western cultures and further afield. The distinction excludes, for example, a great deal of 'African philosophy' by virtue of the cultural embeddedness of much traditional African thought in a 'story-telling' format. This is not such a problem in the quest for 'authentic Indian philosophy' since there is much in Indian culture which conforms to the narrow confines of the '*logos*' rubric. However, even here the distinction excludes material that might be of interest in the Vedic hymns, the *Upaniṣads*, and the Buddhist *sūtras* etc. Even within western philosophical circles one encounters problems with the rigid dichotomy between myth and philosophy (Hatab, 1990: ch. 6). The classification of works such as Plato's *Timaeus* as 'philosophical texts' has generally involved ignoring or suppressing the cosmogonic and mythological framework in which Plato's exposition proceeds.

Similarly, the rigid dichotomy between myth and history which characterises western modernity is also quite misleading. As French thinker Michel de Certeau has suggested, all histories are in fact 'localised fabrications (or stories) of the present' (Ahearne, 1995: 25). To say that history is fabricated is to blur the myth/history distinction by pointing out that all histories are socially located, that is to say, they provide contextualised meaning for those who adhere to them. Histories always function as sacred stories which give meaning to particular communities – i.e. they are also myths. To take a modern example, whether Darwin's theories about the origins of the human species are correct or not, they function in modern western societies as one of the primary myths for explaining human origins. This is not to say that Darwin was absolutely right in what he said, nor is it to deny the validity of what he said, it is simply a statement about the way in which Darwinian theory (or at least a popularised version of it) functions to give some sense of meaning to many groups within modern western societies.

Let me make it clear at this point what I am saying. To describe histories as 'localised fabrications' is, indeed, to undermine any notion of an objective and universal account of history. This goal is simply impossible in my view since human beings remain socially located and therefore tend to see things from a particular perspective. However, this does not mean that we cannot decide between competing histories, that we cannot appeal to events or historical facts, say, the date that Caesar crossed the Rubicon, in debates about historical events. Rather, my point is that such events or 'facts' do not exist in a vacuum – they are always embedded within particular discursive processes and histories. One can question, therefore, why Caesar crossing the Rubicon might be seen as historically important. The appeal to facts in order to establish the objective certainty of history is misleading. The point at issue is not whether certain events may or may not have happened (which, of course, can also be subject to sceptical scrutiny), rather, the issue is why such events are considered sufficiently important to include within one's historical account. What do such histories say about the interests and context of their advocates and what do they say about the people, events and movements that are ignored or silenced by such accounts?

To say that all history is fabricated, therefore, should not be seen as an attempt to falsify history, or to render historical accounts 'merely subjective'. The claim that all historical accounts are subjective privileges the historian as an autonomous and free-thinking individual. There are in fact a variety of 'voices off-stage', namely the tradition of previous and contemporary accounts in which the historian is located, as well, of course, as the traces of the past which inform the present moment. History then is neither fully 'objective' (in the sense of providing a neutral or universal account of historical events) nor is it subjective; all histories are socially located.

For most westerners it is largely taken for granted that much of their cultural heritage ultimately derives from the ancient Graeco-Roman world. This self-conception has for centuries been enshrined in the construction and continued legitimation of a 'classical' tradition represented by specific Latin and Greek texts, as well, of course, as the interpretations placed upon various artefacts and ancient monuments which are said to stand as a testament to the 'birth of western civilisation'. These materials are taken to be representative of the gradual (and largely linear) unfolding of western culture. However, as Martin Bernal (1987) has shown, the location of the roots of western culture in ancient Greece is as problematic as the exclusion of Africa and Mesopotamia from histories of western culture.

It is perhaps no exaggeration to say that intellectual resistance to engagement with 'other cultures' is severely hampered by the tendency to reify the concept of 'culture' and to conceive of these 'cultures' as self-contained and static entities. Creative hindsight allows the perception that one belongs to a fixed and well-determined history specific to a particular group or community of people. Of course, we should not ignore the very real differences between cultures which make cross-cultural engagement such a difficult but interesting proposition, but these differences are not as insurmountable as they are often represented. The tendency to treat 'cultures' as isolated and largely autonomous entities misrepresents the dynamism and internal diversity of cultures.

As has often been said, history is written by the victors. Being aware that this is the case is a beginning but is scarcely enough. One must also attempt to unearth the silences of history, the voices of the marginalised and the forgotten, the heterogeneity which is buried by singular versions of history. In one sense, the goal of unearthing the silences of our past – the subaltern perspectives on history – is an impossible task to achieve in its entirety. However, this is precisely why we can never accept a definitive account of history. As French theorist Michel Foucault points out, all histories inevitably construct their own silent spaces. For Foucault in fact it is precisely the excavation of these discursive locations which makes the work of the scholar both an ongoing and forever incomplete project. On this view the place of the intellectual is to problematise the 'normative' by focusing attention upon the way such 'received wisdom' legitimates the authority of some and silences others.

– SECULAR REASON AND THE DICHOTOMY OF TRADITION VS MODERNITY –

Modern western philosophers are heirs to the Enlightenment tradition which established a firm dichotomy between 'rationality' and 'tradition' and the explicit favouring of the former over the latter (Habermas, 1970: 90). Amongst western thinkers it is perhaps German philosopher Hans-Georg Gadamer who has paid most attention to this aspect of modern, western consciousness. Gadamer calls for a 'rehabilitation' of tradition and a rejection of the Enlightenment dichotomy between the rational and the traditional. He bases his argument upon the insight that rational thought, however critical and 'free-thinking' it might claim to be, must always occur from within a tradition itself. It makes no sense at all, Gadamer suggests, to think of rational criticism as a free-floating, neutral and ungrounded activity which can be carried out in a cultural or social vacuum.

Gadamer, in his emphasis upon the normative power of tradition, seems to imply on occasions that attempts to understand texts which belong to a different culture (and hence a different 'tradition') are deeply problematic.

> Although in the meantime the research in Eastern philosophy has made further advances, we believe today that we are further removed from its philosophical understanding. The sharpening of our historical awareness has rendered the

> translations or adaptations of the texts ... fundamentally problematic. ... We cannot speak of an appropriation of these things by the Occidental philosophy. What can be considered established is only the negative insight that our own basic concepts, which were coined by the Greeks, alter the essence of what is foreign.
> cited in Halbfass, 1988: 164

However, the so-called 'European tradition' is itself a mixture of diverse cultural sources, and there is no reason to assume that the problem of understanding *between* cultures is qualitatively different from that of understanding *within* cultures, or between different time periods of the same culture (Halbfass, 1988: 165).

Moreover, the emphasis placed upon detached and abstract rationality by western philosophers since the Enlightenment is not without its problems. Through a highly perceptive analysis of Immanuel Kant's famous essay 'What is Enlightenment?', Talal Asad demonstrates that Kant's critique of religious authority – an important theme of Enlightenment thought – occurred within a context where ecclesiastical power was already in retreat and where the distinction between public (politics) and private (religion) was already taking hold. Asad points out that the role of rationality in Kant's essay was not extended towards a critical examination of political authority. The principle of rationality has often been upheld in the west as a culturally independent and neutral faculty capable of promoting freedom of thought and thereby firmly distinguished from a dogmatic adherence to (religious) tradition. Thus, the notion of rationality which has predominated in the modern west since the Enlightenment has been unambiguously secular in form and has often been aligned with the natural sciences as the basis for a universal and objective foundation of knowledge. However, far from establishing a universal, neutral and critical faculty of reason, Asad demonstrates that Kant in fact 'proposes both a *sociological* limit (the literate, scholarly minority to whom the privilege of public criticism belongs) and a *political* one (the conditions in which one must refrain from open criticism)' (Asad, 1993: 204).

Asad examines the issue of contemporary Saudi Arabia and demonstrates that western rhetoric about 'Islamic fundamentalist opposition to the progress of modernity' is a manifestation of European Enlightenment values which ignore the possibility of the application of critical reason from within a religious tradition. Such rhetoric, of course, also occludes the sense in which many Islamic movements are reacting against what they see as a steady process of westernisation (or 'westoxification' as it is sometimes called). The western tendency to oppose tradition and modernity, when combined with an unwillingness to see this as a culturally specific distinction conditioned by cultural changes in modern European history, is clearly a major factor in the failure of the west to fully appreciate the Islamic position.

One of the obstacles confronting a proper consideration of classical Indian thought as a legitimate form of philosophising is the widely held belief that Indian thought is culturally specific (in contrast to European universalism), and fundamentally bound to a particular religious world-view. One feature likely to be pounced upon in such a context is the acceptance of authoritative testimony (*śabda*) as a valid means of knowledge (*pramāṇa*) by many schools of Indian thought. The modern western philosopher tends to view this as evidence of the theological and context-specific nature of 'traditional' (i.e. non-westernised) Indian thought. Such an attitude, of course, ignores the cultural particularity of western philosophical traditions.

Why is it then that western philosophy is usually seen as philosophy (the universal category) and 'Indian philosophy' as a particular and culturally limited set of beliefs? The major factor in the successful occlusion of the culturally specific, and hence contextually limited, nature of western cultural forms has been the violently enforced universalism imposed as a result of European colonial conquest. The political, economic and ideological supremacy of the western world since the seventeenth century tells us more about the dominance of western discourses and paradigms in contemporary philosophical debates than any claims by western philosophers to have discovered universal truths applicable beyond the confines of European culture and history. It has often been said that a language is merely a dialect backed by an army. What is often represented as philosophical truth should also be seen for what it is, namely the success of the European will to power.

However, such is the dominance of the discourses of modernity and secularism today that it is inevitable that the issue of the apparently theological nature of Indian thought be addressed if constructive progress is to proceed at all. Jitendranath Mohanty, for instance, has argued that the acceptance of tradition and authoritative testimony as a valid means of knowledge (what is known in Indian circles as *śabda-pramāṇa*) is a legitimate philosophical position to hold, relating not just to the religious insights gained from sacred scriptures (such as the Hindu Vedas) but also to any knowledge which cannot be directly verified by one's own experience (Mohanty, 1992: 232). This indeed seems to have been the position of the early Nyāya school, with emphasis placed upon the notion of *āpta* – a reliable authority. Vātsyāyana defines *āpta* as 'a person who has direct knowledge of the object concerned and is motivated by a desire to communicate the object as known by him' (commentary on *Nyāya Sūtra* 1.1.7).

Reliable testimony according to the Nyāya school is of two kinds – related to the perceptible (*dṛṣṭārtha*) and related to the imperceptible (*adṛṣṭārtha*). For example, I do not actually know, based solely upon my own perceptions, that Malaysia exists (sadly, I have never visited), but I can glean information about it from someone who has been there. Valid testimony about that which cannot be perceived in a traditional Nyāya sense related to a whole range of issues such as the nature of liberation (*mokṣa*), and the fruits of virtuous behaviour for which one is said to be reliant upon wise sages (*ṛṣi*). This category, however, also included knowledge about the material world such as the fact that objects are composed of atoms. Even today we do not actually know this to be the case from perception but are reliant for this insight upon the authoritative testimony of the scientist.

Leaving scepticism aside for the moment, it is important to acknowledge the extent to which human beings remain reliant upon the authoritative testimony of others. Taking into account the modern sense of rupture with the traditional and the religious in the post-Enlightenment west, the Nyāya acceptance of authoritative testimony can be seen as a legitimate epistemological claim about a major source of human knowledge about the world. Nevertheless, even here we should bear in mind that many Indian schools rejected the validity of authoritative testimony (see Chapter 6).

The tendency for contemporary western philosophers to reject an appeal to a higher authority reflects the modern prejudice against tradition as well as the highly developed democratic individualism of western capitalist culture which overemphasises the autonomy of the individual at the expense of the role of communities and traditions in the establishment of knowledge. These conditions, of course, did not prevail in traditional India (nor, one should note, in pre-Enlightenment Europe). Even in a contemporary context anthropologist Milton Singer notes that most of the Indians he encountered do not experience 'the coexistence of the "modern" and the "traditional" as a cultural contradiction or even a conflict' (Singer, 1971: 191). This is because much of modern Indian intellectual thought is 'quite firmly rooted in its past and its present' (Shils, 1961: 61).

In a discussion of the status of philosophy *vis-à-vis* tradition, Mohanty argues that the acceptance of Vedic revelation (*śruti*) as a valid foundation for knowledge by many Hindu philosophers does not constitute a rigid adherence to a dogmatic religious orthodoxy, but reflects instead an acknowledgement of the inevitability of tradition. Of course, as subsequent discussion of Indian philosophical works will demonstrate, there are a variety of world-views to be found in the various schools of ancient Indian thought. These have been subject to rigorous debates both between rival schools and within specific schools themselves. The notion that Indian philosophers remain intellectually restricted by their adherence to a particular religious tradition or set of sacred texts ignores the hermeneutical flexibility of such works and the fact that 'meanings of texts are correlates of acts of interpretation by interpreters' (Mohanty, 1992: 273). Indeed, as both Gadamer and Mohanty have suggested, the claim to be detached from all traditions, including one's own, is palpably false. Criticism can only function *as such* from within a particular tradition and from a particular historical and cultural perspective. It is this acknowledgement of the limits of criticism and the role played by tradition and community in such criticism which remains largely unrecognised by post-Enlightenment western liberalism.

– INDIAN MATERIALISM – A COUNTER-EXAMPLE –

The idea that Indian philosophy is too 'religious' or theological to be considered 'properly philosophical' is misleading for a number of reasons. Firstly, such a view involves the projection of western notions of 'religion' onto Indian culture and is often accompanied by a residue of anti-clerical feeling that ultimately derives from the secular displacement of the Church during the Enlightenment period (King, 1999, Chapter 2). In western culture religion is usually associated with theistic belief but many schools of 'Indian philosophy' are explicitly non-theistic (Cārvāka, Mīmāṃsā, Sāṃkhya, Buddhism) and the relationship of the other schools to theistic belief is a matter of some debate (see Chapter 9). Indeed, as we shall see, there is much that is discussed in Indian philosophical texts that is not specifically 'religious' in nature. Furthermore, why would adherence to a religious tradition make one any less philosophical or open-minded than adherence to a secular or humanistic world-view? The idea then that ancient Indian thought is essentially theological in nature is somewhat misleading. Consider, for instance, the following critique of ancient Hindu brahmanical practices and beliefs:

> There is no heaven, no final liberation, nor any soul in another world, nor do the actions of the four castes, orders etc., produce any real effect. The *Agnihotra* [fire sacrifice], the three Vedas, the ascetic's three staves, and smearing oneself with ashes, were made by nature as the livelihood of those destitute of knowledge and manliness. If a beast slain in the *Jyotiṣṭoma* rite will itself go to heaven, why then does the sacrificer not offer his own father immediately? ... While life remains let a man live happily, let him eat ghee [clarified butter] even if he runs into debt. When the body turns to ashes, how can it ever return again? If he who departs from the body goes to another world, how is it that he does not come back again, restless because of love for his kindred? Hence it is only as a means of livelihood that the Brahmin priests have established here all these ceremonies for the dead –

there is no other fruit anywhere. The three authors of the Vedas were buffoons, knaves and demons.

Sarvadarśanasaṃgraha, Chapter 1

These are not the words of a modern secular critic of Hindu religious practices and beliefs, but are attributed to Bṛhaspati, the reputed founder of an ancient Indian school of materialism (*jaḍavāda*), by the fourteenth-century doxographer Mādhava in his analysis of materialist philosophy. Materialism has ancient roots within India and, as the quote above demonstrates, constituted a major thorn in the side of the religious traditions of India. The materialists are referred to as a distinctive philosophical position in the early Buddhist literature (see *Dīgha Nikāya* I, 2) and evidence of the repudiation of an afterlife is attested to in the *Kaṭha Upaniṣad* (I, 20; 2, 6) and the *Maitrī Upaniṣad* (7, 8–9) where the view is again attributed to Bṛhaspati – this time described as a teacher of the gods. In early Buddhist accounts Ajita Kesakambali is said to have propounded a thoroughgoing materialist philosophy, denying the efficacy of the Hindu Vedic sacrifice and (more importantly from the Buddhist point of view), repudiating the claims to enlightenment of allegedly perfected teachers.

As an established philosophical school the materialists were known as the Cārvākas. This may be the name of their founder, but Cārvāka means 'one who eats' and so may refer to the materialist philosophy of "eating up" all that is given in perception. The Cārvākas accepted only sense–perception (*pratyakṣa*) as an independent means of knowledge (*pramāṇa*) asserting a rigorously empirical 'seeing is believing' philosophy. Alternatively, 'Cārvāka' may denote the school's hedonistic philosophy of 'eat, drink and be merry' ('*cāru*' – sweet and '*vāk*' – speech – making the materialists the definitive 'sweet-talkers'). The school is also known by the name Lokāyata, meaning 'worldly' and members of the school are known as the Lokāyatikas. This epithet clearly denotes the 'down-to-earth' approach of the school since the philosophy of the Lokāyata is said to be based upon a worldly empiricism and involves the explicit rejection of the existence of other worlds (*paraloka*). The term 'Lokāyatika' also appears to mean 'commoner' having some of the connotations of the English phrase 'salt-of-the-earth'. It is not clear to what extent the term reflects the 'plebeian' origins of materialistic thought or even the non-Vedic origins of the school. Nevertheless, we should bear in mind that a literate education and Vedic ritual practice were reserved for the upper three *varṇa* (the priestly, warrior and merchant classes) of ancient Hindu society. Moreover, there is a clear political dimension to the Cārvāka critique of Brahmanical ritual and privilege. However, the epithet 'commoner' may simply reflect a condescending attitude on the part of the upper echelons of ancient Indian society towards 'the common folk' who were deemed incapable of understanding the abstrusities and importance of the various Vedic rituals. This is not that surprising given that they were excluded from it.

According to the Cārvākas we have only one life, there is no after-life in a heavenly realm nor is there a succession of rebirths as most Indian schools believed. As a result the materialists upheld a philosophy of 'live for the moment' – 'a pigeon today is better than a peacock tomorrow' (cited in *Kāma Sūtra* I.2.25–30). The school is often represented as propounding a crude form of hedonism (*sukhavāda*) rejecting any notions of absolute righteousness (*dharma/adharma*) and promulgating a philosophy of pleasure-seeking (*kāma*) as the primary goal of life. The emphasis upon happiness (*sukha*) can be seen perhaps as a direct affront to the emphasis placed upon suffering (*duḥkha*) by the other schools of thought. Life may contain a great deal of pain but it also contains much in the way of pleasure and who in their right mind would 'throw away the grain because of the husk' (*Sarvadarśanasaṃgraha,* Ch. 1).

Traditional Brahmanical culture was based upon a value-system of four basic purposes of human existence (*puruṣārtha*): righteousness (*dharma*), wealth or worldly success (*artha*, literally, 'what is useful'), pleasure (*kāma*) and liberation from the cycle of rebirths (*mokṣa*). Originally, there were probably just three aims, but the fourth – liberation from suffering and rebirth – appears to have been accepted with the development of renunciate trends within ancient Indian society. This is seen in the development of the Vedic 'forest literature' (*āraṇyaka*) – the product of a shift in late Vedic society away from a worldly focus upon sacrificial rituals and towards a life of isolated contemplation and meditation. The forest literature provided the context in which the early *Upaniṣads* (final part of the Veda or Vedānta) were composed. The earliest such *Upaniṣads* like the *Bṛhadāraṇyaka Upaniṣad* is itself part of an *Āraṇyaka*.

The Cārvākas, however, rejected this world-view and its attendant lifestyle centred upon sacrificial ritual. Some accounts suggest that the materialists accepted only the pursuit of pleasure (*kāma*) as the purpose of human existence (e.g. Nīlakaṇṭha's commentary on *Bhagavad Gītā* 16.11), whilst others suggest that the school accepted pleasure and worldly success or wealth (*artha*) as the basic goals of life. We should bear in mind, however, that we are reliant on the accounts offered by opponents of the Cārvāka position and that these are hardly likely to represent the system in a positive light. Later distinctions seem to have developed between crude and refined (*suśikṣita*) materialism. The latter trend seems to have accepted a hierarchical scheme of pleasures and endorsed the validity of intellectual over sensual pleasures. Indeed, despite their repudiation of ethical duty (*dharma*), there is evidence that some Cārvākas took moral stances, such as non-violence (*ahiṁsā*), rejecting the performance of any action that might cause the suffering of others. Like the Buddhist and Jainas this involved a condemnation of Vedic animal sacrifices and a repudiation of the practices of war (Chattopadhyaya, 1968: 31–5). Clearly then, the Cārvāka position was not a form of unsophisticated or unreflective hedonism and in this regard can be compared to the Greek Epicureans. One might ask how the Cārvākas could take a moral stance given their repudiation of righteousness (*dharma*) as an absolute goal of life, but such groups seem to have grounded their stance in the importance of pleasure (*kāma*) as a universal goal for all, promoting a lifestyle based upon the avoidance of suffering for oneself and for others.

The hedonistic rendering of Indian materialism, whilst no doubt a specific feature of this school, is perhaps somewhat overdrawn in the available accounts of Cārvāka philosophy. Our problem here is that there are no extant writings of the Cārvākas themselves, with one possible exception – the *Lion of Destruction of Philosophical Theories* (*Tattvopaplavasiṁha*) by Jayarāśi Bhaṭṭa (c. 650 CE). Jayarāśi aligns himself with the philosophy of Bṛhaspati at the beginning of this work but he seems more intent on promulgating a radical form of scepticism than outlining a materialistic stance. Eli Franco suggests that Jayarāśi was a member of a school of sceptical Lokāyatikas, to be distinguished from the more well-known materialist Lokāyata (Franco, 1983: 147), though we should consider the possibility that Jayarāśi was in actual fact a sceptic with Lokāyata sympathies. Jayarāśi's discussion of sense–perception, for instance, ends with the refutation of all attempts to establish its truth-giving properties, despite the fact that for the materialists, perception was a valid (indeed the only) means of knowledge. There is simply no way to know, Jayarāśi argues, that our sense–perceptions are true. It is clear, therefore, that in many respects Jayarāśi can be more meaningfully classified alongside the Buddhist thinker Nāgārjuna (second century CE) and the Advaita Vedāntin Śrīharṣa (twelfth century CE) as a critic of mainstream Indian epistemology, based as it was upon an appeal to independent means of knowledge (*pramāṇa*) and accepted by most schools as the basis for philosophical disputation (see Chapter 6). Thus, Jayarāśi concludes his work with the following words:

> So with [all] philosophical theories in this way leading to [their own] destruction, conventional views may be enjoyed only for as long as they remain unexamined.

According to the Cārvāka school sense-perception is the only valid means of knowledge. The materialists rejected the status of the Vedas as revelation (*śruti*) and the authority of brahmanical priests. Both of these stances are also implicit in a third feature of the school, namely its rejection of the efficacy of Vedic rituals. The Cārvākas also rejected the validity of inferential reasoning (*anumāna*) as an independent means of knowledge (*pramāṇa*, see Chapter 6). This stance clearly reflected anxieties about the ways in which logical inferences could be applied to justify belief in the existence of various metaphysical entities, such as gods, demons and heavenly realms that draw our attention away from the here and now. This position, of course, created problems for the Materialists since they used arguments to substantiate their own position and refute the views of others. Materialists such as Purandara (seventh century CE) distinguished between inferences about the past and inferences concerning the future (for example, about an afterlife). Only the former was valid since it could be directly verified by sense–perceptions (*Nyāyamañjari*: 124; Chattopadhyaya, 1968: 28–30).

This material world is all that exists, there are no celestial beings or gods (*deva*) to whom we must bow in supplication and pay homage nor any other worlds in which we might be reborn. The doctrine of rebirth first occurs in the earliest *Upaniṣads* (c. eighth century CE) and within a matter of a few centuries seems to have established itself as a virtually universal belief, being a central teaching not just of the Vedic/Brahmanical traditions, but also of Jainism and Buddhism. The Cārvākas, however, rejected this doctrine, arguing that there was no well-established evidence for any form of existence after the death of the body. Indeed, for the Cārvākas, there is no spiritual self. The self is identical with the material body (*dehātmavāda*) and dies when the body ceases to function as a living organism. Rival schools attacked this stance vehemently, arguing that the vital principle (*prāṇa*) within living bodies imply that the self is more than just the body. Thus, in Sadānanda's *Vedāntasāra* (verses 121–4, fifteenth century CE), there are said to be four schools of materialism, distinguishable according to their view on the nature of the self: 1. self = the gross material body (*sthūla śarīra*), 2. self = the sense-faculties (*indriya*), 3. self = the vital breath (*prāṇa*) and 4. self = the mind (*manas*).[4] Nevertheless, all schools agreed that the self is merely a product of complex material formations.

According to the materialist school the various objects and entities of the world have come into existence through the development and combination of complex material processes. There is no external agent or efficient cause, such as God, involved in the creation of the universe. Objects simply obey their own fundamental natures (*svabhāva*).

> The fire is hot, the water cold, refreshing cool the breeze of morn;
> By whom came this variety? From their own nature was it born.
>
> cited in *Sarvadarśanasaṃgraha*, Ch. 1

The objects that we perceive are constituted by four primary elements – earth, water, air and fire. Other schools accept space (*ākāśa*) as a fifth primary element but this is rejected by the Cārvākas since it is not directly perceived by the sense-organs. This empiricist stance, however, created problems for the Cārvākas. One cannot know that atoms exist based solely upon sense-perceptions since they are too small to be perceived. Atoms are inferred from the perception of qualitative material differences between objects and from our experience of objects as aggregates that are divisible into smaller forms. There must be a point, so the atomist argues, where this division must stop otherwise matter would be reducible to nothingness. The Cārvāka acceptance of atomism is confronted by Jayarāśi at the beginning of his work, arguing that Bṛhaspati mentions the theory of the four elements only because they are so widely accepted by others and not because of his own acceptance of the theory (Franco, 1983: 148).

If only matter exists how then do the Cārvākas account for sentience and the possibility of experience itself? There is clearly a difference between dead, inert matter and the animated consciousness of living beings. For the materialists consciousness is merely a very sophisticated by-product or function of complex material formations. The emergence of consciousness is explained in terms of an analogy with the brewing of alcohol (an analogy that no doubt occurred to the Cārvākas whilst living up to their ideal of enjoying life to the full!). Although fermented yeast produces the intoxicating quality of wine in a certain combination and subject to certain environmental conditions, one would not expect to find wine within the separate ingredients themselves. In a similar fashion, consciousness is a complex result of the amalgamation and interaction of various material factors within the body – 'matter secretes mind, like liver secretes bile'. The mind, therefore, is an epiphenomenon of complex material organisms, but ceases to function when the body perishes. There is no afterlife, just the here and now.

If the frequency with which they are referred to and refuted are anything to go by, the Cārvākas have had a very significant role to play in the history of Indian philosophical thought, not least as a thorn in the side of those schools wishing to postulate the existence of immaterial forms of existence. Yet, even this seems to underplay the significance of the materialists as an independent school of thought in their own right. This is no doubt due to the lack of Cārvāka primary source-texts, meaning that accounts of the school are always from the point of view of their opponents. However, on the positive side the *pramāṇa-vāda* framework within which Indian philosophical debate developed places a great deal of emphasis upon providing as comprehensive an account of a rival school as possible as the initial position (*pūrvapakṣa*), if only to undermine that position in the subsequent refutation.

The fact that so little is known about the Cārvākas may stem from their suppression by other groups, but it may also reflect their own repudiation of tradition. Ancient Indian philosophical systems have survived for millennia not just because their views and arguments have proved compelling and worth taking seriously by adherents, but also because they have been associated with institutional structures and traditions. The rejection of authoritative testimony (*śabda-pramāṇa*) or tradition (*āgama*) in any form as a valid source of knowledge (as exemplified in their critique of the Hindu, Jaina and Buddhist adherence to their own sacred texts), made it less likely that the materialists would be able to preserve their views as a sustained tradition with some form of institutional backing or lineage (*saṃpradāya*). This is a lesson that modern western philosophers with their similar rejection of tradition might learn something from. Moreover, since the nineteenth century, western orientalists and Hindu reformers such as Swāmi Vivekānanda have emphasised the 'spiritual' dimensions of Indian culture, at the expense of schools like the Cārvāka.

Indian materialism has clear resonances with contemporary cultural and philosophical trends in modern, urban, western culture. In this context one might expect to see a renaissance of interest in Cārvāka philosophy. This has not occurred, however, since the representation of Indian philosophy in the west has generally functioned as an example of the 'exotic other' that helps to define the 'modernity' and normativity of Euro-American culture. There are also many resources for materialist perspectives within the west and many westerners remain so deeply attached to the romantic conception of Indian philosophy as essentially spiritual or mystical in nature that the Cārvākas are unlikely to be seen as sufficiently interesting to warrant greater attention. Indeed, it is those aspects of Indian philosophical thought that remain most amenable to 'spiritual' or 'mystical' characterisations that are likely to continue to provide the major point of interaction between Indian philosophy and western culture. The existence of other trends within ancient Indian thought, however, should not be forgotten in this process.

– NOTES –

1. A distinction between philosophy and theology is also clearly made before the Enlightenment. Thomas Aquinas (thirteenth century CE), for instance, suggests that philosophy (a category which included what is now called 'natural theology') is based upon reason alone. The point to note, however, is that it is for this reason that philosophy is to be seen as subordinate to theology since pure reason will leave one 'in the greatest darkness of ignorance' (*in maximis ignorantiae tenebris*). Thus, while philosophy and theology are distinguished, they are not seen in oppositional terms and in so far as they

are distinguished it is theology and not philosophy which can claim to provide the surest forms of knowledge.

2. One could argue that western society, under the influence of the Protestant Reformation, the Enlightenment and increasing literacy, has facilitated a democratisation of philosophy in the modern era. To a certain degree this has undoubtedly been the case. However, in the modern era we have seen the development of "professional philosophy" as an academic subject, institutionalised within universities within a departmental structure. When this is combined with the increasingly specialised and technical nature of philosophical discourses, however, one finds that philosophy, in the narrow professionalised sense of the term, still remains the province of an intellectual, male and largely middle-classed elite.
3. It has often been said that history is written by the winners, that is, by those in positions of authority. It would seem that one technique for marginalising the 'foreigner' is to ignore them or to provide only a cursory analysis of their ideas. Clearly, one has an additional problem with Indian thinkers since they are even further on the margins and are not even considered part of the apostolic traditions of western philosophy.
4. The association of the self with the vital breaths is attributed to the materialist Kambalāśvatara by the eighth-century Buddhist Śāntarakṣita, see *Tattvasaṃgraha*, v. 1864.

CHAPTER 2

Can Philosophy be Indian?

– IS THERE 'PHILOSOPHY' IN ANCIENT INDIA? –

> There is nothing more agreed than, that all the Learning of the Greeks was deduced originally from Egypt or Phoenicia; but, Whether theirs might not have flourished to that Degree it did by the Commerce of the Ethiopians, Chaldeans, Arabians, and Indians is not so evident, though I am apt to believe it.
>
> William Temple [1690] 1970: 8

> There are some who say that the study of philosophy had its beginning among the barbarians. They urge that the Persians have had their Magi, the Babylonians or Assyrians their Chaldaeans, and the Indians their gymnosophists ... If we may believe the Egyptians, Hephaestus was the son of the Nile and with him philosophy began ... These authors forget that the achievements which they attribute to the barbarians belong to the Greeks, with whom not merely philosophy but the human race began.
>
> Diogenes Laertius, third century CE, cited in Hicks, 1972: 3–5

Is 'Indian philosophy' really a type of 'philosophy'? Part of the problem with attempting to answer such a question is that any discourse about philosophy is historically and culturally specific and is thus implicated in an (already presupposed) conception of the nature of philosophy. Indeed, one might argue that the term "Indian philosophy" is problematic not only because it presupposes that a particular product of western cultural history (viz. philosophy) can be applied beyond its western context, but also because of the political implications of such a designation. The geographical demarcation of Asian thought (the East) from the West and the subordination of the former to the latter, politically, economically and culturally, make Indian thought and culture particularly vulnerable to manipulation, domination and distortion by western interests.

The acceptance of the existence of "Indian philosophy" might be seen as a positive acknowledgement of the existence of rational modes of thinking in India. On the other hand, the geographical specificity of the phrase can also function to marginalise Indian thought by focusing attention upon its own cultural particularity – its "Indianness". This can then be contrasted with the apparently global [*sic*] nature of 'western philosophy'. It is important, therefore, to emphasise the role played by European colonial expansion in the production of the myth of European universalism since the Enlightenment.

> For the point is not that Enlightenment rationalism is always unreasonable in itself but rather a matter of documenting how – through what historical process – its 'reason', which was not always self-evident to everyone, has been made to look 'obvious' far beyond the ground where it originated. If a language, as has been said, is but a dialect backed up by an army, the same could be said of the narratives of 'modernity' that, almost universally today, point to a certain 'Europe' as the primary habitus of the modern.
>
> Chakrabarty, 1992: 20–1

The association of systematic thought, theoretical abstraction and philosophy exclusively with European culture is a common feature in the works of many modern western intellectuals. Western accounts of the history of philosophy can be broadly characterised in terms of two main "strands". The first offers a pluralistic account of the origins of philosophy and is represented in the eighteenth and nineteenth centuries by writers such as Friedrich Ast (1778–1841), Christian Wolff (1679–1754), Arthur Schopenhauer (1788–1860) and Paul Deussen (1845–1919). The second strand represented by German scholars such as J. J. Brucker (1696–1770), Dietrich Tiedemann (1748–1803), G. W. F. Hegel (1770–1831) and the English historian of philosophy Thomas Stanley (1625–1678) came to the fore in the late eighteenth century and, following Diogenes Laertius, attempted to locate the origins of philosophy in ancient Greece. Martin Bernal has argued that the renewed interest in the Greeks and their establishment as the source of Germanic/European culture, particularly amongst German intellectuals reflected 'the German crisis of identity in the eighteenth century, along with a desire to return to authentic German roots' (Bernal, 1987: 214). Tiedemann, for instance, a student at the influential University of Göttingen, seems to have been the first to associate the birth of philosophy with the Pre-Socratic thinker Thales in his 1791 work *Geist der spekulativen Philosophie*. Tiedemann's account, in a manner reminiscent of *The Lives of Eminent Philosophers* by Diogenes Laertius (third century CE) is based upon the myth of the 'autonomous agent', that is, the elitist historiography which views the history of philosophy (and the development of culture) in terms of the reflections and actions of certain key figures. This de-contextualised approach separates the philosopher from the wider socio-cultural and political context in which their thinking occurred and has proven particularly popular in modern accounts of the history of philosophy since it privileges the philosopher as an independent, free-thinking and autonomous agent.

The most famous exponent of the view that philosophy originated in Greece, however, is probably G. W. F. Hegel. Philosophy, Hegel argued, is the development of the consciousness of freedom and was a Greek invention that reaches its apex in the modern Germanic nations. Consequently, Hegel rejected the older pluralistic accounts which suggested that there were a number of different types of philosophy originating from a variety of cultural and geographical locations. Hegel became aware, through the work of the English Indologist Henry Thomas Colebrooke (1765–1837), of the apparent existence of Indian forms of philosophy and used Colebrooke's account to revise his lectures on the history of philosophy. He conceded, for instance, that Indian thought was abstract and had developed its own formal logic but believed that India represented the 'childhood' of humanity with nothing of significance to say to the modern philosopher:

> In the massively wild religion of the Indians, which is totally devoted to fantasy they distinguish indeed one thing as ultimate, namely Brahm or Brahma, also called Brahman. This unity is regarded as the Supreme, and the characterization of man is to identify himself with this Brahm.
>
> cited in Viyagappa, 1980: 192

Hegel therefore dismissed Indian thought as insufficiently distinguished from religious and mythological ideas to count as 'philosophy' in the mature (Greek) sense of the term.

In a similar vein, German phenomenologist Edmund Husserl (1859–1938) has argued that 'only in the Greeks do we have a universal ("cosmological") life-interest in the essentially new form of a purely "theoretical" attitude' (Husserl, 1970: 280). The uniquely Greek invention of *theoria* is here contrasted with the religious-mythical attitude of Indian thought which has a much more straightforwardly practical orientation according to Husserl. This is a common feature of modern western conceptions of 'Oriental thought'. Aristotle distinguishes between practical wisdom (*phronēsis*), theory (*theoria*, or *epistēmē*) and technical knowledge or expertise (*technē*). Husserl's position is just one example of the tendency of the modern west to claim superiority in the areas of theoretical and technological thought, whilst conceding that the east has generally developed a higher degree of practical wisdom (*phronēsis*). According to Husserl, the theoretical approach is characterised by a detachment from practical concerns resulting in the thinker's ability to view the world from a disinterested and non-participatory manner. *Theoria* also allows for a contrast between the world and its representation to be made, resulting in a universally applicable means of assessing truth claims and applying critical thought to all truth–claims including those of one's own tradition. For Husserl, the exclusive possession of 'philosophy' in the sense of 'pure theory' furnishes European culture with a self-awareness that is historically unique. Europe, therefore, had a universal and globally relevant mission which Husserl describes as 'the Europeanization of all foreign parts of mankind". In particular, the Indians will have to 'Europeanize themselves, whereas we, if we understand ourselves properly, will never, for example, Indianize ourselves' (cited in Halbfass, 1988: 167). However, as contemporary Indian philosopher Jitendranath Mohanty points out:

> It is indeed true that a certain practical interest motivated much of recorded Indian thought ... But it is no less true that philosophical knowledge, in Socratic thinking, was regarded as the means to a good life. It is only we moderns who have divorced theory from practice, and have ascribed that separation, and consequent purity of theory, to the Greeks (and have learned to deny it to the Indians).
>
> Mohanty, 1992: 284

Mohanty rightly points out that Platonic thinking was equally as mythic as that of the *Upaniṣads* and that Husserl's position reflects 'an inadequate factual knowledge, combined with a too hasty "theoretical" interpretation of the concept of *theoria*, and the all-too-common (in nineteenth century Europe) romantic view of the oriental mode of thinking' (Mohanty, 1992: 285). One should also bear in mind that *theoria* in Christian and Neoplatonic circles was closely associated with *contemplatio* and the spiritual path and had a much closer association with the 'mystical' than is implied by Husserl's analysis and modern English derivations of the term.

Unlike his teacher, Husserl's student Martin Heidegger (1889–1976) remained ambiguous about the benefits of 'the Europeanization of the Earth' and seems to have been much more receptive to the potential insights to be gained from an engagement with eastern thought. He remained convinced, however, that it is a mistake to talk of 'Indian philosophy'.

> The often heard expression 'Western-European philosophy' is, in truth, a tautology. Why? Because philosophy is Greek in nature; Greek, in this instance, means that in origin the nature of philosophy is of such a kind that it first laid claim to the Greek world (Griechentum), and only it, in order to unfold.
>
> Heidegger, 1956: 29–31

The claim that 'philosophy' and more generally the distinctive features of western thought developed in ancient Greece, however, is highly questionable (Bernal, 1987). Such a claim involves a highly dubious series of historical jumps, a questionable conception of human nature, and a simplistically linear vision of cultural development as homogeneous, teleological and autonomous. One should also note the implicit secularism exemplified in the polarisation of the mythic (*mythos*) and the rational (*logos*, see Hatab, 1990). Similar notions and attitudes towards Indian thought can be found in the works of almost all of the influential philosophers in the west, whether explicitly stated or conspicuously present in the resounding silence with regard to the relevance of non-western thought to the philosophical quest for knowledge.

This situation leads us to ask the following awkward question: 'What is one to make of the apparent tension between the alleged universality of reason and the fact that its upholders are so intent on localising its historical instantiation?' (Bernasconi, 1997). In this regard even the sophisticated and insightful work of Jitendranath Mohanty remains tied to a post-Kantian conception of philosophy when he restricts the application of that term to reflective thinking (*manana*), excluding all knowledge that might be gained through contemplation or meditation (*nididhyāsana*):

> philosophical knowledge by itself ends with *manana*; something else, some other sort of cognitive achievement, brings that practical realization, but this sense of 'knowledge' is beyond philosophy, and philosophy is in no interesting sense practical. It does not itself bring about, but only demonstrates the possibility of a practical goal the conception of which is internal to the system.
>
> Mohanty, 1992: 281

According to Mohanty, in so far as schools of Indian thought like Advaita Vedānta and Yoga promote the attainment of meditative and non-conceptual (*nirvikalpa*) forms of 'mystical' insight (*jñāna*), they are moving beyond the scope of philosophy. Note also that the distinction between 'theory' and 'practice', which Mohanty decries elsewhere as a modern distinction, is here applied to establish the 'purely theoretical' nature of philosophy.

The thesis that 'Indian philosophy' is not particularly concerned with liberation (*mokṣa*) is consonant with an increasingly popular trend, particularly amongst Indian scholars, to reject the conventional picture of Indian thought as profoundly soteriological in intent (for example, Daya Krishna, 1991: Chapter three). Clearly, in the context of the hegemony of western secular reason, this has become an important strategy in establishing the respectability of Indian thought in a modern, secular context. Indeed, such a claim can be seen as a clear example of a post-colonial attempt to displace the popular image of India as mystical and 'otherworldly' in nature.

It is clear that western accounts have placed far too much emphasis upon the supposedly soteriological basis of Indian thought. Nevertheless, attempts to distinguish Indian thought from a cultural context which, in contrast to modern western culture, is profoundly religious, tends to secularise Indian thought and thus 'domesticate' it in terms of dominant western presuppositions about the nature of 'philosophy' and the types of questions that it asks. To exclude the so-called 'spiritual' (*ādhyātmika?*) aspects of Indian thought from the category of 'philosophy' is to project the Enlightenment dichotomy between philosophy and religion onto materials where such a polarity does not exist.

The association of Indian thought with a 'mythic mode of thinking' is a predominant theme in western conceptions of the subject. Consider the following comment made by the seventeenth-century English empiricist John Locke:

> Had the poor Indian philosopher (who imagined that the earth wanted something to bear it up) but thought of this word 'substance' he needed not to have been at the trouble to find an elephant to support it, and a tortoise to support his elephant; the word substance would have done it effectively.
>
> Locke, 1689: II. XIII, 19, cited in Matilal, 1986: 3

Locke is here referring to a Hindu cosmological myth which suggests that the world is ultimately supported by a tortoise. However, as B. K. Matilal has suggested, 'It would be impossible to find a text in classical Indian philosophy where the elephant–tortoise device is put forward as a philosophic explanation of the support of the earth' (Matilal, 1986: 4). Thus, to suggest that this is the sort of notion that Indian philosophical texts seriously postulated is a gross misrepresentation. Using the same criteria we could reject the Greek philosophical tradition on the basis of the Greek belief that the world is held aloft by the shoulders of Atlas. The way to avoid such misrepresentations is clear – consult the texts and traditions themselves. In fact, as Matilal points out, if Locke had been in a position to do so (because, to be fair, Indology was fairly undeveloped in this time), he would have found a whole host of notions corresponding to that of 'substance', the most notable being '*dravya*' – that in which qualities inhere, a notion which dates back to the *Vaiśeṣika Sūtra* (200 BCE–1 CE).

Locke, of course, was living in a time when it was commonly held that European civilisation (as opposed to the savage and uncivilised) was technologically, culturally and racially superior to the non-Europeans. We are now living, so we are told, in a post-colonial age and a society which has 'transcended' such prejudices. However, despite the multitude of works which have appeared in the west discussing a wide diversity of types of Indian thought, the overwhelming majority of professional philosophers remain uncompromisingly Eurocentric in their failure to engage with non-western modes of thought. Matilal, for instance, quotes the following incidental remark from Anthony Flew's 1971 book, *An Introduction to Western Philosophy*:[1]

> philosophy as the word is understood here, is concerned first, last and all the time with argument. It is, incidentally, because most of what is labelled *Eastern Philosophy* is not so concerned – rather than any reason of western parochialism – that this book draws no materials from any source east of Suez.
>
> Flew, 1971: 36

According to Flew it would seem that it is only those people who have been fortunate enough to live west of the Suez Canal who have been able to pursue "real" philosophy. Flew's statement contains so many presuppositions that one hardly knows where to begin. Notice that by making this statement in the context of a modern western democratic and pluralistic culture Flew shows an awareness of the possibility that his project might be conceived of as overtly parochial. This is even reflected in the title of his book – An Introduction to *Western* Philosophy. Flew perhaps should have come clean at this point and admitted that what he wished to discuss was western philosophy (hence the title), and that he had no interest in the thoughts of those peoples and cultures existing 'east of Suez'. The problem with Flew's statement as it stands, however, is that it represents yet another example of Eurocentricity and the phenomenon that Edward Said described as Orientalism – a colonially inspired attitude of mind which accepts a radical and unbreachable dichotomy between the East and the West.

Western philosophers, taking their lead from the literal rendering of *philosophia* as 'the love of wisdom', claim to be interested in the pursuit of knowledge for its own sake. This, in fact, is implied by Anthony Flew's suggestion that philosophy is exclusively concerned with argumentation, presumably leading to some reasoned conclusion. Why then does Flew suggest that eastern thought is not also interested in argumentation? Flew, as far as I know, did not spend time studying the thought-forms of non-European cultures and so has no right to make the claim that he does about 'eastern philosophy'. As we shall see, the history of classical Indian thought is a long history of intense intellectual debate and argumentation.

Nevertheless, Flew's statement reflects a tragically simplistic view of both 'western' and 'non-western' philosophy, neither of which can be said to be universally interested in 'pure argumentation'. What, one might ask, would such a phenomenon look like? Can one argue in a cultural vacuum? Here again we encounter the Enlightenment belief that it is possible to theorise in an abstract manner, devoid of context, agenda or ideological motivation. The myth of pure theory, modelled as it is on the notion of an objective, detached and neutral scientist discerning the true nature of reality, is again guilty of ignoring the historically situated and culturally specific nature of all discursive practices. Worse than this, however, is Flew's ethnocentric belief that the cultures, languages and intellectual traditions of the non-western world can be completely ignored, having been surpassed by the historical traditions of the west.

Let us consider Flew's argument more closely. Presumably what is being suggested is that whilst one might find the occasional philosophical argument in 'eastern philosophy', much of it is tainted by mythological, dogmatic and theological motivations. Let us unpack these ideas further. Flew's position amounts to a variant on the secularist thesis which suggests that 'Indian philosophy' cannot be real philosophy (i.e., philosophy as modern westerners practice it) because it involves explicitly theological criteria (for instance, a reliance upon revelation or *śruti*) and traditional religious beliefs rather than on neutral and objective philosophical grounds, such as argumentation based upon the exercise of pure rationality.

We have already had cause to reject the claim that western philosophical traditions are any more detached from a tradition than those of classical India. It is also worth noting that an uncompromising appeal to tradition (*aitihya*), that is, to the proclamations of a succession of elders (*vṛddhāḥ*), is only accepted as a valid and independent means of knowledge (*pramāṇa*) by the Paurāṇikas, a relatively minor school of Indian thought which never succeeded in gaining the authority and importance of the classical *darśanas*. *Śabda-pramāṇa* is, as we have seen, an acknowledgement of one's reliance upon the authority of others, including, but not exclusively representing, the testimony of *śruti*. To claim that such sources are inappropriate and unverifiable is to ground one's own perspective in a secularism which is just as theological (or ideological if you prefer) as the position of the classical Indian schools of thought. Indeed, one should note that, in the acknowledgement of the importance of teachers (*guru*), the function of tradition (*saṃpradāya*) and the inevitability of speaking from a particular perspective (*darśana*) in the exercising of critical reasoning, the Indian approach is both more realistic and more honest about its particularity and social location.

The problem with the thesis that Indian thought is theological rather than philosophical is that it does not allow the discussion to proceed on a level playing field, or, to mix my sporting metaphors, the rules of the game have been set to favour one team over another. Not only does such an approach imply that western philosophical works (by contrast) are autonomous and detached from the prejudices of a particular tradition, the thesis also presupposes the normative status of European cognitive categories and contemporary western debates. I shall label these presuppositions, Eurocentric-cognitivism and Euro-contemporocentrism. The former is the tendency to favour the disciplinary and cognitive boundaries of modern European thought, as seen, for instance, in the separation of philosophy from religion, literature, art, science and other cognitive pursuits. The historical factors behind this separation are, of course, to be found in the Enlightenment spat between science and religion and attempts to model modern western philosophy on the former (usually seen as the winner of the dispute!). Differentiation between cognitive disciplines is now endemic in the modern university, and is institutionalised in the form of departmentalisation, academic specialisation and the professionalisation of philosophy in the academic sphere.

The historical factors behind the distinction between the disciplines of philosophy and religion as two separate spheres of activity arise from the dispute and subsequent divorce of the two as a result of the Enlightenment, the rise of science and anti-clerical feeling in the 'Age of Reason'. Of course, beyond the European context such socio-historical factors did not prevail. Traditional Indian culture simply did not carve up the conceptual world in this manner since the antagonism between a secularised discipline of philosophy (making overtures to the rising disciplines of the natural sciences) and "superstitious" religion never took place. Related to this is a second presupposition – Euro-contemporocentrism, a wonderfully convoluted example of academic jargon that I am using here to denote the privileging of the philosophical boundaries and questions of European thought since the seventeenth century as the yardstick for conceptual issues in general. This can be seen, for instance, in the retrospective tendency to read contemporary and in vogue debates back into the canon of accepted philosophers of the past.

Bearing all of this in mind, I must agree with Heidegger and Flew that in the pre-colonial era there is nothing which directly corresponds to the modern European notion of 'philosophy' as a cognitive discipline distinct from such spheres as religion in the diverse and rich cultures that exist east of the Suez. This, however, should no longer be of surprise to us. Such a discovery in and of itself will not convince us to ignore the thought-forms of other cultures unless one also accepts the Enlightenment (and Eurocentric) assumptions that secular rationality alone leads to wisdom and that non-western cultures have nothing of relevance to add to contemporary philosophical debates.

To illustrate this point let us consider an example from the wider Asian context recently put forward by the Japanese scholar Hajime Nakamura. When Japanese intellectuals first encountered modern western philosophy in the nineteenth century they thought that it was something new. The nineteenth-century Japanese thinker Amane Nishi (1829–97) coined the term '*tetsugaku*' to refer to this new import from the west. Of course, this is not to say that no 'philosophical' thinking of any kind had ever occurred in traditional Japan, but rather that there was no separate branch of scholarship called 'philosophy', forged in the historical and cultural conflicts of Europe. One reason for this, as Nakamura himself suggests, is that 'there was no antagonism toward religion, and intellectuals saw no need to develop a separate discipline with a different name' (Nakamura, 1989: 138). Again, we should note that traditional Japanese intellectuals divided up their intellectual world in a manner which differs from that of post-Enlightenment Europe. This should not surprise us.

The situation is not quite so straightforward in traditional India. A number of pre-existing Sanskrit terms have been used by modern intellectuals to correspond to the English term 'philosophy'. '*Darśana*' (from the root *dṛś*: 'to see') is a Sanskrit term meaning 'sight', 'vision', or 'perspective'. Traditionally, the term was used in a doxographical sense to refer to the various schools of thought in traditional Indian debating circles. Today, however, the term is most frequently used as a broad synonym for the western idea of 'philosophy'. Thus, it has become customary to refer to a *darśana* as a "philosophical school". In classical Indian texts *darśana* has various meanings, dependent upon context, but the term itself appears to have two important uses in a traditional Indian philosophical context:

1. '*Darśana*' as 'perspective', 'point of view', or 'school of thought' – what might be called a 'neutral', descriptive or doxographical usage.
2. *Samyagdarśana*, meaning 'correct view', which leads to liberation from the cycle of rebirths (*saṃsāra*) – what might be called a prescriptive usage.

What contemporary scholars most often mean by *darśana* is one of the six traditional schools of Hindu thought, viz. Nyāya, Vaiśeṣika, Sāṃkhya, Yoga, Mīmāṃsā and Vedānta. This usage is closer to *darśana* as a descriptive equivalent of the English 'perspective' or 'point of view', but retains an element of modern Hindu ideology in so far as it draws a line between what is seen as orthodox (i.e. the various Hindu schools of thought), and heterodoxy (the various schools of Buddhism and Jainism etc.), which is dismissed and left unconsidered. Such an approach to Indian thought is parochial and narrow in that it fails to grasp the fact that 'Indian' does not equal 'Hindu', and that the six traditional schools of Hindu thought have not developed in a cultural vacuum divorced from, for example, Buddhist or Jain influences.[2]

The term *ānvīkṣikī* ('investigation through reasoning') has also been put forward as a Sanskrit equivalent of 'philosophy'. For instance, in his *Arthaśāstra* Kauṭiliya distinguishes between four cognitive disciplines (*vidyā*), namely *trayi* (Vedic learning), *daṇḍanīti* (jurisprudence), *vārttā* (economics), and finally *ānvīkṣikī* . The *Arthaśāstra*, dating in its present form from around the third century CE, further explains *ānvīkṣikī* as representative of the Sāṃkhya, Yoga and Lokāyata schools of thought. Further elaboration of this term in the text demonstrates that *ānvīkṣikī* is primarily an investigative method which provides reasons for evaluating what is appropriate and what is not appropriate in the other cognitive disciplines. Kauṭiliya, citing an older source, describes *ānvīkṣikī* as 'a source of light for all knowledge' (*pradīpaḥ sarvavidyānām*), 'a means for all activities' (*upāyaḥ sarvakarmaṇām*) and as 'a foundation for all social and religious duties' (*āśrayaḥ sarvadharmāṇāṃ*) (see Halbfass, 1988: 263–86).

However, one wonders if the attempt to find a semantic equivalent to the term 'philosophy' is ill-conceived, if only because the meaning of the term and the nature of the discipline remains the subject of continued debate in the west. Paul Hacker, for instance, has suggested that *ānvīkṣikī* is an investigative method which can be applied to a number of cognitive spheres and which bears no specific relationship to philosophy. In a stinging critique of H. Jacobi, who was the first Indologist to suggest 'philosophy' as a translation of *ānvīkṣikī* (Jacobi, 1911), Hacker argued that Jacobi's 'ingenious reflections tell much more about their author (i.e., that he was so obviously impressed with the Occidental emancipation of philosophy from theology that he projected this conflict into his own area of research, India) than about actual events in the history of Indian thought' (Hacker, 1958, cited in Halbfass, 1988: 274).

Thus, beyond the context of the European Enlightenment there has been no explicit antagonism between intellectuals and religious authority which might have precipitated the construction of a secular discipline such as modern western philosophy. The result of this is that classical Indian 'philosophers' include as part of their discussion what most westerners would conceive of as fundamentally 'religious' questions.[3]

However, despite differences between traditional Indian and modern western thought, there are various factors which reconcile both 'philosophy' and 'religion' in a pre-modern context in both Asia and Greece. The traditional conception of philosophy as the 'search for wisdom in life' encompasses both aspects, an interest in matters of ultimate concern (relegated to the sphere of religion in the modern secular west), the nature of reality, and questions of the meaning and purpose of life etc. Such issues are the lifeblood, I would suggest of traditional (i.e. pre-professionalised) philosophy.

Interestingly enough, this is close to popular conceptions of what philosophy is, though it is not so close to modern academic notions of philosophy as espoused by the professional academic working in western (or westernised) departments of Philosophy in the modern university. One result of this divorce from ultimate concerns in 'professional philosophy' has been the tendency for its practitioners (alongside western scholarship in general), to be perceived by society at large as "purely academic" in the full and pejorative sense of the phrase, that is, as divorced from the fundamental issues of life and the leading of an authentic lifestyle. As one author has recently noted:

> Where the Anglo-American tradition tends to trivialize the great questions that preoccupied philosophers of old by subjecting them to increasingly technical analyses of the language in which they are cast, the continental tradition has steered itself clear of the trivial only to end up in the box canyon of nihilism. Thus, philosophy in the twentieth century, following the subjective, the historical, and the linguistic turns, has ended up in a double dead-end. Take your choice: technical trivialization or poetic nihilism. Neither is terribly appealing to the poor person in the street who, if interested in philosophy at all, is more likely to turn to Plato than to Donald Davidson or Derrida.
>
> Ogilvy, 1992: xiv

Whilst I would not want to endorse a characterisation of modern western philosophy en masse which is so obviously dismissive and sweeping, one cannot help but think that the author has made a salient point about the practice of modern professionalised philosophy and its reception in wider society. My own first encounter with western philosophy was through the works of the ancient Greek philosopher Plato. I soon learned as a university undergraduate that philosophy, particularly as exemplified in contemporary Analytic circles, tended to ignore what I thought of as the central questions – those ultimate questions about life that inspired my initial interest in the subject, in favour of a rigorous kind of linguistic analysis of statements and a highly specialised (and thus both alienating and elitist) series of debates that seemed to bear little resemblance to those issues which I had considered to be the 'lifeblood' of philosophy in my earlier reading of Plato.

Should 'Indian philosophy' be called philosophy at all then? Let us consider the parallel case of the category of 'religion'. Attempts to provide a universal definition of religion are doomed to failure, as Talal Asad notes, 'not only because its constituent elements and relationships are historically specific, but because that definition is itself the historical product of discursive processes' (Asad, 1993: 29). This point is equally applicable to misguided attempts to define the 'nature' or 'essence' of 'philosophy'. It is clear that 'philosophy' in the most specific sense of the term is a western phenomenon. To attempt to find such an entity in pre-colonial India will inevitably lead to a westernisation of the material under consideration. For the interpreter of Indian thought, to play this game is not only to conform to European rules, it is also to play away from home. The result of this activity, of course, has been the development of an image of 'eastern philosophy' as mystical and antithetical to rational reflection. This is an image constructed according to the normative paradigms of Orientalist concerns and founded upon the inequality of power relations between the west and 'the rest' (see King, 1999).

What is generally called 'philosophy' in the west then is indeed a European invention. Thus far we can agree with western thinkers such as Husserl, Heidegger and Hegel. However, rejecting the straightforward translation of Sanskrit terms like *ānvīkṣikī* or *darśana* as 'philosophy' need not imply a position of Eurocentric hubris. The historicist realisation of the culturally specific nature of contemporary western philosophy is precisely the reason why western philosophers should be more interested in engaging with the intellectual thought of other cultures.

In maintaining a position of Eurocentric isolationism the western philosopher is left arguing that because other cultures have not distinguished 'philosophy' from other spheres of human intellectual activity, and in particular, because they have failed to purge the discipline of its traditional association with religious forms of discourse, it cannot be worthy of consideration. This secularist position presumes *a priori* that the distinction between philosophy and theology, which is, as we have seen, an historically specific consequence of social and political events in European society, is a *natural* distinction to make. From this stance it becomes relatively easy to argue that the distinction should be applied universally in order to liberate humanity from the limitations of religious traditionalism and dogmatism. Thus,

> In the name of the universality of values, European colonialism violently universalized its own singular particularity and annihilated the historicality of the colonized. In this context, western philosophy – in the guise of a disinterested, universalistic, transcendental, speculative discourse – served the indispensable function of being the ultimate veracious buttress of European conquest. This service, furthermore, was rendered in the name of 'Man' and the emancipation of 'Man'.
>
> Serequeberhan, 1991: 3

As westerners move into the globalised world of the twenty-first century the encounter with apparently 'alien' world-views has become an inevitability. The western philosopher would do well to adapt Mr Spock's famous line from the television series *Star Trek*, and admit that – 'It's *philosophy* Jim, but not as <u>we</u> know it!'

– WHY CONSIDER 'INDIAN PHILOSOPHY'? –

Accepting that there are perspectives which are broadly comparable with 'philosophical' or 'theoretical' thought in non-western cultures (even if the specifically modern connotations of 'philosophy' remain historically and culturally specific to the west), one might very well ask why westerners should still feel it necessary to consider such alien world-views. There are, of course, a number of good reasons why one might consider it worth examining the philosophical reflections of a culture other than one's own, apart from the obvious interest in learning about other cultures and perspectives for their own sake. For instance, it is clear that one way in which European culture has tended to define itself is in contradistinction to 'the East'. Thus, a proper engagement with these cultures will undoubtedly result in a greater appreciation and understanding of the cultural roots and identity of 'the West'. This is particularly important since we no longer live in a world which can be strictly divided into East and West. In a supposedly post-colonial era Eurocentric and neo-colonial attitudes must be abandoned if one is to engage with the pluralistic and multicultural nature of contemporary society and come to terms with the way in which this affects both the issues under consideration and the modes of their representation.

Secondly, a sensitive examination of non-western culture furnishes the analyst with the possibility of a greater appreciation of the contours of western culture. By examining theoretical perspectives from another culture one is more likely to become aware of some of the cultural blind-spots in the philosophical traditions of both cultures. A third reason for investigating non-western philosophy might be to engage in a properly conceived and balanced philosophical debate in global terms. Such a debate would need to reflect the cultural and intellectual diversity of humankind. Considering Indian philosophy (or Chinese or African philosophy etc.) is also likely to provide intellectual stimulation, new and creative syntheses of old ideas, and the potential for the development of new approaches, orientations and world-views which properly reflect the diversity of human experience. This is already happening in other spheres of human activity, for instance in the appropriation and adaptation of eastern philosophical ideas in the works of transpersonal psychologists, in the realm of complementary and alternative therapies with the adoption (and adaptation) of Acupuncture, Shiatsu and Āyurvedic medicine in the west, and in the realm of religion with the rise of various eastern-inspired "New Age" movements. Given this context it is high time that western philosophers took the thought-forms and arguments of other cultures more seriously.

Let us consider a few examples of some areas which might prove of interest to western philosophers in terms of contemporary philosophical debates. These examples are, of course, only my own thoughts. No doubt there are many other interesting points that might be found.

Within Indian culture there exists a firmly dualistic strand, best exemplified by the Sāṃkhya school of thought, which distinguishes *Puruṣa* (pure consciousness) from *Prakṛti* (primal matter, see Chapter 8). What might strike the westerner as odd, however, is the fact that those factors which might be described as "mental" (i.e. *buddhi*, the intellect, and *manas*, the mental organ which perceives ideas and organises sensory information into a coherent picture) are classified by the Sāṃkhya school as a subtle form of matter, to be distinguished from consciousness itself. In Indian culture *manas* is often classified as a sixth sense organ (see Chapter 6). This intriguing notion might provide interesting new ways of circumventing the problems of Cartesian dualism and the separation of the mind and body. Again if we consider the Buddhist tradition we find a highly sophisticated analysis of experience which does not presuppose the notion of a permanent subject of those experiences. Buddhist philosophical texts (the Abhidharma) provide a highly complex "meta-language" for discussing experience (see Chapters 5–7). These works are not only interesting from the point of view of psychology and the philosophy of mind but also have implications for notions of ethics. The reception of the work of Derek Parfit (1984, *Reasons and Persons*) amongst western philosophers reflects how strange it seems to most westerners to conceive of an ethical system which does not presuppose the notion of a person or a persisting ethical subject. Buddhist thought thus provides an interesting counterpoint to "person-based" ethical systems.

Contrary to the firmly held belief that Indian philosophical thought is highly speculative and metaphysical, the various *darśanas* place supreme importance upon perception (*pratyakṣa*) as a valid source of knowledge (*pramāṇa*). Overall this has given a highly empirical emphasis to much Indian philosophical thought. Debates about the role of conceptualisation in perceptual knowledge and the nature of the perceptual act itself provide interesting food for thought for western philosophers (see Chapter 7). Notable again, however, is the wider conception of experience conveyed by the term *pratyakṣa*. Indian philosophers have spent centuries investigating, classifying and discussing the nature of consciousness (*cit*), including the nature and status of what are often called in the west "altered states of consciousness". The wider scope of Indian speculations in this area open up realms of experience mostly ignored by contemporary western philosophers and psychologists. For some schools the general category of perception (*pratyakṣa*) includes the extraordinary perception of the yoga practitioner (*yogī-pratyakṣa*). Insights derived from such experiences are sometimes used to justify certain claims (for instance, as evidence of the existence of atoms on the grounds that the advanced yogin is able to perceive the atomic level of reality), but they are generally put forward as additional support for a position rather than as substantive evidence in their own right. The reason for this is clear, most of us are not capable of verifying *yogī-pratyakṣa* and thus it cannot possibly convey the same degree of epistemological validity as more universally available forms of perception. However, the inclusion of *yogī-pratyakṣa* reflects the acceptance of a wider range of perceptual and non-sensory experiences than those usually examined by modern western philosophers working from within a secularist paradigm.

The rejection of insights and experiences gained from so-called 'altered states of consciousness' by western philosophers is characteristically made on the grounds that such experiences are non-veridical or at least non-verifiable and that they reflect a commitment to a particular metaphysical or religious perspective. This secular approach reflects social and ideological shifts that have occurred in western culture since the Enlightenment. In so far as the secularist paradigm rejects out of hand those claims which are based upon such states of consciousness it remains equally bound to a particular metaphysical position of its own. In fact, it is not clear, particularly in the light of Gadamer's insights, that it is possible for any school of thought to be free from a metaphysical position of some kind, nor even that such a situation would be desirable!

Further evidence against the claim that Indian thought involves a multitude of fanciful speculations can be deduced from the marked absence of the diverse hypothetical and abstract entities postulated in the western metaphysical tradition. Mohanty suggests that the predominance of pure unactualised possibilities and abstract entities in western thought reflects the influence of Christian monotheism and the doctrine of creation *ex nihilo* in particular. Without the postulation of a 'Divine Mind' creating the universe out of nothing, there was no need for the Indian traditions to postulate such abstract entities:

> In the absence of possibilia and of abstract entities such as propositions, some standard concepts of necessary and its opposite, contingent truth, cannot find any formulation in the Indian systems. Thus, we have an account of what the world does consist in, but not of what might have been or could not possibly be.
>
> Mohanty, 1992: 233

Mohanty goes on to suggest that in Indian inferences one finds the extensional 'it is never the case that' rather than the modal 'it is impossible'. The inferential structure of logic developed by the Nyāya school of Indian thought also differs from its Aristotelian "cousin". Whereas Aristotelian syllogistic inference moves from the universal to the particular, Nyāya logic grounds itself in particularity, moving from the particular to the universal. Thus, the Nyāya inference demands a particular instantiation as an example in order for the conclusion to follow (see Chapter 6). This, Mohanty argues, provides an empirical grounding to Nyāya logic that is not necessarily present in Aristotelian syllogisms. This defence of Nyāya logic of course is not new and dates back to the writings of sympathetic western Orientalists of the nineteenth century (see Ganeri, 1996).

One might also point to interesting distinctions in Indian logic, such as that between implicatory negation (*paryudāsa-pratiṣedha*), that is, negation which implies the opposing thesis, and non-implicatory negation (*prasajya-pratiṣedha*) which negates without presuming the affirmation of the opposing thesis. Consideration of Indian systems of logic open up the possibility of the cross-cultural study of logical systems. Indian notions of two levels of truth (in the Buddhist and Advaita Vedānta schools) may also prove stimulating to western philosophical debates about the nature of meaning, truth and the role of language. Moreover, while western formal logic closely follows mathematics in its formulation, Indian formal logic (*navya-nyāya*) has tended to model itself on grammar. There is a wealth of interesting and highly developed linguistic and grammatical speculation in the Indian works of Panini, Patañjali and Bhartṛhari (see Chapter 3), as well as the rival theories of the Buddhists. Much of this remains relevant not only to contemporary Analytic philosophers but also to continental and post-structuralist thinkers such as Derrida and Lacan.

Thus, even when applying the culturally specific categories of the modern western world and the distinctions between the cognitive sub-disciplines of philosophy one can find much that would be of interest to the contemporary western philosopher. No doubt there is also a wealth of material relevant to the specific areas of metaphysics, ontology and the philosophy of religion, though these are less fashionable areas of research in the modern era.

– NOTES –

1. In this respect one can see the relevance of Jacques Derrida's suggestion that it is in the "margins" of the text, in the incidental remarks of the author, that one can find that which is suppressed, the 'hidden agenda', the presuppositional basis of the project undertaken.
2. That it is legitimate to use the term *darśana* to refer to Buddhist as well as Hindu schools of thought can be gleaned from the fact that it is used in such a broad doxographical fashion by both Bhāvaviveka in his *Verses on the Heart of the Middle Way* (*Madhyamaka Hṛdaya Kārikā*) and Candrakīrti in his *Prasannapadā* (on *Madhyamaka Kārikā* 15.11).
3. The Sanskrit term *Dharma* is probably the closest approximation to the western idea of 'religion', but does not fit easily with the western tendency to classify in terms of "-isms".

In Hindu terms *Dharma* denotes the fundamental truth about the nature of reality and connotes a particular moral and obligatory sense of one's duty to conform with the regulated flow of the cosmos in general terms and in more caste-specific terms. As such, it is not easily classifiable in terms of any particular group of people or cultural manifestation without distorting its usual meaning.

CHAPTER 3

The Varieties of Hindu Philosophy

– THE ORIGINS AND NATURE OF HINDU PHILOSOPHY –

There is a joke about the Buddha visiting New York City and approaching a hot-dog vendor. 'Make me one with everything', the Buddha requests. Having received his hot dog, the Buddha hands a ten-dollar bill to the vendor. 'What about my change?' the Buddha asks, to which the street vendor replies: 'Change comes from within'.

As we shall see in the next chapter, the idea that Buddhist philosophy promotes a philosophy of universal oneness is misleading since the Buddhist tradition has consistently reduced unities into their more complex constituents (*dharmas*). In a sense then, the Buddhist goal is to become aware that everything and everybody is inherently complex and diverse, rather than part of some universal oneness. It is the realisation of the complexity of everything that impels the Buddhist to reject the notion of autonomous individuality. Ironically, this philosophical step opens up the possibility of a greater recognition of the mutual inter-dependence of all things, though, strictly speaking, this is not the same as a doctrine of 'universal oneness'.

Nevertheless, in the west the popular image of 'eastern philosophy' is that it is world-denying, mystical and monistic in nature. Broadly speaking, this image is a caricature of one particular school of Hindu philosophy – the Advaita Vedānta tradition of Śaṅkara (c. 700 CE). The reasons for this cultural association are complex but they reflect the interest shown in Śaṅkara's monism by European and American intellectuals in the nineteenth and early twentieth centuries (see King, 1999: Chapter 6). During this time the non-dualist (*advaita*) philosophy of Vedānta also became a focal point for certain key figures in the rise of Indian nationalism such as Swāmi Vivekānanda, Mohandas Gandhi and Sarvepalli Radhakrishnan. Vivekānanda, in particular, embarked on extensive lecture tours in Europe and North America and established organisations such as the Vedānta

Society and the Ramakrishna Mission. He, more than any other figure, was probably most responsible for promoting the idea that Advaita Vedānta was the 'essence of Hinduism' and the culmination of Indian philosophical development. Such a view is highly misleading and homogenises the rich diversity of Indian culture under a single Neo-Vedāntic banner.

It is often said that there are six schools of 'orthodox' Hindu philosophy. This view is problematic for a number of reasons. Firstly, because it is a mistake to impose the idea of 'orthodoxy' onto Indian religion and culture. Even when discussing philosophical perspectives it is clear that there has never been a centralising institution comparable to the Christian Church to oversee and define doctrinal correctness within India. Sometimes an appeal is made to the classification of schools into *āstika* (affirmer) and *nāstika* (non-affirmer) traditions as evidence of an indigenous Hindu notion of 'orthodoxy'. This mode of classification is usually taken to imply that acceptance of the Vedas as revelatory knowledge (*śruti*) provides the grounds for distinguishing orthodox Hindu schools from their 'heterodox' rivals – the Cārvākas, Buddhists and Jainas. It is clear, however, that the *āstika–nāstika* distinction is a fluid and changeable mode of classification and differs in its meaning and application according to context. The Buddhist philosopher Nāgārjuna, for instance, refers to the Vaiśeṣika school as one of several *nāstikas* (non-affirmers) in *Ratnāvalī* I, v. 60–1, in this sense denoting those who deny the authority of the Buddha. There are also many shades of meaning of *āstika* in an Indian philosophical context. Within the so-called 'orthodox fold' of Hindu philosophy attitudes towards the Vedic scriptures are quite diverse. Whilst the Mīmāṃsā and Vedānta schools accept the ultimate authority of the Vedas, they place emphasis upon different aspects of the Vedic corpus. Schools like the Sāṃkhya and Vaiśeṣika exhibit little more than a token acceptance of revelation (*śruti*). Indeed, for the Vaiśeṣika school only perception and inferential reasoning are valid and independent means of knowledge – *śruti* is accorded no independent status of its own.

The earliest usage of the *āstika–nāstika* distinction seems to occur in the context of the rise of medical science in ancient India, particularly in relation to the practice of scholastic disputation. In the *Caraka Saṃhitā* (second century CE) – the major source for the theory and practice of *Āyurveda* medicine – *nāstika* denotes one who refutes a position within the context of a scholastic debate (*vāda*) rather than an expositor of heterodox philosophies (Heesterman, 1968–9).[1] Indeed, according to Dasgupta, the origins of Indian traditions of debate are to be found not in philosophical works or doctrinal disputations but in the more pragmatic and empirical context of Indian medical science:

> We hear of debates, discussions or logical disputes in literature earlier than the *Caraka-saṃhitā*; but nowhere was the acquirement of this art deemed so much a practical necessity for earning a living as amongst the medical men. And, since there is no mention of the development of this in any other earlier literature, it is reasonable to suppose that the art of debate and its other accessories developed from early times in the traditional medical schools, whence they are found in Caraka's work.
>
> Dasgupta, 1988, Vol II: 401–2

The *Caraka Saṃhitā* thus endorses the use of practical or heuristic reasoning (*yukti*) as a valid and independent means of knowledge (*pramāṇa*) as a pragmatic and experimental approach to medical diagnosis and treatment (1.11). Medical practitioners are advised to avoid dogmatic positions on questions such as the origins of humanity and disease etc.:

> Do not let yourselves become embroiled in complex arguments and counter-arguments, nor let yourself pretend that truth is obvious and easy to attain if one adheres to a single philosophical position (*pakṣasaṁśraya*). By your clever argumentation you will all end up going in circles, like a person sitting on an oil press that moves round and round. Free yourself from simplistic biases and search for the truth dispassionately.
>
> *Caraka Saṃhitā* 1.25.32, translated in Larson, 1993: 111

The origins of Indian philosophical speculation can also be discerned in the early Vedas with accounts of verbal contests between ritual officiants. These '*brahman*-riddles' (*brahmodya*) represent an exchange of views couched in terms of an enigmatic question testing the participants understanding of the mystery of the ritual. The answers to such questions remain suitably enigmatic themselves and involve a recognition of underlying correspondences (*bandhu*) between ritual practice and the cosmos as a whole. Examples of such debates can be found throughout Vedic literature (e.g. Ṛg Veda 1.164). The earliest *Upaniṣads* – the *Chāndogya* and *Bṛhadāraṇyaka* – dating from the eighth to the sixth century BCE, both refer to councils for the discussion of various metaphysical issues such as the nature of the self (*ātman*), the ritual and *brahman* – the underlying ground of the universe (see Ch Up 5.31 and Bṛ Up 6.2.1). Again, in the *Praśna Upaniṣad* (c. beginning of Common Era) we find an account of various questions (*praśna*) offered by learned Brahmins in a debate concerning the origins of the universe and the nature of the vital breath (*prāṇa*).

The term most often used to denote a school of philosophy in India is '*darśana*' (from the root *dṛś* – 'to see'). In the specific context of an examination of traditional Indian philosophy *darśana* can be translated as a 'point of view' or 'perspective'. The use of the term *darśana* to denote a 'school of philosophy', however, does not occur until the fifth century of the

Common Era where it is used by the Buddhist Bhāvaviveka in his *Verses on the Heart of the Middle Way* (*Madhyamaka Hṛdaya Kārikā*). Bhāvaviveka's work is the earliest clear example of a doxographical account of Indian philosophical schools (Qvarnström, 1989). As well as outlining his own Madhyamaka Buddhist philosophy, Bhāvaviveka discusses the *śrāvaka* (non-Mahāyāna) Buddhists and the doctrines of the Yogācārins. In terms of non-Buddhist schools he discusses the Sāṃkhya, Vaiśeṣika, Mīmāṃsā and Vedānta schools. This establishes a scheme of six basic schools, but three of these are Buddhist. Towards the end of the eighth century CE the Jaina scholar Haribhadraśuri composed his *Outline of the Six Schools* (*Ṣaḍdarśanasamuccaya,* late eighth century CE), further reinforcing the notion that there were six schools. We should note, however, that the schools discussed here are the Buddhists (here represented as a single school), the Nyāya, Sāṃkhya, Jaina, Vaiśeṣika and Mīmāṃsā schools. No mention is made of Yoga and Vedānta as distinctive philosophical traditions in this work. Similarly in the tenth century Jayanta Bhaṭṭa discusses six schools in his *Summary of Nyāya* (*Nyāyamañjarī*), but again his list of six is different with the Vaiśeṣika replaced this time by the Cārvākas. Again, Yoga and Vedānta are omitted. Clearly, the notion that there are six basic systems of thought gained considerable authority during this period, but authors continued to provide radically different accounts of what constituted those six, sometimes including Śaiva philosophy as a school and also constructing categories such as 'the *Nāstika* school' to accommodate a 'multitude of sins'.

In the modern era it has become standard practice to identify the six schools as 'Hindu', that is, exhibiting some allegiance to Hindu brahmanical culture and lifestyle, in particular an acceptance of the Vedas as authoritative. Following this scheme the six schools are:

Nyāya – the School of Logic
Vaiśeṣika – the School of Atomism

Sāṃkhya – the School of dualistic Discrimination
Yoga – the School of classical Yoga

Mīmāṃsā – the School of Vedic Exegesis
Vedānta – the School based upon the end of the Vedas (i.e. the *Upaniṣads*)

The schools are usually grouped into couples (as above) according to their perceived affinities. Thus, Nyāya and Vaiśeṣika represent the 'empirico-logical' strand of Hindu culture, Sāṃkhya and Yoga share an interest in attaining liberation (*mokṣa*) through the isolation of pure consciousness from matter, whilst Mīmāṃsā and Vedānta exemplify an approach to philosophy grounded in the exegesis of the sacred Vedas. This understanding of the 'six schools' has become dominant in modern accounts of Indian philosophy and conveniently ignores the diversity of doxographical accounts offered before the modern era. The designation of these schools as 'Hindu' and therefore the legitimate representatives of Indian philosophical culture of course also succeeds in silencing the role played by Buddhist, Jaina and Cārvāka schools in the history of Indian philosophy.

In the modern era one also finds the claim that the six 'Hindu' schools represent complementary perspectives upon the same basic reality. As such, they are said to be in the final analysis in agreement with each other about the nature of reality. This trend, although amenable to Neo-Hindu and modern nationalist assumptions about the underlying unity of Indian history and culture, fundamentally misrepresents the rich diversity and contestatory nature of Indian philosophical thought. Although there are inclusivist trends within Indian culture, even a cursory analysis of the literature of the various *darśanas* will demonstrate that the schools uphold radically different positions on a whole range of topics. Moreover, it is clear that there is considerable diversity within as well as between the various *darśanas*, particularly when such schools are viewed over an extended period of time.

The development of specific *darśanas* is a history of the development of a variety of well-established philosophical traditions or schools of thought. The scope of interest of the *darśanas* is much wider than that of modern philosophy and has more in common with ancient forms of philosophical speculation which tended to include the study of humankind and the 'empirical sciences'. Even today, physics, chemistry and biology are sometimes referred to by their more traditional nomenclature of 'natural philosophy'. Similarly, in India, as we have seen, the boundaries between cognitive disciplines is not drawn up in the same way as the modern disciplinary boundaries of the post-Enlightenment era. Although this point has been overstated far too often, it is true that most forms of Indian philosophical thought have an interest in what might be described as theology or soteriology (the science of salvation).

– BHARTṚHARI AND THE PHILOSOPHY OF LINGUISTIC ANALYSIS (*VYĀKARAṆA*) –

Considerable attention has been paid to the apparent certainties of mathematics in western philosophical discussion (from Plato through Descartes to Frege). It is worth noting the role played by Islamic and Indian mathematicians in the furtherance of such pursuits. It was in India after all that the concept of 'zero' was first discovered. There may indeed be some connection between this and the development of the Mahāyāna Buddhist notion of 'emptiness' (*śūnyatā*) as that which is neither positive (+) nor negative (–) in its implications. The Indian discovery of the 'zero' of course has allowed not only the development of the decimal system of enumeration but also the binary system which underlies the technological revolution of the computer age. Nevertheless, overall ancient Hindu philosophy displays a much greater interest in the apparent certainties of grammar – in the sense of language (*śabda*) but also in the sense of the grammar of ritual. These two dimensions are intertwined in a Vedic context, though the former has generally been seen as the remit of the grammarian, whilst the latter has been the primary concern of the Mīmāṃsā tradition.

The most influential figure in the establishment of linguistic analysis (*vyākaraṇa*) as a *darśana* in its own right is Bhartṛhari (fifth century CE). For Bhartṛhari, understanding the operations of language is not only a valid philosophical tradition but remains the most important *darśana* since it is the task of the grammarian to preserve the purity of the Vedic message and prevent the corruption of its language (*Vākyapadīya* 1.11). Indeed, Bhartṛhari has high expectations for linguistic analysis arguing that it is the door leading to liberation (1.14) and leads to a realisation of the Absolute (i.e. *brahman*, 1.22).

Why does Bhartṛhari make such bold claims about a correct understanding of grammar? To appreciate his position we should note that linguistic analysis in this context is indistinguishable from the study of the Vedas – the ancient sacred teachings of the Hindu brahmanical traditions. For grammarians such as Bhartṛhari, Sanskrit (or at least that form of it in which the Vedic hymns were composed) represents the archetypal example of a natural language (hence its name '*saṃskṛta*' – perfected). In the Vedic-brahmanical world-view the universe conforms to the grammatical structure of the sacred language of the Vedas.

Indeed Bhartṛhari, like his modern Lacanian and Derridean counterparts, rejects the view that one can know anything outside of language. All knowledge is linguistic in nature (*śabda*). Even those things that might be described as indescribable (*avācya*) are describable (*vācya*) precisely in so far as we can refer to them as indescribable. There is an eternal connection between knowledge and language which cannot be broken.

> If this eternal identity between knowledge and the word were to disappear, knowledge would cease to be knowledge; it is this identity which makes identification possible.
>
> *Vākyapadīya*, 1. 124, translation in Iyer, 1965: 110–11

Bhartṛhari did not require the postulation of an innate structure to the human brain, as Chomsky does, to account for difficult cases such as the experiences of new-born babies because of the Indian belief in rebirth (*saṃsāra*). Thus, even the new-born child carries with it karmic baggage and a linguistic mode of apprehension resulting from its experiences in past lives (*Vākyapadīya* 1.121).

For Bhartṛhari the fundamental unit of meaning is the complete utterance. If one knows a language well, meaning is apprehended as a complete sentence and is an instantaneous flash of comprehension (*pratibhā*). This became known as the *sphoṭa* theory of meaning. The authentic experience of meaning occurs through a holistic grasp of complete utterances and not individual words – as a kind of *gestalt*. However, if one does not know a language well meaning is artificially derived by grasping the meaning of individual phonemes and words and determining their relationship to each other. An analogy can be drawn here with a work of art, a painter conceives of a picture as a unitary whole despite using a variety of colours and brush strokes to create the picture. Similarly, when we appreciate a painting we experience it as a whole, not as a collocation of disparate brush strokes.

The linguistic structure of reality, according to Bhartṛhari, is unitary and cannot really be divided into smaller atomic units except for the heuristic purpose of grammatical analysis. Language is indivisible (*akhaṇḍa*) and ultimately refers to a single monistic reality (*śabda-brahman*). Thus, as Mādhava explains this view

> *brahman* is the thing denoted by all words; and this one object has various differences imposed upon it according to each particular form; but the conventional variety of the differences produced by these illusory conditions is only the result of ignorance. Non-duality is the true state; but through the power of 'concealment' [exercised by illusion] at the time of the conventional use of words a manifold expansion takes place.
>
> *Sarvadarśanasaṃgraha* XIII: 219

How is it then that the one appears as many? It is easier to see why Bhartṛhari viewed language as indivisible and ultimately unitary if we note that the Sanskrit language has no real sense of punctuation (or as Mark Tully puts it there are 'no full stops in India'). Indefinitely long expressions can be formed by nominal composition, that is by adding terms onto compounds according to certain basic grammatical rules. Speech then is potentially infinite in extension. The history of the universe can be viewed as the utterance of one very long sentence!

For Bhartṛhari the manifold universe is a creation of *śabda-brahman* – the Absolute as Word (see *Bṛ Up* 4.1.2). This is reminiscent of similar conceptions of creation found in Judaeo-Christian and Hellenistic circles focusing upon the notion of *logos*. For Bhartṛhari creation occurs through the creative power of the word (*śabda*). The early Vedic hymns had already praised Vāc, the Goddess of Speech, as creator (Ṛg Veda X. 71.7) and the source of friendship and social cordiality (X. 71). Speech is the final abode of *brahman* (Ṛg Veda 1.164.35) and creates with merely a quarter of her being with the remaining three-quarters transcending human speech (1.164.45). She is responsible for the establishment of a rhythmic (syntactical?) order (*ṛta*) to the universe (1.164.37). Bhartṛhari describes the sacred syllable Om as 'the source of all scripture and the common factor of all original causes.' (*Vākyapadīya* 1.9). Om symbolises *brahman* – the totality or the Absolute. In the *Māṇḍūkya Upaniṣad* Om is analysed into its three constituent letters A, U and M and related not only to time and the passage of past, present and future but also to the waking, dreaming and deep sleep states. As a totality, however, Om symbolises the fourth state (*turīya*) – an experience of non-duality (*advaita*) which transcends the previous three. Similarly, 'A' is identified by Śaṅkara as the sound (*śabda*) emitted when one opens one's mouth and 'M' as the sound when it closes. 'A-U-M' therefore represents the creation, subsistence and eventual destruction of the universe.

For Bhartṛhari, the power of time (*kāla*) is central to the apparent manifestation of a multiplicity from the unity of the Word-Principle (*śabda-brahman*). Time is like a thread or a piece of string (*Vākyapadīya* 3.9.15) which allows for movement and causal activity, like the pulling of the strings of a puppet (Ibid., 3.9.4). It is a dynamic force which pushes things (*kalayati*) in and out of existence like a revolving water-wheel (3.9.14). Time functions through permission (*abhyanujñā*) and prevention (*pratibandha*) to bring things into existence (i.e. establish them in the present) and prevent others from occurring (by establishing them in the future). Time allows things to arise but also pushes them, through the process of decay, out of the present and into the past (*Vākyapadīya* 3.9.4). In this fashion time can be said to have three powers, allowing all things to arise, subsist and then cease. Nevertheless, the unrolling (*vivarta*) of the universe is, from the ultimate perspective, an eternal 'now'. Time is eternal and undivided and the final goal of linguistic analysis for Bhartṛhari is the apprehension of the whole, of *śabda-brahman* in its absolute non-duality.

> Time is the creative power of Śabda *brahman* and is thus responsible for the birth, death, and continuity of everything in the cosmos. Time is one, but when broken or limited into sequences appears as moments or actions ... All of ordinary life is sequenced by these three powers of time [i.e. past, present and future]. Yet all the while, declares Bhartṛhari, there is really no sequence at all. From the ultimate viewpoint all three powers of time are constantly present. Time is one.
>
> Coward and Raja, 1990: 44

There has been some discussion as to the relationship between Bhartṛhari and the emerging non-dualistic strand of Advaita Vedānta and also questions about his relationship to various Buddhist strands of thought. Bhartṛhari has clearly influenced the Buddhist Dignāga and is cited respectfully by him on a number of occasions. As a proponent of the Buddhist philosophy of process-dynamism, however, Dignāga rejects the *sphoṭa* theory of meaning in favour of a theory of meaning based upon the mutual exclusion (*apoha*) of linguistic signs (see Chapter 4). Similarly, some scholars have argued that Bhartṛhari's philosophy shows significant resemblances to the philosophy of Advaita Vedānta (Iyer, 1969; Sastri, 1959). Bhartṛhari's philosophy, although grounded in the monistic reality of *śabda-brahman*, does not seem to imply that the world is an illusion (*māyā*) as the Advaita Vedānta philosophy does. His use of terms like '*vivarta*' to denote the 'unrolling' of the universe clearly pre-dates the illusionistic connotations of this term as it is used in later Advaita Vedānta thought (see Chapter 9).

Nevertheless, Bhartṛhari is an important figure in Indian philosophy and was influential in the development of the non-dualistic philosophy of Maṇḍana Miśra (late seventh to eighth century CE), a Mīmāṃsaka philosopher and an older contemporary of Śaṅkara, reputed founder of the Advaita (non-dualist) school. Maṇḍana defended Bhartṛhari's *sphoṭa* theory of meaning and, with a little borrowing from the Buddhist Dignāga, extended Bhartṛhari's claim that language ultimately denoted an underlying unity (*brahman*) to the experiential realm (see Chapter 7).

– THE VARIETIES OF HINDU PHILOSOPHY –

Although one should be wary of attempts to elide 'Hindu' with 'Indian' in the study of Indian philosophy, the remainder of this chapter offers a brief account of the six Hindu schools mentioned earlier. Sadly, there is insufficient space to discuss the considerable role played by Jaina and Śaivite schools within Indian philosophical circles and I will leave that task to minds better prepared than my own. Nevertheless, we will not remain bound in our discussion to an analysis of Hindu philosophy alone. We have already encountered the dissenting voices of the Cārvāka materialists and will proceed in the next chapter to examine the varieties of Buddhist philosophical thought in India.

Each of the six schools of (so-called) 'Hindu' philosophy have a foundational text of aphoristic sayings which together constitute the basic 'thread' or '*sūtra*' of teachings for that particular school. The term *sūtra*, literally meaning a thread or a strand, refers to the acceptance of these texts as the fundamental "strands" of the school which they represent. The one exception in this regard is the Sāṃkhya school where the primary foundational text is a collection of verses (*kārikā*) rather than *sūtra*-style aphorisms (there is a *Sāṃkhya Sūtra* but it is much later than the *Sāṃkhya Kārikā* and clearly composed in order to substantiate the Sāṃkhya's position as an established school with a foundational *sūtra* of its own). This caveat aside, therefore, the various *sūtras* outline the fundamental stance of each school (*darśana*).

Sūtras usually consist of brief and cryptic aphorisms, most of which are incomprehensible without the aid of a commentary (*bhāṣya*). For instance, the *Brahma Sūtra* (or *Vedānta Sūtra* as it is sometimes known) consists of a series of short phrases, often containing little more than a few short words. The extreme brevity and cryptic nature of these texts made memorisation easier. This allowed for the continuation of a consistent, oral tradition. It is possible that many of these early *sūtras* are the condensation of a long process of intellectual debate. It is probably fair to say, therefore, that all of the early *sūtra* materials are composite, having gone through a number of redactions, and it remains difficult to pinpoint their exact origin and date. As such it is perhaps more appropriate to consider these texts as the product of a specific scholastic community or tradition (*saṃpradāya*) than as the work of a single author.

Sūtras in general came to take on a sort of semi-revelatory status for the particular school that they belonged to. The authority of such texts is usually thought to be beyond question, though this certainly did not stop later thinkers from 'creatively reinterpreting' the text and on some occasions disagreeing with it. However, as we have noted, the *sūtra* is a highly condensed text making it highly amenable to a variety of interpretations. The various philosophers following each tradition wrote what are called *śāstras*, which are basically philosophical texts offering a more comprehensive and systematic exposition of the topics of the *sūtras*. Simplistically, therefore, one could say that the *sūtras* tell us what the truth is and the *śāstras* attempt to explain why.

The *bhāṣya* is a particular type of *śāstra* (an explanatory exposition of doctrine), in the form of an authoritative commentary upon the *sūtras*. The main task of a *bhāṣya* is to explain the meanings and allusions contained within the *sūtra* itself. For example, the *Brahma Sūtra* has been commented upon by a number of Vedānta thinkers, the most famous being the *bhāṣyas* of Śaṅkara (Advaita Vedānta, eighth century CE), Rāmānuja (Viśiṣṭādvaita, eleventh century CE), and Madhva (Dvaita, thirteenth century CE). *Bhāṣyas* soon became the most important forum for the exposition of each school's basic philosophical position, providing an interpretation of the meaning of the *sūtra* as well as an opportunity to refute the views of rival schools of thought. They became indispensable tools for unlocking the meaning of the *sūtras*.

– THE PRIOR EXEGESIS SCHOOL (PŪRVA MĪMĀṂSĀ) –

The Mīmāṃsā tradition is primarily concerned with a correct understanding of the Vedas. Traditionally, a distinction is made between Dharma Mīmāṃsā – The Exegesis of the Dharma school, later called the Prior Exegesis school (Pūrva Mīmāṃsā) and Brahma Mīmāṃsā, later called the Later Exegesis (Uttara Mīmāṃsā) or Vedānta tradition. *Dharma* is a term that will be familiar to all students of Hinduism, denoting the cosmic, social and moral order of the universe. On a microcosmic level all Hindus have their own *svadharma*, that is a prescribed set of obligations and modes of behaviour based upon their caste-status, gender, social position, familial status etc.

It might surprise some to discover that the Pūrva Mīmāṃsā is an atheistic tradition. By this I mean that the school believes that the Vedic revelation is self-authenticating and authorless and therefore cannot be said to derive from a particular deity. Of course, the Mīmāṃsā accepts the existence of a whole variety of gods. After all, the Vedic hymns are full of references to such beings and most hymns pay homage to one deity or another. The Mīmāṃsā, however, understood the revelation of the Vedas (*śruti* – 'that which is heard') to be supreme and resisted any notion of an over-arching Supreme Deity or divine Creator.

The primary concern of the Prior Exegesis school was in the nature and sanctity of the Vedic ritual, the preservation of which was seen as vital to the maintenance of the cosmic order (*ṛta*, later '*Dharma*'). On this view the primary significance of the Vedas is to be found in a series of injunctions or imperatives it offers as a guide to human behaviour. The school, therefore, propounded its own form of Vedic fundamentalism, combined as it was with the beliefs that the Vedas were not of human origin (*apauruṣeya*) and that the language in which the hymns occur (an early form of Sanskrit) was sacred and transcendent to our use of it. There is no possibility that language could be conventional. Language, for the Mīmāṃsā, was the verbal expression of reality and the linguistic rules of Sanskrit constituted the naturally occurring rhythms of the universe. As we saw in our discussion of Bhartṛhari and the Hindu grammarians, the ancient Vedic seers (*ṛṣi*) were not seen as the composers of the Vedic hymns but were those in whom the revelation was heard. Mīmāṃsā exegesis then did not base itself upon the principle of authorial intention since the Vedas have no author.

The foundational text of the school is the *Mīmāṃsā Sūtra* of Jaimini

(c. 200 BCE–200 CE), a voluminous text consisting of twelve chapters divided into sixty sections, followed by an appendix of four chapters (known as the *devatā-kāṇḍa*) addressing various deities. Although clearly containing ancient material the *Sūtra* is aware of the *Brahma Sūtra* of Bādarāyaṇa and seems to presuppose it on a number of occasions (Nakamura, 1985: 423). The earliest extant commentary upon the *Sūtra* is by Śabara Svāmin (c. third to fourth century CE) and this *bhāṣya* constituted the main point of departure for subsequent Mīmāṃsā works. There are two main schools of Mīmāṃsā both named after their founders – Kumārila Bhaṭṭa and Prabhākara.[2]

Kumārila (seventh century CE) is thought to be an older contemporary of Śaṅkara and composed an independent exposition of Śabara's *Bhāṣya* in three parts, the most important being the *Śloka Vārttika* discussing the philosophical themes of the first chapter of Śabara's commentary. Maṇḍana Miśra, a disciple of Kumārila, wrote a number of important Mīmāṃsa treatises, but also became renowned as an exponent of the non-dualistic (*advaita*) philosophy of Vedānta. Prabhākara was a contemporary of Kumārila and shows some awareness of his work.

– THE LATER EXEGESIS (UTTARA MĪMĀṂSĀ) OR 'END OF THE VEDAS' (VEDĀNTA) SCHOOL –

Vedānta means 'end of the Vedas' and denotes the final section of Vedic literature known as the *Upaniṣads*. As we have seen a distinction developed between two traditions of Vedic interpretation – the 'Prior Exegesis' (Pūrva Mīmāṃsā) and the 'Later Exegesis' (Uttara Mīmāṃsā) schools. The establishment of the Uttara Mīmāṃsā or 'Vedānta' as a distinctive exegetical trend within brahmanical circles is based upon a distinction between those sections of the Vedas that are concerned with the proper execution of ritual actions (*karma-kāṇḍa*) and those sections concerned with the attainment of metaphysical knowledge (*jñāna-kāṇḍa*). The former denotes the concerns of the Mīmāṃsā school, whilst the latter represents the primary interest of the various Vedānta traditions.

There are a number of Vedānta traditions (*saṃpradāya*), despite the tendency of many to conflate the Advaita tradition of Śaṅkara with Vedānta as a whole. All schools of Vedānta accept the classical *Upaniṣads*, the *Brahma Sūtra* and the *Bhagavad Gītā* as the triple foundations (*prasthānatraya*) of their tradition, though there are differences of opinion concerning the number of authoritative *Upaniṣads* as well as divergent interpretations of the import of these central Vedāntic texts.

The *Brahma Sūtra* (or *Vedānta Sūtra*) is an early attempt to systematise the doctrines of the *Upaniṣads*. It is attributed to Bādarāyaṇa but clearly contains materials spanning a 700 year period, culminating in a final redaction some time around 400–50 CE. The primary target of the *Brahma Sūtra* is a repudiation of the Sāṃkhya position that reality is the product of an interaction between consciousness (*puruṣa*) and matter (*prakṛti*). *Brahman* alone is the cause of the universe. The central concern of the *Upaniṣads* was the nature of the relationship between *ātman* (the essential self) and *brahman*. According to the *Brahma Sūtra* the self is a portion (*aṃśa*) of *brahman* (BS 2.3.43), that is, it is not separate from *brahman* but it is also not identical (see BS 2.3.43 and Chapter 9). Subsequent schools of Vedānta attempted to make sense of this position in a variety of ways.

– THE PHILOSOPHY OF NON-DUALISM (ADVAITA VEDĀNTA) –

The Advaita Vedānta school of Śaṅkarācārya (eighth century CE) put forward the radical position that there is in fact no difference at all between *brahman* and the self. Reality is non-dual (*advaita*) and only *brahman* is ultimately real. The earliest available work attributable to the Śaṅkarite tradition of Advaita is the *Gauḍapādīya Kārikā* or *Māṇḍūkya Kārikā* (c. sixth century CE) – comprising of 215 verses divided into four chapters. This short text is attributed to a mysterious figure known as Gauḍapāda – the supreme teacher or grand-teacher (*paramaguru*) of Śaṅkara (eighth century CE). It is not clear whether this implies the primary inspiration of Śaṅkara or literally denotes someone in a direct lineage of teachers (*guru-paramparā*). The Advaita tradition, however, generally reveres Gauḍapāda as the teacher of Śaṅkara's own teacher Govinda. Whatever the precise identity of this figure, the *Gauḍapādīya Kārikā* constitutes a major source of ideas for Śaṅkara. The text propounds the view that the world of diversity is nothing more than an illusory appearance (*māyā*) of a monistic, or more accurately non-dualistic, reality. The final truth is that nothing has really come into existence (*ajātivāda*) in the first place. Plurality is an illusion. *Brahman* – the divine Absolute – is the sole reality and is identical with *ātman* – the immutable, essential self that constitutes the ultimate reality of all beings. The *Gauḍapādīya Kārikā* is infused with the philosophical terminology of Mahāyāna Buddhism, especially in the fourth chapter. This has led some (for example, Dasgupta, 1988, vol. 1: 423) to argue that the author was himself a Buddhist, though it seems more likely that we have here a further example of the interactive nature of Hindu and Buddhist philosophical schools. The *Gauḍapādīya Kārikā* is clearly a Vedāntic text and utilises Buddhist arguments and analogies to suit its own ends (King, 1995).

Śaṅkara is best known for his commentary on the *Brahma Sūtra* which is usually deemed to be the definitive exposition of his thought. He also wrote commentaries on a number of *Upaniṣads*, the *Bhagavad Gītā*, the

Gauḍapādīya Kārikā and possibly a sub-commentary on the *Yoga Sūtra*, though determining which of these works are authentic and which are spurious is a difficult and exacting task (see Mayeda, 1973, 1992). Śaṅkara also wrote at least one independent scholastic treatise (*śāstra*) known as the *Thousand Teachings* (*Upadeśasāhasrī*). The central philosophy of Śaṅkara's Advaita school is summed up in certain key phrases occurring in the early *Upaniṣads*. These became known as 'great sayings' (*mahāvākya*) and were believed to represent the final teaching of the Vedas. Such phrases were also thought to induce a state of enlightenment when studied under the proper conditions in the form of a liberating awareness of the undifferentiated unity of one's essential self (*ātman*) with the ground of the universe (*brahman*). The most famous *mahāvākya* is probably 'That is You' (*tat tvam asi*), denoting the identity of *ātman* and *brahman*, but other 'great sayings' include: 'I am *brahman*' (*aham brahmāsmi*), 'This *ātman* is *brahman*' (*ayam ātmā brahma*) and 'All this (i.e. the universe) is *brahman*' (*sarvam khalu idam brahma*).

For Śaṅkara the world is a false appearance (*māyā*) of *brahman* brought about by ignorance of the identity of the self (*ātman*) with *brahman*. There are two levels of truth, the ultimate truth – that is, reality as viewed from the non-dualistic perspective of *brahman*-realisation (*brahmānubhava*), and practical truth, that is, reality as viewed from the perspective of the unenlightened. From this vantage point the universe is manifold and exists separately from *Īśvara* – the Personal Creator of the Universe.

It is common to find Śaṅkara represented as the most influential and important figure in the history of Hindu philosophy but this is clearly not justified by the historical evidence. In the immediate centuries after Śaṅkara his works seem to have been overshadowed in Vedānta circles by his older contemporary Maṇḍana Miśra. It is Maṇḍana who receives most attention as a representative of the Advaita position during this period (Potter, 1981: 17) and it was not until the teachings of the two figures became harmonised in the work of Vācaspati Miśra that Śaṅkara's status came to the fore (Hacker, 1964: 30). Śaṅkara is said to have established a number of Advaita monasteries (*maṭha*) throughout India, though even here Hacker suggests the credit should go to Vidyāraṇya in the fourteenth century (Hacker, 1964: 31). We should bear in mind also that there were a variety of non-dualistic philosophies within ancient India ranging from the linguistic non-dualism (*śabdādvaita*) of the grammarian Bhartṛhari, the non-dualistic philosophy of the Recognition (*pratyabhijñā*) school of Śaivism in Kashmir and the devotional non-dualism of the *Bhagavatā Purāṇa*, though these are often forgotten in the rush to pay homage to Śaṅkara.

Nevertheless, the consolidation of the Śaṅkarācārya tradition of Advaita occurs in the works of Śaṅkara's chief disciples Sureśvara and Padmapāda. Subsequently, the Advaita tradition produced two strands of interpretation with regard to Śaṅkara's philosophy. The Vivaraṇa strand follows the interpretations of Śaṅkara's student and youngest contemporary Padmapāda. The Bhāmatī strand synthesises Śaṅkara's views with those of Maṇḍana Miśra, his older contemporary and rival, and is first put forward in the *Bhāmatī* of Vācaspati Miśra (c. 960 CE), a sub-commentary on Śaṅkara's *Brahma Sūtra Bhāṣya*. There are a number of subtle differences between these two sub-schools, but the significant factors are that the Bhāmatī strand maintains the importance of yogic practice and contemplation (*nididhyāsana*) in the attainment of liberative knowledge, whilst the Vivaraṇa rejects the Mīmāṃsaka emphasis upon activism in favour of Vedic study and a direct apprehension of *brahman*. Secondly, the two sub-schools differ over the question of the nature and locus of ignorance (*avidyā*). For the Bhāmatī strand ignorance is located in and differs according to the individual self (*jīvātman*), whereas for the Vivaraṇa there is also a cosmic aspect to ignorance (*māyā*) which relates to *brahman* itself.

– NON-DUALISM OF THE QUALIFIED (VIŚIṢṬĀDVAITA VEDĀNTA) –

The illusionism (*māyā-vāda*) of Śaṅkara's Advaita stance came under considerable criticism from rival Vedānta traditions. Particularly noteworthy in this regard is the Viśiṣṭādvaita Vedānta tradition of Rāmānuja (traditional dates: 1017–1137 CE, though 1056–1137 is also possible). Rāmānuja wrote a commentary on the *Brahma Sūtra* (often called the *Śrī-Bhāṣya*) and is said to have composed eight other works, including an influential commentary on the *Bhagavad Gītā*. Frequently one finds the name 'Viśiṣṭādvaita' rendered as 'qualified non-dualism' but it is better rendered as 'the non-duality of that which is qualified (*viśiṣṭasya*)'. Rāmānuja accepts that the self is not-different from *brahman* and thus accepts a form of non-dualism. He rejects, however, the idea that *brahman* is an impersonal reality without qualities. Rāmānuja also rejected any notion that the world was somehow unreal (*māyā*) and considered Śaṅkara's adoption of this position to be both an affront to the creativity of the deity and evidence that he was a crypto-Buddhist (*pracchana bauddha*).

The Viśiṣṭādvaita tradition incorporates Vaiṣṇava devotionalism (*bhakti*) into the Vedānta tradition. The relationship between *brahman* and individual selves is the same as the relationship between the individual self and the body which it inhabits. *Brahman* 'ensouls' the universe and is its inner controller (*antaryāmin*). *Brahman* remains the sole reality – the ground of being – but the individual self is a 'mode' (*prakāra*) of *brahman* and in this sense at least is not different from *brahman* itself.

Other schools of Vedānta include Dvaita or Dualist Vedānta, a tradition initiated by Madhva (1238–1317) in reaction to Advaita and (to a lesser extent) Viśiṣṭādvaita. Madhva composed commentaries upon the *Brahma Sūtra*, the *Bhagavad Gītā* and the *Upaniṣads* and a number of independent works. The Dvaita school promulgated an uncompromising form of monotheism, worshipping Viṣṇu as the Supreme Deity and Creator of the universe. Individual selves are creations of Viṣṇu and are separate from Him, though they remain wholly dependent upon Viṣṇu for their existence. The material world is also separate from both God and each individual self, being the evolute of primal matter (*prakṛti*). Madhva therefore differs from all other schools of Vedānta in making Viṣṇu the efficient cause of the universe but not its material cause. God is not that out of which the universe is moulded!

– THE PARTICULARIST SCHOOL (VAIŚEṢIKA) –

The Vaiśeṣika school displays an interest in examining and classifying fundamental realities. The school upholds the reality of the external world, propounds an atomic theory of matter and is seen by many as a prototypical example of early 'scientific' speculation in ancient Indian culture. The Vaiśeṣika system is one of the oldest schools of Indian philosophy and is first expounded in the *Vaiśeṣika Sūtra*. These aphorisms are ascribed to a figure known as Kaṇāda (or *ulūka* – 'the owl'). Vaiśeṣika is primarily interested in an analysis of nature and the school takes its name from its preoccupation with particularity (*viśeṣa*). The Vaiśeṣika displays an interest in investigating the fundamental categories (*padārtha*) of reality. How many types of entity make up the world? As such, the Vaiśeṣika can be seen as a very early attempt to provide a comprehensive ontological classification or 'inventory' of existence.

The difference in the orientation of the Vaiśeṣika in comparison to a tradition such as the Mīmāṃsā can be seen from their respective attitudes towards the notion of *Dharma*. The *Vaiśeṣika Sūtra* begins 'Now we shall consider the nature of *Dharma*'. This is an interesting beginning and has perplexed those who wish to interpret the Vaiśeṣika as a kind of proto-scientific movement in ancient India. It may be the case that the earliest forms of Vaiśeṣika represented a divergent strand of Mīmāṃsā, though it has usually been thought that the origins of the school lie outside the Vedic fold. The *Vaiśeṣika Sūtra* defines *Dharma* as 'the object or good marked by a Vedic injunction or command' though the text makes it quite clear that Vedic injunctions are good because they proclaim the *Dharma* rather than because they are the Vedas! This is to be contrasted with the position taken in the Pūrva Mīmāṃsā school where *Dharma* is self-certifying (*svataḥ pramāṇya*) and emphasis is placed upon the primacy of the revealed word (*śruti*). Crucially, the Vaiśeṣika school accepts only two independent sources of valid knowledge (*pramāṇa*): perception and inference. The Vedas are a valid source of knowledge, but are not independently established since they are based upon the perception (*pratyakṣa*) of wise sages (*ṛṣi*). Similarly, Vedic injunctions are said to be based upon the use of logical inference (*anumāna*).

The *Vaiśeṣika Sūtra* displays an awareness of Sāṃkhya and Mīmāṃsā ideas but shows no knowledge of Nyāya as a system of thought. The earliest reference to the Vaiśeṣika can be found in Buddhist Abhidharmic literature of the first century CE, though the medical theories of the Āyurvedic text the *Caraka Saṃhitā* seem to presuppose some Vaiśeṣika (as well as Sāṃkhya) concepts. We have no real idea how old some of the Vaiśeṣika aphorisms really are, but the composition of the *Sūtra* as a whole can probably be placed in a two hundred year period from 200 BCE to the beginning of the Common Era.

The next five hundred years have been described as the 'Dark Period' of Vaiśeṣika history since so little is known about the development of the system and there is no extant literature from this period to examine. A Chinese Buddhist tradition suggests that there were eighteen schools of Vaiśeṣika and Sāṃkhya in ancient India (Matilal, 1977: 59) but the early period between the composition of the *sūtras* and later works of Vaiśeṣika philosophy is mostly lost until the composition of the *Compendium of the Nature of Fundamental Categories* (*Padārtha-dharma-saṃgraha*) of Praśastapāda (c. 550 CE). This work is referred to by both Uddyotakara (Nyāya) and Dignāga (Buddhism) and gradually became the standard reference work of the Vaiśeṣika school. Although ostensibly a commentary (*bhāṣya*) upon the *Vaiśeṣika Sūtra* Praśastapāda does not provide a close discussion of the aphorisms making a number of organisational changes to the order of the *sūtras* as well as adjustments to the early Vaiśeṣika position. Thus, Praśastapāda replaces the *sūtra*'s original list of seventeen qualities with a list of twenty-four and introduces a theistic cosmology to the Vaiśeṣika system.

Praśastapāda shows clear evidence of influence from the works of the Buddhist Dignāga (c. 600 CE) in his discussion of the nature of perception (*pratyakṣa*) and from the Nyāya school in his discussion of inference (*anumāna*). Subsequent commentaries on Praśastapāda, by Vyomaśiva, Śrīdhara (ninth century CE) and most significantly Udayana (eleventh century CE), show an increasing reliance and interaction with Nyāya thought to such an extent that by the time of Udayana's commentary the *Kiraṇāvalī* one can no longer speak of the schools as two separate traditions.

– The School of Reasoning (Nyāya) –

The primary concerns of the Nyāya school represent a shift away from the ontological orientation of the slightly earlier Vaiśeṣika towards a concern with the nature of knowledge itself. How do we know what we know? What are the valid sources of knowledge? The Nyāya displays a keen interest in the nature of perception and the ways in which truth is established. In particular, the Nyāya became concerned with the nature of inferential reasoning (*anumāna*) and constructed a system of rules for conducting debates. The school shares many of it presuppositions with the Vaiśeṣika and defends a form of pluralistic realism, grounded in the reliability of 'common-sense' perceptions.

The *Nyāya Sūtra* is traditionally ascribed to Akṣapāda Gotama (c. 250–450 CE). The *sūtras* are more organised than those of the Vaiśeṣika school and some aphorisms from the *Vaiśeṣika Sūtra* are repeated with a slight variation in the *Nyāya Sūtra* (e.g. NS 1.1.8). The Nyāya aphorisms have clearly undergone a number of redactions and the present form of the *sūtras* seems to incorporate material from earlier manuals on debating procedures (*vāda-śāstra*), particularly evident within the fifth of its five chapters. These *sūtras* seem to have originated in the disputations and debates between scholars and brahmin ritual specialists in ancient India and consisted of a list of logical-cum-theoretical categories pertinent to a debating context and thereby included the rules and regulations whereby such debates could take place. As the early Nyāya position developed, the first two of the sixteen categories mentioned in the text, viz. *pramāṇa* (the means of knowledge) and *prameya* (that which is known) became the focus of particular interest and by the time of the final redaction of the *Nyāya Sūtra* the issue of epistemology (what do we know and how do we know that we know it?) had become the central preoccupation of the Nyāya school.

Consequently, it is highly unlikely that the *Nyāya Sūtra* in its final form constitutes the work of a single author. Crucial in the attempt to ascribing a date for the final redaction of the text is its awareness of the Buddhist philosophy of emptiness (*śūnyatā*). Nāgārjuna's critique of *pramāṇa*-theory in the *Vigrahavyāvartanī* seems to presuppose the Nyāya position and in his *Vaidalya-prakaraṇa* Nāgārjuna mentions all sixteen categories of the *Nyāya Sūtra*. Moreover, the *Nyāya Sūtra* is aware of Nāgārjuna's critique and refutes his position. It is likely then that the final redaction of the text was contemporaneous with Nāgārjuna, placing it sometime in the late second century of the Common Era.

The first available commentary on the entire *Nyāya Sūtra* is the *Nyāya Bhāṣya* of Vātsyāyana (c. 350–450 CE). The author is perhaps more famous in the west for his composition of the *Kāma Sūtra* – a Hindu text on the etiquette of courtship and love and not just a manual of sexual positions as it is often represented in the west. The *Nyāya Sūtra* is not nearly so titillating unless one is excited by a detailed discussion of Indian logical and philosophical categories! Vātsyāyana is aware of alternate views to his own, implying the existence of other commentaries, though his may have been the first commentary upon the entire *Nyāya Sūtra* (Matilal, 1977: 80).

Vātsyāyana's *Nyāya Bhāṣya* was criticised in the writings of the Buddhist philosopher Dignāga, thus precipitating a long history of Nyāya responses to Dignāga's critique. First in line was Uddyotakara ("the Enlightener") who composed the *Elucidation of Nyāya* (*Nyāya Vārttika)* in the sixth century. The text provides a comprehensive rebuttal of the views of the "quibblers" with specific reference to the Buddhist position of Dignāga and introduces a clearly theistic emphasis to the Nyāya position. There are a number of important Nyāya works from this period (including lost works by Sānātani and Trilocana), but worthy of particular mention is the *Summary of Nyāya* (*Nyāyamañjarī*) of Jayanta Bhaṭṭa (c. 900 CE). This is an independent Nyāya treatise dealing with Buddhist thought (mainly the work of Dharmakīrti, Dignāga's pupil) and the views of the Mīmāṃsakas (e.g. Kumārila).

It is clear that by the time of Jayanta, the Nyāya tradition had firmly established the *Bhāṣya* of Vātsyāyana and the *Vārttika* of Uddyotakara as the central authorities since he refers to a distinction within the Nyāya tradition (*saṃpradāya*) between 'masters' (*ācāryas*) specialising in the *Vārttika*, and the expositors (*vyākhyātṛs*) – experts on Vātsyāyana's *Nyāya Bhāṣya*. An example of the former is Vācaspati Miśra (c. 960 CE) in his *Gloss on the Elucidation of Nyāya* (*Nyāya-vārttika-tātparyaṭikā)* – a commentary on Uddyotakara's work. Vācaspati was a polymath, composing works on a variety of Hindu philosophical schools, earning him the title 'master of all systems' (*sarvatantrasvatantra*). What is characteristic of Vācaspati's works is that they are all written from the perspective of the school under consideration. He is not easily classifiable as a Naiyāyika and indeed he is also famous as a philosopher of the Advaita Vedānta tradition. Whilst wearing his Nyāya hat, Vācaspati provided a defence of Uddyotakara's position from the Buddhist critique of Dharmakīrti (seventh century CE) and his followers.

In the eleventh century we encounter the work of Udayana, author of a number of Nyāya and Vaiśeṣika works. Udayana, for instance, composed the *Kiraṇāvalī*, widely acknowledged to be the best commentary on the work of Praśastapāda. Udayana also wrote a number of independent works including *Distinguishing the Truth of the Self* (*Ātmatattvaviveka*, also known as *Bauddhadhikkāra* 'A Critique of the Buddhists') – a defence of the doctrine of self (*ātman*) in response to the Buddhist teaching that there is no abiding-self. Within this work Udayana refuted a variety of Buddhist perspectives from both the Abhidharma and Mahāyāna traditions with special emphasis upon his immediate predecessor – the Buddhist Jñānaśrīmitra. Udayana also wrote a number of smaller works on Nyāya thought but is probably most famous for his *Nyāyakusumāñjali*, another independent work in seventy-two stanzas, providing a philosophical defence of the notion of 'God' (*īśvara*) from a Nyāya standpoint.

From the time of Udayana it becomes increasingly difficult to see any difference between the Nyāya and Vaiśeṣika positions. The two schools have clearly shared a great deal in common throughout their history, frequently being represented as sister-schools, but as a result of the work of Udayana and figures such as Śasadhara and Maṇikaṇṭha (late thirteenth century CE) the old (*pracīna*) Nyāya became absorbed into a "New Nyāya" (*navya-nyāya*) tradition that accepted the four *pramāṇas* of traditional Nyāya alongside the seven categories (*padārtha*) of the Vaiśeṣika school.

The central figure in the establishment of Navya-Nyāya is Gaṅgeśa (c. 1320 CE), author of the *Jewel Reflecting Reality* (*Tattvacintāmaṇi*). Although Gaṅgeśa is often seen as the principal founder of Navya-Nyāya his work is dependent upon the ground laid by Udayana and his successors in synthesising the Nyāya and Vaiśeṣika systems. We should also bear in mind the sense in which Indian philosophical schools developed as a result of their encounter with other schools. A major influence upon the development of Navya-Nyāya, therefore, was Śrīharṣa, not a Naiyāyika at all but a member of the non-dualistic (Advaita) Vedānta tradition of Śaṅkarācārya. It is Śrīharṣa's critique of Udayana in his *Khaṇḍanakhaṇḍakhādya* which precipitated a response in terms of the technical language that characterises subsequent Navya-Nyāya treatises. The main focus of Gaṅgeśa's critiques, however, was not Vedānta but instead the philosophy of the Prabhākara Mīmāṃsakas. Moreover, from the twelfth century onwards Buddhist philosophy and practice went into a period of severe decline in India from which it never recovered (at least that is until the late twentieth century) and the traditional Naiyāyika dispute with Buddhist philosophy became supplanted by disputations between the Nyāya and Mīmāṃsā schools.

The consolidation of the new (*navya*) style of Nyāya exemplified by Gaṅgeśa was achieved by one of his sons Vardhamāna, with the establishment of a commentarial tradition based upon the methodology of his father's work. Vardhamāna wrote nine Navya-Nyāya commentaries (collectively entitled *Prakāśa* – 'The Elucidation') on classics of the Nyāya and Vaiśeṣika traditions and founded a school in Mithilā. The Navya-Nyāya tradition continued to develop with the work of Yajñapati and the founding of a sub-school or tradition (*saṃpradāya*) based upon the 'Light' (*Āloka*) commentary on Gaṅgeśa by his disciple Jayadeva Pakṣadhara (fifteenth century CE). A Bengali tradition of Navya-Nyāya was also established, the most famous exponent being Raghunātha (c. 1500 CE), particularly interesting for his willingness to criticise established Nyāya-Vaiśeṣika categories and Gadādhara (seventeenth century), author of a commentary on Raghunātha's account of inference (the *Anumāna-dīdhiti*).

– The School of Enumeration (Sāṃkhya) –

Sāṃkhya thought represents some of the most ancient strands of Indian philosophical thinking and occurs in a variety of forms. As a systematic school (*darśana*), Sāṃkhya upholds a radical dualism between consciousness and matter and sees the final purpose in life in terms of the separation of the two and the attainment of isolation (*kaivalya*) for the pure consciousness (*puruṣa*). Although the goal is to disentangle oneself from the activities of the material world, Sāṃkhya does not reject the reality of this world (as happens for instance in the Advaita school). Consciousness and matter constitute the two basic ontological principles which underlie the manifestation of the universe.

The history of the Sāṃkhya philosophy can be roughly divided into three periods: 1. an early period of proto-Sāṃkhya ideas (c. 900 BCE–300 CE), 2. the (so-called) classical period when the *Sāṃkhya Kārikā* was composed and the tradition flourished as an independent school or *darśana* (350–1000 CE) and 3. later Sāṃkhya, exemplified by the composition of the *Sāṃkhya Sūtra*, a period of relative decline for the philosophy (1000 CE onwards).

The dualistic philosophy that became characteristic of Sāṃkhya thought can be discerned in the early speculative hymns of the Vedas. The distinction between consciousness and materiality, for instance, is foreshadowed in the *Nāsadīya Sūkta* (Ṛg Veda X. 129.3–5) where creation occurs not through the intervention of some deity but through the arising of desire (*kāma*) and the transforming process of cosmic heat (*tapas*). Such formative influences can also be discerned in early dualistic cosmogonies such as the interaction of (male) Puruṣa and (female) Virāj in the *Puruṣa Sūkta* (Ṛg Veda X. 90), or in the 'heating up' of the primordial golden egg (*hiraṇyagarbha*, Ṛg Veda X. 121).

Sāṃkhya elements can be discerned in the Brāhmana and Āraṇyaka literature, especially in the tendency to establish mystical homologies or correspondences (*bandhu*) between microcosm and macrocosm. Many of the items, later accepted as fundamental principles (*tattva*) by the Sāṃkhya school, are already outlined by the time of the composition of the later parts of the *Bṛhadāraṇyaka Upaniṣad*, that is by the fifth century BCE (e.g. Bṛ Up 4.5.12). In the *Kaṭha Upaniṣad* we find a hierarchical gradation of principles with the *puruṣa* at the top and sense-organs and their objects at the bottom (1.3.10–11) and in the *Śvetāśvatara Upaniṣad* we can see the further development of Sāṃkhya ideas.

Early Sāṃkhya ideas within the *Upaniṣads* were realist in nature, but tended more towards a form of monism than the dualism of spirit and matter that has become characteristic of the school in subsequent times. Before their development into a distinctive *darśana* Sāṃkhya ideas can also be found in the *Mokṣadharma* portion of the *Mahābhārata* (chapters 168–353 in the Critical Edition of Book 12), and in the *Bhagavad Gītā* (chapters 23–40 of Book 6). These portions of the *Mahābhārata* date roughly from the fourth century BCE to the second century of the Common Era. In the *Bhagavad Gītā* the term 'Sāṃkhya' occurs on a number of occasions, often related to the notion of *Jñāna* or *Buddhi Yoga* (Path of Knowledge, see *Gītā* 2.39; 3.3; 5.4–5; 13.24; 18.13; 18.19). Crucial in this regard is Chapter 13 which describes the phenomenal world in terms of the distinction between the field (*kṣetra*, i.e. *prakṛti*) and the 'knower of the field' (*kṣetrajña*, i.e. the *puruṣa*). The *Gītā*, however, is a highly idiosyncratic text and integrates Sāṃkhya dualism within a hierarchical synthesis which places final emphasis upon the path of devotion (*bhakti-yoga*) and identifies the impersonal *brahman* of the *Upaniṣads* with the lower nature (*prakṛti*) of the Supra-Personal Godhead of Kṛṣṇa.

– THE CLASSICAL SĀṂKHYA OF ĪŚVARAKṚṢṆA –

The first systematic exposition of Sāṃkhya philosophy as an independent school of thought that is available to us is the *Sāṃkhya Kārikā* of Īśvarakṛṣṇa (350–450 CE). The *Sāṃkhya Kārikā* performs the same function within the Sāṃkhya tradition as the *sūtras* of the other schools of Hindu thought, in that it provides a foundational and authoritative source-text for Sāṃkhya philosophy and a basis for a tradition of commentarial elucidation based upon Sāṃkhya principles. However, the *Sāṃkhya Kārikā* is clearly not the earliest attempt to systematise Sāṃkhya philosophy. The text refers to an earlier exposition (now apparently lost) known as the *Science of Sixty Topics* (*Ṣaṣṭitantra,* see SK v. 72) and is probably preceded by alternate schemes of fundamental principles (*tattva)* such as that found in the *Ahirbudhnyasaṃhitā*, a Pañcarātra (Vaiṣṇava) text. The *Kārikā* was brought to China by the Buddhist scholar Paramārtha in 546 CE and then translated by him into Chinese some time between 557 and 569 CE. The standard number of verses in the text is often stated as 72, but this remains a source of contention. Paramārtha translated 71 *kārikās* (with verse 63 omitted), with other commentaries varying between 69 and 73 verses.

Apart from Paramārtha's commentary (entitled 'The Golden Seventy' or *Suvarṇasaptati*, despite its 71 verses!), there are a number of extant commentaries on the *Sāṃkhya Kārikā*. The most popular has tended to be the *Gauḍapāda Bhāṣya*, attributed to Gauḍapāda, the reputed teacher of Śaṅkarācārya's teacher Govinda. This figure is identified as the author of an important early text of the Advaita (non-dualistic) lineage of Vedānta – the *Māṇḍūkya-Kārikā* or the *Gauḍapādīya Kārikā* (see King, 1995). The attribution of common authorship seems unlikely, however, given their philosophical differences. Common authorship, however, is not impossible given the example of scholars, such as Vācaspati Miśra, who were able to compose authoritative commentaries and treatises from the point of view of a variety of philosophical stances. As we have seen, training and involvement in the science of Indian philosophical debate (*vāda-śāstra*) required one to be able to present the evidence of a rival perspective as an initial step (the *pūrvapakṣa*), before refutation and the establishment of one's own definitive position (*siddhānta*). Such practices required participants in Indian philosophical debates to develop a keen appreciation of a rival's perspective and an ability to present it in a clearly formulated and systematic fashion.

Of the remaining commentaries on the *Sāṃkhya Kārikā* the most significant are the *Light of Argumentation* (*Yuktidīpikā*) and Vācaspati Miśra's *The Moonlight on the Sāṃkhya Principles of Reality* (*Sāṃkhyatattvakaumadī*). The former has been assigned to the sixth century CE (Frauwallner 1973: 226) but may be later since it seems to contain an earlier work known as the *Rāja Vārttika* (*Rāja's Elucidation* or perhaps '*The King's Elucidation*') within the body of its own exposition (Wezler, 1974: 434–5). Vācaspati's work dates from the tenth century CE and became a standard authority on Īśvarakṛṣṇa's verses throughout India.

The Sāṃkhya system of Īśvarakṛṣṇa is characterised by a fundamental dualism between pure spirit or consciousness (*puruṣa*) and primal materiality or nature (*prakṛti*). The world is a multiplicity that has evolved from this primordial matter, but the motivating force behind the creation of the universe derives not from *prakṛti* itself but from *puruṣa* – the principle of consciousness (see Figure 2). A useful metaphor for picturing this is to imagine *prakṛti* as an inert mass of dark matter that comes into view once the light (of the *puruṣa*) is shone upon it. Despite setting the wheels of evolution in progress through its interest in *prakṛti*, the *puruṣa* does not participate in the creation of the world since it is merely a witness-consciousness (*sākṣin*) and not an agent (*akartā*).

Prakṛti – the primordial source of everything (except, of course, pure consciousness or *puruṣa*) – is made up of three fundamental aspects: *sattva*, *rajas* and *tamas*. These three aspects or constituents (*guṇa*) are the fundamental strands (rather than emergent properties or qualities) of *prakṛti*. Before the *puruṣa* becomes absorbed in its new-found interest, the now 'animated' *prakṛti* existed in a state of pure potentiality (*pradhāna*) with all three *guṇas* established in perfect equilibrium. The *puruṣa*, however, upsets this balance and thereby causes the first evolute of *prakṛti* to emerge. This is *buddhi* or Intelligence (known as *mahāt* – 'the Great One' in its cosmological aspect). *Buddhi* is a mirror-reflection of the consciousness of the *puruṣa*. It is, however, a product of *prakṛti* and not to be confused with the real thing.

The emergence of intelligence from the interaction of *puruṣa* and *prakṛti* also leads to the next evolute – *ahaṃkāra* – 'the feeling of I am'. It is at this stage that notions of ego and individuality come into play. *Ahaṃkāra*, the individualising or 'subjective' aspect of our experience, manifests itself in terms of five sense-capacities (*buddhīndriya*), five action-capacities (*karmendriya*) and the mind (*manas*), which functions as the centralising organ which co-ordinates all of our sensory perceptions, thoughts and actions. Together these constitute the sattvic or cognising aspect of *prakṛti*. Similarly, *prakṛti* produces five subtle elements (*tanmātra*) – sound, touch, form, taste and smell, and five gross elements (*mahābhūta*), viz. space, wind, fire, water and earth. These constitute the basic constituents of the objectified world and correspond to the *tamas guṇa* – the 'objective' or determinate aspect of *prakṛti*. In the Sāṃkhya system, the third *guṇa* – *rajas* – exemplifies motion and agency and is something of a mediating principle between *sattva* and *tamas*. All three 'strands' co-exist and mutually support each other's functions. Thus, *rajas* provides the energy or movement that allows both intelligence or subjectivity (*sattva*) and reification or objectification (*tamas*) to occur. Purposive movement, however, requires both an intellect or a subjective will and determinate forms. Finally, the world of objective forms, that is gross and subtle matter, requires conscious will and agency in order to proliferate and change.

All in all the Sāṃkhya system outlines a scheme of twenty-five fundamental principles of reality (*tattva*), including the two most basic *prakṛti* and *puruṣa*. The school upholds a thoroughgoing realism. The world around us is real and independent of our perception of it being a series of material evolutes (*pariṇāma*) deriving from *prakṛti*. Nevertheless, our true self is *puruṣa* – the principle of pure consciousness that has mistakenly become associated (*saṃyoga*) with the manifestations of *prakṛti* and thereby forgotten that it is a transcendent witness rather than an active participant in the activities of material existence. The goal of the Sāṃkhya system, therefore, is to discriminate through a process of intellectual abstraction the fundamental principles of reality in order to extricate oneself from the incessant processes of birth and death (*saṃsāra*) that characterises embodied existence. Consistent with its thoroughgoing realism, and in stark contrast to the monism of schools like Advaita Vedānta, the Sāṃkhya system accepts that there are a plurality of *puruṣas*.

An interesting feature of the Sāṃkhya scheme is the way in which it can be interpreted both in psychological and cosmological terms. The twenty-five *tattvas* can be seen as a conceptual map of the basic categories of experience – an analytical picture, if you like, of what you are actually experiencing now, or as a cosmological account of the creation of the universe. A variety of scholarly views have been put forward to explain this apparent confusion (see Parrott, 1986). We should bear in mind, however, that it is inappropriate to draw a sharp division between the cosmological and the psychological in an early Vedic context (especially given the homologies (*bandhutā*) between cosmic, social and individual realms in ancient Indian thought), but a more 'psychological' emphasis is more likely to come into play once Sāṃkhya developed into a system of thought concerned with the liberation of the individual aspirant from the suffering (*duḥkha*) induced by repeated re-embodiment (Larson, 1979: 178).

The frequency and ferocity of refutations of the Sāṃkhya position decline considerably towards the end of the first millennium of the Common Era. The Sāṃkhya school was already the odd one out in that it did not have an ancient *sūtra* as the basis for its reflections. The *Sāṃkhya Pravācana Sūtra* (c. fourteenth century CE) is clearly a late attempt to remedy this situation and thereby justify the antiquity and authority of the Sāṃkhya school. This suggests that as an independent school of thought Sāṃkhya had entered a period of declining influence. The Muslim scholar Alberuni (tenth century CE), however, refers to the Sāṃkhya school as an important resource for understanding Hindu philosophical thought, though even here the independence of the Sāṃkhya tradition is somewhat undermined by its strong association with the Yoga tradition. Indeed, it is perhaps through the development of the philosophy of the Yoga *darśana* that Sāṃkhya ideas can be seen to continue in their development. It is perhaps misleading, therefore, to describe this era of Sāṃkhya history simply as a period of decline. Moreover, the importance and influence of Sāṃkhya philosophy has far and away exceeded its activities as an independent school of thought.

– The Classical Yoga School –

Many westerners see yoga as a variation on the modern concern for health and fitness and a means of overcoming the stresses and strains of modern day living. Most of what passes for yoga in this context, however, bears little relation to traditional practices, institutionalised as they were within established traditions or lineages (*saṃpradāya*) of teacher (*guru*) and pupil (*śiṣya*), structured according to hierarchical and initiatory stages of development and bound up with an ascetic lifestyle and world-view very different from the concerns of the modern western urbanite. Yoga in the more traditional sense of the term has been practised throughout South Asia and beyond and involves a multitude of techniques leading to spiritual and ethical purification. Hindu and Buddhist traditions alike place a great deal of emphasis upon the practice of yoga as a means of attaining liberation from the world of rebirth and yogic practices have been aligned with a variety of philosophical theories and metaphysical positions.

The term '*yoga*' seems to derive from the root '*yuj*' meaning to 'bind or yoke together'. In theistic traditions yoga is primarily conceived of as a pathway leading to union with the divine, but this is by no means the only understanding of the term. An alternate rendering of the term sees it as the quest for the unification of the mind or the self in the attainment of *samādhi* or meditative concentration (see, for instance, Vyāsa's commentary on YS 1.1). The latter rendering, of course, is amenable to a modern psychological interpretation and has proven popular in the west since it allows yoga practices to be secularised and divorced from the specific religious or metaphysical world-views in which such practices were originally located.

There are a variety of different types of yoga. The *Bhagavad Gītā* outlines three main types: the yoga of knowledge (*jñāna*), the yoga of good works (*karma*) and the yoga of devotion (*bhakti*). The *Gītā* integrates all three into a single theoretical framework, marginally favouring the yoga of devotion, but seeing all three in terms of the cultivation of an attitude of selfless action, that is, the performance of actions without personal attachment to its consequences (*niṣkāma-karman*). The ideal outlined in the *Gītā*, therefore, is a life of duty (*dharma*) for duty's sake with no thought of personal gain. The yoga of knowledge is particularly emphasised within the Advaita Vedānta tradition of Śaṅkara where actions (even yogic ones) are not seen as necessary, liberation requiring the attainment of knowledge of the identity of *ātman* and *brahman*. Similarly, the yoga of devotion has appealed more to the various monotheistic traditions within India, though in the *Gītā* *bhakti* does not seem to imply the emotional longing for the deity that it later connotes, implying instead contemplation of the deity and a dedication of all actions to the service of the Lord (Viṣṇu/Kṛṣṇa).

Generally speaking, however, we can identify two main forms of Hindu yoga. The first is known as Rāja-yoga or Royal Yoga and is usually identified with the *Yoga Sūtras* of Patañjali, which thereby function as the paradigmatic textual exposition of 'classical yoga' within Hindu circles. The second form is known as Haṭha Yoga or the Yoga of Force and places much more emphasis upon self-realisation through the perfection of the body, the utilisation of a variety of postures (*āsana*) and the purification of the various energy channels (*nāḍī*) within the body.

– THE CLASSICAL YOGA OF PATAÑJALI –

The first comprehensive systematisation of yoga techniques and theory can be found in the *Yoga Sūtra* of Patañjali (third to fourth century CE). This figure, sometimes spuriously identified with a famous Hindu grammarian of the same name, may indeed be the author of this text, though it is possible that Patañjali was the editor, bringing together a wide range of practices and providing a short handbook on yoga theory and practice. The *Yoga Sūtra* is usually divided into four chapters (*pāda*), though this division seems rather odd at times and is suggestive of a later attempt to organise the material. Nevertheless, chapter one (51 verses) discusses the nature of meditative concentration (*samādhi*). Chapter two (55 verses) outlines the path to attainment (*sādhana*). Chapter three is said to outline the supernormal powers (*vibhūti*) attained during yogic practice, whilst chapter four is concerned with the nature of liberation (or isolation (*kaivalya*) as the Sāṃkhya and Yoga traditions call it).

The metaphysics of the *Yoga Sūtra* is similar to that of the Sāṃkhya traditions, though there are notable differences (see Chapter 7). The goal of the Yoga tradition is to realise the isolated status of pure consciousness (*puruṣa*) from matter (*prakṛti*). Commentators on the *Yoga Sūtra* include the influential *bhāṣya* of Vyāsa, responsible more than any other text for anchoring the interpretation of Patañjali's system within a broadly Sāṃkhya framework, and the ubiquitous Vācaspati Miśra, author of the *Tattvavaiśāradī*, a gloss on Vyāsa's commentary. Also important is the commentary by King Bhoja (eleventh century CE), known as the '*Royal Sun Bird*' (*Rājamārtaṇḍa*). This work, also called the *Bhoja-vṛtti*, follows Vācaspati Miśra in most respects but remains critical of aspects of the earlier commentaries. Mention should also be made of the *Yoga Bhāṣya Vivaraṇa*, a sub-commentary on Vyāsa's work and believed by some to be an authentic work of Śaṅkarācārya (eighth century CE) of the Advaita Vedānta tradition, and the *Yoga Vārttika* of Vijñānabhikṣu. Both works display a clearly Vedāntic imprint in their interpretation of the Yoga system.

In chapter two of the *Yoga Sūtra* Patañjali seems to outline two alternative schemes of yoga. The first is known as *Kriyā-yoga* or the yoga of action (not to be confused with the *karma yoga* of the *Bhagavad Gītā*). This practice involves ascetic discipline (*tapas*), self-analysis (*svādhyāya*)[3] and devotion to the deity (*īśvara-praṇidhāna*) and leads to the cultivation of meditative concentration (*samādhi*) and the attenuation of defiling hindrances (*kleśa*, YS 2.1–2). The second form of yoga, more usually associated with Patañjali himself, is the Eight-Limbed Yoga (*aṣṭānga-yoga*, YS 2.28–55, III.1–8). Since more time is devoted to outlining this scheme within the *Yoga Sūtra*, most scholars have associated the eight-limbed system with Patañjali himself, though Feuerstein (1980: x) has argued that this scheme is adopted from older sources by the author 'for the sake of expositional convenience' (see also Feuerstein, 1979: 59). The eight limbs are as follows:

1. Restraint (*yama*): outer control, i.e. the ethical rules to be followed by a yogin. These are akin to Buddhist and Jaina precepts and involve a vow of non-violence (*ahiṁsā*), truthfulness, non-stealing, sexual restraint and greedlessness.
2. Self-discipline (*niyama*): inner control. Again this has five aspects involving moral, mental and physical purity, contentment, ascetic practice (*tapas*), self-analysis (*svādhyāya*) and contemplative devotion to the lord (*īśvara-praṇidhāna*). The last practice does not seem to imply devotion in the sense of the emotive and monotheistic *bhakti* traditions of India but rather a sustained meditative reflection upon the divine form. Devotion to the Lord may denote a form of visionary meditation (e.g. concentrating upon a particular icon or artistic representation of the divine), or an interiorised reflection upon the nature of God. Nevertheless, the practice seems to be tied up with contemplation of the syllable Om which is said to be the name of the Lord (YS I.27).

   Some forms of yoga are based upon repetition of a sacred phrase or mantra. The most sacred mantra of all is the syllable Om which often appears before and after Indian religious texts and prayers. If the yogin listens intently he or she is said to be able to hear the sound of the syllable Om as it resonates throughout the universe. Meditation on Om is also found in various *Upaniṣads*.[4] The *Yoga Sūtra* clearly endorses such techniques, but stresses that recitation is not enough (YS 1.28), one must also reflect upon the meaning of the syllable. In mantra-yoga (that is, yoga specifically based upon the mantra technique) recitation is usually all that is required. In modern westernised forms of yoga such as transcendental meditation a mantra is usually chosen which has no meaning for the practitioner. This is so that no preconceptions are brought to the practice of recitation which might otherwise become an obstacle in focusing the mind. For Patañjali, however, mere recitation is not enough and will result in a state of trance rather than a state of greater awareness.

3. Posture (*āsana*). There are many different yogic postures but the most famous is *padma-āsana* or lotus position. Attentiveness to posture, even on western reductionist principles is sound physiological advice.[5] Correct posture is necessary to facilitate the flow of vital energy or breath (*prāṇa*) throughout the body and allows for increased awareness.
4. Control of Breath/Vital Energy (*prāṇāyāma*). This is probably the most common form of meditative practice in South Asia and in some fashion has also been utilised in a variety of cultural and religious contexts the world over. In Yoga the technique involves the development of a rhythmic pattern of breathing. The term '*prāṇa*' refers not just to breath, but also to the vital energy of the body in general. *Prāṇa* is the 'principle of life' which makes something alive or animate. There are different levels at which *prāṇa* is concentrated. The most subtle material form is the breath, but *prāṇa* is also to be found in blood and in its most concentrated form as semen in men and vaginal fluid in women. This leads the yogin, especially in the later Haṭha Yoga traditions (see below), to practice techniques for improving the circulation of the vital energy through one's body as a means of achieving an immortalised or diamond-body (*vajra-śarīra*). Concentration of vital energy within certain limbs (*prāṇa-dhāraṇā*) is also accepted as a therapeutic technique for healing ailments. Loss of vital energy (either through lack of breath or the loss of blood or sexual fluids) is seen as detrimental to the well-being of the yogin as well as clouding one's perception of reality. In the Rāja Yoga tradition this usually results in a vow of celibacy for most yogins (female: *yoginī*).
5. Sense-withdrawal (*pratyāhāra*). The introversion of awareness and withdrawal of attention from the activities of the sense-organs is deemed necessary if one is aiming to concentrate upon the self as a pure witness-consciousness (*sākṣin*). Sense objects are distractions and cause one to make an erroneous identification of oneself with the material products of *prakṛti*.

These five limbs are known as the outer-members (*bahir-aṅga*) of the eight limbs of Rāja Yoga. This is because they are largely the physiological and psychological prerequisites of advanced yoga practice. The last three limbs are known as the inner-members (*antar-aṅga*), since they are concerned specifically with the control of consciousness (*saṃyama*, YS 3.4).

6. Concentration (*dhāraṇā*). This denotes the practice of holding the mind upon an object of meditation for an extended period of time. The object of concentration can be a figure (*yantra*), a diagrammatical representation (*maṇḍala*) or a symbolic phrase or word (*mantra*). The aim of *dhāraṇā* is to achieve a one-pointedness (*ekāgratā*) of mind.
7. Meditative-awareness (*dhyāna*). This is a meditative insight into the nature of the object being concentrated upon. In modern western psychology this would be described as an 'altered state of consciousness' and is a deepening of the previous stage of concentration which is little more than the ability to hold the mind on an object for a fixed period of time.
8. Meditative-concentration (*samādhi*). This represents the pinnacle of yogic

practice. There are two main types. The first is known as *saṃ-prajñāta-samādhi* and involves conceptualisation (*vikalpa*) and concentration upon an object of consciousness (*ālambana*), whether external or mental in nature. The second type – *asaṃprajñāta-samādhi* – is a non-conceptual awareness (*nirvikalpa*) of reality and denotes a fully interiorised awareness without a corresponding external or mental object. Such states are initially transient and the waking state is soon re-established by latent subliminal or sub-conscious impressions (*saṃskāra*) that are the products of previous karmic actions. Through repeated cultivation and mastery, however, such states can last for longer and longer periods of time and gradually undermine the production of further subliminal impressions. Eventually one attains a state where all karmic seeds are eliminated (*nirbīja-samādhi*). At this stage one attains a liberating knowledge of the self as an isolated seer (*draṣṭā*) or pure witness-consciousness.

– THE YOGA OF FORCE (HAṬHA YOGA) –

Although rarely considered as a philosophical school (*darśana*), Haṭha Yoga represents an important development in the theory and practice of yoga in India and has provided the model for much that goes by the name of yoga practice in the contemporary western world. Haṭha Yoga seems to have developed out of the classical tradition of Rāja Yoga around the ninth century CE, beginning as a specific practice of the Kānphata or 'ear splitting' sect, a name denoting the group custom of slitting the ear cartilage to accommodate a large earring. This originally ascetic movement is said to have been founded by the legendary Gorakṣānatha (or Goraknāth, c. ninth to tenth centuries CE), traditionally the author of the two oldest Haṭha Yoga works (both of which are no longer extant, unless one accepts authentic authorship of the *Gorakṣa Paddhati*). Nevertheless, Haṭha Yoga is a highly eclectic set of practices and undoubtedly contains highly archaic elements. Mircea Eliade (1973: ch. 8) has even suggested that yoga in general has its origins in the aboriginal religion of the Indus valley community which existed in India before the invasion of the Āryans, making such practices thousands of years old. The classical texts of the Haṭha tradition tend to conceive of themselves as a ladder for attaining the heights of Rāja Yoga and so do not see themselves as incompatible with the classical yoga of the *Yoga Sūtra*. This is particularly true with regard to the most famous Haṭha Yoga text – *Light on the Yoga of Force (Haṭha Yoga Pradīpika*, c. fourteenth century CE), where Haṭha Yoga is said to be taught for the benefit of those unable to aspire to Rāja Yoga (I.I.3).

The primary aim of Haṭha yoga is to prevent the dissipation of the vital breath (*prāṇa*) by centralising it within the middle channel (*suṣumṇā-nāḍī*). This is thought to awaken the 'serpent force' (*kuṇḍalinī*) – a powerful manifestation of the Goddess and symbolising the power (*śakti*) inherent in the universe.

> The Kuṇḍalinī-śakti, who sleeps above the *kanda* [the source of the energy channels located between the navel and the scrotum], gives liberation to Yogin-s and bondage to the ignorant. He who knows her knows Yoga.
>
> *Haṭha Yoga Pradīpika* III.107, trans. in Tatya, 1972: 56

Ordinarily, the *kuṇḍalinī* is coiled up at the lower end of the spinal column, but is awakened through yogic practice. According to the *Yogaśikhā Upaniṣad* (I. 133) '*Haṭha*' derives from '*ha*' (sun) and '*ṭha*' (moon), signifying the union of the two polar aspects of the human personality, most commonly understood to be the male and female aspects of each individual person which are usually in a state of mental and physical separation and requiring integration.

Haṭha Yoga promotes various psycho-somatic techniques for the transformation of the human into a divine body (*divya-śarīra*), also known as the diamond or thunderbolt body (*vajra-śarīra*), endowing the practitioner with immortality. Hindu thought is often represented as devaluing embodiment but the Haṭha Yoga tradition views the body as a useful instrument for effecting emancipation. Consequently, the tradition emphasises the psycho-physiological aspects of yogic practice. For critics such as Gauḍābhinānda (author of the smaller *Yoga-Vāsiṣṭha*, ninth century CE) (V.6. 86; 92), Haṭha Yoga does not lead to liberation it merely causes pain and discomfort! Indeed, even within the Haṭha Yoga tradition the practice of the yoga of force without knowledge of the broader context of Rāja Yoga is said to be fruitless

> There are the mere Haṭha-yogin-s without the knowledge of Rāja-yoga. I regard them to be practitioners who do not obtain the fruits of their efforts.
>
> *Haṭha-Yoga-Pradīpika* IV.79; Tatya, 1972: 77

The field of activity for Haṭha Yoga is the subtle body (*sūkṣma śarīra*) which transmigrates from one gross material body to another. This subtle body is composed of *prāṇa* – the subtle breath of life which animates the gross body. The axial current of the body is the 'middle duct' (*suṣumṇā-nāḍī*) has six power centres or *cakras* (seven in total, since the highest *cakra* is above the crown of the head).[6] By focusing the life-force (*prāṇa*) through control of one's breath (*prāṇayāma*) and concentration of the mind (*dhāraṇā*) at the lowest energy-centre one causes the *kuṇḍalinī* (serpent-power) to awaken and rise up the axial current, like mercury in a thermometer. Then one concentrates upon the next *cakra*, causing the power to rise up to this level. Finally, one reaches the crown of the head (*sahasrāra*-

cakra), where one attains full meditative concentration (*samādhi*) and the *kuṇḍalinī* power transforms the consciousness and body of the practitioner. In the Tantric traditions of Haṭha Yoga the male yogin learns to control and prevent the ejaculation of semen during sexual intercourse as a means both of retaining *prāṇa* but also of transforming sexual desire and energy (*rajas*) into spiritually transformative energy and power. Similarly, the female *yoginī* learns to control her own vaginal ejaculate after a conjoining with a male practitioner. Such highly ritualised sexual acts are carried out by male and female practitioners as a means of re-integrating the male and female principles of existence. Such practices are also seen as ritualised embodiments of the creative conjunction of God (Śiva) and Goddess (*Śakti*).

Hindu philosophy is diverse and multi-faceted in the interest, issues and theoretical stances that are discussed. The diversity of philosophical positions adopted by the various traditions belies the modern notion that there are only six schools of Hindu thought and that they represent complementary perspectives. The history of Indian thought reflects the pluralistic context of ancient India and is a history of disputation and philosophical debate between a variety of traditions, thinkers and schools. Moreover, as we shall see in the next chapter, these brahmanical traditions had to contend not only with each other but with the philosophical perspectives of the various schools of Buddhism in ancient India. It is to these that we shall now turn.

– NOTES –

1. Āyurveda – 'the science of life' – is classified as a supplementary portion (*upāṅga*) or supplementary knowledge to the Vedas (*upaveda*) but is undoubtedly very ancient, being practised well before the time of the Buddha (c. fourth century BCE). The *Caraka Saṃhitā* is purportedly a revision of an older text of Indian medicine known as the *Agniveśā Tantra*, edited and revised by Caraka (first century CE), possibly a court physician to King Kaniṣka. The work was probably completed by Dṛḍhabala around 500 CE.
2. There appears to have been a third Mīmāṃsā school founded by Murāri Miśra. This school was not as influential as the Bhaṭṭa and Prabhākara schools and Murāri's works are lost to us except for fragments cited in the works of others.
3. Vyāsa, the most influential commentator on the *Yoga Sūtra* makes it clear that self-analysis (*svādhyāya*, literally: 'one's going into') involves contemplation of sacred *mantras* such as the syllable Om or the study of texts concerning liberation (*mokṣa-śāstra*).
4. Particularly noteworthy examples of the use of the syllable Om in the Upaniṣadic literature are the *Maitrī Upaniṣad* which describes the body as a bow and the syllable Om as an arrow which focuses the mind upon its target and the *Māṇḍūkya Upaniṣad*, a short text devoted exclusively to an explanation of the syllable Om and its symbolic significance.
5. Modern physiological reductionists might argue that increasing the flow of oxygen to the brain explains some of the altered states of consciousness attained by yoga practitioners.

Too much oxygen can lead to hallucination. Yogins, of course, would deny that they are having hallucinatory experiences, arguing instead that they are merely increasing their capacity for awareness. If this happens to correspond to (or even in some sense be caused by) a greater flow of oxygen to the brain then so be it, but that in and of itself does not detract from the question of the truthfulness of the yogic experience itself.

6. The six energy centres are often represented as lotuses which open up as the serpent-power ascends. The final attainment of the seventh level (the *sahasrāra-cakra*) is depicted as a thousand-petalled lotus. There the serpent force, as Goddess, unites with the static transcendental God Śiva. At first this union is brief but it can be prolonged through constant practice. In ascending order the six energy centres are: 1. the root base (pelvic region) – *mūla-ādhāra*, 2. own place (abdominal region) – *sva-adhiṣṭhāna*, 3. jewel town (navel) – *maṇi-pura*, 4. unstruck (solar plexus) – *anāhata*, 5. pure (throat region) – *viśudhaḥ*, and 6. insight (brow) – *ājñā*.

CHAPTER 4

Buddhist Philosophy in India

– BUDDHISM IN INDIA –

An account of philosophical perspectives in traditional India would be impossible without a consideration of the various schools of Buddhist philosophy that flourished in India for over a millennium from the time of King Aśoka (269–232 BCE), to the demise of Buddhism in India in the twelfth century of the Common Era. The reasons for the subsequent decline of Buddhism in India are complex. Having become a pan-Indian phenomenon under the Buddhist King Aśoka, Buddhism successfully migrated further afield in South, East and Northern Asia. The fortunes of Buddhist monastic communities (*saṅgha*), however, have always been somewhat reliant upon royal approval. Political changes, the adoption of many distinctively Buddhist ideas by Hindu movements like Advaita Vedānta and the proliferation of Hindu devotional (*bhakti*) movements, all combined to undermine the distinctiveness of Buddhism as a religious and philosophical tradition. Moreover, many Buddhist sites, such as the great Buddhist university in Nālandā, were comprehensively destroyed by Muslim invasions from the tenth century onwards. In the modern era, however, with the Tibetan diaspora and modern interest in Buddhism in India and the west, Buddhism is today making something of a comeback in the land of its origin.

Many accounts of Indian philosophy either conflate 'Indian' with 'Hindu', thereby ignoring or offering only a cursory analysis of Buddhist philosophical thought, or provide a rather ahistorical and static account of the various *darśanas*, ignoring the interactive and developmental nature of the variegated philosophical traditions of India. However, one cannot hope to understand the theoretical developments that have occurred within the various Hindu schools without examining the impact of Buddhist philosophical ideas upon the debates and histories of these traditions. Schools such as the Nyāya and Advaita Vedānta would not exist in the form in which they do if it were not for the centuries of debates with the various schools of

Buddhism. Indian philosophical schools, particularly in so far as they engaged in inter-scholastic debates, were neither static nor predetermined in the trajectory of their intellectual development. The history of Indian philosophy is, *pace* Anthony Flew, a history of debate and argumentation both within and between various schools of thought. In this chapter, therefore, I wish to provide a brief account of the various schools of Buddhist philosophy in India as a prelude to more in-depth discussion in later chapters.

– THE DOCTRINAL FOUNDATIONS OF BUDDHIST PHILOSOPHY –

In his first public teaching (known as the 'Turning of the Wheel of *Dharma*'), Siddhārtha Gautama, the historical Buddha, is said to have set out the fundamentals of Buddhist doctrine and practice:

> There are two extremes, monks, which are to be avoided. What are these two extremes? A life given to pleasures, dedicated to pleasures and lusts – this is degrading, sensual, vulgar, unworthy and useless; and a life given to self-torture – this is painful, unworthy and useless. By avoiding these two extremes, the Perfected One (i.e. the Buddha) has gained the knowledge of the Middle Path which leads to insight and wisdom, which produces calm, knowledge, enlightenment and *nirvāṇa*.
>
> *Saṃyutta Nikāya*, V, 420

The Buddha then proceeded to outline the four noble truths – the kernel of Buddhist doctrine. These are:

1. Birth, old age, sickness and death are unsatisfactory (*duḥkha*).
2. The cause of unsatisfactoriness is craving (*tṛṣṇā*).
3. There is an end to unsatisfactoriness and craving and it is known as *nirvāṇa*.
4. The way to achieve *nirvāṇa* is to follow the middle path between all extremes. This path has eight steps and involves the development of 1. appropriate view, 2. appropriate intention, 3. appropriate speech, 4. appropriate action, 5. appropriate livelihood, 6. appropriate effort, 7. appropriate mindfulness, and finally, 8. appropriate meditative-concentration.

This constitutes the 'bare bones' of the Buddhist world-view and provides both the basis and context of all subsequent Buddhist philosophical reflection. Note the emphasis the Buddha places upon a 'middle path between extremes'. This has been understood by Buddhists both as a reference to lifestyle and ethical practice (avoiding the extremes of self-indulgence and self-denial) and as the key to a correct understanding of reality (avoiding all extreme views). In the latter context the early Buddhist tradition distinguished its own doctrinal position from those who posited the existence of an unchanging self (*ātman*) that passes from one lifetime to the next. This position, characteristic of the various Hindu brahmanical schools of thought discussed in the previous chapter, is called the extreme of eternalism (*śāśvata-vāda*). On the other hand there are other positions, such as that of the materialist Cārvākas, for whom there is no continuation of life after the death of the body. This is known as the extreme of annihilationism (*uccheda-vāda*) by the Buddhists.

The Buddhist 'philosophy of the Middle Way' then involves the acceptance of the idea of a cycle of rebirths (*saṃsāra*), but a rejection of the idea that there is an underlying identity or essential self (*ātman*) passing from one lifetime to another. All that there is, if you like, is the process of rebirth itself, perpetuated by cravings, ignorance and the coming to fruition of the results of past actions (*karma*). Imagine, for instance, that the cycle of rebirths is a flowing river. The Buddhist view is that there is no 'river' over and above the flowing water itself. There is a process of rebirth, but no substances or unchanging entities undergoing this process. To understand this view requires us to explore in greater detail the Buddhist conception of reality. This can be summed up in what have been called the three marks of existence (*tri-lakṣaṇa*):

All compounded things are unsatisfactory (*duḥkha*)
All compounded things are impermanent (*anitya*)
Everything lacks an-abiding-self (*anātman*)

Although we can and (hopefully) sometimes do experience a state of happiness, the Buddha pointed out that such states never last. As long as we crave for something we cannot hope to achieve lasting contentment. Even when the object of our desires is grasped this too will not bring everlasting satisfaction. Perhaps it will not be enough and we will want more, or again at some level we will worry about losing that which we cherish so much. Fundamentally this is because everything is impermanent – nothing lasts. Even if one experiences happiness and contentment, the inevitability of change and eventually of one's own death prevents this state of affairs from providing the kind of permanent contentment that the Buddha is striving for. Of course, in Buddhism there is a state of permanent contentment and that is *nirvāṇa*. It is achieved through the cessation of all craving (*tṛṣṇā*) and the attainment of enlightenment (*bodhi*). This amounts to a full existential realisation and acceptance of the four noble truths and the three marks of existence.

The last of the three marks is said to lead on from the first two. Life is unsatisfactory. Primarily this is because it is impermanent. If all things are impermanent, that is, subject to change and decay, then they cannot be said to have a durable essence. Everything, then, lacks an abiding-self or essence of its own. The doctrine of no-abiding-self (*anātman*) is the most distinctive feature of Buddhist thought and constitutes the fundamental starting point of virtually all schools of Buddhist philosophy in India.

– THE BUDDHIST PHILOSOPHY OF NO-ABIDING-SELF (*ANĀTMAN*) –

Although the various Hindu schools of thought disagreed about a number of issues, the six schools discussed in Chapter 3 all agreed that sentient beings were subject to an incessant cycle of rebirths, that this was largely an unsatisfactory state of affairs and that there was a way out – the attainment of liberation (*mokṣa*). This metaphysical scheme was also accepted by the various Buddhist (and Jaina) traditions and provided something of a canvas upon which intellectual debate could proceed. Another unifying factor within the Hindu brahmanical fold was the belief in an essential self (*ātman*) – an immaterial entity which transmigrated from life to life. For all six schools the postulation of such an entity was deemed necessary to establish identity during and between lives and provided a causal explanation of sentience. This immaterial self or *ātman* established a fixed identity throughout the fluctuating changes of the mind–body complex, like a thread holding together a pearl necklace.

The various Buddhist traditions, however, rejected such an entity, seeing it as an unwarranted and unverifiable metaphysical postulate. For the Buddhist there is no *atman* or essential self underlying the changing stream of events which constitutes the mind–body complex. The Buddhist doctrine of no-abiding-self (*anātman*) provided a stark philosophical contrast to brahmanical notions of a substantial self (*ātman*). According to the Buddha, a succession of rebirths does indeed occur but there is no substantial or essential self which persists or ' passes through' this series. This is explained by the Buddha in terms of the doctrine of inter-dependent-origination (*pratītyasamutpāda*). This is a scheme which explains the dynamics of existence from life to life and moment to moment without the necessity of positing a persisting agent or "possessor" of experience. For the Buddhist traditions of India the cycle of rebirths represents a 'common flowing' (*saṃsāra*), an ever-turning wheel or a flowing river, with no substantial entity or soul (*ātman*) transmigrating from life to life. To be philosophically accurate therefore, Buddhist philosophy does not accept reincarnation (the re-embodiment of an abiding-self) though it does postulate a continuous series of rebirths (and re-deaths) so long as ignorance and selfish desires perpetuate the cycle.

There are three ways in which the notion of no-abiding-self (*anātman*) has been utilised in the early Buddhist literature. Clearly, the concept represents a doctrine about the nature of reality (the right view of no-abiding-self). On this philosophical level, *anātman* is seen by the Buddhist as an accurate description of reality – the way things really are (*yathābhūta*). Emphasis has also been placed, however, on the teaching as a moral instrument in the quest for liberation, inculcating a life of selfless altruism, that is, as an aid to the purification of mind, speech and action. A third dimension of the *anātman* teaching, and one that has often been overlooked, is the sociological significance of the no-abiding-self as a cultural symbol in ancient India. It is unlikely that the wider community of lay followers (and even ordained members of the *saṅgha*) understood the full import of the Buddhist teaching of no-abiding-self, but this does not mean that they were not aware of it or that it did not influence them. The *anātman* teaching has spawned a range of processual metaphors within Buddhist culture, reflecting the emphasis placed upon change and impermanence. In the hegemonic context of brahmanical India the distinctiveness of the idea of *anātman* also functioned as a specific cultural symbol representing allegiance to the Buddhist tradition. As such, the Buddhist teaching of no-abiding-self provided an ideological means of differentiating the Buddhist community from the brahmanical philosophies of *ātman* (Collins, 1982: 12).

A number of analogies are used to illustrate the Buddhist philosophy of process. Swinging a torch around at a rapid rate creates an illusion of a circle of light hanging in the air. Similarly, sentient existence is like a flowing river, an ongoing process of changing events and not a fixed or static state of being. Early Buddhist thought placed a great deal of emphasis upon the intentions (*cetanā*) of actions. These are the thoughts which motivate actions (*karman*) and perpetuate the cycle of rebirths. There is no persisting-self throughout this series of lives however, merely a succession of causally conditioned, mental and physical processes that persist for as long as full enlightenment (*bodhi/nirvāṇa*) remains unattained.

The most popular metaphor for expounding the Buddhist doctrine of no-abiding-self is that of the bundle of fire-sticks (*skandha*). According to the Buddha, all of our senses and thoughts are on fire with lust and desire. Although there is no abiding-self or soul (*ātman*), we cannot deny the reality of our experiences. Thus, the Buddha provided a five-fold classification of what he thought was really going on when we experience something. He described these as the five bundles and they constitute one of the earliest attempts at a definitive analysis of what it is to experience something. They are:

1. *Rūpa* – Material Form – the material givenness of experience
2. *Vedanā* – Sensation – the initial sensory apprehension of forms
3. *Saṃjñā* – Cognition – the determinate classification of experience
4. *Saṃskāra* – Disposition – the volitional response that colours experiences
5. *Vijñāna* – Consciousness – awareness of the six sensory ranges (*indriya*)

These five 'bundles' are no doubt an allusion to the bundles of fire-sticks used by the brahmanical priests in the administering of their five ritual fire sacrifices. The allegorisation of the fire sacrifice had already taken place within the early Upaniṣadic material where fire (*agni*) had become closely associated with the notion of the five breaths (*prāṇa*, see *Bṛhadāraṇyaka Upaniṣad* 1.5.3f.) and sacrifice was interpreted in certain circles as an interiorised ritual involving the control of one's breath. For the early Buddhists, however, the five *skandhas* provided their own conceptual map of the entirety of our experience. Where is there a self to be found within this scheme? The Buddha is said to have declared with reference to each of the five *skandhas* – "It is not mine. He is not me. He is not my self", thereby rejecting the existence of some mysterious entity that might be thought to 'own' or 'possess' the *skandhas* and to deny that any such substantial self can be found within the *skandhas* themselves. The five bundles are themselves continually undergoing transformation and do not constitute a persisting or abiding self of any kind.

All five bundles are inter-connected and mutually condition each other. It is inappropriate to talk of material forms or sensations before we become aware of them, nor should we, so the Buddha argued, talk of consciousness without talking about what one is being conscious of. The distinction between the five *skandhas* then is largely conceptual and should not be taken as implying that the *skandhas* can exist in isolation from each other. Nevertheless, the early Buddhists clearly believed that one could make a distinction between wholesome (*kuśala*) and unwholesome mental states and dispositions, and cultivate the former along with analytical wisdom (*prajñā*) in order to see things more clearly.

To appreciate the philosophical differences between the Buddhist and brahmanical traditions in this respect consider the ways in which they both appeal to the example of the chariot to illustrate their respective positions. In the brahmanical schools of thought the essential self (*ātman*) of beings is a spiritual essence to be distinguished from the changing mental and physical processes that one normally associates with the self.

> Know the self (*ātman*) as a rider in a chariot,
> and the body (*śarīra*), as simply the chariot.
> Know the intellect (*buddhi*) as the charioteer,
> and the mind (*manas*), as simply the reins.

> The senses (*indriya*), they say, are the horses
> and sense-objects (*viṣaya*) are the paths around them;
> He who is linked to the body (*ātman*), senses, and mind,
> the wise proclaim as the one who enjoys (*bhoktṛ*)
>
> *Kaṭha Upaniṣad* 3. 3–4, translation in Olivelle, 1996: 238–9

Such a stance is reiterated by Kṛṣṇa in a famous verse from the *Bhagavad Gītā* (2.22)

> Just as a man casting off worn-out clothes takes up others that are new,
> so the embodied self, casting off its worn-out bodies, goes to other, new ones.
>
> Johnston, 1994: 9

In contrast, in the Buddhist text the *Questions of King Milinda* (*Milinda-pañha*), we are offered a Buddhist version of the chariot analogy. Here the Buddhist monk Nāgasena (not to be confused with the Mahāyāna philosopher Nāgārjuna) argues that 'chariot' is merely a designation used to denote the combination of disparate parts that enable it to be useful as a vehicle. He challenges King Milinda to find a chariot over and above the parts that constitute it. Similarly, Nāgasena argues, an analysis of the person (*pudgala*) will demonstrate that there is no transcendent self or subject that 'owns' or possesses experiences. What is conventionally referred to as 'the self' is merely a changing stream of mental and physical processes (*dharmas*) that are constantly undergoing transformation. There is no 'ghost in the machine'.

As we have seen, this world-view has implications for one's conception of the cycle of rebirths (*saṃsāra*). Buddhists believe in re-birth but do not accept that there is any substantial entity of self (*ātman*) being reborn in this process – there is simply the process itself. For the various Hindu schools *saṃsāra* is like a pearl necklace. The succession of lives are a series of pearls held together by a single connecting thread – the *ātman*. In contrast, Buddhist philosophical texts tend to represent rebirth using analogies of dynamic and ever-changing processes, such as the flowing of a river or the flickering flame of a candle. Thus, according to the *Questions of King Milinda* to talk of either 'identity' or 'difference' between lives (and for some Buddhists even from one moment to the next) is inappropriate.

> 'He who is reborn, Nāgasena, is he the same person or another?'
> 'Neither the same nor another.'
> 'Give me an illustration.'
> 'In the case of a pot of milk which turns to curds, then to butter, then to ghee; it would not be right to say that the ghee, butter and curds were the same as the milk but they have come from that so neither would it be right to say that they are something else.'
>
> *Milindapañha* chapter 2, translation in Pesala, 1991: 10

Identity or sameness involves the mistaken assumption of a permanent element or substance that must persist throughout an ever-changing process. On the other hand, the assertion of absolute difference involves a denial of causal continuity between past, present and future. One cannot say that the flame of a candle is identical to the flame of a moment ago, but it would also seem wrong to say that it is a different flame altogether (since it is in some sense causally connected to the flame of a moment ago). Thus, Buddhists have generally accepted that there is causal *continuity* throughout our physical and mental lives but deny that this means that there is an underlying *identity* holding the process together. This may strike the reader as an odd position, so used are we to conceiving of ourselves as persisting entities, but the Buddhist point (at least at a philosophical level) is to steer us away from a model of reality that divides the world up into fixed substances (*dharmin*) that possess qualities (*dharma*). There are no unchanging substrata, only a stream of causally connected qualities (*dharma*).

Within the Mahāyāna Buddhist tradition the doctrine of inter-dependent-origination came to represent not just a means of explaining the dynamics of rebirth without an abiding-self but also a kind of universal theory of relativity. For the Mahāyāna traditions everything arises and exists in dependence upon something else. Like a house of cards, no one entity supports the others – the structure of the universe is maintained through the mutual supportiveness of its constituent factors. Such a conception of reality involves the rejection of an underlying ontological ground or substratum (*sad-adhiṣṭhāna, āśraya*) to explain the continuation of the cycle of rebirths (*saṃsāra*). As we have seen in their use of the chariot analogy, Buddhists have therefore tended to approach entities in a 'deconstructive' or reductionist spirit. For the Buddhist philosopher the notion of a 'subject' or 'agent' of experience is an illusion. The personal self (*pudgalātman*) is a second-order entity that can be reductively analysed into the inter-dependently arising *skandhas*. The overwhelming emphasis within Buddhist thought, therefore, has been to conceive of objects and entities as compositions (*saṃskāra*) made up of more basic realities (the *dharmas*).

The Buddhist teaching of no-abiding-self (*anātman*) seems to require some form of distinction to be made between conventional discourse – involving the frequent use of personal pronouns such as 'she' or 'he' – and theoretical discourse which necessitates strict scholastic precision. The distinction between conventional and ultimate, however, seems to have been explicitly drawn for the first time by Buddhist scholars in an attempt to reconcile conflicting statements within the canon (Collins, 1982: 154). In this context, statements made by the Buddha were divided into two categories – texts of final import (*nītārtha*) and texts of secondary import (*neyārtha*). The scholastic precision of the teaching of *anātman* was further developed by Abhidharma scholars. As we have seen, the Buddha denied the existence of an-abiding-self and yet continued to use personal pronouns in everyday discourse. How is this possible? It would seem that the Buddha denied the efficacy of terminology presupposing 'an abiding self' only in contexts where he was being precise and definitive and *not* in everyday, conventional language. The refusal to adopt the language of personhood that characterises conventional discourse would have made everyday teaching and discussion virtually impossible.

The implicit antecedents of the distinction between the two truths, however, can be traced back to the *sūtras* of the *Tripiṭaka*. The distinction between conventional and ultimate truth may be prefigured in the early Buddhist references to an 'individual truth' (*pacceka sacca*). There seems to be no clear-cut distinction between these two kinds of truth in the Pāli canon, though the very fact that the Buddha used personal pronouns and referred to persons in everyday parlance, whilst stating in his more theoretical moments that there is no-abiding-self (Sanskrit: *anātman*/Pāli: *anattā*), suggests an implicit distinction between the everyday and the theoretical contexts of discourse. The idea, for instance, is already implicit in the conception of the Buddha as a 'healing physician'. This conception of the Buddha (and of the four noble truths as his diagnosis and cure for the unsatisfactory conditions of life) exemplifies a teacher who teaches according to the spiritual condition of his audience. According to one famous sermon the *Dharma* (that is the teaching of the Buddha) is but a raft to be relinquished once one has reached the shore, i.e. *nirvāṇa* (*Majjhima Nikāya* i.134). From the voluminous evidence of the Buddha's teaching (accepting, of course, that much of it is late and perhaps apocryphal), different statements appear to have been made at different times to different audiences. The apparent conflict between these teachings when examined together is overcome by later Buddhist scholars via the hermeneutical distinction between definitive and interpretable levels of meaning.

The Buddha is said to possess the ability to intuit the capacity and propensity of his student and adapt his teaching according to circumstance. This is apparent from a number of occasions where the Buddha responds differently to the same question, the criterion for determining an answer being the level of understanding and intent of the questioner. There is much evidence of the Buddha adapting his answer to the level of understanding and intent of the enquirer. The most famous incidents are those involving Vacchagotta and Māluṅkyāputta (see *Majjhima Nikāya*, suttas 63, 72). On both occasions, the Buddha refused to be drawn on certain metaphysical questions. These became known as the *avyākṛta* (Pāli: *avyākata*) or 'unanswered questions' (see Chapter 9).

– MAINSTREAM BUDDHIST PHILOSOPHY (ABHIDHARMA) –

The account of a series of philosophical discussions between the Buddhist monk Nāgasena and King Milinda (possibly Menander – an Indo-Greek king ruling in North-East India in the second century BCE) reflects ongoing attempts to explain the import of the Buddhist doctrine of no-abiding-self. The *Questions of King Milinda* is probably the most popular (and readable) text of a specific genre of Buddhist literature known as the Abhidharma. Early Buddhist sacred teachings were classified in terms of three baskets (PIṬAKA): the Sūtras (or Āgamas), that is the general discourses of the Buddha, the Vinaya-piṭaka, containing explanations of the rules of monastic discipline, and the Abhidharma-piṭaka – a collection of works outlining a systematic understanding of the Buddha's teachings (the Dharma).

The term 'Abhidharma' has various possible meanings ranging from 'understanding the Dharma', to 'that which surpasses the Dharma'. The early Abhidharma literature appears to have developed from early matrices (*mātṛkā*) or lists of doctrinal topics. These lists generally served as headings for philosophical and meditative reflection and constituted early attempts both to systematise the Buddha's teaching in a manner conducive to memorisation and to provide a categorisation of the various types of mental and physical processes (*dharmas*). These matrices are reminiscent in some respects of the early lists of fundamental categories (*padārtha*) provided by the Hindu Nyāya and Vaiśeṣika schools. However, it is important to distinguish here between the ontological realism of the Nyāya and Vaiśeṣika schools and the phenomenological orientation of Buddhist Abhidharma. Whilst the Hindu schools were concerned with providing a definitive inventory of what really exists (ontology), the Abhidharma tradition shows a much greater concern to provide an accurate account of the way objects appear to our pre-reflective consciousness (phenomenology). Over time, however, it seems that the Buddhist *dharma* lists were taken more and more seriously by the various Abhidharma schools as accounts of what really exists rather than as attempts to classify phenomena as they appear to us. As we shall see, this shift precipitated a critical response from the Madhyamaka and Yogācāra schools of Mahāyāna Buddhism.

The early Abhidharma lists constituted an attempt to formulate a compact abridgement of the Buddha's fundamental ideas, as found in the broader corpus of his teachings. It is likely then that the earliest form of the Abhidharma Piṭaka consisted of little more than a list of headings (the matrices or *mātṛkā*). Only later did these lists develop into a comprehensive system of classifications, categories and highly refined distinctions. According to the Buddhist tradition it was the monk Śāriputra, upheld as the exemplar of wisdom or analytical insight (*prajñā*) in mainstream (i.e. non-Mahāyāna) Buddhism, who was appointed by the Buddha to produce elaborations of the Dharma along such lines. The summaries of Abhidharma teachings available today, however, are likely to be much later (probably c. third century BCE). Despite attempts at a reconstruction of these 'proto-Abhidharma' lists (e.g. from the first book of the Pāli *Abhidhamma-piṭaka* – the *Dhammasaṅghaṇi*) little can be deduced about their philosophical intent since they are too highly condensed.

– THE STHAVIRA-VĀDA (PĀLI: THERAVĀDA) –

Sthavira-vāda means 'doctrine of the elders' and is the epithet of the early followers of the Buddha. Today the dominant tradition of Buddhism in South-East Asia is known as Theravāda which is the Pāli rendering of *sthavira-vāda*. Although much of the sacred literature of Indian Buddhism seems to have been composed in some form of Sanskrit (sometimes in a variant known as 'Buddhist Hybrid Sanskrit'), the canonical works of the Theravāda tradition are composed in Pāli and were preserved by the tradition in Śri Laṅka, Myanmar and Thailand. Members of the Theravāda tradition of Buddhism claim to be the oldest tradition of Buddhism and trace their identity back to the earliest followers of Gautama, the historical Buddha (c. fourth century BCE). This identification, however, is problematic. Much of the Pāli canonical material contained within the Theravāda *sutta-piṭaka* corresponds very closely to similar discourses in the canons of rival schools of Buddhism and is no doubt quite ancient. On the other hand, much of this material no doubt dates from a few centuries after the Buddha's lifetime and it is not possible, therefore, to accept the Pāli materials as incontrovertible accounts of the Buddha's teaching.

It is often said that there are two traditions of Buddhism: Mahāyāna (the Great Vehicle) and Hīnayāna (the Little Vehicle). This is misleading for a number of reasons. Traditionally, there are said to have been eighteen schools of Buddhism in ancient India, all belonging to what might be called 'mainstream Buddhism'. The Mahāyāna did not constitute one of these eighteen sects (*nikāya*) of Buddhism, because it initially emerged as a spiritual and philosophical trend rather than as a distinctive school of its own. In this sense the emerging Mahāyāna movement was more akin to Christian Pentecostalism in so far as it rode roughshod over a variety of established divisions between traditions and was more of a transformative trend than a well-defined sectarian movement.

In any case schism (*saṅghabheda*) in Indian Buddhism was always based upon differences over correct practice (orthopraxy) amongst the monastic community and not over differences of opinion concerning doctrine (orthodoxy). Buddhist sects (*nikāya*) arose as a result of disputes over the nature of practice within the monastic *saṅgha* (i.e. over the rules of conduct – known as the *vinaya*) and doctrinal affairs became relevant to such schisms only when differences of opinion impinged upon the rules of monastic practice and therefore the unity of the *saṅgha* (community of Buddhist monks and nuns). The issue of being a Mahāyāna Buddhist, therefore, did not necessarily impinge upon one's own sectarian affiliation. Consequently, although the Mahāyāna trends within Indian Buddhism produced a bewildering variety of new sacred texts (*sūtras*) proclaiming to be the word of the Buddha, the *vinaya-piṭaka* of mainstream schools such as the Mūla-Sarvāstivāda and the Dharmaguptakas were adopted, since there was felt to be no requirement to produce their own body of literature on the rules of monastic practice.

The term 'Hīnayāna' (little or inferior vehicle) is an inappropriate name for the Theravāda school for two reasons. Firstly, the term is highly pejorative, being adopted in later Mahāyāna literature as a swipe at the 'small-mindedness' of mainstream Buddhism. Since the Mahāyāna movement always remained a minority trend within Indian Buddhism, I will use the more neutral term 'mainstream' Buddhism to denote what is often referred to as Hīnayāna Buddhism. Secondly, we must avoid assuming that the terms 'Hīnayāna' and 'Theravāda' refer to the same type of entity. Although the Theravāda tradition tends to identify itself with the Sthaviravādins of early Buddhism, this involves considerable historical creativity. The Theravāda represents the only surviving sect of mainstream Indian Buddhism. The tradition survived because it became established within other regions of South-East Asia (such as Śri Laṅka) and continued after the demise of Buddhism on the Indian sub-continent. The Theravāda represents only one of the original eighteen sects of Buddhism and was supplanted in India by more successful sects such as the Sarvāstivāda. Consequently, the school did not play a significant role in the development of either Hindu or Buddhist philosophy in India.

– The Sarvāstivāda or Vaibhāṣika School –

The Sarvāstivāda school of Buddhism had the widest geographical spread of any of the mainstream schools of Buddhism and historically has probably been the most influential. It is the doctrines of the Sarvāstivāda that constitute the major point of departure for the emerging Mahāyāna trends in the first millennium of the Common Era. The schism that resulted in the establishment of the Sarvāstivāda school seems to have occurred between 244 and 237 BCE (the latter being the year of King Aśoka's 'Schism Edict'). After the schism the school spread from Pāṭaliputra to Mathurā before moving to Kashmir and establishing itself as the dominant form of Buddhism in North-Western India. From here the school acquired its alternate name – the Vaibhāṣika, denoting an adherence to the teaching contained in the *Mahā-Vibhāṣā* – a voluminous compendium of Sarvāstivāda doctrine.

The Sarvāstivāda and Theravāda are the only traditions of mainstream Buddhism that are known to have a complete canon of Abhidharma works. The Sarvāstivāda *Abhidharma-piṭaka* consists of seven works: the *Jñāna-prasthāna* and six supplementary works, including the aforementioned *Mahā-Vibhāṣā*. The philosophical stance of this school is summed up in its name – Sarvāstivāda, literally 'the doctrine that everything exists'. This literal rendering requires further explanation if we are to understand the Abhidharma context to which it refers. For the Sarvāstivāda, 'everything' denotes 'all *dharmas*' – that is, the momentary mental and physical 'events' that collectively constitute our experience of the world. These *dharmas* are characterised by origination, duration, decay and cessation (*Abhidharma-kośa* II.45cd). For the Sarvāstivāda although *dharmas* are momentary in the present they have a real, durable essence (*svabhāva*) that persists through the three realms of time. Clearly, the Sarvāstivāda saw problems in establishing causal and karmic continuity between past, present and future times unless there was some sense in which *dharmas* continued to be real even if not currently associated or manifested to consciousness (*citta-viprayukta*). As a result, the school posited *dharmas* such as 'possession' (*prāpti*) – a kind of impersonal force which holds some characteristic or property within a given stream of consciousness. Such *dharmas* were deemed necessary by the school not only as a means of establishing causal and karmic continuity both within and between lives, but also to provide a criterion for distinguishing between enlightened and unenlightened beings in terms of the qualities that they possessed.

The most influential summary of the Vaibhāṣika position has undoubtedly been the *Abhidharma-kośa* of Vasubandhu (late fourth century CE). This exposition of the Sarvāstivāda position was something of a watershed within Indian Abhidharma. The *Kośa* became highly revered as an authoritative exposition of the Vaibhāṣika system and became the major scholastic source for Sarvāstivāda Abhidharma. Vasubandhu, the author of this text, however, displayed clear leanings towards a position known as the Sautrāntika and wrote a commentary (*bhāṣya*) upon the *Abhidharma-kośa*, which refuted many Vaibhāṣika doctrines from a Sautrāntika standpoint.

– THE SAUTRĀNTIKA –

The two main centres of Sarvāstivāda doctrine were in Gandhāra and Kashmir. As we have seen, Kashmir saw the development of the dominant position known as the Vaibhāṣika. In Gandhāra, however, more progressive elements within the Sarvāstivāda led to the development of a school known as the Sautrāntika or 'those who adhere to the *sūtras*'. As this name suggests, the Sautrāntika emphasised the authority of the *sūtras* of the *Āgama-piṭaka* over the proliferating Abhidharma literature which they saw as the work of later authors and not the authentic words of the Buddha. This is not to say that the Sautrāntika repudiated the *Abhidharma-piṭaka*. Abhidharma philosophy remained a valid system of reflections upon the Buddha's teachings, but were not as authoritative as the Buddha's verbatim teachings in the general discourses (*sūtras*).

The Sautrāntika philosophy explained karmic continuity not in Vaibhāṣika terms as the actualisation of an existent but previously latent cause (the existence of *dharmas* across the three time periods) but rather in terms of the transformation of the stream of consciousness (*citta-saṃtāna*). Crucial to the Sautrāntika account was the notion of karmic seeds (*bīja*). Actions produce karmic seeds within specific streams of consciousness that bear fruit (*phala*) at a later time. Differentiation between individuals, therefore, was possible on the basis of the different seeds implanted within the various streams of consciousness. Sentient experience on this view is a continuity of transformations (*pariṇāma*) of consciousness caused by the fruition of the seeds of previous actions. The school also became known as the Saṅkrāntivāda, denoting belief in the transmigration of the five bundles (*skandha*) from one life to the next. According to this view, the *skandhas* continued in a post-mortem state of intermediate existence (*antarabhāva*) between lives in the form of a subtle (but still changing) consciousness (*sūkṣma-manovijñāna*).

The Sautrāntika position involved a comprehensive paring of the Vaibhāṣika list of *dharma*-categories. *Dharmas* such as 'shape' (*samsthāna*) were not substantial-existents (*dravya-sat*), nor do *dharma*-categories such as *prāpti* (possession) refer to anything other than the state of possessing or not possessing certain qualities. In this sense the Sautrāntika attempted to avoid what it saw as the unnecessary reification of categories. *Dharmas* only 'exist' for as long as they manifest themselves. They do not exist in the past or the future as the Sarvāstivāda position implied. The Sautrāntika doctrine of momentariness (*kṣaṇa-vāda*), therefore, involved the rejection of duration as a feature of *dharmas* (see *Abhidharma-kośa* II.45cd). The Sautrāntika position is that *dharmas* manifest when they have causal efficacy (*kriyā*) and cease to exist when they do not. To exist is to perform a function. This account of *dharmas* focused upon the immediacy of what is presented to consciousness and explicitly repudiated the Vaibhāṣika analysis which distinguished the existence of *dharmas* from their causal efficacy. In many respects the Sautrāntika position seems to have been an attempt to return the Abhidharma to the status of a 'pure phenomenology', that is, an account of what actually appears to consciousness rather than a theory about what exists (ontology). Consequently,

> Atomism, the existence of past and future, and of all kinds of categories the Vaibhāṣikas had devised to forge a coherent system (such as prāpti, a kind of metaphysical glue linking related but diverse elements), are all thrown out by Vasubandhu, who in his argumentation follows a principle somewhat like Occam's Razor ('If it is not an absolutely necessary category, throw it out!')
>
> Stefan Anacker, 1975: 64

The Sautrāntika, like the Sāṃkhya and Vedānta schools, believed that we do not perceive external objects directly but rather experience mental images (*ākāra*) of them. Although external objects are real and cause our experiences, what we encounter in perception is a mental image of an object and not the object in itself. They therefore propounded a philosophy of indirect realism (see Chapter 7). The central philosophical text of the Sautrāntika school of Buddhism is the *Abhidharma-kośa Bhāṣya* of Vasubandhu, which is written from the Sautrāntika perspective.

– THE SAṀMATĪYAS –

Although the Buddhist doctrine of no-abiding-self constitutes one of the most distinctive contributions to the history of philosophy, not all schools of Buddhism seem to have been comfortable with the *anātman* doctrine as it has generally been represented in mainstream Buddhist philosophy. A school known as the Saṁmatīyas denied mainstream interpretations of this doctrine, arguing that in some sense it is permissible to speak of a personal self (*pudgala*). For the Saṁmatīyas it remains legitimate to speak of a 'person', though such an entity is neither identical with nor different from the five *skandhas*. This school, however, remained a minority (if numerically significant) position within Indian Buddhism and was condemned by all other Buddhist schools for its apparent denial of the doctrine of no-abiding-self.

It remains a moot point as to what the Saṁmatīyas meant by their adherence to the language of 'personhood'. Since there are no surviving texts of the Saṁmatīyas our only evidence is the refutation of their views (where they are called the '*pudgala-vādins*') in the Theravāda *Kathā-Vatthu* and the Vaibhāṣika *Vijñānakāya*. From these texts it seems that the Saṁmatīyas conceived of the '*pudgala*' as some kind of epiphenomenon that occurs in conjunction with the five *skandhas*. As a result the 'person' is neither exactly the same as the five bundles (and so cannot be reduced to them) nor is it completely separate from them. In the absence of any texts composed by members of the school itself, however, it is unclear what the position of the Saṁmatīyas might have been and if it is indeed correct to describe them as '*pudgala-vādins*'. The school may be a proponent of some kind of dialectical methodology, rejecting the establishment of a fixed philosophical position. The Saṁmatīyas may have been dialectically inclined meditators looking to avoid the rigidity of 'extreme views'. There is certainly plenty of evidence in the earliest strata of Buddhist teachings (e.g. the *Sutta Nipāta*) where the Buddha is represented as one who does not hold a view (*dṛṣṭi*). This 'no-view' strand of Buddhist thought is one which comes to the fore in Nāgārjuna's philosophy of emptiness (*śūnyatā*) and the subsequent Madhyamaka school of Mahāyāna Buddhism (see Chapter 6). Nevertheless, whatever the problems in reconstructing the philosophical position of the Saṁmatīyas, we should note that their position is still expressed in terms of a particular interpretation of *anātmatā* – so central has this teaching been in the history of Buddhist thought in India.

– THE MAHĀSAṄGHIKA –

The Mahāsaṅghikas are said to have split from the *sthavira-vādins* in the fourth century BCE in a dispute over the stringency of monastic rules, with the former taking the more lenient view with regard to the rigorous standards to be adhered to as an ordained member of the *saṅgha*. A sub-sect of the Mahāsaṅghikas, known as the *Lokottāra-vāda* propounded the doctrine of the supramundane nature of the Buddha, who is said to have transcended the world and be in possession of all of the perfections (*pāramitā*). As a result of the Buddha's immense accumulation of merit, it was suggested that the Buddha's lifespan and power must be immeasurable. This type of speculation provided a basis for the development of later Mahāyāna conceptions of Buddhahood. The Mahāsaṅghikas also rejected the mainstream position that there could only be one Buddha in each historical epoch. Consequently, others could follow the *bodhisattva* path and the school outlined a system of ten stages on this path which probably influenced the later Mahāyāna scheme of ten stages (*bhūmi*).

For these kinds of reasons the Mahāsaṅghikas are often seen as important forerunners of the Mahāyāna strand of Buddhism which developed from the first century BCE onwards. The association of the Mahāsaṅghikas with the early Mahāyāna, however, is highly problematic since what subsequently became known as the Mahāyāna has clearly developed from a variety of heterogeneous sources and displayed no particular sectarian allegiance (*nikāya*). In fact, the term 'Mahāyāna' ('Great Vehicle') is an umbrella term encompassing a multitude of positions, movements and trends within Indian Buddhism at the beginning of the Common Era, mainly centred upon the notion of the *bodhisattva* – those beings who are destined to become fully enlightened Buddhas.

– MAHĀYĀNA BUDDHISM IN INDIA –

In philosophical terms Indian Mahāyāna produced two philosophical schools – the 'Middle Way' (Madhyamaka) school of Nāgārjuna and the 'Practice of Yoga' (Yogācāra) school. Both traditions contributed significantly to philosophical debate within India in the first millennium, before the demise of Buddhism within its homeland from the tenth century onwards.

– NĀGĀRJUNA AND THE MADHYAMAKA OR 'MIDDLE WAY' SCHOOL –

The central philosophy of the Madhyamaka school is the doctrine of emptiness (*śūnyatā*), that is, the view that everything (*absolutely* everything) is empty of or lacks an independent-existence or own-being (*svabhāva*). As we shall see, this doctrine struck at the core of mainstream Abhidharma thought and ontological speculation in general (see below and Chapter 5). Very little is known about the early history of the Madhyamaka or 'Middle Way' School, though it seems to have developed as an attempt to systematise the philosophical implications of a genre of early Mahāyāna sacred texts known as the Perfection of Wisdom literature (*Prajñāpāramitā sūtras*). These *sūtras* represent one of the earliest expressions of Mahāyāna Buddhist thought, and first seem to have arisen in the first century BCE.

The reputed founder of the 'Middle Way' school is Nāgārjuna, a Buddhist monk living in the second century of the Common Era and author of the seminal text of the school – the *Foundational Verses on the Middle* (*Mūla Madhyamaka Kārikā*, or MMK). This work is an independent scholastic treatise (*śāstra*) rather than a commentarial text and provides the first systematic philosophical exposition of the Mahāyāna doctrine of emptiness (*śūnyatā*). A Tibetan tradition refers to Rāhulabhadra, the author of a number of hymns, as Nāgārjuna's teacher, but other Tibetan and Chinese traditions of a more reliable nature refer to this figure as a disciple rather than a teacher of Nāgārjuna. Only quotational fragments remain of Rāhulabhadra's works, and so very little can be ascertained as to his respective position in early Madhyamaka thought.[1]

It is unlikely that Nāgārjuna is the actual 'founder' of what later became the 'Madhyamaka' school (the term is not found as the designation of a specific school until Candrakīrti's *Madhyamakāvatāravṛtti* in the seventh century CE), but he was certainly the crucial source of its distinctive approach. The *Verses on the Middle* constitute Nāgārjuna's definitive work, and the root (*mūla*) text of the Madhyamaka school. The prevailing trend within modern scholarship has been to accept the authenticity of another five texts, which together with the *Verses on the Middle* (MMK) constitute the logical or analytic (*yukti*) corpus (Tibetan: *rigs chogs*) of Nāgārjuna's literary output.[2] The confinement of authenticity to these logical works alone, however, can lead to a misleadingly negative appraisal of Nāgārjuna's philosophy (Lindtner, 1982: 249, Ruegg, 1981: 33–6). The question of authorship is rather a complex issue since we have virtually no clearly substantiated historical evidence for assigning a given text to Nāgārjuna. Thus the modern academic definition of Nāgārjuna has tended to become a rather limited and philosophically narrow one, ignoring the fact that poetic works eulogising the Buddha such as the 'Four Hymns' (*Catuḥstava*) constitute the most frequently cited of Nāgārjuna's apparent compositions.[3] In terms of a discussion of Madhyamaka philosophy, however, it is primarily the works of Nāgārjuna's logical (*yukti*) corpus that concern us.

The question of the relationship between Nāgārjuna and the mainstream Abhidharma schools remains an area of considerable debate. The notion of emptiness (Sanskrit: *śūnyatā;* Pāli: *suññata)* can be found in early Buddhist literature and the concept is certainly utilised in the non-Mahāyāna systems of Abhidharma. Nāgārjuna shows a lucid grasp of many central Abhidharmic concepts and his exposition in the *Verses on the Middle* seems to have been instigated primarily as a reaction to the perceived finality of mainstream Abhidharmic analysis. The central target of Nāgārjuna's work, therefore, is the Abhidharma notion of the independent-existence (*svabhāva*) of *dharmas*. Most scholars have tended to view the *Mūla Madhyamaka Kārikā* (MMK) as a work composed in response to the Sarvāstivāda Abhidharma (Murti, 1955: 69; Streng, 1967: 33), though there is some evidence that is suggestive of a Sautrāntika context to Nāgārjuna's critique.[4] Moreover, Sarvāstivāda Buddhism predominated in North-Western India and there is a strong tradition which ties Nāgārjuna to Southern India.

The question of Abhidharmic influences upon Nāgārjuna is also tied up with the question of his authorship of the voluminous *Mahāprajñāpāramitā-śāstra* – a commentary on *The Perfection of Wisdom in*

25,000 Lines and a Mahāyāna 'Abhidharma' text in its own right. Modern scholarship has cast doubt upon the text as an authentic work of Nāgārjuna, since it spends some time explaining Indian customs and Sanskrit idioms as if intended for a non-Indian audience. The work is not available in Sanskrit, perhaps because it was intended for a Chinese audience, where it is known as the *Ta-chih-tu-lun*. There is no known Tibetan version of the text which also implies that the text was unavailable in India by the eighth century CE (indeed, the text appears to have been unknown to both the Indian and Tibetan traditions). It seems likely that Kumārajīva, the professed translator of this work, was involved in the composition of at least parts of the work, and certainly edited the text to make it more amenable to a non-Indian audience. The *Mahā-prajñāpāramitā-śāstra* has a wide knowledge of the Sarvāstivāda Abhidharma, and also seems to presupposes the MMK, which it quotes many times.[5]

Whatever the specific targets of Nāgārjuna's critique, the main focus of his attack in the *Verses on the Middle* is the way in which the mainstream Abhidharma schools took their own *dharma*-lists to be definitive classifications of the way things really are (*yathābhūta*). Nāgārjuna launched a comprehensive attack on the idea that any *dharma* could have an independent-existence or inherent-nature of its own (*svabhāva*). Not only is there no personal self (*pudgala nairātmya*) but the *dharma*-categories are themselves lacking any substantial essence or selfhood (*dharma nairātmya*). Thus, Nāgārjuna propounded the doctrine that all *dharmas* (Abhidharma shorthand for 'everything') are empty or devoid of independent-existence or an essence of their own (*svabhāva-śūnya*).

Care must be taken, however, to avoid reading too much of the philosophy of later Mahāyāna into Nāgārjuna's thought. A. K. Warder (1973: 376) has argued that the author of the *Verses on the Middle* (*Madhyamaka Kārikā*), the *magnum opus* of Nāgārjuna, displays no allegiance to the Mahāyāna schools and in fact 'writes simply as a Buddhist trying to establish the correct interpretation of the Tripiṭaka as recognized by all Buddhists'. Certainly, there are no obvious references to any Mahāyāna *sūtras* in the work and the only *sūtra* alluded to by name is the *Katyāyānavavāda* (at MMK 15.7), a mainstream Buddhist canonical text of the *Saṃyuktāgama* (cf. *Samyuttanikāya*, ii, p.17).[6] It has been suggested that this reflects Nāgārjuna concern to convince mainstream Buddhists of the validity of his position, therefore rendering an appeal to Mahāyāna *sūtras* both superfluous and counter-productive (Robinson, 1967: 63; Lindtner, 1982: 27–8).

As far as his authorship of the *Verses on the Middle* is concerned, we can perhaps agree with Warder that:

> If Nāgārjuna really had any sympathy with the Mahāyānists, he was certainly against that complete break with early Buddhism which many Mahāyāna *sūtras* advocate. If he had such sympathies, we must conclude that his aim was to prevent a break, to reunite all Buddhists on the basis of the texts which all accepted, to restore the original Buddhism.
>
> Warder, 1973: 84

However, Warder has assumed too much in the way of early Mahāyāna polemic against the non-Mahāyāna schools in the period in which Nāgārjuna lived. Early Mahāyāna texts generally represent themselves as an expansion (*vaipulya*) rather than a repudiation of mainstream Buddhism. Moreover, early Mahāyāna is made up of a bewildering variety of groups, movements and orientations and displays neither the unanimity nor sufficient self-awareness to distinguish itself as 'Mahāyāna' (The Great Vehicle) in contradistinction to the 'Hīnayāna' (Little Vehicle) of mainstream Buddhism. Warder has overstated his case in claiming that Nāgārjuna was not a Mahāyānist. We know little of the intellectual milieu in which Nāgārjuna flourished and at this early stage in the development of Mahāyāna ideas the use of later scholastic distinctions between 'Hīnayāna' and 'Mahāyāna' only succeeds in clouding the issue.

Nāgārjuna provides us with an insight into some of the central teachings of the emerging Mahāyāna traditions of Indian Buddhism. All *dharmas* (basically, everything) are empty of an intrinsic nature or independent-existence of their own (*svabhāva-śūnya*). The Madhyamaka tradition also made a distinction between two levels of truth – conventional and ultimate truth. Moreover, in the Mahāyāna traditions liberation (*nirvāṇa*) and the wheel of rebirth (*saṃsāra*) are not different. The perceived difference between them is a quality of the perceiver and not a feature of reality itself. Indeed, *nirvāṇa* and *saṃsāra* are more like two sides of the same coin. If you are enlightened then you see reality in terms of *nirvāṇa*; however, if you are unenlightened the world is a source of continual re-embodiment and suffering (*duḥkha*). Indeed, for the Mahāyāna traditions one no longer seeks an end to rebirth as a spiritual goal since this is deemed too individualistic and lacking in compassion (*karuṇā*). The advanced Mahāyāna practitioner (known as a *bodhisattva* – 'one destined to be enlightened') continues to take part in the realm of *saṃsāra* even after attaining complete enlightenment, for the sake of the alleviation of the suffering of all sentient beings.

Important figures within the Madhyamaka tradition are Āryadeva and Buddhāpalita, both said to be disciples of Nāgārjuna. Subsequent interpretations of Nāgārjuna's philosophy of emptiness, however, owes much to the works of Bhāvaviveka (c. 500–70 CE) and Candrakīrti (c. 600–50 CE). Bhāvaviveka's work provides the basis for the Svātantrika school of

Madhyamaka and reflects the integration of the epistemological system of Dignāga (see below) into the Madhyamaka philosophy. The Svātantrika school accepts the validity of offering independent arguments to convince others of the truth of emptiness and is an attempt to bring Nāgārjuna's philosophy closer to the epistemological theories *(pramāṇa-vāda)* offered by other schools. This allowed the tradition to take part in the inter-scholastic practice of philosophical debate (*vāda*) that was at this time the dominant mode of philosophical interaction. This also explains Bhāvaviveka's interest as a doxographer – a classifier of the various *darśanas*. In contrast to this stance however, Candrakīrti rejected the 'domestication' of Nāgārjuna in terms of the debating schemes offered by other schools and is seen as the instrumental figure in the development of the Prāsaṅgika school of Madhyamaka. For Candrakīrti Nāgārjuna's view that he does not have a thesis (*pratijñā*) to put forward should be taken at face value. The middle path involves the repudiation of all fixed views (*dṛṣṭi*) and is to be arrived at through the refutation of all philosophical theories. Thus, the goal of the Madhyamaka system, as Candrakīrti represents it, is to arrive at the truth of emptiness not by offering independent arguments of one's own, but rather by refuting all possible opinions through the practice of *reductio ad absurdum* (*prasaṅga*). We should note, however, that an explicit distinction between Svātantrika and Prāsaṅgika traditions does not occur within Indian Madhyamaka itself, being a scholastic distinction which arose once Mahāyāna Buddhism migrated to Tibet.

– THE 'PRACTICE OF YOGA' (YOGĀCĀRA) SCHOOL –

The second important philosophical school to develop in Indian Mahāyāna Buddhism, the Yogācāra school, seems to have developed the distinctive features of its philosophy from a comprehensive analysis of meditative experience (hence the name 'Yogācāra' – 'the practice of yoga'). The radical critique of ontology offered by Nāgārjuna and the rejection of any attempt to posit an independent-existence (*svabhāva*) to anything was something of a 'speculation-stopper' but this in itself did not prevent later Mahāyānists from developing fresh insights and 're-formulations' of old themes.

After Nāgārjuna, one can discern two distinctive and general features, both inter-related, in later developments of Indian Mahāyāna thought. The first is an increasing emphasis upon skill-in-means (*upāya-kauśalya*) as a major factor in the salvation of beings. Skill-in-means is the central concept in the *Saddharmapuṇḍarīka Sūtra* or *Lotus of the Wonderful Law Sūtra* (*Lotus Sūtra* for short), probably the most famous Mahāyāna text and especially revered in East-Asian Buddhism. Skill-in-means refers to the ability of Buddhas and advanced *bodhisattvas* to adapt their actions according to circumstances and pitch their teachings according to the particular proclivities and attainment levels of their audience. This gave early Mahāyāna teachings a certain pragmatic flair, grounded in the twin ideals of wisdom (*prajñā*) and compassion (*karuṇā*) for the suffering of others. With much in the way of metaphysical speculation curtailed by Nāgārjuna's analysis, the skill-in-means notion allowed for the further construction of provisional 'teachings', on the grounds that many followers could not understand the abstruse ramifications of the doctrine of emptiness.

As well as an increasing interest in the exposition of Buddhist teachings at a pragmatic and pedagogical level, the second feature of post-Nāgārjunian Mahāyāna is a renewed focus upon the various stages of the Buddhist path (*mārga*) and an investigation of the theoretical aspects of yogic *praxis*. Both features can be found in the literature of the early Yogācāra school.

The Yogācāra or 'Practice of Yoga' school is known by a variety of names. It has been called 'the Doctrine of Consciousness' (*vijñāna-vāda*), 'the Doctrine of Cognitive-Representations-Only' (*vijñaptimātratā*) and the 'Mind-Only' (*cittamātra*) school. The school shares a great deal in common with its Mahāyāna sibling – the Madhyamaka school, accepting the doctrine of two truths, the universalised ideal of the *bodhisattva*, the non-difference of *nirvāṇa* and *saṃsāra* and the doctrine of emptiness (*śūnyatā*), and displays a similar orientation towards the Perfection of Wisdom genre of Mahāyāna *sūtras*.

The earliest Mahāyāna *sūtra* with an obvious Yogācāra leaning is *The Sūtra which Unravels the Knots* (*Saṃdhinirmocana Sūtra*, third century CE). This text is of great historical interest, not only because it is an example of a particularly early phase in the development of Yogācāra philosophy (in chapters four and eight), but also because of the first mention of the notion of the 'three turnings of the wheel of Dharma' (*dharma-cakra*). The first turning represents the attainment of enlightenment by Gautama Buddha and the teachings passed on by the *śrāvaka* (non-Mahāyāna) schools of Buddhism. With the advent of the Perfection of Wisdom *sūtras* one first encounters the Mahāyāna teachings. This constitutes the second turning of the wheel. The *Saṃdhinirmocana Sūtra*, however, declares that these teachings have been misunderstood (perhaps by the Madhyamaka?) and offers what it describes as 'the third turning' of the wheel of Dharma. The *Sūtra* denies any innovation in this third revolution arguing that each turning is simply a more explicit rendering of previous attempts to express the Buddha's teachings.

The central philosophical interest of the Yogācāra school involves an analysis of the nature of consciousness-events (*vijñāna*). Traditionally,

Buddhist philosophy postulated six types of consciousness-event. These arise as a result of the contact of the six sense-organs (i.e. the five sense-organs and the mind or *mano-vijñāna*) with their respective object and are constantly undergoing transformation. According to the Yogācāra, these six types are coordinated by a seventh – the centralising or organising faculty of the mind (*manas*) which processes all sensory data and creates a coherent picture of reality. However, unless one has attained enlightenment, the mind is afflicted by defilements (*kliṣṭa manas*) and constructs a false picture of reality, conditioned by individual proclivities, attachments and karmic actions carried over from previous lives. Underlying all of these conscious processes, therefore, is an eighth layer of consciousness – the store-consciousness (*ālaya-vijñāna*). This is a repository of the seeds left by past karmic actions. These karmic seeds (*bīja*) gradually come to fruition and present themselves in the form of the previously mentioned consciousness-events. Thus, when one becomes conscious of something, this is said to be a 'fruition consciousness' (*vipāka-vijñāna*), being the coming to fruition (the 'coming into view' if you like) of a previously undeveloped karmic seed embedded within the store-consciousness. The final goal of the Yogācāra tradition is to purify the store-consciousness of all karmic defilements and thereby initiate what it calls 'a revolution of the foundation' (*āśraya-parāvṛtti*). This is a transformative experience of enlightenment and tantamount to liberation (*nirvāṇa*) itself.

Such an account allowed the early Yogācāra philosophers to dispense with the 'language of externality' in favour of a fully internalised and phenomenological account of what appears to consciousness (see Chapter 7). This no longer requires one to posit external objects as the cause (*nimitta*) of one's experiences since one can talk about consciousness-events (*vijñāna*) without recourse to metaphysical postulates such as an external world. The Yogācāra position can be further explained if we examine the school's notion of the 'Three Own-Beings' (*trisvabhāva*). Nāgārjuna and the Madhyamaka school rejected the notion of 'own-being' or 'independent-existence' in favour of a vision of the world as a network of mutually dependent (and insubstantial) events. In the Yogācāra school, however, the notion *svabhāva* is reintroduced but for very different purposes. According to the school there are three levels, aspects or dimensions of experience:

Parikalpita Svabhāva – the Constructed or Imagined realm of experience,
Paratantra Svabhāva – the Dependent realm of experience,
Pariniṣpanna Svabhāva – the Perfected realm of experience.

Unenlightened beings construct a false picture of the world as consisting of enduring subjects and objects which they superimpose (*samāropa*) onto their experiences. This is the *'parikalpita'* or constructed dimension of experience and refers to our inherent tendency to 'reify' experience, that is, to attribute an 'independent-existence' (*svabhāva*) to the impressions that we encounter in perception. '*Paratantra*' or the 'dependent' realm refers to what is actually there, namely, the stream of momentary *dharmas* that arise in dependence upon each other and subject to various causal conditions. This is what is finally and ultimately real for the Yogācāra school. It is the basic and irrefutable 'givenness' of our experiences that cannot be reduced away into nothingness. What we see when we perceive a blue pot is not a pot but a visual patch of blue. This is irrefutably given. Whether it corresponds to and is caused by an independently existing pot is another matter entirely. '*Parinispanna*' or the 'perfected' aspect is that same causal flow of consciousness-events but without the errors and false attributions which constitute the *parikalpita* realm. It involves seeing patches of blue for what they are without the superimposition (*samāropa*) of concepts (*vikalpa*) and categories (*jāti*) like 'pot'. Thus, the scheme of the Three-Own-Beings (*trisvabhāva*) establishes that the experiences of ignorance and enlightenment are both present within consciousness itself and both focus upon the same given reality – the dependent-realm (*paratantra*) of momentary *dharmas*.

Thus, at a stroke the scheme integrates the problem (ignorance) and the solution (enlightenment) of Buddhist practice within consciousness as the field of activity. Such an account does not require the postulation of anything other than a continual transformation of consciousness (*vijñāna-pariṇāma*) to explain the transition from one state to another. Clearly, the scheme is also another way of expounding the classic Mahāyāna position that the world of bondage and rebirth (*saṃsāra*) and the goal of liberation from it (*nirvāṇa*) are two orientations towards the same basic reality. The various Buddhas, therefore, experience and live in the same reality as us, though they see it for what it is rather than from a perspective conditioned by ignorance and attachment.

For the Yogācāra, then, one should attempt to pacify the constructivist tendencies of the mind through the practice of yoga until one is able to see what is really presented to consciousness once one takes away one's predetermined beliefs about the nature of reality. The Yogācāra path is in this sense an exercise in phenomenological reductionism within a context of Buddhist meditative *praxis*. By relinquishing the language of subject and object one apprehends the bare awareness itself, devoid of the baggage of conceptual thought (*prapañca*). This involves giving up deeply ingrained distinctions between one's sense of self, so-called external objects and internal thoughts and realising that they are nothing more than a flow of changing perceptions. For the Yogācārin we do not know that there is something 'out there' beyond our awareness itself. We are aware of colours, shapes, tactile data and so on but not of objects. These are constructed by the mind out of the manifold of sensory impressions that are presented to consciousness. We also do not know that we ourselves are anything other than a further series of experiences. Conceived as a whole then, all that we can really describe as real is the ever-changing flow of perceptions (*vijñaptimātra*). Due to ignorance (*avidyā*), however, we continue to construct these momentary perceptions into enduring subjects and objects. This is more than what presents itself to consciousness and leads to attachment, suffering and frustration.

For the Yogācāra school the doctrine of emptiness (*śūnyatā*) is 're-located' into a phenomenological and meditative context. To realise that everything is empty is to understand that the entirety of one's experience is devoid of a subject (*grāhaka*, 'one who grasps') and an object (*grāhya*, 'that which is grasped'). This does not mean that there is nothing at all but rather to clarify precisely what is real and in what sense it is so. Reality for the Yogācārin is constituted by a stream of mutually dependent and momentary *dharmas*, or, if you like, the flow of consciousness-events (*vijñāna*).

– Asaṅga and Vasubandhu –

Asaṅga (fourth century CE) is widely held to be the 'founder' of the Yogācāra school. This tradition should, as always when dealing with ancient philosophical or religious traditions, be taken with a fairly substantial pinch of salt. A 'founder' in classical Indian philosophy rarely refers to the first person to put forward a new philosophical innovation. In many cases 'founder' denotes the primary systematiser or populariser of an established (if ill-defined) 'way of viewing' (*darśana*) the world. Moreover, it is not clear what Asaṅga's attitude to earlier figures such as Nāgārjuna was. Did he conceive of himself as a founder of a new system of thought or merely as a faithful expositor of Mahāyāna teachings? (see King, 1994).

According to Mahāyāna tradition Asaṅga, through the practice of meditation, had a visionary experience of the *bodhisattva* Maitreya (the future Buddha) in the Tuṣita heaven, whereupon five new texts were 'revealed' to him.[7] Some scholars have noticed a difference between the works of Asaṅga and these five 'root' texts but are reluctant to take the tradition at face value. Consequently, it has become customary to refer to the author of these texts as Maitreyānatha in the belief that they probably originate from a teacher of Asaṅga whom later became associated with the *bodhisattva* of the same name.

The attribution of this 'revelatory' insight to Maitreya reflects the fact that

Asaṅga is said to have spent many years cultivating the meditative path in the hope of having just such an experience. This is not to say that Asaṅga merely 'imagined' his experience, nor is it to accept uncritically the tradition which says that he was in fact inspired by Maitreya; it is merely to suggest that given the prevailing conditions under which the 'revelation' took place, its occurrence is hardly surprising. Whether or not one accepts the 'revelation' theory of the tradition itself one must not forget that the texts themselves were compiled within an atmosphere of the prolonged practice of meditation. Under such conditions it would not be surprising to experience a heightened awareness within which inspiration would be forthcoming.[8]

From his own literary output, it is clear that Asaṅga was a great systematiser and expounder of the Buddhist tradition. His voluminous *Stages of the Yogic Path* (*Yogācāra-bhūmi*) is an enormous compendium of doctrine and practice in both Mahāyāna and non-Mahāyāna schools alike. Of its five main divisions, the first contains seventeen volumes, the fifteenth and probably the most famous of which is the *Bodhisattva-bhūmi* (translated into Chinese by Dharmakṣema in 418 CE). The sheer size of the text probably led to Asaṅga's composition of an abbreviated summary of its contents, the aptly-named *Compendium of the Mahāyāna* (*Mahāyānasaṃgraha*). As well as this, and a few commentaries on various Mahāyāna works (e.g. on the *Ratnagotravibhāga* and the *Vajracheddikā Prajñāpāramitā Sūtra*), Asaṅga is also said to have composed the *Abhidharma Collection* (*Abhidharmasamuccaya*), a text outlining a Mahāyāna Abhidharma system based upon the insubstantiality of all *dharmas* (*dharma-nairātmya*) and Mahāyāna meditative practices. Asaṅga himself is said to have attained the level of a third-stage bodhisattva (*prabhākarī*, 'Light-giving one') and his mastery of yoga is perhaps an important factor in the subsequent development of the Yogācāra's practical orientation.

Mention should also be made of Asaṅga's half-brother Vasubandhu (also fourth century CE). It is unclear whether this is the same Vasubandhu who wrote the *Abhidharma-kośa* and its *Bhāṣya* from the Vaibhāṣika and Sautrāntika perspectives, but the Mahāyāna tradition does assert that Vasubandhu was converted to the Mahāyāna by his half-brother after a number of years as a mainstream (*śrāvaka*) Buddhist practitioner (see King 1998). Unlike Asaṅga, Vasubandhu the Yogācārin is most famous for short compositions such as the *Twenty Verses* (*Viṃśatikā*) and the *Thirty Verses* (*Triṃśikā*). It is said that these verses represent condensed summaries of years of teaching by Vasubandhu. There are many other works attributed to Vasubandhu including the *Teaching on the Three Own Beings* (*Trisvabhāva-nirdeśa*), and a variety of commentaries on Mahāyāna *sūtras* and various works by Asaṅga and Maitreyānatha.

There is evidence of considerable doctrinal diversity within the Yogācāra school in India. Some strands emphasise what one might call a 'No-Mind' (*acitta*) interpretation, seeing the 'revolution of the foundation' (*āśraya-parāvṛtti*) as the cessation rather than the transformation of the *ālaya-vijñāna* or store-consciousness. From this perspective the final goal involves a transcendence of mental activity and the attainment of a non-conceptual awareness (*nirvikalpa jñāna*) of reality as it is. On the other hand, there is also much in the early Yogācāra literature which is suggestive of a 'Pure Mind' interpretation. On this view the goal of Yogācāra practice is to purify the store-consciousness of defilements rather than to eradicate it. The 'revolution of the foundation' does not require the cessation of mind but rather the uncovering of the intrinsic purity of consciousness, which then shines through. Non-conceptual awareness on this view is pure consciousness reflecting reality like a mirror that has been cleaned of all defilements.

Subsequent thinkers within the Yogācāra school include Sthiramati and Dharmapāla (sixth century CE), both of whom were contemporaries and philosophical rivals of the Mādhyamika philosopher Bhāvaviveka. This is a period of great academic rivalry, not least between the Valabhī sub-school of Yogācāra, of which Sthiramati was the most famous representative and the Nālandā sub-school of Dharmapāla, though the two groups seemed to have kept to their own locality and avoided becoming embroiled in disputes with each other. Of the two strands of Yogācāra thought Dharmapāla is perhaps less faithful and more innovative in his representation of Vasubandhu. Thus, a central philosophical phrase for Vasubandhu was the notion of 'the transformation of consciousness' (*vijñāna-pariṇāma*), used to refer to the changes that occur within a given flow of consciousness over time. Dharmapāla, however, understood '*vijñāna-pariṇāma*' to denote the evolution of an external world out of consciousness. This is clearly a form of idealism and formed the basis for the subsequent Fa Hsiang school of Chinese Yogācāra, brought to China by Dharmapāla's disciple Hsüang-tsang. It is not clear, however, that this is what Vasubandhu implied by the term (Ueda, 1967: 159; Takeuchi, 1977).

Mention should also be made of Paramārtha (499–569 CE) whose work as a translator of many Mahāyāna Buddhist (especially Yogācāra) texts resulted in the establishment of the She-lun school of Chinese Yogācāra. This school was subsequently eclipsed by Hsüang-tsang and the Fa Hsiang school of Dharmapāla, but Paramārtha was nevertheless an important figure in the introduction of Yogācāra philosophical ideas to China. Paramārtha posited a ninth level of consciousness – an undefiled consciousness (*amala vijñāna*). This constituted the fundamental level of reality underlying the phenomenal activities of the defiled store-consciousness. Thus, Paramārtha firmly anchored his rendering of Yogācāra theory within the 'Pure Mind' strand of interpretation, making it more amenable to associations with those aspects of the Mahāyāna tradition which emphasised a pure 'buddha-nature' or 'buddha-seed' (*tathāgatagarbha*) within all sentient beings.

– THE EPISTEMOLOGICAL (PRAMĀṆA-VĀDA) SCHOOL OF DIGNĀGA AND DHARMAKĪRTI –

Dignāga (480–540 CE) and Dharmakīrti (600–660 CE) are important figures in the history of Indo-Tibetan Buddhist philosophy and are responsible more than any other thinkers for the integration of Mahāyāna Buddhist philosophy into the epistemological (*pramāṇa-vāda*) structure of mainstream Indian philosophical debate. This was a considerable task given the critique of *pramāṇa*-theory offered by Nāgārjuna (see Chapter 6), but their work is clearly an attempt to bring the Mahāyāna philosophy of emptiness (*śūnyatā*) into the forefront of scholastic discussion. Dignāga and Dharmakīrti are usually classified as Yogācāran in terms of their general philosophical orientation but their works often defend a minimalist Abhidharma stance based upon broadly Sautrāntikan principles. Thus, *dharmas* persist only for as long as they exhibit causal efficacy (*artha-kriyā-samartha*). Indeed, causal functionality, they argue, is precisely what one means by 'existence'. However, because each *dharma* is impermanent, this existence is only momentary in duration. This goes some way towards explaining the apparent discrepancy between the broadly Sautrāntikan realism defended by Dignāga and Dharmakīrti within their works and the Yogācāran phenomenalism that they propound in certain key sections of those same works. Dharmakīrti's 'strategy of ascending scales' (Dreyfus, 1997: 103–5) allows him to defend Sautrāntikan realism at a provisional level, whilst propounding Yogācāra philosophy as his definitive position (*siddhānta*).

Such a strategy becomes an increasing feature of Mahāyāna scholasticism in subsequent centuries with figures such as Vimuktisena (sixth century CE), Śāntarakṣita (725–83 CE) and Kamalaśīla (740–95 CE) providing a creative and hierarchical synthesis of Madhyamaka and Yogācāra thought. Śāntarakṣita and his disciple Kamalaśīla, for instance, were key figures in the early migration of Mahāyāna Buddhism to Tibet. Their philosophical position can be described as Yogācāra-Svātantrika-Madhyamaka. In other words, whilst the two thinkers accepted the validity of the Yogācāra denial of externality, they saw this as a stepping stone to the Svātantrika-Madhyamaka position which thereby represented the highest expression of the Buddha's teaching. Such syntheses were made possible by a recognition of the differing concerns of the two schools and because of the explicit acknowledgement of 'levels of truth' within the Buddhist tradition.

– NOTES –

1. On Rāhulabhadra and his hymns see Ruegg (1981: 55–6), especially for a discussion of the *bhakti/tathāgatagarbha* elements of Rāhulabhadra's apparently early form of Madhyamaka. As Ruegg notes (Ibid: 56): 'Rāhulabhadra thus represents a fairly distinct current in early Madhyamaka thought that was not elaborated in the theoretical scholastic texts of the classical school based on the MMK, but which is reflected in the hymns ascribed to Nāgārjuna.'
2. The texts of Nāgārjuna logical corpus are the *Verses on the Middle* and the following additional works: 1. *The Sixty Verses on Reason* (*Yukti-ṣaṣṭika*), 2. *The Seventy Verses on Emptiness* (*Śūnyatā-saptati*), 3. *Discriminating the Arguments* (*Vigraha-vyāvartanī*), 4. *The Treatise of Subtle Pulverisation* (*Vaidalya-prakaraṇa* – a critique of Nyāya), and 5. *The Establishment of the Practical* (*Vyavahāra-siddhi*), now lost and often replaced in Tibetan circles by the *Ratnāvalī*, or the *Akutobhayā*. These six treatises are all said to be authentic Nāgārjunian works by the Tibetan historian Bu-ston. Tāranātha, however, omits the *Vyavahāra-siddhi*. These works (listed above, with the exception of the *Ratnāvalī*) have generally been ascribed to a single author. Even if such texts were found not to be by Nāgārjuna their importance for the Madhyamaka school is clear from the frequency with which they are cited by early Mādhyamikas such as Bhāvaviveka (550 CE). This makes such texts indispensable as sources of early Madhyamaka thought.
3. In terms of establishing the authenticity of a text, Nāgārjuna is identified as the author of the *Verses on the Middle* (*Madhyamaka Kārikā*). Any claim of authorship, therefore, must demonstrate considerable doctrinal and linguistic resemblance to this foundational text. It is not surprising, therefore, to find many scholars refusing to deal with those texts which do not display the same logical and analytical approach as the *Verses on the Middle*. Lindtner (1982), however, has collected a variety of texts all of which he thinks are likely to be authentic compositions of Nāgārjuna.
4. On Nāgārjuna and the Sarvāstivāda school see Conze, 1978: 93–4; Ruegg, 1981: 7. Nāgārjuna discusses three marks of the conditioned rather than four (MMK 7.1 ff). This is a Sautrāntika rather than a Vaibhāṣika position (see *Abhidharma-kośa*, II. 45cd). According to Robinson (1967: 67), 'The Middle Stanzas particularly attack the doctrine of momentariness (*kṣaṇikatva*) and reject both the Sautrāntika and the Vaibhāṣika positions.' Thomas Dowling (1976: 208) also refers to chapter 17 of the MMK, where Nāgārjuna discusses a theoretical entity the *avipraṇāśa*, but does not deal with the *avijñapti-rūpa*. This may cast doubt upon the suggestion that Nāgārjuna is criticising the Abhidharma of the Vaibhāṣikas within this text.
5. Richard H. Robinson (1967: 37–8) counts thirty-five references to the MMK in the text, of which there are undoubtedly many more. See also Ruegg, 1981: 32.
6. David Seyfort Ruegg (1981: 6), however, suggests that MMK 13.8 presupposes the *Kaśyapaparivarta* (T 310, 43), one of the early Mahāyāna *Ratnakūṭa sūtras* (see also Robinson, 1967: 91). This *Sūtra* is believed to have been originally translated into Chinese between 178–84 CE making it a relatively early example of Mahāyāna philosophy in formation.
7. The five texts 'revealed' to Asaṅga are: 1. *Abhisamayālaṃkāra* – a treatise on the Perfection of Wisdom, 2. *Madhyānta-vibhāga* – 'The Discrimination of the Middle from the Extremes', 3. *Dharmadharmatā-vibhāga* – 'The Discrimination of *Dharmas* from their Essential Nature', 4. *Mahāyāna Sūtrālaṃkāra* – 'The Ornament of Mahāyāna *Sūtras*', 5. *Ratnagotra-vibhāga* (or *Uttara-tantra*) – an exposition of the Buddha-nature

(*tathāgatagarbha*) teaching. The works of Maitreya (notably 2., 3. and 5.) are terse, concise and cryptic. In contrast to this, the works of Asaṅga are clear and verbose.

8. Such an experience, on an admittedly cruder and preliminary level, is open to the vast majority of humans at some time in their lives. The phenomena of automatic writing is one which has much documentation in the west, particularly with the advent of hypnosis as a psychological technique for tapping into the 'unconscious' mind. In the rarefied heights (or should we say 'depths') of yogic experience one is likely to open up similar avenues into the 'unconscious' (or in a Yogācāra context, the *ālayavijñāna*).

CHAPTER 5

Ontology: What really exists?

– VAIŚEṢIKA: CLASSIFYING REALITY –

'To be or not to be – that is the question' – or at least it was one of the central philosophical questions of ancient Indian philosophy. The early Vedic hymns and UPANIṢADS offered a variety of speculative views as to whether being (*sat*) or non-being (*asat*) constituted the basic ground from which the universe ultimately originated. This is an issue that has perplexed thinkers since time immemorial. What really exists and what does it mean to say that something exists? The Nyāya and Vaiśeṣika systems represent an ancient Indian attempt to investigate and justify what is often called a 'common-sense' view of reality. However, as students of western philosophy are well aware, such a task often leads to philosophical positions that involve a movement away from reality as it is experienced. As Bertrand Russell famously remarked, 'Naive realism leads to physics and physics, if true, shows that naive realism is false' (Russell, 1940: 13).

The Nyāya and Vaiśeṣika schools uphold a thoroughgoing, pluralistic realism. The world of objects are directly perceived and exist independently of our experience of them. The two schools are often grouped together and this reflects a long and successful alliance and cross-fertilisation of ideas, culminating in their fusion in the work of Udayana (eleventh century CE) and the subsequent New Nyāya tradition (*navya-nyāya*) from the thirteenth century onwards. However, the traditions do differ in some respects, particularly within the early period of their development. Early Nyāya shows much less interest in the Vaiśeṣika project of providing a comprehensive classification of what exists and indeed such a goal is regarded as unattainable by Vātsyāyana (author of the highly revered *Nyāya-bhāṣya*).

Nevertheless, most of the basic presuppositions of the Nyāya school are shared with its sister-school the Vaiśeṣika, which is slightly older than the Nyāya if the extant literature is anything to go by. The earliest text of the Vaiśeṣika – the aptly named *Vaiśeṣika Sūtra* – was compiled some time between 200 BCE and the beginning of the Common Era. The *Sūtra* displays no knowledge of Nyāya as a specific school at this time, but there is some awareness of Sāṃkhya and Mīmāṃsā ideas. Reference is made to the text in the first century CE which suggests that it had already become a popular and authoritative text by this time, though, of course, we cannot be sure that the *Vaiśeṣika Sūtra* that we have before us is identical to the one referred to nearly two thousand years ago. The Vaiśeṣika is primarily interested in an analysis of nature and the name of the school derives from the Sanskrit *viśeṣa*, meaning 'particularity'. The system, therefore, establishes itself on the basic principle that the world is made up of a variety of distinguishable particularities.

For the Vaiśeṣika there are five basic material substances – earth, water, fire, air and ether (*ākāśa*). These substances or elements (*bhūta*) may have a variety of qualities but they each possess a specific quality that is unique to that substance. Indeed, this unique quality is the means whereby that particular substance can be known to exist. Thus, what distinguishes earth from the other primary substances is that it possesses the unique quality of smell. Similarly, for water there is the quality of taste, fire that of colour, air corresponds to touch and ether or space to sound. Moreover, for the Vaiśeṣika each of the five sense-capacities are constituted by their respective substance. Our capacity to smell, therefore, is a result of the presence of the earth element.

> Earth possesses the qualities of colour, taste, smell and touch.
> Water possesses the qualities of colour, taste and touch and is also fluid and viscid.
> Fire possesses the qualities of colour and touch.
> Air possesses the qualities of touch (e.g. when 'feeling a breeze'), despite its invisibility.
> Ether has no perceivable qualities, but must be a substance since it is through space that sound vibrations travel to the ear.
>
> *Vaiśeṣika Sūtra* II.1.1–11

All material objects are made up of atoms (*paramāṇu*) and these are eternal and indestructible realities. However, the compounded entities that they produce are finite and constitute the aggregated objects that we normally perceive and interact with. Differences between material objects reflect differences in the ratio of basic substances contained within them. Thus, hard objects like stone contain more earth, whilst milk contains more water. The existence of an irreducible atomic level of material reality cannot be perceived but it can be inferred, so the Vaiśeṣika argued, from the divisible nature of objects and as a way of accounting for the differences between them. A stone is smaller than a mountain and this is because the mountain is an aggregate containing more atoms. Furthermore, if the process of reduction did not reach some level of basic irreducibility, existence (*sat*) would in the final analysis be made of nothingness (*asat*). This was not a position that the Vaiśeṣika was prepared to entertain seriously. Atoms combine to make dyads. Three dyads combine to make a triad and this constitutes, for the Vaiśeṣika, the smallest perceivable object (exemplified for this school by the particle of dust in a sunbeam). All material objects then are made up of various complex combinations of these triadic combinations. The atom is thought to contain six sides (since three dyads make a triad) allowing the various atoms to connect with each other. Critics of atomism, such as the Yogācāra Buddhist Vasubandhu (fourth century CE) emphasised the problems of discussing purely inferential entities that could not be verified by perception.

> The object of perception is neither single, nor composed of many atoms, nor an aggregate of them, because no atom can be established.
>
> One atom joined at once to six other atoms must have six parts. On the other hand, if they are said to occupy the same space, then their aggregate would mean nothing more than a single atom.
>
> *Viṃśatikā*, verses 11 and 12

The basic concern of the Vaiśeṣika school was an investigation of the world in a search for the primary categories of what is real. The term that the Vaiśeṣika uses for the primary categories of reality is *padārtha* or category (literally, 'the meaning (or referent) of a word'). This term reflects the Vaiśeṣika attempt to construct a systematic analysis of reality based upon a 'common-sense' approach to the world. What is it that words refer to? The school has clearly been influenced in this regard by the philosophical speculations of the grammarians and the Vaiśeṣika position reflects a realist approach to the relationship between a word and the thing which it denotes.

In the early Vaiśeṣika tradition there are said to be six fundamental categories: substance (*dravya*), quality (*guṇa*), action or motion (*karman*), universal (*sāmānya*), particularity (*viśeṣa*), and the relation of inherence (*samavāya*).[1] Later, a seventh category was added – absence (*abhāva*). All in all this provides us with a metaphysical system which postulates three senses in which one call talk of reality (*padārtha*). The first three categories (substances, qualities and actions) are existents (*sattā*). However, to appreciate the Nyāya-Vaiśeṣika position we must appreciate the distinction between reality and existence. For the Vaiśeṣika, the former denotes the categories or *padārtha*, whilst the latter denotes those specific realities (the first three *padārtha*) in which 'existent-ness' (*sattā*) occurs. 'Existent-ness' is a difficult concept to explain but it is something like a universal principle of being, i.e. that universal and singular property which characterises all things that exist (VS I.2.7-9, 17).[2]

The next three categories (universals, particularities and the relation of inherence) whilst not existing in the sense of the first three are nevertheless real presences (*bhāva*). Finally, the seventh category of absence (*abhāva*) denotes the reality of absence, i.e. that which renders negative statements true. From a Nyāya-Vaiśeṣika point of view if something can be known, that is, possesses knowability (*jñeyatva*) then it must in some sense be real. Thus, whilst we cannot talk of absences existing (i.e. as a *sattā*), nor of an absence being a real presence (i.e. *bhāva*), absence or 'lack' is something that is directly experienced (for instance when I am looking for a pencil and cannot find one). Hence in some sense, the later Nyāya-Vaiśeṣika argued, it must be a reality.

– SUBSTANCE (*DRAVYA*) –

Crucial to an understanding of both the Nyāya and Vaiśeṣika philosophies is the notion of substance (*dravya*). In both systems a substance is that which possesses qualities (*guṇa*) and actions (*karman*, see VS I.1.15). It is not possible, so the Nyāya-Vaiśeṣika contends, to have qualities or characteristics without an underlying substance in which they inhere. A substance can also be characterised as the substratum of change. Change cannot occur without some existing substance underlying it (VS I.1.17). Thus, when we say 'the tree has grown considerably over the past five years' we imply that there is some support or substance to which these changes have occurred. According to the *Vaiśeṣika Sūtra* there are nine fundamental substances (VS I.1.5). Five of these are material and constitute the five elements (*bhūta*) already discussed (VS II.1.1-5, 9). The remaining four are non-material substances, namely, time (*kāla*), space (*dik*), the soul (*ātman*) and the mind (*manas*).

Space is that substance which allows material objects to move freely and must exist in order to make sense of spatial notions such as far and near. According to Praśastapāda space is eternal, indivisible and all-pervading and can be inferred from our experience of directions (left, right, north, south, near and far etc.). Similarly, time is known through our experience of different temporal modes (now, later, yesterday etc.). Time, therefore, constitutes the substratum or cause of all temporal cognitions. Both time and space, however, are in reality indivisible and eternal (VS II.2.9). The divisions that we make in time and space, therefore, are merely figurative (PDS 5.42).

The soul or self (*ātman*), like time and space, is an immaterial, eternal and all-pervading substance. There are a plurality of individual souls and their existence can be inferred from the quality of sentience or consciousness. The self, therefore, is the substance of the quality of consciousness. The *ātman* also possesses secondary qualities such as desire, aversion, pleasure and pain. The crucial feature of all of these qualities is that they are not material. Given that, so the Nyāya-Vaiśeṣika argues, the substance (the *ātman*) in which they inhere or dwell must also be non-material. The *ātman* is a witness to our experiences and must be distinct from material objects (including the body) and from consciousness, sensations and the mind because it is the knower of them. However, it should be borne in mind that for the Nyāya and Vaiśeṣika systems consciousness is not an essential attribute of the self. Consciousness is a contingent quality of the self deriving from its association with a material body. Thus, when an *ātman* attains liberation from rebirth (*mokṣa*), it no longer possesses consciousness, though it is believed to retain its own individuality (*viśeṣa*).

What this means is that everything that we can know can become an object of knowledge, but must therefore be distinguished from the subject of all knowledge, that is, the *ātman*. Notice how even consciousness is known, and is therefore an object in relation to the subject – the *ātman*. Nevertheless, liberation (*mokṣa)* is freedom from pain and from all constraints – including the limitations of consciousness. This is because consciousness is intentional – that is, it is always a 'consciousness of' something, implying a duality of subject and object. In such a state the *ātman* remains in bondage since it has not yet been properly distinguished as a substance. So, all that one can say about the state of *mokṣa* is that it is a liberation from embodied existence (*saṃsāra*), a freedom from all constraints, and a state where the *ātman* resides in its own element, if you like, as a unique and particularised substance. This conception of the self and the nature of liberation (*mokṣa*) has a clear resonance with the Sāṃkhya and Yoga schools of thought in which the essential self (*ātman* or *puruṣa*), is said to reside in its own form (*sva-rūpa*, see *Yoga Sūtras* I.3), in a state of blissful isolation (*kaivalya*).

The ninth and final substance is mind (*manas*). Unlike ether (*ākāśa*), space, time and the self, the mind is atomic but it cannot produce new composites like the four types of material atoms (ether remember, although material, is not atomic). The mind remains in association with the self until liberation is achieved. According to the Vaiśeṣika the mind cannot be directly perceived but its existence must be inferred in order to explain the apprehension of sensory information from the sense-organs and to account for the internal perception of the self and a whole host of affective and mental states. Although our sense-organs might be in contact with an object at any given time, the selective attention of the mind is required for a perception to occur.

– QUALITY (*GUṆA*) –

The notion of substance requires something that subsists within it. This brings us to the notion of qualities (*guṇa*). Just as substances can be inferred from our perception of qualities, from a Nyāya-Vaiśeṣika perspective, qualities cannot occur without a substance in which they can inhere. Substances therefore constitute the fundamental substratum for the existence of qualities whilst qualities are characterised as those perceivable attributes by which substances can be known to exist. The *Vaiśeṣika Sūtra* outlines seventeen qualities (*guṇa*), but these are supplemented by Praśastapāda to make a list of twenty-four.[3] This list includes material qualities such as colour, taste, odour and touch, and mental qualities such as pleasure and aversion, volition and cognition. The list also includes what one might describe as qualities of relation such as remoteness and proximity, separateness, conjunction (*saṃyoga*) and disjunction etc. The list (whether of seventeen or twenty-four qualities) seems somewhat arbitrary but the definitive number of qualities is not as important as the realist metaphysical position that the substance-quality ontology represents.

– ACTION (*KARMAN*) –

Like qualities, action (sometimes translated as motion) can only occur within substances, which constitute the primary substrata of reality.[4] Although both require substances to occur, qualities are static and passive whilst action by its very nature is dynamic and short-lived. There are five kinds of movements or actions: 1. upwards, 2. downwards, 3. expansion, 4. contraction and 5. locomotion. Since qualities are passive (they are after all merely attributes), the category of action is required to account for causation and the arising and cessation of composite entities. All actions are directly perceivable except for those carried out by the mind. The activity of the mind, however, can be inferred by changes in our internal perceptions and mental state.

– UNIVERSALS (*SĀMĀNYA*) AND PARTICULARITIES (*VIŚEṢA*) –

One issue that particularly concerned the Nyāya and Vaiśeṣika thinkers was the relationship between the words we use to refer to things (*pada*) and the things themselves (*artha*). When I come across a tree or a horse or a river how do I know that they are what they are? What makes a horse a horse and not a cow? In order to make sense of the world in which we live and also in order to communicate with others we use a variety of terms that function as universal categories for a variety of phenomena. Thus, the word 'horse' has come to be used in such a way that I am not required to come up with a new word each time I come across another horse. Nevertheless, although we can talk of a category of horses, what is it that they have in common? Furthermore, to say that Red Rum and Champion the Wonder Horse are both horses is not to say that they are the same thing. There must be some sense, therefore, in which they are similar and different.

According to the Nyāya-Vaiśeṣika system words like 'horse' are class-names. All member of the class of 'horse' share a universal feature (*sāmānya*) in common, namely 'horseness'. Similarly, trees share the category of 'treeness' in common and cows all share 'cowness' and so on. Without such commonalities, the school argues, one would be unable to establish any grounds for using such terms or making connections between discrete particularities (*viśeṣa*). What kind of ontological status should one assign to such class-categories?

The various Buddhist schools generally took a nominalist position with regard to the status of universals, arguing that common essences or universals are merely mentally imputed categories. What 'horses' share in common is that they have all been classified under the same name according to convention. Universals, on this view, are not intrinsic properties of entities but are, in contrast, conceptual constructs deriving their validity from conventional acceptance and past usage. The view that language was conventional was also accepted by the Nyāya-Vaiśeṣika but the later tradition interpreted this as meaning that it was established by the Creator and not by the network of human social relations as implied by the Buddhist analysis. The Buddhist approach, of course, struck at the heart of the traditional Brahmanical world-view, best exemplified in the Mīmāṃsā traditions with the belief in the perfected (*saṃskṛta*) nature of the Sanskrit language and the Vedas.

> For Hindus, language is grounded in the Vedas, the source of their culture. The intense preoccupation of Indian culture with grammar and linguistics derives largely from this Vedic connection ... In denying that language is naturally meaningful, the Buddhists refuse to grant the Vedas any privileged epistemological status.
>
> Dreyfus, 1997: 214–15

Dignāga, for instance, postulated a theory of language known as the doctrine of exclusion (*apohavāda*) in order to rebuff the Nyāya-Vaiśeṣika acceptance of the reality of universals. According to Dignāga class-names such as 'horse' are constructed negatively, that is, according to a principle of negation or exclusion. A horse is defined as such not because there are certain essential attributes that pertain to each and every horse and not to anything else, but because the term functions within a broader network of signifiers that allow it to be defined in terms of a series of exclusions. A 'horse' then is 'not-cow, not-tree, not-dog, not-sunflower' etc. The advantage of this scheme (which is reminiscent of the theories of the French structuralist Ferdinand de Saussure) is that it allows the Buddhist to account for the differentiation between entities within language without requiring the postulation of a positive entity. It is a theory of language based upon a metaphysics of no-abiding-self (*anātman*). Universals on this view are merely imputed and should not be thought of as anything other than conventional designations.

In contrast to the Buddhist view the Nyāya-Vaiśeṣika position propounds a staunch realism. Universals are real. However, in what sense can one say that a universal exists? Have you ever seen 'horseness' by itself without horses? For the Buddhist this demonstrates that the idea of 'horseness' is just that, merely an idea. Other schools such as the Jainas and the Advaita Vedāntins argue that universals do exist but that they never exist separately from particularities. Thus, 'horseness' is real but one would never expect to find 'horseness' anywhere other than in a particular example of a horse. Universals are real but cannot be distinguished from their particular instances. The Nyāya and Vaiśeṣika schools, however, do not accept this mediating position, believing that universals and particularities can in fact be differentiated and are of equal ontological status. Following the view of Uddyotakara, in identifying Red Rum as a horse we recognise a common feature (*anuvṛtti*) running through all individual examples of 'horseness' (*Nyāya Vārttika* 2.2.4). It is precisely our experience of this common characteristic (*anuvṛtti-pratyaya*) and our recognition that the universal is different in nature from the particular example of it which establishes the independent reality of universals. We can make no sense of the notion of 'horses' as a class-term unless universals have some form of reality that is distinguishable from their particular instantiations.

Universals then are real, but in what sense? According to the Nyāya-Vaiśeṣika system, universals are not existents (*sat*) like substances and the qualities and actions that they possess. Instead, universals should be understood as subsistents (*bhāva*), that is, they do not "exist" as such (because the universal principle of existence (*sattā*) does not inhere in them), but they are presences revealed to us through perception and our experience of the efficacious use of language. This position is often compared to Plato's theory of the reality of ideal forms. Both Plato and the Nyāya-Vaiśeṣika system believe that universals, or in Plato's sense the ideal forms, are real and independent of particular material examples or instantiations of them.

However, for Plato, the forms exist in a suprasensible realm and cannot be apprehended in the sensory world. In contrast as Matilal notes

> Nyāya-Vaiśeṣika universals exist nowhere but in this world of ours, and particulars do not 'copy' them but 'manifest' them, or allow the universals to *reside* in them. We can say, in accordance with Nyāya, that the particulars provide a 'home' for the universal. The only mystery in this is that when the 'home' is destroyed, the universal is rendered 'homeless'; but it is not destroyed thereby! It maintains a 'homeless', i.e. unmanifest existence. It is spatially locatable and observable, provided the relevant particular is observable.
>
> Matilal, 1986: 383

To clarify Matilal's point here we should note that universals in this system of thought do not exist as such, though they are real presences (*bhāva*) distinguishable, yet never appearing separately, from their particular instantiations (Matilal, 1968: 123ff).

Particularity (*viśeṣa*) is probably best understood in this context as the opposite of a universal (*sāmānya*). Particularity belongs to all substances that are indivisible and eternal i.e. the four types of material atoms, ether (*ākāśa*), time, space, souls and minds (PDS 8.146). Although earth atoms, for instance, are all of the same type, there must be some sense in which they are distinguishable, otherwise it would only make sense to talk of a single earth atom. The principle of individuality, therefore, which distinguishes particular instantiations of the same substance, is what is meant by particularity (*viśeṣa*). Thus, although all souls (*ātman*) are characterised as the substratum of consciousness, they are not identical. Each soul is distinguishable from all others. Similarly, minds are unique particularities and cannot be reduced to each other. However, it should be pointed out that particularity can only be predicated of ultimate entities or substances such as these and does not apply to composite entities such as tables and chairs. These everyday objects are distinguishable based upon their relative position in space and fundamentally by the fact that they are compounded of different atoms, but since they are capable of reduction to their more basic components, such objects cannot be described as particularities since these are absolutely discrete by their very nature.

– INHERENCE (*SAMAVĀYA*) –

Inherence (*samavāya*), like universals (*sāmānya*) and particularities (*viśeṣa*) is a subsistent (*bhāva*) and not an existent (*sattā*) category. Inherence denotes a necessary conjunction and is to be distinguished from contingent conjunction (*saṃyoga*) which is the bringing together of two previously separate objects that can be conjoined or separated without changing their fundamental natures. I can place a book on my desk and remove it and on both occasions both book and desk remain intact in their basic nature and properties. Inherence however, denotes a necessary conjunction. Entities related by inherence cannot remain as they are once they are separated. For this reason inherence has been defined as 'the relation (*saṃbandha*) between two inseparables (*ayuta-siddhas*)' (Shastri, 1964: 275).

> Inherence is the relationship between things that are inseparably connected, and which stand to each other in the relation of the container and the contained, – the relationship, namely, that serves as the ground of the notion that 'such and such a thing subsists in this.'
>
> PDS 9. 157, in Radhakrishnan and Moore, 1957: 422

The relation of inherence is a kind of metaphysical glue and is probably best illustrated using examples. Qualities are related to substances by the relation of inherence. Thus, the blue colour of a blue pot inheres within that pot. Similarly, a whole (*avayavin*) inheres within its parts and cannot subsist in isolation from them. Thus, a clay pot is inherent within its various clay constituents. The pot cannot exist anywhere without its parts, but it is still, on Nyāya-Vaiśeṣika terms, distinguishable from them. However, to separate the clay constituents of the pot (e.g. by hitting them with a hammer) is to destroy the pot. Similarly, what is the relationship between a cloth and its threads? The cloth inheres in the threads as the new whole that is created by the conjunction of its parts. This is a vitally important point to note about the Nyāya-Vaiśeṣika conception of wholes. The cloth did not exist before the various threads were woven together, nor will it exist if the threads are unravelled. One is perhaps tempted to say that the cloth is nothing more than the interwoven threads. This, however, is not the Nyāya-Vaiśeṣika position. The cloth, according to this system, is distinguishable from its parts and has been brought into existence by the contingent act of conjunction (*saṃyoga*) that has woven the threads together. The relationship between the threads and the cloth is, as we have seen, one of inherence (*samavāya*). It is a necessary relation – the cloth inheres within its parts and could not subsist without them and it is because they are in a necessary relation that we do not perceive them as different.[5] As a newly created whole, the cloth remains distinguishable from its parts and cannot be reduced to them.

What happens then if the cloth is cut into two, making two smaller cloths? In this case the old cloth has been destroyed and two cloths have been newly created. Again, if a piece of chalk is used to write on a blackboard, the line of chalk on the board constitutes a newly created whole inhering in the various chalk particles that constitute it. The piece of chalk is also a newly created whole, since it is no longer caused by exactly the same parts. As D. N. Shastri (1964: 376) remarks, this is 'realism with a vengeance'. What these examples demonstrate rather well, however, is the way in which the

Nyāya-Vaiśeṣika systems, premised as they are upon an attempt to provide a theoretical basis for 'common-sense' realism, end up positing categories such as inherence which, on the face of it, seem to contradict our common-sense experience of reality. Cloths, pots and pieces of chalk do not seem to be separate from their constituent parts.

– ABSENCE (*ABHĀVA*) –

We have seen that the realism of the Nyāya and Vaiśeṣika schools is rigorous and thoroughgoing in its attempt to classify everything that might count as real. Indeed, the original list of six *padārthas* represents not just the types of things that exist, but also those realities that do not exist as independent entities – the presences or *bhāvas*. As the school developed, a seventh category was added to the original list, namely absence or non-existence (*abhāva*). This was in many respects a controversial development but demonstrates an ongoing concern to elucidate all aspects of what it is to be real. As I have already stated, the Nyāya school based itself upon the principle that if something could be known then it must in some sense be real. How then could you know absence or non-existence (*abhāva*)?

Consider the following statement: 'My wallet is empty' (a regular occurrence I might add). If this statement is true then what reality does that statement correspond to? Framing the question in this fashion demonstrates the rigorous adherence to a correspondence theory of truth in the Nyāya and Vaiśeṣika schools. Truth is what corresponds to the real nature of things. For 'my wallet is empty' to be a true statement, later Naiyāyikas argued, the emptiness or lack (*abhāva*) of that wallet must in some sense be real because it is both knowable (*jñeya*) and nameable (*abhidheya*). When I cannot find my keys, the perception of the absence of my keys is accurate and therefore corresponds to a real situation. These cases, so it is said, are to be distinguished from those things which are palpably unreal, such as the horns of a hare (hares do not have horns) or a square circle, on the grounds that real absences are causally efficacious whilst unreal entities are not (Udayana, 1950: 108). There are a number of types of absences, including prior absence (for example, my keys before they were made), destructional absence (my keys once they have been melted in a furnace), absolute absence (for example, of colour in air) and mutual absence (for example, my keys are not my wallet and vice versa).

– REALITY AS PROCESS: THE ABHIDHARMA RESPONSE –

The Nyāya-Vaiśeṣika systems clearly began as an attempt to provide a systematic account or reflection upon the nature of reality based upon common-sense notions and our experience of the world. Both schools ground their philosophies in a firm acceptance of the basic truthfulness of sense-perceptions. The Nyāya and Vaiśeṣika engaged in a fierce debate with the various Buddhist schools that lasted until the twelfth century CE when Buddhism entered a period of demise in India that is only now ending. The Buddhists remained much more sceptical of the reliability of our perceptions, emphasising the role played by attachments and negative emotional states (such as anger, aversion and craving) in the distortion of our experience of reality. For the Nyāya and Vaiśeṣika schools we are not fundamentally deceived in our apprehension of reality. However, as we have seen, even in their attempts to provide a philosophical account of so-called 'common-sense' reality the Vaiśeṣika school was led to the postulation of imperceptible entities such as atoms and inherence. For the emerging Buddhist schools, another unwarranted assumption of the brahmanical schools in general was the postulation of an immaterial and abiding principle of identity – a soul or self (*ātman*) that is said to transmigrate from life to life.

The central issue for the emerging schools of Buddhist philosophy (for that is what the Abhidharma became) was the search for a way of speaking about reality (the way things are) without slipping into the conventional discourse of persons, objects and substances. Their answer was to develop a form of discourse based upon the notion of a *dharma*. This term has innumerable meanings in Indian culture and within Buddhism generally refers to the Buddha's own teachings. In the specific and highly rarefied context of Abhidharma theory, however, a *dharma* denotes the primary level of reality – what is really present (rather than imputed) in experience. As such, *dharmas* are the mental and material 'micro-events' that constitute reality as we know it. The world as analysed by the Abhidharma is not one of trees, plants, mountains, tables, books or persons – it is a world of momentary events or *dharmas*.

It is important to be philosophically specific about the Abhidharma notion of a *dharma*. The *Abhidharma-kośa Bhāṣya* defines a *dharma* as 'that which bears its own characteristics' (*svalakṣaṇa-dhāraṇa*, I.2). This sounds rather like the Nyāya-Vaiśeṣika notion of substance (*dravya*), but Buddhist tradition is sceptical of the knowledge gained through experience, whereas in the Nyāya and Vaiśeṣika schools we find a philosophical defence of the reliability of everyday sense-experiences. For Buddhists *dharmas* are not objects or entities such as tables, chairs or sentient beings, but the fundamental and momentary events that make up such phenomena. For schools such as the Sautrāntika a *dharma* is a moment (*kṣaṇa*) of experience, and in Abhidharma terms there are thousands of *dharmas* occurring in every instant of experience. For the Vaibhāṣika school, however, there are also a number of *dharmas* that are not associated with consciousness (*citta-viprayukta*), i.e. do not manifest themselves to consciousness. This category reflects the Vaibhāṣika concern to provide a comprehensive taxonomy of all possible instances. Here we see a clear example of an attempt to construct a basic Buddhist ontology, with *dharmas* as the underlying supports (*dhātu*) of our experience. This approach seems to differ from the Sautrāntika emphasis upon the Abhidharma as a phenomenological account of what "appears". In contrast, for the Vaibhāṣikas *dharmas* seem to become the fundamental categories of reality.

The Abhidharma task then is to be able to talk about the world as it really is (*yathābhūta*) rather than as it might appear (*yathābhāsa*) to the untrained and unenlightened mind. Thus, the Abhidharmic enterprise involves the cultivation of analytical insight (*prajñā*) as a means of reducing second-order entities into their fundamental and primary constituents. The result is that the Abhidharma schools tended to propound a doctrine of radical momentariness (*kṣaṇa-vāda*), itself a systematisation of the Buddhist notion of universal impermanence (*anityatā*). What we conventionally refer to as a 'person' therefore, is really a continually changing continuum of moments of experience – a stream of evanescent *dharmas* following each other in such quick succession that the illusion of persistence is maintained so long as one observes with an uncritical and untrained mind. The flow of consciousness arises and ceases in every moment 'as if it were the stream of a river' (*Visuddhimagga* 458, cf. 554).

The Abhidharma, therefore, postulated a two-fold analysis of reality – the conventional level (of entities – e.g. tables, chairs, persons etc.) and an ultimate level of momentary mental and material events (*dharmas*). The existence of the former is purely nominal (*prajñapti-sat*), whilst the latter persist as the fundamental constituents of reality (*dravya-sat*). In Abhidharma terms anything that can be reduced to more basic constituents comprises a nominal or conventional entity rather than a substantial or ultimate reality. The various Abhidharma texts, therefore, provide lists and accounts of what they see as the fundamental and irreducible constituents of phenomena.

The Nyāya-Vaiśeṣika view of a substance (*dravya*) as that in which qualities (*guṇa*), actions (*karman*) and universals inhere was refuted by the various Buddhist schools in their attempt to avoid what they saw as the mistaken tendency to reify our experience into static entities which possess certain qualities. For the Buddhists, the world was a process of fluctuating and momentary events (*dharmas*) and did not consist of substances and a separate category of qualities that these substances are reputed to possess. Consequently, the Nyāya-Vaiśeṣika notion of inherence (*samavāya*) became the subject of sustained attack by the various Abhidharma schools of Buddhism.

As we have seen for the Nyāya and Vaiśeṣika schools qualities (*guṇa* or *dharma*) require the existence of a substance (*dravya* or *dharmin*) in which they can inhere. We usually think of chairs and tables as existing over and above their specific attributes. Substances were also required as the underlying substrata that allow change to occur. Thus, I enter a room and sit down on a chair, not on a blob of hard, brown and oblong qualities. With this as a basis, it was argued that an immaterial self (*ātman*) must exist as a substance because of the existence of immaterial qualities (e.g. consciousness, emotions etc.).

In contrast to the Nyāya-Vaiśeṣika position the Buddhist world-view is grounded in the metaphysics of no-abiding-self. Where is the chair other than the hard, brown and oblong qualities that one perceives? From a Buddhist Abhidharma perspective what is real is what is actually perceived – namely the momentary and fluctuating stream of causally connected qualities themselves. To translate this into Nyāya-Vaiśeṣika terms, this means that what really exists are the momentary qualities themselves (*dharmas*) with no substrata acting as the possessor or bearer (*dharmin*) of such qualities. There is no mysteriously abiding substance or self in which qualities inhere. For the Naiyāyika realist this position is preposterous. Of course there is a chair there. The practicalities of worldly life necessitate making a distinction between the qualities of the chair and the chair as the object that possesses those qualities. From an Abhidharma perspective, however, rigorous analysis of our own experience demonstrates that what we call 'the chair' is merely a conceptual construct imputed by the mind which reifies momentary perceptions and constructs unified entities out of the complex and dynamic series of mental and material *dharmas*. For the Buddhist then, the postulation of a relation such as 'inherence' (*samavāya*) is the mistake of thinking that a stream of events requires an underlying substance in order to occur.

The overwhelming emphasis within Buddhist philosophical thought, therefore, has been upon the reduction of 'wholes' into their constituent factors (*dharmas*, i.e. factors). This 'anti-wholism' is reflected in two basic Buddhist principles:

1. Wholes do not ultimately exist if they are capable of reduction into their constituent parts.
2. The whole is no more than the sum of its parts.

The appearance of an entity is dependent upon the parts from which it is constituted. Therefore, that entity or 'whole' cannot exist in an ultimate sense. This approach is endorsed by the Abhidharmists in their reduction of all everyday or conventional realities *(saṃvṛti-sat)* into their momentary constituents (*dharmas*). In Mahāyāna Buddhist thought, this view is extended even further to include even these *dharma*-constituents on the grounds that all *dharmas* arise in mutual dependence and thus are devoid of their own independent-existence (*svabhāva-śūnya*).

The Buddhist Dharmakīrti, for instance, attacks the Nyāya-Vaiśeṣika idea that wholes (*avayavin*) inhere throughout their parts on the grounds that this contradicts our experience. If the material body is an indivisible whole that inheres in its parts then moving one's hand would cause the entire body to move. Similarly, covering one's face with a cloth would be enough to cover the whole body and painting one's face blue would result in the entire body appearing blue (*Pramāṇavārttika* II. 84–6). The later tradition of New (navya) Nyāya conceded this point to the Buddhists, accepting that qualities do not always pervade the entirety of substances. This concession, of course, undermines the unity of the whole (*avayavin*), which is precisely the Buddhist point. It is perhaps significant, however, that by the time of the New Nyāya school, Buddhism had already entered a terminal decline in India, and thus constituted less of a philosophical threat to the integrity of the Nyāya-Vaiśeṣika system.

Nevertheless, the debate between the Nyāya-Vaiśeṣika traditions and the Buddhists over this and related issues lasted for centuries. Neither side, of course, could accept the stance of the other since their respective approaches to the question of ontology were directly incommensurable. The Nyāya and Vaiśeṣika schools promulgated a pluralistic and substantialist realism, based upon a metaphysical distinction between substance and qualities. In contrast, the various Buddhist schools advocated a phenomenalistic philosophy of dynamic processes (rather than fixed substances) which conceived of reality in terms of unique and momentary particulars known as *dharmas*.

– REJECTING ONTOLOGY: THE MAHĀYĀNA PHILOSOPHY OF EMPTINESS –

In the first century before the Common Era we see the beginnings of a new trend within Indian Buddhism, mostly centred around the notion of the compassionate *bodhisattva* ('buddha-to-be') as a universal ideal for all Buddhists to aspire to. With the advent of what became known as 'Mahāyāna' ('Great Vehicle') Buddhism in India, we find a radicalisation of the Abhidharma critique of substance-realism. Central to this development is the figure of Nāgārjuna, a Buddhist monk living in the second century of the Common Era. Nāgārjuna is thought to be the first major philosopher of the Mahāyāna Buddhist tradition and the founder of the Madhyamaka or 'Middle Way' school of Buddhism. The central theme of Nāgārjuna's work is the systematic utilisation of the concept of 'emptiness' (*śūnyatā*) – a rigorous extension of the Buddhist doctrine of no-abiding-self (*anātman*) to everything. In the Abhidharma traditions *anātman* was usually understood to be the fact that there is no persistent or abiding person (*pudgala*) as the subject of our experiences. What is real are the momentary *dharmas* which constitute each stream of consciousness (*citta-saṃtāna*). For Nāgārjuna, however, even these *dharmas* lack an intrinsic-nature or an independent-nature of their own (*niḥsvabhāvatā*) since they are causally dependent upon other *dharmas* for their arising. Emptiness, therefore, is a realisation of inter-dependent-origination (*pratītyasamutpāda*) – the mutual relativity of all things. All *dharmas* (basically everything that might be thought to really exist in Abhidharma terms) lack an independently established nature of their own, because they depend upon (*pratītya*) other factors for their existence. There are no self-sufficient 'absolutes' anywhere.

> Inter-dependent-origination is what we call 'emptiness'.
> It is a dependent designation and is itself the Middle Path.
>
> MMK 24.18

For Nāgārjuna and the subsequent 'Middle Way' (Madhyamaka) school there can be no such thing as an independently established object or entity. All entities are dependent for their origination upon other factors (*parabhāva*). The book that you are now reading is dependent upon the tree from which the paper originated, the logger who felled the tree, the word-processor on which the work was typed, the actions of the author, the decision-making of the publishers etc. All of these factors, of course, did not arise out of nowhere free from conditioning. The tree grew from a seed in the ground and was reliant on sunlight, rain and mineral nutrients in the soil. The logger, author and publishers are all reliant upon their biological parents for their existence, as were their parents before them. In fact, the more one reflects upon the complex web of conditional relations that constitutes reality, the more one realises the full import of the Buddhist doctrine of inter-dependent-origination. For the Buddhist, no entity escapes this web of conditional relations. No matter how long we search we will never find an uncaused cause – an absolute and self-established reality. Enlightened beings such as Gautama the historical Buddha remain as caught up in this web of relations as the rest of us and are devoid of an independent-existence (MMK 22.16). The difference in the case of enlightened beings, however, is that they have fully realised this fact – the emptiness or inter-dependence of everything – and since we have not we continue to experience suffering (*duḥkha*).

Nevertheless, as Nāgārjuna points out, if there is no autonomous entity within this web of conditional relations the conventional notion of 'arising in dependence upon another' becomes problematic:

> In the absence of 'independent-existence' (*svabhāva*) how can there be such a thing as 'existence-dependent upon another' (*parabhāva*) for 'existence-dependent upon-another' simply means the 'independent-existence' of that other.
>
> MMK 15.3

The problem then is that 'existence-dependent-upon-another' (*parabhāva*), that is, being reliant upon another for one's existence, implies the independence of that other. However, if we turn our analysis onto that other it too dissolves into a web of conditional relations and so on *ad infinitum*. Since there are no absolute, independent or self-established entities to be found anywhere even the notion of 'existence-dependent-upon-another' (*parabhāva*) must be abandoned (MMK 1.3). Nāgārjuna therefore argues that a full understanding of the inter-dependent-origination of all things is a realisation that all things are empty of an independent-existence or nature of their own (*svabhāva-śūnya*). This involves a rejection of the whole enterprise of ontological discourse (that is, speaking about what does or does not exist) since 'existence' and 'non-existence' both miss the mark (MMK 15.4–5).

As a corollary to this, even the notion of emptiness itself is not to be clung onto as a view (*dṛṣṭi*) about an ultimate reality of some sort (MMK 27.30). One should not talk of emptiness (*śūnyatā*) as if there is something called 'Emptiness' – "out there" as it were, which constitutes an ultimate or absolute reality. Emptiness is nothing more than the fact that all things are empty of their own autonomous existence (*svabhāva-śūnya*). As such, whilst one can use the adjective 'empty' (*śūnya*) to describe a universal characteristic of all things, there is no substantive reality other than this fact to be designated by the term 'emptiness' (*śūnyatā*). One can say that a cup is empty but not that there is something called emptiness over and above the cup. Candrakīrti (seventh century CE), for instance, compares the mistake of reifying 'emptiness' with the example of the person who, upon being told that a merchant has nothing to sell, asks if he can buy some of that nothing (*Prasannapadā* 247–8). Thus, Mādhyamikas also discuss what they call the 'emptiness of emptiness' – even the concept of emptiness itself is empty of inherent existence (*Madhyamakāvatāra* VI.185–6). Thus, to grasp onto the concept of emptiness as a philosophical theory is like grasping onto the wrong end of a snake – watch out or you will get bitten! (MMK 24.11)

Nāgārjuna is rigorous in his insistence that we do not mistake the adjectival nature of 'emptiness' as a term denoting an ultimate or absolute reality. Similarly, abstract discussions of emptiness mean little unless one specifies what it is that is empty and what that empty thing is empty of. For Nāgārjuna, what all things lack (or are empty of) is *svabhāva* – an independent-nature or essence, an autonomous existence of their own. This means that the language of ontology (what exists and does not exist) must be abandoned since both existence (*bhāva*) and non-existence (*abhāva*), in Nāgārjuna's view, presuppose the notion of autonomous-existence (*svabhāva*). To say that something exists, Nāgārjuna argues, is to imply that it has a separate existence of its own. This is contradicted by a realisation that all things arise in a relationship of dependence upon other things. However, to say that nothing exists within this framework is to say that there is absolutely nothing. Try banging your head against a brick wall (you may already be doing this) and you will soon find out why Nāgārjuna thinks that 'nothing exists' is an extreme view (on second thoughts, take my word for it). So, the declaration that everything lacks autonomous-existence does not mean that there is absolutely nothing, nor does it mean that there is a world of independently established objects as we conventionally assume.

The Abhidharma distinction between nominal existence (*prajñapti-sat*) and substantial existence (*dravya-sat*) is crucial to the development of the Madhyamaka perspective since what we find in the notion of emptiness is a radicalisation of Abhidharma reductionism. We have already seen in Chapter 4 that the issue of reconciling divergent teachings within the Buddhist canonical literature was circumvented by the notions that the Buddha's words, whilst always true and wholesome in nature, were context-sensitive. The Buddha was known to have adapted the form of his teaching according to the circumstances and propensities of those addressed. Some teachings of the Buddha were definitive (*nītārtha*) and could be taken at face value. Other teachings, however, were of provisional or secondary import (*neyārtha*) and required further elaboration if they were to be understood as the Buddha's final position on things. Based upon such epistemological notions, Abhidharma philosophers felt that a similar distinction needed to be made concerning the way in which things exist, depending upon whether they were ultimate or provisional realities. In this manner the Abhidharmists distinguished between what they called 'nominal existence' (*prajñapti-sat*) and 'substantial existence' (*dravya-sat*). Although the Buddhists use the notion of substance (*dravya*) here, we should not confuse this with the use of the term in the Nyāya and Vaiśeṣika schools. In an Abhidharma context a substantial-existent (*dravya-sat*) denotes the momentary *dharma*-event and not a fixed substrata in which qualities inhere. The classical definition of the distinction between nominal and substantial existents is found in the *Abhidharma-kośa* of Vasubandhu (fourth century CE):

> If the awareness of something does not operate after that thing is physically broken up or separated by the mind into other things, it exists conventionally like a pot or water; others exist ultimately.
>
> *Abhidharmakośa* VI.4

In the Madhyamaka school everything (that is, all *dharmas*) are merely nominal in their existence (*prajñapti-sat*) – there are no substantial existents (*dravya-sat*). The distinction between ultimate and conventional truths, however, is retained by the school in order to circumvent the dangers of adopting a nihilistic position (*ucchedavāda*). Emptiness, Nāgārjuna reminds us, is not mere nothingness but is another way of declaring the mutual relativity of all things!

We should not underestimate the radical nature of Nāgārjuna's critique. Traditional Indian metaphysics made a distinction between two states of being: *saṃsāra* – the "common flowing" of rebirth, which is characterised by suffering (*duḥkha*) and ignorance (*avidyā*) and *mokṣa* or *nirvāṇa* – liberation from rebirth, seen as an end to all suffering and the attainment of complete enlightenment. For the Nyāya tradition liberation is attained through the eradication of ignorance (*mithyā-jñāna*, literally, 'false knowledge'). Through the control of one's mind (*manas*) one can attain an undistorted picture of reality. According to *Nyāya Sūtra* I.1.2 the cycle of rebirths follows a causal chain: Misapprehension (*mithyā-jñāna* or *avidyā*) leads to faults or defects (*doṣa*), such as envy, hatred, jealousy etc. All of these negative dispositions, therefore, are caused by the attachment and revulsion caused by a misapprehension of reality. Such defects or faults result in the performance of karmically tinged actions and the consequences that lead from them. This leads to rebirth (i.e. continued existence in *saṃsāra*), which for the Nyāya in common with the other schools of Indian thought is fundamentally a source of *duḥkha* – pain, suffering and unease in the broadest sense of the term. One can eradicate suffering, however, through the cultivation of a correct knowledge of reality (*tattva-jñāna*) and the practice of yoga (NS ch. 4). Meditative practices aid the subject in attaining a clear perception of reality and are to be encouraged. The *Sūtra* also suggests that one should make efforts to be in constant conversation with the wise in order to grasp true knowledge.

Nāgārjuna and the subsequent Mahāyāna traditions of Buddhism, however, reject this basic soteriological distinction.

> There exists no feature which distinguishes *saṃsāra* from *nirvāṇa* and no feature of *nirvāṇa* which distinguishes it from *saṃsāra*.

> The boundary (*koṭi*) of *nirvāṇa* is also the boundary of *saṃsāra*, there is not even a subtle difference between them.
>
> MMK 25.19–20

For the Mahāyāna schools of Buddhism the only difference between rebirth and enlightenment is in one's orientation towards them. For this reason the advanced Mahāyāna practitioner (the *bodhisattva)* does not renounce worldly norms (*laukika dharma*) upon enlightenment (*Śūnyatāsaptati* 70) but continues to manifest in the world of rebirth out of compassion and for the sake of others. Moreover, the teaching of the ultimate truth is dependent upon the correct usage of the conventional for its explication (MMK 24.10). *Saṃsāra* and *nirvāṇa* are the result of the dichotomising activities of an unenlightened mind and are not separate ontological realities.

> At bottom, the two realms of ultimate meaning and worldly convention refer to the different modes of understanding of the saint and the common worldling. The actual world is itself not two but one, and therefore the two truth realms cannot be made so completely other as to refer to separate worlds of meaning.
>
> Gadjin Nagao, 1989: 110

In the Mahāyāna traditions, the enlightened being 'remains within *saṃsāra*' upon realising the perfection of wisdom (*prajñāpāramitā*). The conventional level of meaning, therefore, far from being abandoned upon enlightenment, is positively re-affirmed or redeemed through the notion of emptiness. The dichotomy (*dvaya*) between existence (*bhāva*) and liberation (*nirvāṇa*) cannot be found because on this view *nirvāṇa* is nothing more than a 'complete knowledge of existence' (*Yuktiṣaṣṭika* verse 6).[6]

We should also bear in mind that for the Madhyamaka the postulation of two truths is a distinction between 'levels of meaning' (*artha*) or understanding (*jñāna*) and should not be taken to imply that there are two specific 'levels of reality' or a distinction between appearance on the one hand and some underlying reality on the other. To interpret the two truths in this fashion would be to undermine Nāgārjuna's rejection of a difference between the world of embodied rebirths (*saṃsāra)* and final enlightenment (*nirvāṇa*). *Saṃvṛti-satya* is the conventional and 'concealing' level of meaning, while *paramārtha-satya* is the supreme or 'ultimate meaning' (*parama-artha*). The Madhyamaka distinction is semantic or cognitive and is not to be interpreted as making an ontological statement about some underlying (and therefore ultimate) reality.

The Madhyamaka point is simple but profoundly difficult to grasp. All discourse is conventional and should be utilised with this insight in mind. Language is valid only in so far as it merely points towards the ultimate truth, which in turn is a reflection upon its own purely conventional nature:

> The Mādhyamika theme of the identity of emptiness and dependent co-arising explains awakening as awareness of emptiness, beyond words and images, but expressed conventionally in the dependently co-arisen words of our making. Those words are valid when they are in harmony with ultimate meaning, that is to say, when uttered in full awareness of their dependently co-arisen and empty status.
>
> Keenan, 1989: 195

One way of clarifying the Madhyamaka position on the two truths is to point out that in having perfect wisdom (*prajñāpāramitā*), that is knowledge (*jñāna*) of the ultimate truth (*paramārtha-satya*), enlightened beings possess the ability to explain this truth in conventional language. This is not to say that ultimate truth is fully expressible in conventional language, for if it were, everyone would be enlightened (Candrakīrti, *Madhyamakāvatāra* VI.30). Nevertheless, there is no way for the Buddha to point to the ultimate without utilising the tools of the conventional. Teaching the ultimate truth to others therefore involves the correct application (*prayojana*) and understanding (*prajñā*) of the limits and uses of conventional truth (*saṃvṛti-satya*). In fact, ultimate knowledge (*paramārtha-jñāna*) is the realisation that *dharmas* are dependently co-arisen and empty of an essential nature, i.e. that they are in actual fact conventional existents (*saṃvṛti-sat*) and nothing more. In one sense then, 'ultimate' (*paramārtha*) and 'conventional' (*saṃvṛti*), therefore, are not concepts referring to separate levels of 'existence' (*sat*) but relate to separate levels of awareness (*jñāna*).

The bottom line for the Madhyamaka school is that the ultimate truth is that *there are no ultimate or independently established existents*, which amounts to a rejection of the entire enterprise of constructing an ontological theory about what really exists. Some scholars (such as Mark Siderits, 1989) have rendered the Madhyamaka position as 'the ultimate truth is that there is no ultimate truth', but this would seem to undermine the ultimate truth of the Buddha's Dharma (and lead to a paradox). For Nāgārjuna clearly there is an ultimate truth and that truth is that there is no entity that exists as an ultimate reality. The distinction between these two interpretations is a subtle one but is crucial in avoiding a nihilistic interpretation of emptiness. To deny that there is an ultimate truth is to collapse the distinction between conventional and ultimate truth which, Nāgārjuna argues, is central to understanding the import of the philosophy of emptiness (MMK 24.8–9). Fully realising that all entities are conventionally real but ultimately devoid of independent-existence (*svabhāva-śūnya*), therefore, is the realisation of the ultimate truth and the attainment of enlightenment.

Critics of the doctrine of two truths, of course, pointed to the apparent discrepancy between the two. Kumārila the Mīmāṃsaka (seventh century

CE), for instance, asks why, if both can be described as truth, they seem so diametrically opposed in their implications. Kumārila's answer is, of course, that so-called conventional truth is really just a euphemism for untruth (*mithyā*) or falsity (Matilal, 1971: 153). For Nāgārjuna and his followers, however, to conflate conventional and ultimate truth is to miss the Madhyamaka point entirely. The distinction is crucial to Nāgārjuna's philosophy since without the recognition of some degree of truth to conventional entities, emptiness would be indistinguishable from the nihilism that its opponents ascribe to it.

The debate between the Hindu brahmanical traditions and Buddhism continued for over a millennium. The Nyāya and Vaiśeṣika schools appeal to 'common-sense' experiences as a basis for their account of what is real. The various Buddhist philosophical traditions (the Abhidharma) also appeal to experience but tend to emphasise its processual and fluctuating nature, remaining sceptical of the role played by the mind (*manas*) in the construction of our view of reality. Inevitably, in a debate about ontology (what is real), attention was bound to turn towards the sources and justification of knowledge itself and this will be the topic of the next two chapters.

– NOTES –

1. However, as Halbfass (1992: 72) notes, the six-fold classification does not really establish itself until the time of Praśastapāda. We should bear in mind then that 'a complete list of all six categories as well as the term *padārtha* [or "category"] itself is found in only one single Sūtra of questionable authenticity. In the version of the Vaiśeṣika Sūtra that forms the basis of Śaṅkaramiśra's commentary *Upaskāra*, it appears as I, 1, 4. It is missing, however, in the versions used by several apparently older commentaries.' (Ibid: 75).
2. Praśastapāda characterises all six categories under the rubric of 'is-ness' (*astitva*). He also describes substances, qualities and actions as having 'connection to reality' (*sattāsambandha*), and universals, particularities and inherence as having 'being by virtue of self-identity' (*svātmasattva*). Later Vyomaśiva argued that 'existent-ness' (*sattā*) could be applied metaphorically to the latter three categories on the grounds that they are 'concomitant properties' (*sādhāraṇadharma*) within the same substrates. This step allowed later thinkers such as Udayana to place all six categories under the rubric of *sattā* (Halbfass, 1992: ch. 7). From the time of Raghunātha (fourteenth century CE) then, the New Nyāya school held that existent-ness (*sattā*) and presence (*bhāva*) were indistinguishable, though this created new issues in itself regarding the precise ontological status of the presences. See Shastri, 1964: 146–52; Potter, 1957: 48.2–3 to 49.2 and Ingalls, 1952: 54.
3. According to Praśastapāda's *Padārthasaṃgraha* (II.5) the twenty-four qualities (*guṇa*) of the Vaiśeṣika school are: 1. colour, 2. taste, 3. smell, 4. touch, 5. sound, 6. number, 7. size, 8. distinctness, 9. conjunction (*saṃyoga*), 10. disjunction, 11. nearness, 12. farness, 13. cognition, 14. pleasure, 15. pain, 16. desire, 17. aversion, 18. effort, 19. heaviness, 20. fluidity, 21. viscidity, 22. volition (*saṃskāra*), 23. moral virtue and 24. immorality.

4. Indeed, the Naiyāyika Bhāsarvajña argues that the Vaiśeṣika category of action (*karman*) should be subsumed under that of qualities (*guṇa*) though his position has not generally been followed in Nyāya-Vaiśeṣika circles and he was criticised in this regard by Udayana.
5. In this regard Uddyotakara puts forward the rather odd position that a whole weighs more than its parts but that the difference is indistinguishable and difficult to ascertain because one does not know how much of the total weight belongs to the causal parts or the whole as effect (Shastri, 1996: 130).
6. The idea then that the distinction between the two truths and between worldly existence (*saṃsāra)* and liberated awareness (*nirvāṇa*) is an affirmation of some form of ontological absolutism which distinguishes between phenomenal appearances (*saṃvṛti-sat*) and a subjacent ground (*paramārtha-sat*, i.e. 'what actually is') is a misreading of the Madhyamaka position. See T. R. V. Murti (1955) for a classic example of an absolutistic interpretation of Nāgārjuna.

Chapter 6

Epistemology: How do we know what we know?

– The Foundations of Knowledge (*Pramāṇa*) –

How do we know what we know? This is a question that has plagued thinkers throughout history in a variety of different cultures and philosophical traditions. In classical Indian thought questions about the nature, means and source of knowledge – the discipline known as epistemology to modern philosophers, is summed up in the Sanskrit notion of *pramāṇa*. *Pramāṇa* is defined in the Nyāya school as a 'source' or 'means' (*karaṇa*) of valid apprehension or valid knowledge. One cannot expect to possess valid knowledge (*prama*) without first having some means or way of apprehending it. The means for such knowledge is known as *pramāṇa*.

The number of sources of valid knowledge differs according to the philosophical school (see Figure 1). The Cārvākas as materialists accepted only sense-perception (*pratyakṣa*) as a valid source of knowledge. The Vaiśeṣika and most Buddhist schools tended to accept perception and logical inference (*anumāna*) as valid,[1] whilst the Sāṃkhya school accepted perception, inference and authoritative testimony (*śabda*, see *Sāṃkhya Kārikā* v. 4, *Sāṃkhya Sūtra* I. 99–101).

The Nyāya school accepts perception, inference and authoritative testimony (usually taken to be the three central *pramāṇas*) but also defends analogy (*upamāna*) as a fourth independent source of knowledge.[2] Analogy refers to the type of knowledge that derives from the combination of things that one already knows. Imagine a situation where you have never encountered a camel but a friend who has recently been to Egypt says to you 'a camel is like a horse, only it usually lives in the desert and has a humped back'. When you later encounter a camel you are now in a position to determine that it is one – based upon the analogous description that you have been given. Other schools argued that analogy was not an independent source, being reliant upon authoritative testimony or inference and so on.

Name of School	Perception	Inference	Testimony	Are External Objects Real?	Does the Self Exist?
Cārvāka	Yes	No	No	Real	Only as Body
Nyāya	Yes	Yes	Yes	Real	Yes
Vaiśeṣika	Yes	Yes	No	Real	Yes
Advaita Vedānta	Yes	Yes	Yes	Empirically Real	Yes
Pūrva Mīmāṃsā	Yes	Yes	Yes	Real	Yes
Sāṃkhya	Yes	Yes	Yes	Real	Yes
Yoga	Yes	Yes	Yes	Real	Yes
Abhidharma	Yes	Yes	No	*Real as Dharmas*	No
Prāsaṇgika	Conventionally	No	No	Conventionally Real	No
Svātantrika	Conventionally	Yes	No	Conventionally Real	No
Yogācāra	Yes	Yes	No	Unreal	No
Viśiṣṭādvaita	Yes	Yes	Yes	Real	Yes

Figure 1: The *Pramāṇas* in Indian Philosophy

At first glance Nyāya is, in many respects, the school of Indian thought that appears to have most in common with modern western Analytic or linguistic philosophy. Particular concerns and features of the school include analysis of the nature of inference, a rigorous analysis of propositions, a thoroughgoing advocacy of direct perceptual realism and an interest in establishing the foundations of epistemology. However, it is precisely because of these similarities that one must be careful not to assimilate Nyāya to the concerns and agenda of modern Anglo-American philosophical thought. One must remain mindful of the distinctiveness and 'alienness' of the Nyāya and resist temptations to interpret the school merely in terms of modern, western philosophical concerns.

The importance of the Nyāya for the other schools of Indian philosophy lies not only in its rigorous defence of a pluralistic realism but also in the bringing to the fore of questions related to epistemology – the means (and defence) of knowledge. With regard to the other Hindu schools it has been noted that:

> Though they rejected the metaphysical tenets, they accepted the general methodology of the Nyāya-Vaiśeṣika school and soon, thanks to their efforts, instead of remaining a mere school of philosophy, it attained a position of pre-eminence in the science of methodology. Thus, in ancient India a pupil was first required to learn grammar and then Nyāya or logic. Unless a student took lessons in Nyāya he was not supposed to be competent to study Pūrva Mīmāṃsā or Vedānta.
>
> Barlingay, 1975: 5

The importance of the Nyāya tradition within Indian philosophy can hardly be overestimated. The significance of the Nyāya system lies particularly in its thoroughgoing defence of perceptual realism, its appeal to a pragmatic empiricism and the school's strong commitment to rational debate and clear, logical argumentation. It is a crucial example, therefore, in demonstrating that Indian philosophical debate is thoroughly grounded in the rules of logical debate and is neither irrational nor other-worldly and impractical. As B. K. Matilal remarked:

> Indian philosophical literature did not always deal exclusively with idealism, monism, subjectivism and mysticism. The Nyāya-Vaiśeṣika writers were, instead, critical and positive thinkers, and genuinely interested in logic, analysis of human knowledge and language, and descriptive metaphysics.
>
> Matilal, 1977: 112

– INFERENCE (*ANUMĀNA*) AND THE NYĀYA SCHOOL –

Nyāya means 'that by which one is led to a conclusion' or 'correct reasoning' and is often referred to as 'the science of reasoning' (*tarkaśāstra*). It is for this reason that the school is most well known for the development of logical procedures as a means of establishing a correct inference (*anumāna*). Analysis of inferential reasoning was central to the exercise of 'good philosophical practice' and in establishing the proper rules for scholastic debate that are, as we have seen in an earlier chapter, central to the practice of Indian philosophy and the interactive development of the various *darśanas*.

The roots of the Nyāya no doubt lie in earlier handbooks concerning the nature of debate and its formal procedures (*vāda-śāstra*). Crystallised versions of these manuals can be found in the *Caraka Saṃhitā*, the Buddhist *Upāyahṛdaya* and Asaṅga's *Bodhisattva-Bhūmi*. Many of these categories and rules have also been absorbed into the first and fifth chapters of the existing *Nyāya Sūtra*. According to the *Nyāya Sūtra* there are three types of debate – discussion (*vāda*), disputation (*jalpa*) and destructive criticism or 'wrangling' (*vitaṇḍā*):

> *vāda* is primarily meant for the discernment of truth or the real nature of the thing under investigation and imparting the truth as one understands it to the other party; that is to say, in *vāda*, there is no consideration of victory or defeat. On the other hand, in *jalpa*, victory is the sole end in view ... That same disputation is *vitaṇḍā* (wrangling) when there is no establishing of the counter-view ... (NS 1.2, 3)
>
> Solomon, 1976: 104, 112

In Indian philosophical circles there are two types of inference, that which is designed to alleviate doubt for oneself (*svārtha-anumāna*) and that which aims at convincing another (*parārtha-anumāna*). The latter requires the elaboration of a formal proof but the former does not. This distinction reflects the Indian view that inference concerns the correct application of thought. A formal proof, therefore, is only required as a means of aiding the listener in directing their thought processes in an appropriate manner. The association of formal proofs with the convincing of others (*parārtha-anumāna*) also reflects the context of inferential reasoning in the practice of debate in ancient India. Thus, Karl Potter (1963: 75) argues that 'the purpose of analyzing inference was to establish rules of debate among philosophers, so that the best system of thought could be identified without question'.

The *Nyāya Sūtra* outlines a five-membered argument or proof, though this scheme clearly evolved from earlier forms (Matilal, 1985: 5).[3] An inferential proof, therefore, is made up of the following members:

1. *Pratijñā* – The Statement, Premise or Position that is to be established (*sādhya*)
2. *Hetu* – The Cause or Reason for the statement
3. *Udāharaṇa* – The Example
4. *Upanaya* – The Application of that example
5. *Nigamana* – The Conclusion

The stock example usually given to illustrate this scheme runs as follows:

'This hill has fire' (statement/*pratijñā*)
'Because it has smoke' (reason/*hetu*)
'Since whatever has smoke has fire e.g. an oven' (example/*udāharaṇa*)
'This hill has smoke, which is associated with fire' (application/*upanaya*)
'Therefore, this hill has fire' (conclusion/*nigamana*).

There has been considerable debate amongst contemporary philosophers about the status of this inferential form and its relationship to Aristotelian logic (Ganeri, 1996; Matilal, 1985: 5–8). The classic Aristotelian syllogism has three components:

1. The Statement or Major Premise ('Smoke is always a sign of fire')
2. The Minor Premise ('This hill has smoke')
3. Conclusion ('Therefore, this hill has fire')

Some have argued that the Nyāya explication of inference (*anumāna*) is therefore redundant and can be reduced to the 'slimmer' Aristotelian version. One should note, however, that one feature of the Nyāya inference is the emphasis that it places upon empiricism and particularity. *Anumāna* denotes that type of knowledge (*māna*) which comes after (*anu*) – something else. Inference cannot occur in an empirical vacuum, it must remain at least hypothetically verifiable in some manner if it is to have any validity. It is a mediated (*parokṣa*) form of knowledge and in this regard can be contrasted with the immediacy (*aparokṣatva*) of perceptual knowledge. Furthermore, the Nyāya equivalent of the Aristotelian major premise ('Smoke is always a sign of fire') is always couched in terms of an example (*udāharaṇa*), in this case an oven. There is always a burden of establishing another particular instance within the Nyāya logical framework that is missing in the classic Aristotelian syllogism. Thus, one could say that the Nyāya inference places a much greater emphasis upon particularity, involving an argument from one particular case to another particular case via a universal statement, whereas its Aristotelian counterpart is an argument which moves from the universal to the particular on a purely formal basis. This no doubt reflects the roots of *anumāna* in the formulation of rules for debate and displays a more practical orientation than both Aristotelian logic and modern formal logic where the primary concern is with formal validity and deduction rather than with the soundness of the argument based upon its actual content or relevance to the world of lived-experience.

> Western logic does not consider it its business to inquire whether the premises and the conclusion of an argument are true. It is solely concerned with determining whether a given argument is valid, ... In sharp contrast Indian logic is at once formal and material. Indian logicians reject the verbalist view of logic – the view that logic is only concerned with thought-forms and symbols and not with content and referents ... whereas the Indian view is based on the conviction that logic is an instrument for the discovery and understanding of reality, and not a mere formal discipline wholly unrelated to the world, ... the Western tradition, having sharply divided the formal from the empirical, is faced with the serious problem of accounting for the fact of the application of logic in the study of the world.
>
> Puligandla, 1997: 197–8

Consider the following famous example of Greek syllogistic reasoning:

All men are mortal
Socrates is a man,
Therefore, Socrates is mortal

The Naiyāyika and other Indian logicians would argue that this argument is acceptable only because one knows from experience (i.e. by induction) that men are in fact mortal. Indian logic then is both formal and empirical and does not allow for a purely deductive logic. In this regard one is reminded of a similar critique of syllogistic logic offered by the western philosopher John Stuart Mill (Ganeri, 1996: 9).

The validity of inferential reasoning as an independent means of knowledge, however, was rejected by the Cārvākas. The ancient Indian materialists did not reject the use of arguments as such, but argued that inference required perceptual knowledge in order to establish its validity. The main Cārvāka objection to inferential reasoning was that it could yield probabilities but not certainties. One could never be sure that every case could be definitively established since this was beyond the scope of human experience. The school, therefore, rejected the principle of universal concomitance or pervasion (*vyāpti*) which linked the minor and major terms in the Nyāya five-membered inference. Thus, one might be led to believe that dawn has broken because one hears a cockerel crowing. But the cockerel may have been disturbed by a fox, or we may be the victim of an April Fool's joke. The materialist-sceptic, therefore, appeals to the partiality of analogies and particular examples (*dṛṣṭānta*) to undermine the independent validity of inferences. The Nyāya response, however, is to suggest that the fault lies here with the example used and not with the inferential process itself. Later materialists such as Purandara (seventh century CE) accepted the validity of inference so long as it remained verifiable by sense-perception. This ruled out speculations about transcendent realms and other worlds (*paraloka*) beyond the empirical realm (Dasgupta, 1988 vol. 3: 536–7, Chattopadhyaya, 1968: 28–30). We should bear in mind, however, that ancient Indian logic never developed a purely formal structure. Inferential reasoning is always seen as grounded in perception and the activity of the mind. In the west this has been described as 'the fallacy of psychologism', that is, the mistake of seeing the formal processes of logical reasoning as relating to mental events rather than to the structure of language or reality itself. Within the ancient Indian traditions, however, a purely formal and deductive logic would be seen as dangerously divorced from empirical reality.

There is no general agreement amongst the traditional Indian schools about the number and types of fallacious reasoning (*hetvābhāsa*). The Nyāya generally accepts five main types (NS 1.2.4–9), but Praśastapāda of the Vaiśeṣika school lists only four such fallacies. The five types accepted by the Nyāya are: 1. wandering (*savyabhicāra*) or indecisive (*anaikāntika*) reasoning, 2. contradictory (*viruddha*) reasoning, 3. unestablished (*asiddha*) reasoning, 4. reasoning that requires as much proof as the thesis (*sādhya-sama*), and 5. reasoning that is mis-timed (*kālātīta*). This final type was later replaced by reasoning that is sublated or 'overturned by a higher knowledge' (*bādhita*).[4] The Buddhists, Jainas and the Bhaṭṭa Mīmāṃsakas generally accepted the first three as examples of fallacious reasoning. In the context of Buddhist philosophical debates, overcoming these fallacies became known as "removing the thorns" (*kaṇṭakoddhāra*) from your argument.

The Nyāya also postulates an additional category known as hypothetical reasoning or rational critique (*tarka*) which is akin to the western *reductio ad absurdum*. The purpose of hypothetical reasoning is to test the validity of inferential reasoning by demonstrating the absurd consequences that follow from an opponent's position and therefore eliminate doubt (*saṃśaya*) in the mind of the enquirer.[5] Udayana mentions five types of rational critique (*tarka*): 1. Self-dependence (*ātmāśraya*) – where x has been used as a ground for establishing x. 2. Mutual-dependence (*anyonyāśraya*) – an extension of self-dependence where there is no independently established ground to justify either element for example, 'where is x?' 'It is with y.' 'Then where is y?' 'It is with x'. 3. Vicious circle (*cakraka*) – another variant of the fallacy of self-dependence when one presupposition is seen to imply another. 4. Infinite regress (*anavasthā*). This is also a variant of self-dependence and involves an unending regression from one presupposition to another. 5. Undesired outcome or illogical thinking (*aniṣṭaprasaṅga*).[6] Sometimes an additional category – over-complexity or 'heaviness' (*gaurava*) of argument is included in the list. This is similar to the western idea of Ockham's Razor – all things being equal accept simplicity (*lāghava*) of explanation since this involves postulating the minimum of entities.

To illustrate the formal procedures of an Indian *vāda* debate let us briefly examine the following scheme which is based upon a fifteenth century Tibetan Buddhist account of the procedures for participating in a philosophical debate.[7] A formal debate involves two participants – the proponent (*pūrva-pakṣin*, that is, 'one who holds the initial position') and a respondent (*prativādin*) – and a witness or arbiter (*sākṣin*). This may be a distinguished individual (perhaps a respected authority within the community or in the case of interscholastic debates a king) or an assembly of some form. The order and procedure of the debate follows eight basic steps, running as follows:

1. The initial proponent is asked to put forward his thesis (*pratijñā*).
2. If the thesis is thought to be erroneous the respondent may refute it immediately, but if the thesis is accepted, then the respondent asks the proponent to outline the reason (*hetu*) for accepting the thesis.
3. The proponent then offers a proof outlining the reasons why the thesis should be accepted.
4. The respondent asks if the proof offered contains the logical relations required of a sound inference (as we have seen in the case of the Buddhist *pramāṇa* tradition there are three types of fallacious reasoning, for the Nyāya there are usually five).
5. The proponent replies by "removing the thorns", that is, he negates the faulty relations and erroneous reasoning that may have occurred in the outlining of the proof of his thesis.

This concludes the first part of the debate. If the respondent accepts both the thesis and the proof then the debate concludes. However, if the proof is deemed erroneous for some reason we enter the second part of the debate.

6. The respondent offers a statement of refutation of the proponent's thesis which thereby constitutes the initial starting-point (*pūrvapakṣa*) of his own exposition. The refutation that follows aims to demonstrate the errors and inconsistencies of the proponent's position *based upon the reasoning and evidence provided by the proponent*. This stage, of course, may be entered much sooner (at stage 2) if the respondent does not accept the thesis of the proponent at the outset.
7. The proponent responds with a rejoinder if it is thought that his critic's refutation is in some way erroneous. However, if the proponent accepts the soundness of the refutation, the respondent is asked to state a formal proof of the refutation in a positive form, that is, as an independent and formally stated inference.
8. Finally, the respondent offers a formal proof of the refutation in inferential form.

There are a number of interesting features to be gleaned from such procedural schemes as this. Firstly, as Esther Solomon points out, the central feature of the *vāda* type of debate is not to defeat your opponent (as in *jalpa*), nor is it to provide a destructive criticism of your opponent's view without offering an alternative position (as in *vitaṇḍā*). Instead, the purpose of such debates is to provide a forum for an exchange of opinions and the clarification of perspectives. Note, for instance, that one is expected to follow the lines of argument offered by one's opponent in the debate and to investigate their proof *in and on its own terms*. This requires one to 'step into the shoes' of one's opponent and interrogate their own evidence. Thus, a skilled Buddhist debater engaged in a discussion with a Mīmāṃsaka would be expected to engage his fellow disputant using independent arguments to convince his opponent (*parārtha-anumāna*) but must also be able to engage with the evidence and the accepted *pramāṇas* of the Mīmāṃsaka. Throwing arguments at each other without a consideration of the perspective of one's fellow disputant will not yield any furtherance of mutual understanding. Thus, the most skilled debater is the one who has a sound and comprehensive knowledge of his opponent's position as well as his own.

The Nyāya tradition remained ambivalent about the validity of disputation (*jalpa*) and mere refutation (*vitaṇḍā*) as debating procedures. The *Nyāya Sūtra* suggests that these two approaches are to be adopted to protect the truth from those who do not conform to the *vāda*-rules of debate:

> *Jalpa* and *vitaṇḍā* are [to be employed] for protecting the ascertainment of truth, just as fences with thorny branches are constructed to protect the seedling coming out of the seed.
>
> *Nyāya Sūtra* 4.2.50 trans. in Gangopadhyaya, 1976: 83

Vātsyāyana adds in his *Nyāya Bhāṣya* that such strategies are acceptable for the inexperienced and for those who might still harbour doubts. The Buddhist *pramāṇa-vāda* tradition of Dignāga and Dharmakīrti, however, unambiguously rejects the use of any debating tricks (*chala*) as inappropriate in a sincere quest for knowledge. Perhaps it is in direct reference to the Nyāya analogy employed above that the Buddhist tradition of Dharmakīrti came to describe this process (exemplified by stage 5) as an act of "removing the thorns" from one's argument.

The *pramāṇa-vāda* tradition initiated by the Nyāya school and subsequently adopted by other Hindu and Buddhist schools of thought provided a public framework within which different philosophical positions could interact, 'fine-tune' their own theoretical perspectives and develop an in-depth understanding of the philosophies of other schools. The development of a wide-ranging and public framework for inter-scholastic debate not only provided an impetus for the refinement of the philosophical positions and arguments of the various schools (*darśana*) and traditions (*saṃpradāya*), it also left an unmistakably discursive imprint upon Indian philosophical writing. The origins of Indian philosophy in the practice of inter-scholastic debates can be seen in the formal structure of their exposition. An initial (and sometimes exhaustive) statement of the opponent's position is first put forward (the *pūrvapakṣa*) before proceeding to a comprehensive examination and refutation of that position. It is only then that the final or definitive position (*siddhānta*) of the author is outlined and established according to a set of proofs.

> From this process emerged a clearer conception of the nature of differences between the individual schools that had survived the pressure of debate. Not all had survived having their basic claims publicly contested, and some new schools grew gradually together until they finally merged. The eventual result was a determinate set of perspectives acknowledged as worthy opponents in debate.
>
> Clayton, 1992: 28–9

Members of particular schools were able to appeal to all of the evidence that they accepted as a valid source of knowledge (*pramāṇa*), even if such evidence was tradition-specific and therefore unacceptable to their opponents. A Naiyāyika, for example, could appeal to the authoritative testimony of Vedic scripture in a debate with a Buddhist despite the fact that his Buddhist opponent neither accepted the Vedas as an authoritative source, nor agreed that verbal testimony (*śabda*) was a valid means of knowledge (*pramāṇa*). In response, the Buddhist might offer a refutation of the Nyāya appeal to the Vedas on its own terms, that is, by providing counter-evidence from the Vedas that seemed to contradict the Naiyāyika's thesis. The primary focus of the Buddhist response, however, would be couched in terms of an appeal to the *pramāṇas* (for example, sense-perception) and the outlining of philosophical arguments aimed at a refutation of the Nyāya position.

The *pramāṇa-vāda* schema thus provided a widely accepted and inter-scholastic framework for the exploration of a variety of different philosophical views. The emphasis upon established procedures of argumentation and philosophical accountability (in the form of appeals to the *pramāṇas*) also provided an opportunity for participants to appreciate the evidence (some of which was internal to particular traditions) that members of other *darśanas* employed as justifications for their own particular belief-system. Such evidence could be appreciated in and on its own terms without requiring assent or consensus over the interpretation or validity of such evidence in a broader context.

– EMPTINESS AND NĀGĀRJUNA'S CRITIQUE OF PRAMĀṆA THEORY –

Acceptance of the *pramāṇa-vāda* framework for philosophical debate, however, was by no means universal in India. The most influential critics of *pramāṇa*-theory have been Nāgārjuna (second century CE), Jayarāśi the materialist-sceptic (seventh century CE) and Śrīharṣa the Advaita Vedāntin (twelfth century CE).

The main problem for Nyāya realism and its adherence to independent means of knowledge (i.e. the *pramāṇa*), as students of western philosophy will be aware, is that of establishing irrefutably that there are independently existing objects 'out there' without appealing to one's own experience of them. The problem here is that one is using that which requires proving (Sanskrit: *sādhya*/Latin: *probandum*) as the proof (Sanskrit: *hetu*/Latin: *probans*) to justify one's position. Critics of the Nyāya school, most notably the second-century Buddhist Nāgārjuna, rejected Nyāya arguments on the ground that the school failed to provide any independent proof for their own position. Nāgārjuna did not explicitly deny the 'outwardness' of objects and indeed his subsequent followers in the Madhyamaka school developed realist arguments akin to those used by the Nyāya to rebut the philosophies of the Yogācāra school of Buddhism – a tradition which did, in some sense, deny the external reality of objects. Nāgārjuna's criticism of the Nyāya was a much broader attack upon the whole edifice of *pramāṇa* theory and the ontological speculations that it attempts to justify.

Nāgārjuna's rejection of the ontological discourses of 'existence' and non-existence' led him to declare that the philosophy of emptiness (*śūnyatā*) is the 'Middle Way' between the extreme positions of eternalism (*śāśvata*) and nihilism (*uccheda*). Nāgārjuna also states that in discussing this theme he is not asserting a proposition or thesis (*pratijñā*) of any kind.

> If I would put forward any thesis (*pratijñā*) whatsoever, then by that I would have made a logical error. But I do not put forward a thesis. Therefore I am not in error.
>
> *Vigrahavyāvartanī* v. 29

There has been some debate as to the precise import of this bold statement. How can Nāgārjuna claim not to have a thesis to put forward? Is it possible to argue strategically, that is, without taking a fixed position of one's own? Is emptiness itself not a philosophical theory? David Seyfort Ruegg (1986: 233–5) has argued that in denying that he has a *pratijñā* to put forward, Nāgārjuna is rejecting any thesis which posits the existence of an entity (*bhāva*) or a *dharma* as independently existent (i.e. possessing *svabhāva*) and does not mean thereby that he has no doctrinal position or scholastic allegiance (*darśana*) at all.[8] One might also appeal to the classical Indian distinction between implicatory negation (*paryudāsa-pratiṣedha*) and non-implicatory negation (*prasajjya-pratiṣedha*) in order to make sense of Nāgārjuna's claim.[9] The former is a negation which implies its contrary, whilst the latter represents negations that require no such commitment. In this case Nāgārjuna's negation would be an example of the latter.

However one interprets Nāgārjuna's claim not to have a thesis, his critique of prevailing epistemological theories focuses upon the Nyāya understanding of the relationship between the means of knowledge (*pramāṇa*) and that which is known (*prameya*). For Nāgārjuna the Nyāya belief in the inseparability (*miśra*) of the two leads to a vicious circle (*cakraka*, VV 46–9).

> Now if you think that through the establishment of the *pramāṇas* are established the *prameyas*, and that through the establishment of the *prameyas* are established the *pramāṇas*, then neither the *prameyas* nor the *pramāṇas* are established by you.
>
> If the son is to be produced by the father, and if that father is to be produced by that very son, tell me which of these produces which other?
>
> *Vigrahavyāvartanī* 46–9, trans. in Bhattacharya, 1990

Moreover, Nāgārjuna argues, if the *pramāṇas* constitute the independent means and criteria of various types of knowledge, what is it that establishes their status as independent means? (VV 31). Appeal to a further set of criteria will lead to an infinite regress (*anavasthā*, VV 32, see NS 2.1.17).

However, if there are no further criteria, then the assertion of the *pramāṇas* remains without foundation and amounts to an abandonment of the initial thesis (*pratijñāhāni*) that all knowledge is established via independent means (VV 33). Notice how in this argumentation Nāgārjuna uses the Nyāya's own categories of hypothetical (i.e. *reductio ad absurdum*) reasoning (*tarka*) to refute the Nyāya theory of *pramāṇas*.

Subsequent developments within the Madhyamaka school in India led to the formation of two distinct interpretations of Nāgārjuna's project. The Prāsaṅgika Madhyamaka (exemplified by Candrakīrti, seventh century CE) argued that the truth of emptiness could be established only through the use of *reductio ad absurdum* (*prasaṅga*) arguments. On this view the Madhyamaka does not put forward independent arguments of its own but instead establishes internal inconsistencies in the presuppositions of others, thereby undermining their position from within. The basic Prāsaṅgika stance is expressed rather well by Gadjin Nagao:

> As a theory Mādhyamika is unable to articulate its own true insight (*darśana*) through its own forms of expression, inasmuch as theoretical conclusions (*siddhānta*) would contain within themselves the cause of their own collapse. Mādhyamika can be brought to speech only through the reasoning of others, only in virtue of reasons and examples admitted as valid by others ... Mādhyamika is therefore not the presentation of its own view through its own reasoning. Rather it brings the propositions and theses (*pratijñā*) advocated by others to self-deconstruction within the criteria advocated by those others, and guides them to emptiness. Its efficacy lies in the disclosure of internal contradictions in what is advocated by the other party through the other's own criteria.
>
> Nagao, 1989: 131–2

In contrast, the Svātantrika Madhyamaka tradition (exemplified by Bhāvaviveka, sixth century CE) believed that the establishment of the truth of emptiness required the use of independent (*svatantra*) argumentation. We can see this as an acceptance of the *vāda* framework of disputation, motivated no doubt by the perceived need to construct inferential arguments for convincing others (*parārtha-anumāna*), if only at the conventional level. Bhāvaviveka is clearly influenced by Dignāga's construction of a Buddhist *pramāṇa* scheme and he displays a doxographical interest in the exploration of and engagement with rival scholastic positions.[10] It would seem then that the Svātantrika stance allowed the Madhyamaka tradition to maintain its involvement in the wider scholastic context and disciplinary framework of Indian philosophical debate (*vāda*) in a manner that would have been prohibitive, strictly speaking, on Prāsaṅgika grounds.

Viewed through Nyāya and western Analytic spectacles, Nāgarjuna's critique has often been described as a radical form of scepticism. Perhaps the most famous modern exponent of such an interpretation has been the late Bimal Krishna Matilal. Matilal tended to represent Nāgārjuna's stance as that of the sceptic, though he notes that

> By calling Nāgārjuna a sceptic, or rather by using his arguments to delineate the position of my sceptical opponent of the *pramāṇa* theorists, I have only proposed a probable extension of the application of the term 'scepticism'.
>
> Matilal, 1986: 50

However, as Mark Siderits has argued, to see Nāgārjuna's use of argumentation as sceptically motivated is

> to take him as viewing epistemology as First Philosophy (with philosophy itself seen as the queen of the sciences). That this was not Nāgārjuna's view can be seen from the overall dialectical structure of his writings. Epistemological issues are conspicuous by their virtually total absence from the *Mūlamadhyamakakārikās*, the whole point of which is just to show the impossibility of constructing a coherent metaphysics given the requirement that a real be a *svabhāva*, i.e. something that bears its own essential nature.
>
> Siderits, 1997: 76

Nāgārjuna's institutional and religious location as a practising Buddhist should not be ignored in the assessment of the nature and consequences of his critique. The repudiation of *pramāṇa*-theory did not lead Nāgārjuna to a sceptical or agnostic position about the truthfulness of Buddhist teaching. We can know, Nāgārjuna argues, that all things (including the *pramāṇas*) are empty of independent-existence (*svabhāva-śūnya*). The refutation of the *pramāṇas*, therefore, merely establishes that they too are empty, i.e. dependently co-arising (see *Vaidalya-prakaraṇa* 4) and remains consistent with the establishment of emptiness (*śūnyatā*) as the ultimate truth.

The primary interest of the Nyāya school, in response to Nāgārjuna's critique, was in the preservation of *pramāṇa* theory in the light of Nāgārjuna's devastating criticism. The *Nyāya Sūtra* argues that the *pramāṇas* are like a lamp, in illuminating the object of knowledge (*prameya*) they also illuminate themselves (NS 1.1.19). This will not satisfy Nāgārjuna, however, because he views the analogy as inappropriate. Moreover, the example still fails to address the issue of how one can know that the *pramāṇas* are a reliable and independent authority. Vātsyāyana adopts a different strategy arguing that the justification of the *pramāṇas* does not lead to an infinite regress (*anavasthā*) because everyday practice (*vyavahāra*) requires a distinction to be made between the means of knowledge and the object of knowledge. Without an acceptance of the epistemological truth of the *pramāṇas*, Vātsyāyana argues, accomplishment of one's goals (*prayojana*) would be impossible (NB 2.1.20). Here truth is justified by an appeal to worldly pragmatism.

The Mādhyamika is also seen by the Naiyāyika as the arch practitioner of destructive criticism or wrangling (*vitaṇḍā*). Vātsyāyana suggests that a debater who merely refutes the views of others (*vaitaṇḍika*) should be asked what their own position (*pratijñā*) is. If they reply, as Nāgārjuna does, that they have no thesis to put forward, Vātsyāyana argues that they have forfeited the right to engage in debate since they have no position to defend. However, Vātsyāyana also believes that *vitaṇḍā* cannot occur without an underlying aim or purpose (*prajoyana*) such as removing doubt (*saṃśaya*). Even this is a position of sorts. Moreover, in such a context, he argues, there could be no ascertainment of truth (*nirṇaya*, *Nyāya Bhāṣya* on NS 1.1.1). In response to Vātsyāyana one could agree that the *vaitaṇḍika* does indeed have some kind of motive – namely the refutation of other views and the establishment of truth – but that this does not in and of itself involve the assertion of a positive thesis (*pratijñā*) (Matilal, 1986: 87; Matilal, 1985: 16–17). Objections to Vātsyāyana's stance were made by Śrīharṣa, the twelfth century Advaita philosopher. He argued that the Nyāya insistence upon the recognition of *pramāṇa*-theory (epistemology) as a prerequisite for engaging in philosophical debate is an attempt to set up the debate on their own terms. Śrīharṣa seems to have accepted the *pramāṇas* as conventionally or practically valid (*vyavahārika*) but rejected the Nyāya view that they point to ultimate existents or realities (*paramārtha sattā*).[11]

As we have seen in Chapter 5, Nāgārjuna's response to his critics involves an appeal to the notion that there are two levels of truth. Grasping this point, he argues, is essential for understanding how the notion of emptiness functions. The *Madhyamaka Kārikā* (MMK) stresses the importance of the distinction between conventional truth (*saṃvṛti-satya*) and the ultimate import (*paramārtha*) of the Buddha's message:

> The teaching of the Dharma by the Buddhas rests upon the two truths: worldly conventional truth and truth in the ultimate sense. Those who do not discern the distinction between these two do not discern the profound truth (*tattva*) in the teaching of the Buddha. Without relying upon the practical, the ultimate is not taught. Without understanding the ultimate, one cannot attain *nirvāṇa*.
>
> MMK 24.8–10

Notice that here, like Vātsyāyana, Nāgārjuna appeals to worldly practicalities, this time, however, as support for the concept of emptiness. Indeed for Nāgārjuna, without an acceptance of emptiness no practicalities or actions are possible (MMK 24.15). One simply cannot explain causation or the possibility of change, he argues, without relinquishing the idea of autonomous existence (*svabhāva*) and embracing inter-dependent-origination or emptiness as the fundamental characteristic of all things (MMK 24.15–17).

Nāgārjuna accepted the practical necessity of a distinction between ultimate and conventional truth and this protects the analysis of all *dharmas* as essentially nominal entities (*prajñapti-sat*) from veering towards a nihilistic position. It is worthwhile reiterating that this central Madhyamaka teaching should not be interpreted as a distinction between two independently existing realms. The emphasis upon the doctrine of two truths as an ontological distinction in the Madhyamaka system has perpetuated the misconception that 'emptiness' denotes some kind of absolute reality underlying appearances. Nāgārjuna's point is precisely that there is no underlying absolute reality – all that there is is what is going on right now – an inter-dependent flow of mental and physical events (*dharmas*), mutually conditioning and conditioned by each other and therefore lacking any substantial essence of their own.

However one interprets Nāgārjuna (and the subsequent Madhyamaka traditions provide a number of alternative interpretations on this and other issues), Nāgārjuna makes it clear that the terms 'emptiness' (*śūnyatā*) and 'inter-dependent-origination' (*pratītyasamutpāda*) have the same meaning (*ekārtha*) and strike a middle path between all fixed views (see VV.71). As such they are designations or pointers (*prajñapti*), and as the Mahāyāna saying suggests 'the finger that points at the moon is not the moon!'

> Emptiness was proclaimed by the conquerors as the giving up of all views, but those for whom 'emptiness' is a view will achieve nothing.
>
> MMK 13.8

It is perhaps because the Madhyamaka reductive analysis (*prasaṅga*) is so universal in its application that *śūnyatā* in the final analysis is claimed not to be a philosophical theory *in the same sense* as the competing theories that it rejects. Candrakīrti describes emptiness as a medicine that clears out all defilements, including itself (*Prasannapadā* 249 on MMK 13.8). 'Emptiness' then appears to function at a meta-theoretical level. To put this another way, in discussing the emptiness of all postulated entities, the Mādhyamika is on a 'different wavelength' to his or her (supposed) opponents. The Mādhyamika philosopher sees the critique of philosophical views as occurring from a higher perspective (*darśana*) than the clash of rival views involved in philosophical debate (*vāda*) and argumentation. This view is supported by Nāgārjuna's pupil Āryadeva:

> No criticism can be leveled against someone who does not hold a thesis, be it [about] existence, non-existence, or [both] existence and non-existence, even if [you try] for a long time.
>
> *Catuḥśataka* 16.25, translation in Lang, 1986: 150–1

Such an attitude itself can be traced to much earlier texts of the Buddhist tradition. The conception of the Buddha as free from the quarrelsome disputations of others, and indeed as 'free from all views' can be found in one of the earliest collection of the Buddha's teachings – the *Sutta Nipāta*. It is important to acknowledge the extent to which the fundamental ideas of the Madhyamaka can be found to have antecedents in the earlier traditions of Buddhism since in my view there has been a tendency to over-emphasise the discontinuities between schools of thought in ancient India at the expense of the continuities and interactions of the various *darśanas*. Thus in the *Saṃyutta Nikāya*, the Buddha declares that,

> Although the world may quarrel with me, I have no quarrel with the world. That which is considered to exist in the context of the world I also assert as existent; and that which is considered not to exist in the world I also assert as nonexistent.
> *Saṃyutta Nikāya* 22, 64.103, translation in Huntington, 1989: 67

One way to understand the language of emptiness then is to see it as a kind of meta-language or meta-theory. The insight (*prajñā*) into the universality of emptiness therefore is expressed by means of a 'deconstructive' meta-philosophy whereby all fixed views (*dṛṣṭi*) are subverted by the establishment of inconsistencies and unwarranted conclusions derived from their own basic premises. Without a recognition of the radically deconstructive nature of the Mādhyamika approach one is likely to misinterpret the school's position as a form of nihilism (*uccheda-vāda*) or even as a form of absolutism (*śāśvata-vāda*). The correct utilisation (*prayojana*) of the language of emptiness, however, is the means whereby the ultimate truth (*paramārtha-satya*), as embodied in the Buddha's teaching (*dharmadeśana*) can be expressed through the language of conventions (*saṃvṛti*). This is the skilful and purposeful use of concepts advocated by the Madhyamaka, which is of course at the same time a purification and a redemption of conventional truth (*saṃvṛti-satya*).

Whilst one is by no means obliged to accept the Madhyamaka position as true, if we are to take the works of Nāgārjuna and his followers seriously we must also take seriously the expressed intentions and meanings which they have applied to them. *Śūnyatā* then is not to be understood as a definitive doctrinal position (*siddhānta*) in the sense of being a rival theory amongst theories jostling for supremacy in philosophical debate.[12] In the final analysis the notions of 'emptiness' and 'dependent-origination' are examples of conventional-talk. In this sense they function as indicators which point to the ultimate truth but should not be grasped onto as 'ultimates' in themselves. As a result Nāgārjuna describes such terms as 'dependent designations' (*prajñaptir upadāya,* MMK 24.18), implying no ontological commitment whatsoever (MMK 22.11).

On a semantic level the distinction between ultimate and conventional performs the function of rehabilitating the conventional purpose (*prayojana*) of language (MMK 24.7). The meaning of words is established through common consensus, that is, they are conventional and do not relate to some underlying ultimate reality. This does not prevent Nāgārjuna from acknowledging the referential capacity of words, since this occurs in the conventional realm of discourse. Clearly, however, Nāgārjuna's stance is a rejection not only of the *pramāṇa-vāda* framework introduced by the Nyāya but also involves a repudiation of the ontological categories that the Nyāya and Vaiśeṣika see as the real referents of words (*padārtha*).

From a religious perspective the correct understanding of the distinction between ultimate and conventional allows a practitioner to grasp the fact of the 'essenceless-ness' (*niḥsvabhāvatā*) of all *dharmas*; this in itself is an insight into the fact that there is no underlying essence or 'ground' to experience other than the causal conditioning of the experience itself. All *dharmas* are empty in that they are inter-dependently arisen. The ultimate meaning (*parama-artha*) of any given factor (*dharma*) then is determined by its place within the overall scheme (which is conventionally determined, i.e. *saṃvṛtic*), and not by its own independent nature (which it fundamentally lacks). This point, crucial to an understanding of the Madhyamaka position, is described in lucid terms by Huntington:

> Every element of conceptualization and perception owes its individual identity to an interrelated web of causes and conditions, so that it does not bear its meaning or existence in itself, and on this account concepts of a self-sufficient generative matrix or a transcendental ground are inherently problematic. By virtue of its most fundamental nature, as illuminated through the Mādhyamika's deconstructive analysis, all experience is radically contextual. All things are necessarily conditioned and quite empty of independent existence.
>
> Huntington, 1989: 109

The question of whether one can engage in debate (*kathā*) without holding a position of one's own continued in disputations between the Madhyamaka school and other systems of thought. For schools like the Nyāya, Nāgārjuna was a philosophical terrorist refusing to adhere to the rules of the game and yet claiming to have won nevertheless. From a Madhyamaka standpoint, Nāgārjuna was a philosophical 'freedom-fighter' pointing the way to liberation (*nirvāṇa*) and an end to the conceptual proliferation (*prapañca*) produced by the various philosophical schools. In this sense 'emptiness' is a kind of conceptual bomb which explodes the ontological and epistemological presuppositions of *pramāṇa* theory without replacing it with a theory of its own. For opponents of the Madhyamaka this was a nihilistic position. For Nāgārjuna and his followers, however, saying that all things are empty of an independent reality (*svabhāva-śūnya*) is a realisation of the conventional reality of entities and does not imply that there is *absolutely* nothing.

– NOTES –

1. An exception to this rule is the Vaiśeṣika scholar Vyomaśiva for whom *śabda* also was an independent source of knowledge.
2. The exception here is Bhāsarvajña who deviated from the standard Nyāya position in a number of respects (leading to his description by later thinkers as a *Nyāyaikadeśin* – see Matilal, 1977: 95). Bhāsarvajña did not accept comparison (*upamāna*) as an independent *pramāṇa*, and was probably influenced in this regard by the Yoga school (see *Yoga Sūtra* I.7), though such influence may have been indirect since Bhāsarvajña was a native of Kashmir and may have been following the Śaivite *Pratyabhijñā* (Recognition) school at this point.
3. The five members (*avayava*) of the Nyāya inference are made up of three terms – that which is to be proven (*sādhya*), the reason or ground for the inference (*hetu*) and the common locus of the two (*pakṣa*) – and two relations – pervasion (*vyāpti*) – that is, the relation of invariable concomitance between that which requires proof and the reason, and the relation between the reason and the common locus or *pakṣa* (*pakṣadharmatā*). See *Nyāya Sūtra* 1.1.32–9; 1.1.5; 2.1.37–8. For a discussion of the five-membered argument see Matilal, 1985: 29–42 and Potter, 1963: 59–78.
4. Vātsyāyana explains that the fallacy of 'mis-timing' refers not to examples of overly drawn-out argumentation but to the fallacies of equivocation in general. We can see that the formulation of the *vāda* rules and fallacies of reasoning occurred in a context of debating contests if we consider other examples of fallacies sometimes mentioned, such as 'proving what has already been accepted' (*siddhāsādhanatā*) – a technique of time-wasting during a debating session, and tautology (i.e. none of the terms offered in an inference should be identical to each other). For a discussion of the various types of fallacious reasoning see Potter, 1963: 75–89 and Matilal, 1985: 42–58.
5. Technically speaking, *tarka* is the means of assessing the validity of the relation of pervasion or universal concomitance (*vyāpti*) between the thesis requiring proof (*sādhya*) and the reason offered (*hetu*). As such it is the procedure for establishing the conclusion of an inference. Since one of the functions of *tarka* is to remove doubt, it is also an ancillary element to the establishment of the *pramāṇas* in general.
6. Maṇikaṇṭha argues that undesired outcome should more properly be classified as a fallacy of reasoning (*hetvābhāsa*) and is not an example of *tarka*. See Potter, 1977: 207; 671.
7. The account is based upon the scheme outlined in the *Tshad ma rigs gter dgongs rgyan* of Shākya-mchog-ldan, a fifteenth-century Tibetan Buddhist work on the Buddhist rules of debate (see Jackson, 1987: 197–9).
8. Ruegg (1986: 233–5) argues that 'What the Mādhyamika has disowned, then, is any thesis, assertion or view (*dṛṣṭi*) that posits the existence of some kind of *bhāva* or *dharma* possessing a *svabhāva*, and not all philosophical statements, doctrines and theories (*darśana*) without distinction … Nāgārjuna's statement "I have no *pratijñā*" may be interpreted in accordance with the more specific meaning 'thesis/assertion positing an entity' rather than in accordance with the wider meaning of philosophical

thesis (= doctrine and position) ... The Madhyamaka philosophy is rather a non-speculative and non-constructive discourse relating to non-substantial factors (*dharma*) originating in the structured conditionship of *pratītyasamutpāda*.'

9. The distinction between implicatory (nominally bound) and non-implicatory (verbally bound) negation is discussed by Patañjali the grammarian in commenting upon *Pāṇini Sūtra* 1.4.57 and 3.3.19.
10. One might legitimately ask how Dignāga and Dharmakīrti felt able to construct a system of thought based upon two *pramāṇas* (perception and inference) given Nāgārjuna's stinging critique. Avoiding Nāgārjuna's vicious circle (*cakraka*) may have been a central factor in Dignāga's re-definition of *pramāṇa* not as the instrument or cause of knowledge but as valid cognition itself. Conflating the means of knowledge with its fruit (*phala*) thereby provides support for the Yogācāra rejection of a distinction between cognitions and external objects and also represents an attempt to side-step Nāgārjuna's critique of the mutual dependence of *pramāṇa* and *prameya*. See Dignāga, *Pramāṇa-samuccaya* I. 8–11.
11. Unlike the Prāsaṅgika Madhyamaka and Cārvāka schools who both rejected the *pramāṇa* scheme, Śrīharṣa is a member of the non-dualistic (*advaita*) Vedānta tradition of Śaṅkara and accepts the practicalities of *pramāṇa* theory on a conventional or practical level. Phyllis Granoff (1978) and B. K. Matilal (for example, 1986: 65) tend to represent Śrīharṣa as a *vaitaṇḍika* with no positive program of his own but it is clear that Śrīharṣa upholds a radical monism (*advaita*) which he believes is established through the refutation of rival views. As Ram-Prasad (1993: 169–203) suggests, Śrīharṣa accepted the *pramāṇa-vāda* scheme but only as a means to an end, namely the refutation of all rival views and the establishment of non-dualism as the final position (*siddhānta*).
12. Cp. Nāgārjuna's *Vaidalyaprakaraṇapadārtha* 6 (*Sūtra* 31), where he denies that he accepts either an initial thesis (*siddhi ādi*) or a final thesis (*siddha anta).*

Chapter 7

Perception: Do we see things as they are?

– The Nature of Perception –

Philosophers have often argued that it is important to go 'back to basics' when trying to understand the nature of knowledge. There has always been a strong 'empiricist' vein within Indian philosophical thought which demands that thinkers take seriously the relationship between their theories and everyday perceptions of the world. Indeed, for schools like the materialist Cārvākas perception (*pratyakṣa*) constitutes the only reliable guide in our quest for true and certain knowledge. Nevertheless, all schools of Indian thought, whatever their specific world-view or ontological persuasion, have accepted the importance of perceptual experience as an independent source of knowledge (*pramāṇa*). Indeed, perception is considered by most schools to be the *pramāṇa par excellence*. As we have seen for instance in the case of the Nyāya school, inferential knowledge (*anumāna*) follows on from perceptual knowledge and lacks its immediacy (*aparokṣatva*). Certainly, any philosophical account of reality must take seriously the question of how it relates to our experience of the world. However, once one begins to consider what perception is and how it works, one realises that the task is not as easy as one might at first think.

In the early *Upaniṣads* perception is explained in terms of the self (*ātman*) as an inner light which shines outward (through the eyes) and illuminates the objective world (e.g. *Bṛhadāraṇyaka Upaniṣad* 4.3.6). In his anthropological study of Hindu conceptions of seeing (*darśan*) Lawrence Babb notes a similar model at work amongst contemporary Hindus

> In the Hindu world 'seeing' is clearly not conceived as a passive product of sensory data originating in the outer world, but rather seems to be imaged as an extrusive and acquisitive 'seeing flow' that emanates from the inner person, outward through the eyes, to engage directly with objects seen, and to bring something of those objects back to the seer. One comes into contact with and in a sense becomes what one sees.
>
> Babb, 1981: 396–7

According to the Sāṃkhya and Vedānta schools, in sensory perception the mind or 'inner organ' (*antaḥkaraṇa*) projects itself outwards and takes on the form (*vṛtti*) of the external object. Dharmarāja, a seventeenth century follower of Śaṅkara's Advaita Vedānta school describes this process of perception as an outpouring of light (*tejas*), akin to the flowing of water around an object,

> Just as the water of a tank, having come out of an aperture, enters a number of fields through channels assuming like [those] fields a quadrangular or any other form, so also, the internal organ, which is characterized by light, goes out [of the body] through the door [sense] of sight, etc., and [after] reaching the location of the object, say a pitcher, is modified in the form of the objects like a pitcher. This modification [of the internal organ] is called a mental mode (*vṛtti*).
>
> *Vedāntaparibhāṣā,* trans. in Gupta, 1991: 167–8

This view is likely to strike the westerner as highly unusual since western culture has generally assumed that perception occurs as a result of the external world confronting the subject, not the other way around. The ancient Greek atomist Democritus, for instance, explained visual perception in terms of a small number of atoms leaving an object and entering the eye. In a more sophisticated fashion modern conceptions of perception generally involve the idea of light 'bouncing off' objects and entering the eye where nerve impulses on the retina send messages to the brain which then organises the data (as well as inverting the image on the retina). How though do we get the impression that objects are located 'out there' at a distance from us? Contemporary neuropsychologists such as Karl H. Pribram have suggested a holographic model of perception to account for both the 'outwardness' of our experience and its gestalt-like qualities. This seems to have some similarities with the projective model of perception found in the Sāṃkhya and Vedānta schools (Kaplan, 1987) where the sense-organs are seen as 'moving outwards' (*prāpyakāri*) towards their object. Jadunath Sinha (1958: 137) remarks in this regard that 'it is much easier to conceive the *out-going* of the mind intelligized by the conscious self to the object than the *in-coming* of the unconscious object to the mind'.

In the Vedas the senses are described as minor deities (*devatā*) sent out into the world by major deities such as Indra. Hence they are known as 'forces sent out by Indra' (*indriya*). Within later Hindu culture the senses were often viewed as forces (*śakti*) which go out into the world in order to make contact with objects and gather information for the knowing self. As such the Hindu schools of thought generally distinguished between the physical location of the senses and the sense-organs themselves, seeing the latter as a capacity or force or even sometimes a distinct substance and the former as the material location of its activity. The Buddhist schools, however, rejected the Vedic mythological origins implied in such conceptions of the sense-organs and argued that the senses were not mysterious forces but were in fact identical with the material sockets (*golaka*) in which they are found. Thus, the visual organ is nothing more than the eye, the sense of hearing is nothing more than the ear etc.

For many schools of Indian thought the mind is also classified as a sixth sense-organ (*indriya*), apprehending mental objects but also acting as the organising faculty which constructs a coherent picture based upon the knowledge gained from all six (in this case) sense-organs.[1] Indeed, it is common to see the mind represented as a subtle form of matter, a position which avoids many of the philosophical problems entailed in western philosophy by the Cartesian dualism of mind and body. The most striking example of this is the Sāṃkhya school which characterises the mind as an evolute of primal matter (*prakṛti*) and thereby differentiates the immaterial principle of consciousness (*puruṣa*) from mental activity, which is thoroughly material in nature (see Chapter 8). This reflects a widely held view in ancient India that the mind derives its conscious properties not from itself but from a transcendent principle of consciousness or essential self (*ātman*). The Nyāya and Vaiśeṣika schools are sometimes represented as accepting the view that the mind is a material substance (e.g. Chennakesavan, 1980: 18) but this seems to be a misreading of their position (see NS 2.3.41; Shastri 1964: 136; J. Sinha, 1958: 19).

Nevertheless, the mind has rarely been conceived of as a *tabula rasa* or a passive recipient of perceptual knowledge in Indian culture, being actively involved in its acquisition, even in the Nyāya and Vaiśeṣika schools. This conception of the mind's active role in perceptual experiences gave Indian theories of perception a more 'idealistic edge' than one finds in western philosophy before Immanuel Kant (1724–1804). Kant's 'Copernican Revolution' which offered a 'new' understanding of experience as conditioned by the *a priori* categories of the mind (rather than simply a product of the nature of an external object) provided fresh impetus to debates about the nature of perception in modern western philosophy. Similar theories of perception existed in India, however, many centuries before the advent of the 'Enlightenment' period of European history.

> The almost universal acceptance in India of the doctrine of rebirth, along with the consequences of *karma*, could easily have swung all Indian philosophical systems to idealism. This doctrine holds that the multitudinous personal experiences of the present, as well as the expression of past acts carried in some residual and seminal form, by a transmigrating principle. When such a doctrine comes to be implemented by theories of being and knowledge, philosophy enters the discussion.

> And then it turns out that this doctrine could, but need not, give rise to an idealistic philosophy.
>
> Wayman, 1965: 65

The Nyāya and Vaiśeṣika schools both attempt to defend the view that perception involves a direct and unmediated apprehension of a real world of independent objects composed of primal and indestructible atomic substances. According to the *Nyāya Sūtra*

> Perception is that knowledge which arises from the contact (*samnikarṣa*) of a sense-organ with its object, and which is inexpressible (*avyapadeśya*), unerring (*avyabhicāra*) and of a determinate (*vyavasāyātmaka*) nature.
>
> *Nyāya Sūtra* I.1.4

Perception on this view is the result of contact between two independent factors – the sense-organs of a sentient being and a sense-object.[2] The Nyāya school rejects all attempts to say that our perception is in some way 'constructed' or 'created' by the mind. There is an independently existing world of objects 'out there' which one comes into direct contact with in the act of perception via the sense-organs. Such perceptions are immediate sensory apprehensions. They are not bound up with language (one does not need to name something to experience it), do not mislead and remain amenable to determinate classification. The grammarian philosopher Bhartṛhari rejected the Nyāya view that perception did not involve language on the grounds that knowledge would be impossible without the mediation of linguistic forms (*śabda*). Vātsyāyana, however, cites the experience of the child as evidence that perceptions are not always associated with words (NB 1.1.4), though even in this case Bhartṛhari appeals to previous rebirths and the notion of *karma* as evidence that the experiences of infants are also implicated in linguistic structures.

For the Nyāya school there were four types of independently established valid knowledge, viz, perception, inference, reliable-testimony (*śabda* – or as Nyāya puts it – *āpta* – a trustworthy person or reliable source) and analogy. Of these four sources it is probably perception that is considered to be the most basic. Indeed, with the exception of radical sceptics such as Sañjaya (mentioned in the early Buddhist literature) and critics of *pramāṇa* theory such as Nāgārjuna, Śrīharṣa and Jayarāśī, *pratyakṣa* is the only *pramāṇa* accepted by all schools of Indian philosophy. Nevertheless, the Nyāya needed to develop a response to the philosophical gauntlet thrown down by the sceptic – "how do you know," the sceptic asks, "that what you are now perceiving is not an illusion?" Take, for example, the familiar Indian example of the rope which is 'erroneously perceived' as a snake. How can one be sure which (if either) is a correct perception of reality? Is it a rope, a snake or something else? In response to such questions Vācaspati Miśra (apparently influenced in this regard by his teacher Trilocana) made a distinction between two types of perception, or, if you like, two stages in the perceptual process:

1. Determinate perception or perception with concepts – *savikalpaka pratyakṣa*, and
2. Indeterminate or non-conceptual perception – *nirvikalpaka pratyakṣa*

Earlier Naiyāyikas such as Vātsyāyana interpret *Nyāya Sūtra* 1.1.4 as a singular definition applicable to *all* sense-perceptions before the intervention of determinate classifications by the mind. Sense-perception is direct awareness of an object and precedes concept-classification. For Vācaspati and subsequent Nyāya thought, however, Gautama's definition denotes two stages in the perceptual process. The first stage – indeterminate (*nirvikalpa*) perception – referred to the initial contact between a sense-organ and its object that occurs before the object has been named or determined. This is what Gautama refers to as nonverbal and unerring. Non-conceptual or indeterminate perception cannot be erroneous since it amounts to a pre-determinate, sensory apprehension of an object – it is what one actually sees, hears, feels, smells or tastes at a preliminary level. It also cannot be verbalised since it has yet to be determined or subsumed under conceptual categories (*vikalpa*). However, one is still capable of wrongly conceiving what one perceives, as in the case where one sees a rope, but thinks that it is a snake. Thus, as far as the Nyāya is concerned, false perceptions can and do occur but only in the case of determinate or conceptual perception (*savikalpaka pratyakṣa*). In all cases of perception, therefore, whether true or false, there is an initial contact and non-conceptual (*nirvikalpa*) apprehension of reality. For the Nyāya school, therefore, error is the misapprehension of one thing as something else (*anyathākhyāti*). Error occurs because of a defect in the sense-organ, because only partial apprehension of the object has occurred or finally because one mistakenly identifies an object based upon associations remembered from previous experiences.

How does one distinguish then between erroneous and true perceptions? The Nyāya school argues that perceptions are verified in terms of their practical efficacy. For instance, if we consider the rope–snake example, poking the object with a stick (hopefully a very long one!) to see if it reacts, or shining light upon it will help to clarify one's initial perception. If the object does not move then one can assume that it is not a live snake. When light is shed upon it one might then see that it is indeed a rope. At this stage one has established that the initial sight was wrong since it did not stand up to the scrutiny of later evidence and experience. Clearly, the Nyāya principle is one based upon empirical evidence and continued experimentation. The appeal to the practicalities of everyday life (*vyavahāra*), as in Vātsyāyana's defence of the *pramāṇas*, is pragmatically oriented but we should not confuse the Nyāya position with pragmatism, where truth is established according to efficacy. The Naiyāyika strictly adheres to a correspondence theory of truth in the sense that truth is that which corresponds to the way things really are. From a Nyāya point of view the overcoming of errors or false perceptions leads to a clearer apprehension of reality as it is. As a consequence, the Naiyāyika argues, one finds that things tend to work or fit together better and is no longer beset by the anxiety (*duḥkha*) caused by adherence to false views about reality.

The distinction between conceptual/determinate and non-conceptual/indeterminate perception is first drawn by the fifth-century Buddhist Dignāga (c. 480–540 CE), though even here Dignāga was probably inspired by Gautama's definition of perception as 'non-verbal' in *Nyāya Sūtra* 1.1.4. For Dignāga, sense-perception (*pratyakṣa*) does not involve conceptualisation (*kalpanā*) – it is immediate and non-conceptual. This position is directly opposed to that of Bhartṛhari, for whom all experience is implicated in language (i.e. is *savikalpaka*). For Dignāga the initial sensory apprehension of reality becomes mediated by conceptual constructions (*kalpanā*) arising in the mind. What we apprehend with our senses in its unmediated givenness is the particular instant (*svalakṣaṇa*) that characterises what is really there. However, the picture of reality that we, as unenlightened beings, construct is the product of the association of our 'pure sensations' with linguistic forms – such as names (*nāma*), categories (*jāti*) and concepts in general – acquired from our linguistic and cultural context (*Pramāṇa-samuccaya* I.3). These, Dignāga argues, result in a misapprehension of reality since they derive from the construction of universals (*sāmānya-lakṣaṇa*) in a world in which only unique particulars (*sva-lakṣaṇa*) exist.

This is a crucial point worth underlining. For pluralistic realists such the Mīmāṃsakas and the Naiyāyikas the determinate (*savikalpaka*) stage of perception arises purely out of the object itself (*śuddhavastuja*) and involves analysis and judgements about the nature of the bare given (*ālocana*). Determinate perception, therefore, enables one to know precisely what one is perceiving. The conceptualisation process clarifies our experience and does not fundamentally add anything extraneous to it. Indeed, for the New Nyāya the very idea that pre-conceptual perception can be described as a form of awareness is called into question. For Dignāga the Buddhist philosopher however only the initial non-conceptual (*nirvikalpa*) perception of the bare particular (*svalakṣaṇa*) counts as a true perception. Sensory perception cannot involve concepts (*kalpanā*). Conceptualisation takes place however when the initial moment of bare sensory awareness is subjected to a superimposition or addition (*yojanā*) of names and categories, thereby distorting our experience of reality (Hattori, 1968: n. 3.7, 122). We should bear in mind also that the ultimate goal of Dignāga's system of thought is, of course, to liberate the Buddhist practitioner from attachment to these linguistic and cultural forms through the meditative cultivation of the mind (*citta-bhāvanā*), ethical discipline (*śīla*) and the development of analytical insight (*prajñā*). Eventually, through effort and vigilant practice, one is able to overcome these false constructions and see reality as it truly is (i.e. attain enlightenment).

– PERCEPTION IN ADVAITA VEDĀNTA: RECONCILING THE EVERYDAY WORLD AND MONISM –

The Advaita Vedānta school propounds a philosophy of radical monism. Plurality and separateness are an illusion (*māyā*). How is one to make sense of this claim given that it seems to contradict perceptual experience at the most basic level? In the *Gauḍapādīya Kārikā* (sixth century CE), probably the earliest text to propound the Vedāntic philosophy of non-dualism (*advaita*), duality is described unambiguously as an illusory appearance (*māyā*) caused by the vibrations of consciousness (*citta-spanditā*). The experience of diversity in the waking state is compared to the illusory creation of a diverse world by the mind during a dream (3.29). According to Gauḍapāda, the reputed author of the text, 'consciousness does not make contact with an object, nor even the appearance of an object.' This is because the object is unreal and not different from the consciousness which perceives it (4.26). This view is clearly influenced by Yogācāra Buddhist philosophy (see below) and appears to equate dreaming and waking experiences as equally illusory, though there remains some debate about the precise implications of this view (see King 1995; Kaplan 1987).

The thinker most firmly associated with the Vedāntic philosophy of non-dualism is Śaṅkara (eighth century CE). Here we are in no doubt that Advaita philosophy is strongly associated with epistemological realism. In his commentary on the *Brahma Sūtra* Śaṅkara distinguishes between dreaming and waking experience on the grounds that the latter alone corresponds to an independent and external world of objects (BS Bh 2.2.28–9). Of course, from the point of view of the ultimate truth (*paramārtha-satya*) even our experience of a world of many objects must be overturned by the realisation of the non-dual nature of reality, but this does not prevent Śaṅkara from adopting a realist position with regard to the empirical level of truth (*vyavahārika satya*) and providing a staunch critique of the Yogācāra school of Buddhism.

How then does the Advaitin account for the apparently radical discrepancy between our experience of duality and the undifferentiated nature of ultimate reality? Our mistaken perception of a world of many different things is explained by Śaṅkara in terms of the notion of *adhyāsa* – superimposition or projection. This is defined by Śaṅkara in the introduction to the *Brahma Sūtra Bhāṣya* as 'the apparent presentation of something previously observed in some other thing.' It is the error of mixing up the qualities of what is 'not-self' with the qualities of the self and is clearly influenced by the Sāṃkhya idea of discriminating between the principle of consciousness (*puruṣa*) and the inanimate material world (*prakṛti*).[3]

For Śaṅkara the error of superimposition is a result of the beginningless cycle of ignorance (*avidyā*) which perpetuates the cycle of rebirths (*saṃsāra*). As a result there is a false identification of the self (*ātman*) with what is not-self, namely the mind–body complex which undergoes change and the empirical self (*jīvātman*) which transmigrates from one body to another. To grasp the non-dualistic nature of ultimate reality and the essential identity of the self (*ātman*) with the ground of all being (*brahman*), requires the disassociation of one's essential self (*ātman*) from the activities of the empirical self (*jīvātman*). What really constitutes the self is the unchanging principle of identity which persists throughout various incarnations. However, upon discovering that one is an immutable supreme self (*paramātman*) one realises that this real self never really took part in the rebirth process at all, other than as a witness-consciousness (*sākṣin*). Upon attaining enlightenment one realises that the world is nothing more than an illusory appearance (*māyā*) of the absolute *brahman* which appears as a manifold world because of the superimposition of qualities or limiting adjuncts (*upādhi*). Having eradicated the ignorance (*avidyā*) which causes this misapprehension of reality, one understands one's true nature as the unoriginated (*ajāta*) and immutable *brahman*.

The classic example used by Śaṅkara to explain how superimposition causes us to misapprehend reality is the analogy of the rope and the snake. In this regard Śaṅkara is clearly indebted to the theory of error propounded by the Mīmāṃsā thinker Prabhākara. According to this view the perception of a snake in a rope is an apparent perception of a real entity (a snake) previously observed elsewhere and now remembered. One could not mistake the rope for a snake unless one already knew what a snake was. This is how perception works according to Śaṅkara, by the superimposition (*adhyāsa*) of remembered qualities onto things that do not really possess those qualities.[4] Through ignorance (*avidyā*) one makes the mistake of thinking that the self is a changing and transmigrating agent. Preventing this superimposition through the attainment of knowledge (*vidyā*) leads to a correct apprehension of reality.

Śaṅkara's theory of superimposition is reminiscent in some respects of Kant's notion of the 'transcendental imagination' – in that we build a picture of reality based upon the manifold of impressions received through the sense-organs which are then structured according to certain concepts that we already possess. A significant difference, however, is that Kant thought that many of these concepts or categories were *a priori*, that is, given before experience, being a necessary part of our sensory and intellectual make-up. In contrast, Śaṅkara attributed such categories to experiences gained in the past, including previous embodiments. Śaṅkara here utilises the notion of *saṃskāra* – the notion of 'subliminal potencies' – produced by past karmic actions. It is these *saṃskāras* which cause us again and again to see reality in a similarly patterned manner. On an individual level our experiences can be seen to be a peculiar construction of our own tendencies and dispositions. Each person's perception of reality is conditioned by the memory of their past experiences – their *karmic* baggage if you like. We perceive what we are capable of and expect to perceive. The past experiences that we have accumulated in the beginningless (*anādi*) series of embodiments one has undergone leads to the construction of habitual forms of thinking. One becomes accustomed to experiencing the world in a certain way. There is a need, therefore, to uproot the *saṃskāras* which perpetuate our lives in the same old patterns, bad habits and misguided directions.

For Kant, however, the *a priori* categories constitute the unbreachable conditions of possibility for human experience. These are incontrovertible and binding – as humans we must experience the world according to certain structuring categories such as space and time. Śaṅkara, however, constructs his entire philosophical system based upon the principle that one can transcend the cognitive limitations of current modes of perception and attain the immediacy (*aparokṣatva*) of a direct-cognition of *brahman* (*brahmānubhava*). For Advaitins with a Mīmāṃsaka inclination, such as Maṇḍana Miśra and the subsequent Bhāmatī strand of Advaita, such a process involves the purification of one's cognitive faculties through yogic practice. For Śaṅkara, however, actions cannot produce such a knowledge. Rather, one must turn to the insights of the Vedic teachings in order to bring such a realisation of *brahman* to the fore. Only then can one hope to halt the process of superimposing categories or limiting adjuncts (*upādhi*) onto the non-dual reality that is our true and essential nature.

The significance of the adjuncts (*upādhi*) is that they appear to limit that which they are applied to but in reality do not. *Brahman* appears as a diversity but in fact remains forever unchanged. Note also that Śaṅkara's use of the rope–snake analogy reflects his realist stance. False appearances (such as the snake) do not appear from nowhere. Rather, they presuppose an actually existing substrative reality (*sad-adhiṣṭhāna*) i.e. *brahman,* as the ground of all being (the rope).

> Something unreal is denied on the basis of something real, as for instance a snake etc. on a rope etc. And that is possible only if some positive entity is left over (after the denial). For should everything be denied, what other positive substratum will be left over?
>
> *Brahma Sūtra Bhāṣya* 3.2.22, trans. in Gambhirananda, 1977: 625

Śaṅkara clearly propounds a realist theory of perception and attacks the Yogācāra position in his *Brahma Sūtra Bhāṣya* for their apparent denial of the reality of an external world of objects existing independently of our experience of them. In that sense one can describe his position as a form of empirical realism. However, he maintains a distinction between two levels and truth and believes that our ordinary perception of reality is faulty, being based upon our own ignorance. His final position then is that the empirical world is an illusion (*māyā*). The world is empirically real but not absolutely real. Although one can talk of the world as an effect of *brahman*, it is really just *brahman* (see Chapter 9). Our experience of a world of separate things, therefore, must be 'sublated', that is, overturned by the higher knowledge of *brahman*. Thus,

> the world of manifestations standing opposed to the realization of Brahman has to be sublated by one who wants to realize Brahman; for this phenomenal universe of manifestations has Brahman as its essence and not that Brahman has the phenomenal manifestations as Its essence.
>
> *Brahma Sūtra Bhāṣya* 3.2.21, trans. in Gambhirananda, 1977: 620

Śaṅkara's account, however, can hardly be described as a systematic Advaita theory of perception. The earliest attempt to provide such an account is found in *The Demonstration of Brahman* (*Brahma Siddhi*), a work by Śaṅkara's older contemporary and rival, Maṇḍana Miśra (seventh to eighth century CE). Whereas Śaṅkara asks us to focus upon the transcendental subjectivity of our own consciousness in order to distinguish the self from what it is not (see BS *Bhāṣya* 1.1.4), Maṇḍana is more concerned with establishing the non-dual nature of the self and the world. This requires that some account be taken of our experience of the world of objects. In this regard Maṇḍana is clearly influenced, as his predecessor Gauḍapāda was, by Yogācāra reflections upon the same subject.

Maṇḍana's philosophical position is known as *Sattādvaita* or the 'Non-Duality of Being', since it is his view that all things are undifferentiated or non-dual by virtue of their existence – that is, the presence of being (*sat*) within them.[5] What one perceives is the pure form of being (*sad-rūpa*) itself. The problem of perception for the Advaita tradition was how one reconciles the everyday experience of a plurality of different objects with the view that everything is basically undifferentiated or non-dual in nature. On the face of it the Advaita position seems counter-intuitive – how can one claim that everything is one if we do not experience the world as such? The crucial issue here concerns the status of the process of differentiation itself. Maṇḍana discusses three possible views concerning the way in which diversity or difference (*bheda*) is given in perception. They are:

1. Only difference (*bheda*) between things is grasped in perception
2. Both object and difference are grasped in perception.

This itself breaks down into three possible views:

2a. The object and difference are apprehended simultaneously
2b. Difference is perceived and then the object is perceived.
2c. The object is perceived and then difference is perceived.
3. Only the object is perceived.

Maṇḍana argues that 1., 2a. and 2b. are all false because difference is a relational category and therefore already presupposes the existence of objects. One cannot have difference without first apprehending an object. In this regard Maṇḍana is following a similar line of argument put forward by Nāgārjuna in Chapter 14 of his *Verses on the Middle Way*. This leaves Maṇḍana with only two possibilities – 2c. and 3. According to Maṇḍana 2c. is a misunderstanding of what it is to perceive something. Following the distinction first made by Dignāga between perception as the non-conceptual (*nirvikalpa*) apprehension of the bare given and the involvement of conceptual constructions (*vikalpa*) in the subsequent interpretation of that event, Maṇḍana argues that perception is immediate and cannot be analysed into stages. One cannot say then that perception involves grasping an object and then grasping the difference between that object and everything else. Difference is a concept (*vikalpa*) and is the result of the activities of consciousness rather than a feature of reality itself. For Maṇḍana, therefore, difference is not given in immediate perception, it is subsequently superimposed (*samāropa*) upon the experience of the bare object.

> Perception is first, without conceptual distinctions (*avikalpaka*), and has the bare object (*vastu-mātra*) as its sense-object. However, the conceptual distinctions which follow it descend into particulars (*viśesa*).
>
> *Brahma Siddhi* 71. 1–2

This is a clever move by Maṇḍana since it provides a response to the strongest argument put forward by opponents of the Advaita position, namely that the monistic philosophy of Advaita is counter-intuitive, does not conform to our everyday experience and is continually contradicted by our perception of a multiplicity of objects. For Maṇḍana *brahman* is directly given in every perception, but the immediacy of the non-dual nature of reality is lost in the subsequent act of conceptualisation. Thus, it is the conditioning patterns and ignorance of our own minds which cause us to construct a manifold world from the non-duality of the bare given (*vastu-mātra*).

Maṇḍana maintains that the apprehension of difference is dependent upon two factors: an objective-support, that is, a real object which can then be distinguished from something else, and a distinguishing consciousness. Difference then becomes a quality that is derived from the distinguishing faculties of the mind and not a defining feature of the world, and our experience of diversity is in some sense caused by our own faulty apprehension of reality. What is required, therefore, is that we 'cleanse the doors of perception' in order to realise our identity with *brahman* and the rest of the universe. An identity, ironically, that we are directly perceiving at this very moment if we did but know it! Thus, as Allen Thrasher notes,

> [Maṇḍana] works in a different manner from Śaṃkara, less by separating the Self from *avidyā* and the world than by examining the world and finding Brahman in it, showing that difference (*bheda*) is not given in our ordinary direct experience. For him 'the universe is non-dual' [*Brahma Siddhi* 51.8–9; 67.12] it 'has positive being through Brahman's positive being' [*Brahma Siddhi* 20.11–12].
>
> Thrasher, 1993: 31

Maṇḍana, of course, is clearly reliant upon Dignāga's analysis in his refusal to accept that conceptualisation is a part of the perceptual process.[6] Indeed, for both thinkers, perception is the immediate apprehension of an object and in that sense is not a process at all. Where the two thinkers differ, of course, is in the implications that they draw from this position. Dignāga argues that what one directly apprehends is the unique particular (*svalakṣaṇa*) – that is, the momentary *dharma*, and that this ceases upon its manifestation. What is given in the immediacy of perceptual apprehension therefore is a stream of evanescent particulars. Such a view is, of course, in line with a pluralistic Abhidharma ontology of complex momentary processes. Maṇḍana, in contrast, argues that the Buddhist position amounts to theory 1. – the view that difference (*bheda*) is what is given in perception. Clearly, for Maṇḍana the notion of a unique particular (*svalakṣaṇa*) necessarily implies some recognition of difference. However, difference, so Maṇḍana has already argued, is a concept and so cannot be given in the immediacy of the perceptual event. Rather, he argues, what one actually perceives is the undifferentiated mark of the universal (*sāmānya-lakṣaṇa*), or the non-dual nature of reality itself. For the Buddhist Dignāga, of course, universals are mental constructs (*vikalpa*) and are subsequent to the perceptual act. Far from being an undifferentiated unity, the world is constituted by a stream of evanescent processes or events and is considerably more complex and dynamic than one might think.

– THE IMAGE THEORY OF PERCEPTION (*SĀKĀRA-JÑĀNA-VĀDA*) –

Notice the emphasis that the early Nyāya placed upon perception as direct contact (*saṃnikarṣa*) between a sense-object and the sense-organs – a theory of direct realism. This position was found to be problematic by other schools and led to the development of rival explanations of the perceptual process. Unlike Hindu forms of direct realism, the Buddhist Vaibhāṣikas accepted the Abhidharma analysis of external objects into momentary events (*dharmas*). Perception is direct but it is not of material objects such as tables and chairs. Rather, what we perceive are qualities such as colour and taste. Direct realism, however, whether grounded in what might be called a 'common-sense' realism of objects as in the Nyāya, Vaiśeṣika and Mīmāṃsā schools, or in close attention to appearances as in the phenomenalistic realism of the Vaibhāṣikas, has the problem of making sense of the idea that objective realities 'out there' can come into direct contact with the mind of a perceiver. In what sense do I perceive a table rather than a series of visual and tactile sensory impressions which I then make sense of in terms of the notion of a 'table'? This is a particular problem for the Hindu schools though even in the case of the Vaibhāṣikas there is the question of the ontological status of the qualities apprehended in perception. In what sense are these momentary events independent of the mind?

The Buddhist Sautrāntika school upholds a form of indirect realism, that is, external objects exist but are not perceived in an unmediated and direct fashion. The school therefore propounds a representational theory of perception – what we perceive are images (*ākāra*) and not objects in themselves. This was in response to what was seen as the naivety of the direct realism of the Vaibhāṣika school of Buddhism. The image-theory of perception is also propounded in the Sāṃkhya and Vedānta schools of Hindu thought and bears some resemblance to the sense-data theory which Russell describes in terms that are rather reminiscent of Dignāga:

> Let us give the name of 'sense-data' to the things that are immediately known in sensation: such things as colours, sounds, smells, hardnesses, roughnesses and so on. We shall give the name 'sensation' to the experience of being immediately aware of these things. Thus, whenever we see a colour, we have a sensation *of* the

> colour but the colour itself is a sense-datum, not a sensation. The colour is that *of* which we are immediately aware, and the awareness itself is the sensation. It is plain that if we are to know anything about the table, it must be by means of the sense-data – brown colour, oblong shape, smoothness etc. – which we associate with the table; but ... we cannot say that the table is the sense-data, or even that the sense-data are directly properties of the table. Thus a problem arises as to the relation of the sense-data to the real table, supposing there is such a thing.
>
> Russell, 1982: 4

The Yogācāra school of Mahāyāna Buddhism took the Sautrāntika image-theory of perception (*sākāra-jñāna-vāda*) one stage further and argued that if we only perceive images (*ākāra*), we are unable to infer from this that there are external causes (*nimitta*) for these images. The Yogācāra therefore initiated a new system of thought based upon the image-theory of perception and attempted to explain our experiences based upon the dynamics of consciousness and karmic fruition rather than in terms of interactions with an independently existing and external world of objects. All knowledge-events, the Yogācāra argued, are fundamentally mental in nature. Indeed, it makes no sense, so the school argued, for the Sautrāntika to infer the existence of external objects as the cause (*nimitta*) of our experiences as one can never verify this inference since all that one ever experiences are mental images. One does not require the postulation of external objects as the cause of our perceptions to make sense of the world – all that one experiences in perception are the images (*ākāra*) or mental-representations of objects (*vijñapti-mātra*), never any objects-in-themselves. Thus, for the Yogācāra, when perceiving 'external objects' consciousness is actually perceiving itself (*sva-saṃvedana*). Thus the school propounded a sophisticated theory of experience involving eight (later nine) types of consciousness. These involved the postulation of a type of consciousness-event (*citta or vijñāna*) for each sense-organ (six in all, including the mind), an organising faculty (*mano-vijñāna*) and an underlying (sub)-consciousness, known as the store-consciousness (*ālayavijñāna*). In line with the Buddhist emphasis upon process, these eight categories represented cognitive functions and not substantive entities. There is no permanent consciousness that can be grasped onto as an-abiding-self. Rather each type of consciousness (*vijñāna* or *citta*) denotes a series of momentary cognitive events.

The Yogācāra school has often been described as a form of idealism and most of the school's opponents have represented the school as repudiating the existence of an external world. However, this interpretation has been criticised by a number of scholars (Wayman, 1965; Kochumottum, 1982; Sutton, 1991; Harris, 1991; King, 1995) and it is certainly possible to interpret the early Yogācāra literature as an attempt to remain within the confines of a purely phenomenological discourse in a manner reminiscent of the Abhidharma enterprise (King, 1994, 1995, 1998). The issue here is whether the Yogācāra is primarily making an epistemological point (all that we experience are representations or mental images) or an ontological one (only cognitive representations exist, see Griffiths, 1986: 82–3). The former rejects the question of the independent existence of external objects as unanswerable (*avyākṛta*) and irrelevant to a phenomenological account of experience, whilst the latter involves an explicit denial of an external world. Problems here involve making sense of the distinctiveness of the Yogācāra discourse and clarifying what one means by 'idealism'. As I have stated elsewhere, the Yogācāra notions of *citta* and *vijñāna* denote a far wider range of phenomena than those usually associated in the west with the mind,

> The '*citta*' of *cittamātra* includes within it the conscious apprehension of sensory objects (six in all including the *mano-vijñāna*) ... Objects are really *dharma*-constructs and representations (*vijñapti*), dependent upon the complex processes of *citta* for their appearance. Thus, one can talk of apprehending a sensory object only *after* one has become conscious of it. Sensory apprehension is thereby subsumed by the Yogācāra analysis under the broader domain of '*citta*', which now more clearly than ever, remains too rich and all-embracing a term to be rendered by 'mind' or 'consciousness'. As well as an awareness of sensory objects, *citta* also denotes the organizing faculty of the *manas*, the affective distortion of that process by the defiled mind (*kliṣṭa manas*) as well as the subliminal karmic seeds (*saṃskāras*) and latent dispositions (*anuśaya*) that are collectively known as the *ālayavijñāna*.
>
> King, 1998: 12

However one interprets the school (and there seem to have been a variety of perspectives even within the school itself), the Yogācara system clearly rejected the language of 'externality' as superfluous and, building upon the phenomenalistic tendencies of the Abhidharma traditions, developed a sophisticated 'psychological' interpretation of the operations of *karma* and rebirth. The actions (*karman*) that we perform leave 'perfume traces' (*vāsanā*) which become embedded as seeds (*bīja*) within the store-consciousness, which acts as a kind of subconscious repository of past experiences. These karmic seeds come to fruition at a later time and perpetuate our experience of suffering (*duḥkha*) until such time as we learn to uproot them and release ourselves from karmic attachment and the incessant wheel of rebirth (*saṃsāra*). The Yogācāra account, therefore, is an attempt to provide a phenomenological account of experience based solely upon the transformation of consciousness (*vijñāna-pariṇāma*) and does not thereby involve the postulation of ontological entities, such as external objects, in order to explain our experiences.

The Yogācāra position, however, is not a form of subjective idealism or solipsism. We live in a shared world perceived according to our karmic attachments. In his *Twenty Verses* (*Viṃśatikā*), for instance, Vasubandhu argues that one need not resort to the notion of external objects in order to explain the existence of a shared world of experience, since the similarity of karma between the various streams of consciousness is sufficient in itself for the establishment of conventions and a similarity in experiences in different consciousness-streams. Moreover, there are a whole host of other beings whose experience of reality is quite different, such as animal, inhabitants of hellish realms and gods. Reality appears as it does according to our past karmic actions. No other factor is required as an explanation.

The rejection of the postulation of external causes to our perceptions, however, did not prevent the Yogācāra school from making distinctions between 'internal' experiences and experiences of sense-objects, since these are legitimate phenomenological distinctions that present themselves to consciousness. Thus, a distinction can still be drawn between a sense-object (*viṣaya*) and that object as it occurs as an objective support (*ālambana*) of consciousness. Yogācāra philosophy, however, was not limited to image-theory (*sākāra-vāda)* as a feature of all types of experience. As Edward Conze notes,

> The bare statement denying the existence of external objects belongs to a fairly low and preliminary stage of realisation, and though it may loom large in the philosophical discussions with rival schools, it is no more than a stepping stone to better things. The real point of asserting the unreality of an object *qua* object is to further the withdrawal from all external objective supports (*ālambana*), both through the increasing introversion of transic meditation and through the advance of the higher stages of a Bodhisattva's career.
>
> Conze 1962: 252

In the higher stages of yogic practice one is said to attain states of meditative concentration (*samādhi*) that are completely devoid of a determinate or conceptual content (*nirvikalpa*). This led some Yogācārins to propound a doctrine of *nirākāra-vāda* ('doctrine of no images') with reference to the highest stages of meditative attainment. For these Yogācārins all everyday perceptions were constituted by nothing more than mental images (*vijñapti-mātra*). These images, however, could be relinquished through advanced meditative practice and culminated in the eradication not only of 'mental representations' (*vijñapti-mātra*), but also of the idea of a cognising mind (*citta*) or subjective correlate within experience. This 'no-mind' (*acitta*) tradition conceived of the highest stage of attainment in terms of the complete realisation of emptiness, which is understood here as the absence of the duality *(dvaya)* of subject and object within the stream of consciousness-events.

Rigorous defenders of perceptual realism such as the Buddhist Vaibhāṣikas and the Hindu schools of Nyāya-Vaiśeṣika and Mīmāṃsā can also be said to have propounded a theory of perception without images (*nirākāra-vāda*), but for radically different reasons. In these schools the theory of no-images was firmly grounded in a thoroughgoing realism which saw perception as the *direct* contact between the sense-organs and external objects. Consciousness is like a light which shines outward and illuminates objects but does not undergo modification (*vṛtti*) or require any intermediaries. For these schools the lack of an image as a mediating factor in our experience of external objects was taken to be a universal feature of all types of perception. The Nyāya position for instance, is based upon the principle that 'whatever is, is both knowable and nameable' (*astitva jñeyatva abhidheyatva,* cited in Potter, 1977: 48). The Nyāya point is that if something exists, it must be both knowable and nameable, and should not be taken to mean that if one can know and name something then it must exist, since one can know and name things that clearly do not exist. As the preeminent school of realism in Indian thought, it was important for the Nyāya to establish that we know objects *directly* through our perception of them and that they are amenable to definitive classification or designation. Without these features (problematised by an acceptance of some intermediary principle between our perceptions and the world – such as in image-theory) it would have been difficult for the Nyāya to establish the independent reality of the external world based upon its own epistemological criteria.[7]

The various brahmanical schools (Nyāya, Vaiśeṣika, Mīmāṃsā, Vedānta, Sāṃkhya, Yoga and the *vyākaraṇa* or school of linguistic analysis) all tend to accept the necessity of a real substratum as the basis for perception. For the Nyāya and Vaiśeṣika systems even the perception of an illusion (e.g. a snake) requires something real that is being misperceived (the rope). In contrast, the Buddhist Abhidharma traditions rejected 'the myth of the substratum' as the positing of a mysterious and metaphysical level of reality that is not given in experience. On the issue of the reliability of sense-perceptions, however, the schools differ across traditional Brahmanical and Buddhist lines. Pluralistic realists such as the Nyāya–Vaiśeṣika and Mīmāṃsā-Vedānta schools see the conceptualisation process as establishing precisely what it is that one is perceiving. The Advaita Vedānta and Yoga traditions, however, in common with the various Buddhist schools, question the role played by concepts (*vikalpa*) in the establishment of knowledge about reality. For these schools conceptualisation either distorts reality or represents only a provisional representation of it. On this view concepts make reality appear other than it is. The world-views that are derived from this scepticism about conceptual knowledge differ quite radically, nevertheless, ranging from monism in the case of Advaita Vedānta, dualism in the case of Yoga (see Chapter 8) and a pluralism of momentary events (*dharmas*) in the case of the Buddhist Abhidharma systems.

– NOTES –

1. *Nyāya Sūtra* 1.1.9 distinguishes the mind from the sense-organs in its list of the twelve objects of veridical knowledge (*prameya*). Vātsyāyana, however, argues that the mind is a sense-organ but is distinguished from the other five in the *Sūtra* because they are composed of material elements (*bhautika*), have specific objects and can only function when endowed with certain attributes (*guṇa*) corresponding to their objects. The mind, on the other hand, is immaterial (*abhautika*), takes everything as its object (*sarva-viṣaya*) and functions as a sense-organ without requiring the specific qualities pertaining to the object it perceives (*Nyāya Bhāṣya* I.1.4). This view was important for Vātsyāyana as a response to the objection that the Nyāya definition of perception as involving contact between sense-organ and object (see below) cannot occur in the case of internal perceptions such as the experience of pleasure or pain. Within the Advaita Vedānta tradition the Bhamatī interpretation of Vācaspati Miśra accepts Vātsyāyana's view that the mind is a sixth sense-organ, but this is rejected by the Vivaraṇa interpretation which defines perception in terms of immediacy (*aparokṣatva*). Consequently, internal perceptions (e.g. of pleasure and pain) do not require the mind to be classified as a sense-organ.
2. The early Nyāya definition of perception is based upon the paradigm of sensory perception and does not consider the question of the extraordinary perception of yogic practitioners (*yogī-pratyakṣa)* which was ignored by early Naiyāyikas such as Uddyotakara and Vātsyāyana, though this topic is mentioned in *Vaiśeṣika Sūtra* IX.1.11–15. In his *Nyāyasāra* (The Essence of Nyāya), Bhāsarvajña re-defines *pratyakṣa* as right and direct (*aparokṣa*) intuition (*anubhāva*) thus encompassing the experience of yogic perception. On *nirvikalpa pratyakṣa* in Navya Nyāya see Matilal, 1985: 210–15.
3. Certainly there is a sub-commentary (*vivaraṇa*) on the *Yoga Sūtra Bhāṣya* attributed to Śaṅkara and it has been suggested that this may be an early work of Śaṅkara's reflecting former allegiances (Hacker, 1968, in Halbfass, 1995: 101–34).
4. In later Advaita this position was developed into a distinctive theory of error which argued that the objects of erroneous perceptions were not explicable either as existent or non-existent entities (*anirvacanīya-khyāti*). The point is that our experience of snakes, even if erroneous, is a real experience, yet once we have determined that the object of perception is in actual fact a rope, we know that the snake is not real. The snake experience then is neither completely unreal (I did see a snake), nor is it real (I later realised that my experience was caused by a rope). The Advaita tradition develops the notion of 'the inexplicable' (*anirvacanīya*) to explain the 'ambiguous' ontological status of the empirical world. The world is not a completely unreal illusion, but neither is it an ultimate reality. It is *māyā*, that is, unexplainable in terms of the categories of existence (*sat*) and non-existence (*asat*).
5. Maṇḍana argues that there are two types of realities – positive and negative, and that the

existence of negative realities (a view which seems to derive from his Mīmāṃsā background) does not compromise the non-dualistic position that he adopts.

6. Crucially, however, although Maṇḍana accepted that perception was non-conceptual (*nirvikalpa*), he seems to have distinguished conceptual knowledge from linguistic or verbal knowledge (*śabda*), allowing for the possibility of a non-conceptual but nevertheless linguistic mode of apprehension. Maṇḍana's approach then is particularly noteworthy for his attempt to bring together apparently conflicting elements from Dignāga's and Bhartṛhari's philosophies into a grand synthesis. Like Dignāga, Maṇḍana argued that direct-perception was non-conceptual (*nirvikalpa*) in nature. However, he also promulgated a form of *śabdādvaita* (non-dualism of the word), and therefore seems to have accepted Bhartṛhari's view that all knowledge is linguistic in nature. As Allen Thrasher (1993: 98) notes: 'The possibility is left open that to Maṇḍana's mind even the final, non-dual knowledge of Brahman is still verbal, because its object is Brahman, which is also *śabda*. Just as Brahman as "being" and "the bare thing" is the object of *pratyakṣa*, which is *nirvikalpa*, so Brahman as the highest *śabda* is the object of a *nirvikalpa* verbal knowledge. Verbal knowledge is not necessarily relational; a baby's knowledge of its mother's breast apprehends it merely as "this" ... So the highest knowledge of Brahman, in which there is no duality, no relation, no *vikalpas*, may still be verbal.'
7. For further discussions of perception in Indian thought with particular emphasis upon the debate between the Nyāya and Buddhist schools see Matilal, 1971: 21–39; 77–91; Shastri, 1964: Ch. 12, esp. 426–41.

CHAPTER 8

Consciousness and the Body: What are we?

– THE DUALISM OF THE SĀṂKHYA SCHOOL –

Imagine, if you will, all of the things that you are currently aware of. By virtue of the fact that you are aware of these things they can be described as objects of consciousness (*ālambana* in Indian philosophical terminology). One could argue that if you are aware of them – that is, if they are an object of your consciousness, then they cannot be you. What kind of things might we be talking about? Well, we have our familiar tables and chairs, trees, and the floor beneath our feet. Oh yes, our feet. In fact, if you think about it our bodies are also an object of our awareness. Following this line of reasoning, your body is not your self either. Otherwise what sense are we to make of sentences like 'my body won't do what I want' or 'I have a fat body' where we clearly differentiate between ourselves and our bodily form. Obviously such argumentation will not convince a Cārvāka, for whom the self *is* the body (see Chapter 1), but for the sake of exposition let us proceed with the experiment and see where we end up.

What then about the mind? Various thoughts have gone through your mind since this exercise began. Since we can perceive the activities of the mind and it often disobeys us (try revising for an exam), perhaps that too does not constitute the self – the real you. But surely, one might reply, there must be something that can be identified as the experiencer – something that experiences or witnesses all of these things. This kind of procedure, reminiscent in some respects of Descartes' methodology of systematic doubt, led the Sāṃkhya philosopher to postulate the existence of a contentless witness-consciousness (*puruṣa*), distinguishable from the various mental and material processes that it perceives. This, the Sāṃkhya philosopher argued, is the real you.

The Sāṃhkya philosophy takes its stance based upon a recognition that our experience of the world is fundamentally dualistic – sentient beings experience the world as divided up into 'me' and 'what is not-me'. For the Sāṃkhya school this basic dualism is irreducible – we simply cannot overcome it. This position was, of course, repudiated by other schools of Indian philosophy, most notably by members of the Advaita (non-dualistic) school of Vedānta, for whom everything was ultimately reducible to a non-dualistic reality – *ātman* (or *brahman*). Even within the Advaita school, however, the way in which our experience seems to 'arrive' with an in-built division between perceiver and perceived constitutes a major point of enquiry. Note, for instance, Śaṅkara's introduction to his commentary on the *Brahma Sūtra* where the fundamental problem of Advaita is posited in terms of the division between one's self and others. One could argue, therefore, that one of the common threads of Indian philosophy has been the problem of this apparent duality and how to come to terms with it. We suffer because we are constantly confronted by an 'other'. For many schools of Indian thought (notably Sāṃkhya, Yoga, Advaita and the various Buddhist schools) the goal of liberation is to find some way to transcend or overcome the clash between what you are and what is not you!

The central issue in this regard is where do we draw the boundary of our own existence? Where is the point where we end and the world begins? The Sāṃkhya philosophy, representative of some of the most archaic aspects of Indian thought, is an attempt to answer these kinds of questions. We can provisionally distinguish two basic themes within Sāṃkhya philosophy, at least in the classical form that is outlined in the *Sāṃkhya Kārikā* of Īśvarakṛṣṇa. The first theme is an ontological dualism of consciousness and matter and the second is the analysis of the material basis of the world into three basic constituents or strands (*guṇa*).

For Sāṃkhya there are two basic, irreducible and opposing principles of reality – *puruṣa* – the principle of pure consciousness and *prakṛti* – the primordial nature which provides the material basis and source of everything that exists. *Puruṣa* is a masculine noun meaning '(male) person'. The *Puruṣa-Sūkta* or the Hymn to the Cosmic Man (*Ṛg Veda* X.90, c. eighth century BCE), puts forward the idea that the universe was created through the primeval dismemberment of a cosmic Person. This hymn is interesting for a number of reasons. It is the earliest known reference to the stratification of Indian society into four *varṇas*, that is the classification of Vedic society into four class-groupings or estates. This social division is taken to be a universal phenomenon, deriving from the bodily nature of the cosmic Man. Here the respective positions of the Priest (*brāhmana*), the Warrior (*kṣatriya*), the Merchant (*vaiśya*), and the Servant (*śūdra*) are said to correspond to different parts of the *Puruṣa*'s body.

> His mouth became the Brahmin; his arms were made into the Warrior, his thighs the People, and from his feet the Servants were born.
>
> *Ṛg Veda*, X. 90.12, O'Flaherty, 1981: 31

This verse is an attempt to justify the hierarchical nature of class-divisions, through the belief that they are inherently natural, deriving from the nature of the cosmic Man himself. Some scholars have seen this hymn as an early precursor of the Sāṃkhya notion of *puruṣa*. As in the later Sāmkhya philosophy, *Puruṣa* has a female counterpart, here Virāj, the 'Shining One'. *Puruṣa* is born from Virāj and she is in turn born from him (v. 5). There are, however, important differences to note between this hymn and the later Sāṃkhya *darśana*. In Sāṃkhya philosophy there are many *puruṣas*, whilst in the *Puruṣa-Sūkta* there is mention of only one cosmic Person. Again, in the hymn, the world as we know it derives from the sacrificial dismemberment of the cosmic Man, whilst in the Sāṃkhya system *puruṣa* is not the material basis for creation.

The Sāṃkhya notion of *puruṣa* is that of a monad or 'atom' of pure consciousness, though not 'atom' in the quantitative sense of being small (as in, for instance, the notion of *paramāṇu*) since each individual *puruṣa* is limitless and without restricting spatial boundaries. The *puruṣa* is a single, indivisible 'bubble' of pure spirit. It can do nothing but be conscious or witness the activities of *prakṛti*. But, as is immediately obvious to everyone, our experience as individual conscious beings is not that of a detached and inactive witness-consciousness. We do not normally perceive ourselves in this fashion because our consciousness associates itself with the fluctuations of an external world of material objects and an internal world of subjective thoughts (which are also in Sāṃkhya terms constituted by subtle forms of matter). Thus, Sāṃkhya requires another category to explain this aspect of our experience. This is *prakṛti***,** an implicitly female principle, denoting the original or primordial nature, the basic matrix out of which the world is fashioned. *Prakṛti* literally means 'nature' and refers to the basic matter out of which the world is moulded. It is insentient and unconscious and so requires the *puruṣa* to instigate the creative process. We should bear in mind, however, that the *puruṣa* cannot be described as a creator, though it is an indirect and proximate cause of the evolution of the world. Indeed, it is worth noting that the Sāṃkhya tradition (at least in the 'classical' formulation of Īśvarakṛṣṇa) is non-theistic. There is no creator outside of the system – the gods are in fact transmigrating beings enmeshed in the higher echelons of the prakṛtic realm (Kārikā 53).

The Sāṃkhya tradition offers its own type of 'cosmic string' theory. Like a rope *prakṛti* is composed of three intertwining strands or *guṇas*. We encountered the term *guṇa* in our earlier discussion of the Nyāya and

Vaiśeṣika systems. In that context the term denoted the qualities of attributes that inhere within substances and material objects. In the Sāṃkhya system, however, the three *guṇas* denote the primary material constituents of reality – the twines which together constitute the material universe (*prakṛti*). The doctrine of the three *guṇas* is part of the popular world view of ancient Hindu culture. Primordial matter is made up of three fundamental material constituents – the subtle matter of pure thought (*sattva*), the kinetic matter of energy and movement (*rajas*), and the reified matter of inertia (*tamas*). The *triguṇa* is a recurrent theme in the *Bhagavad Gītā* (c. second century BCE) and is probably very ancient. It is similar in many respects to the ancient Chinese sub-division of the Tao into two complementary principles – *yin* and *yang*, though in the case of the Sāṃkhya school, the *guṇas* are the material constituents of primordial nature and not complementary principles present throughout reality.

In ancient Indian medical theory (*Āyurveda*) there are three humours – *pitta*, *vāta* and *kapha* (wind, bile and phlegm). These regulate the respiratory, digestive and integrative systems of the biological organism. When all three are in balance they are known as the three foundations (*tri-dhātu*) of health and harmony. When an imbalance occurs, however, they are referred to as the three pollutants (*tri-doṣa*) or causes of disease. Ideally, one aims to achieve balance and harmony between these three aspects but in most beings some form of imbalance is normal and reflects differences in the character and physical attributes of individuals. Thus, according to Āyurvedic medical analysis, every person is either a *pitta*-type, a *vāta*-type or a *kapha*-type. Again, there are similarities to the Chinese theory of five elements (*wu hsing*) and the associated typology of personal types in traditional Chinese medicine and Acupuncture treatment. An important dimension of Āyurvedic thought is the attention paid to diet and taste (*rasa*). Rice, for instance, is predominantly nourishing for *pitta* (i.e. it is a 'sattvic' food), whilst spices encourage *vāta* (being 'rajasic' in nature). Different ailments and imbalances require appropriate counter-balancing in this regard. Again, similar classificatory schemes occur in traditional Chinese medicine and cookery, the distinction between types of foods being based upon the ancient idea of the complementarity of different foods requiring careful balancing in each meal.

It is tempting to associate the Sāṃkhya theory of the *guṇas* with the Āyurvedic three-fold scheme, but this is misleading since, on Sāṃkhya terms, *pitta*, *vāta* and *kapha* are primarily related to the functioning of the gross, material body and are therefore products of gross material elements (*mahābhautika*). This would make all three predominantly tamasic in nature. Again, the situation is made more complex since, according to the

Sāṃkhya Kārikā (k. 54), the divine realm is primarily sattvic, the human realm is predominantly rajasic, and the animal and plant realm is primarily tamasic. Thus, when dealing with issues of human health and well-being we are already working within a system that is highly rajasic in nature. Nevertheless, as an internal system of differentiation working within the broader cosmological scheme of the Sāṃkhya school, *pitta* does correspond closely to *sattva*, as *vāta* does to *rajas* and *kapha* to *tamas*.[1]

The classificatory scheme of the three *guṇas* is not found in the early Vedic material and some have suggested that it derives from the aboriginal population of India before the invasion of the Vedic Āryans. Such arguments, however, ignore the problems involved in using the Vedas as a definitive source of ancient Āryan society and also tend to represent ancient Indian culture as static and ahistorical, as if cultural change over time cannot be explained from within. Nevertheless, a three-fold scheme does occur in *Chāndogya Upaniṣad* 6.2–5 where the world is classified in terms of three primordial elements – fire (red), water (white) and food (black), corresponding to speech, breath and mind on a microcosmic level. This three-fold typology appears to foreshadow the systematic development of the three *guṇas* in the Sāṃkhya system.

The *tri-guṇa* scheme constitutes a basic categorisation or 'way of looking at things' that has pervaded Indian culture at many different levels. For example, in a social context the scheme has also been used as a further explanation of the nature of the *varṇa* system and the naturalness of perceived differences between the different class-groupings in ancient Indian society.

Varṇa	*Guṇa*	Colour	Attribute/Quality
Brahmins	*Sattva*	White	'Beingness'/Purity/Light/Knowledge
Kṣatriyas	*Rajas*	Red	Activity/Power/Movement/Aggression
Vaiśya	*Rajas*	Yellow	Activity/Power/Movement/Aggression
Śūdras	*Tamas*	Black	Darkness/Obscurity/Inactivity

– The Sāṃkhya Philosophy of Īśvarakṛṣṇa –

The earliest extant text of what has been called 'classical Sāṃkhya' is the *Sāṃkhya Kārikā* of Īśvarakṛṣṇa (350–450 CE), comprising approximately seventy short verses. The text refers to an earlier text known as the *Sixty Topics* (*Saṣṭitantra*) of which the *Sāṃkhya Kārikā* is said to be a summary. This earlier text, however, is lost. Īśvarakṛṣṇa clearly draws upon older traditions and his short work represents an attempt to provide a systematic summary drawn from debates between conflicting Sāṃkhya schools.

Elements of Sāṃkhya thought can be found in texts such as the *Bhagavad*

Gītā and the *Mokṣadharma* portions of the *Mahābhārata*, but these differ in significant respects from the position outlined in the *Sāṃkhya Kārikā* of Īśvarakṛṣṇa, which has become the standard for defining what 'classical Sāṃkhya' is. However, the tendency to focus upon Īśvarakṛṣna's exposition of Sāṃkhya philosophy as the 'definitive formulation' of the school can be misleading because it creates the impression that the history of Indian philosophy is the story of a static clash between a small number of fixed 'classical' positions (the *darśanas*) rather than as an ongoing and developmental history of interactions between vibrant philosophical traditions (*saṃpradāya*) and historical human beings, subject to contestation and re-interpretation throughout its history. As Daya Krishna notes,

> The so-called Sāṃkhya was itself understood differently, even in classical times, by different thinkers and it would be difficult to find grounds for preferring one philosopher's interpretation to anothers ... In fact, a distinction between the thought of an individual thinker and the philosophical position represented by a school is the supreme desideratum if we want to do justice to philosophical thinking in India.
>
> Daya Krishna, 1991: 145; 153

It is equally problematic to settle on a definitive exposition of Sāṃkhya ideas in the period before Īśvarakṛṣṇa. In the *Bhagavad Gītā* '*sāṃkhya*' primarily denotes the idea of 'discrimination' and is virtually synonymous with the attainment of metaphysical knowledge (*jñāna*). The term does not appear to refer to a specific school but to discriminatory knowledge or analysis as a means to liberation. The non-theistic dualism that one finds in Īśvarakṛṣṇa's Sāṃkhya system differs strikingly from the philosophy expounded in the *Bhagavad Gītā* where the dualism of consciousness and matter is superseded by Kṛṣṇa who is represented in the text as a supra-personal Godhead and the source of both *prakṛti* and *puruṣa*. *Prakṛti* is even identified with *brahman* within the text and described as 'the lower nature' of Kṛṣṇa.

It is even more difficult, therefore, to talk of a definitive Sāṃkhya position before Īśvarakṛṣṇa's account became accepted as the standard account of Sāṃkhya philosophy, at least by opponents of the school. Our knowledge of 'pre-classical Sāṃkhya' (i.e. pre-Īśvarakṛṣṇa Sāṃkhya) is largely the result of comparing what we know of his system (defined in terms of the *Sāṃkhya Kārikā* and its commentaries) with certain trends that are present in the literature which preceded it. Thus, in some texts there are seventeen principles of reality (*tattva)*, whilst others offer lists of twenty, twenty-four or even twenty-five as in the work of Īśvarakṛṣṇa himself. There are also widely differing world-views within which 'Sāṃkhya' ideas can be found, ranging from theism and monism to texts upholding a dualistic metaphysics akin to that of Īśvarakṛṣṇa. Occasionally, as in the *Bhagavad Gītā* or the *Upaniṣads,* proto-Sāṃkhya themes such as the dualism of consciousness and material nature can be found but these are often subsumed under a single all-encompassing reality such as Kṛṣṇa, *ātman* or *brahman*. The *Sāṃkhya Kārikā,* however, represents the earliest available attempt to provide a systematic account of Sāṃkhya philosophy.

The *Sāṃkhya Kārikā* begins with a statement of its soteriological intent. The world of rebirth is one of suffering and frustration (*duḥkha*). This is in fact the first noble truth of Buddhism, that life is inherently unsatisfactory. However, it is a general presupposition of all schools of Indian philosophy (with the exception of the materialist Cārvākas), gearing philosophical speculation towards the goal of liberation from this world. According to the *Sāṃkhya Kārikā,* there are three types of suffering: internal or personal (*ādhyātmika*), external (*ādhibhautika*) and divine (*ādhidaivika*). Even the gods suffer since they participate in *saṃsāra*, the wheel of rebirth. In fact, it is the universality of suffering that produces the desire to know (*jijñāsā*) the means for escaping from it.

In terms of epistemology, Sāṃkhya accepts three independent means of knowledge (*pramāṇa*): perception (*dṛṣta*), inference (*anumāna*) and reliable verbal testimony (*āptavacana,* see k. 4–7). Primordial materiality (*mūla-prakṛti*) as the unified source of creation cannot be directly perceived but can be known by inference based upon our perception of its effects (k. 8). The Sāṃkhya system generally follows the scheme outlined in the *Nyāya Bhāṣya* of Vātsyāyana and accepts three types of inference, though this is stated in the commentaries and not in the *Kārikā* itself (see comm. on k. 5).[2] The three types are:

1. Inference based upon prior (perceptual) knowledge (*pūrvavat*) (*Gauḍapāda Bhāṣya*), or inference from a cause to its effect (Paramārtha), as when one infers that it will rain from a perception of rain-clouds.
2. Inference from a part to a whole (*śeṣavat*), as in when one tastes salt in one drop of water and infers that the entire bucket of water is salty (Gauḍapāda), or inference based upon an effect, e.g. inferring that it has rained because the river has flooded its banks (Paramārtha).
3. Analogical inference (*sāmānyato dṛṣṭa*) as in when one infers that the moon and stars move based upon our experience of the movement of persons and objects, or again, reasoning that mango trees are in blossom elsewhere because they are blossoming here.

The *Sāṃkhya Kārikā* in fact, makes a great deal of use of analogical reasoning, appealing to examples such as milk turning to butter to illustrate its theory of causation, and a dancer and her audience and the co-operation of lame man and blind man to illustrate the relationship between pure consciousness and primordial matter. The problem with analogical reasoning, however, is that the analogies also lend themselves to alternative explanations, a point exploited to good effect in Śaṅkara's critique of Sāṃkhya in his *Brahma Sūtra Bhāṣya*.

Īśvarakṛṣṇa begins his exposition by asking the fundamental question: what triggers *prakṛti* to evolve into the complex world that presents itself to us? Why does the world come into being? His answer is that the world evolves as a result of the conjunction (*saṃyoga*) of *puruṣa* and *prakṛti*. Indeed, the world evolves for the sake of the *puruṣa* (*puruṣārtha*). The postulation of a non-material principle was deemed necessary to account for the initial motivating push which starts the creative process. The *puruṣa*, however, is wholly different from *prakṛti* and is not made up of the *guṇas*, being a purely spiritual or conscious principle (k.17).

Puruṣa is normally in the state of isolation or *kaivalya* and reflects nothing but itself. It is inactive and pure consciousness. At this stage, that is before the creation of the universe, *prakṛti* lies in a dormant state as the unmanifest (*avyakta*, k. 14–16). It is also known as the pre-given (*pradhāna*), because it is the primordial matrix out of which the entire created realm is formed. There is one *prakṛti* but innumerable *puruṣas*. When the individual *puruṣa* encounters *prakṛti* it becomes so fascinated that it forgets itself and becomes besotted with its new found object. The presence of *puruṣa* causes the (unmanifested) state of equilibrium of the three *guṇas* (*guṇasāmyāvasthā*) to be disrupted, in a manner reminiscent of the emergence of properties and forms from darkness as a result of the shining of a torch into a dark corner. The result of this interaction is *saṃsāra*, the 'common flowing' of rebirth, the whirlpool of existence. *Puruṣa* forgets that it is separate from nature and associates itself with the activities of *prakṛti*. This is rather like the experience of watching a good play or a movie and identifying with its characters. In such situations the viewer 'loses himself' in the plot and identifies with the events and actions as they unfold. In Sāṃkhya terms what has happened is that the *puruṣa* has forgotten that it is merely a witness (*sākṣin*) observing the activities of *prakṛti* and instead identifies itself with a subtle body (*liṅga-śarīra*). The subtle body thus acts out a variety of roles (by undergoing a series of gross embodiments, see *Kārikā* 42) purely for the sake of the *puruṣa* – the enjoyer (*bhoktṛ*) of the ensuing experiences.

Although the *puruṣa* is described as the enjoyer of experiences, we should bear in mind that in the Sāṃkhya world-view, such enjoyments are a sham. This is not because the world is unreal in some way. Far from it. The Sāṃkhya school rigorously holds onto the reality of both consciousness and the material realm. Rather, the point is that the *puruṣa* has forgotten what it really is and because of its false identification with the activities of the material world is continually confronted by the unsatisfactoriness (*duḥkha*) of life. The method of release from this incessant cycle of unsatisfactory re-embodiments, therefore, is the discrimination (*viveka*) of the true self from the various components of material nature. Indeed, it is from this interest in discriminating the self from the fundamental principles of material reality that the school derives its name – 'Sāṃkhya' or 'Enumeration'.

In the *Sāmkhya Kārikā* of Īśvarakṛṣṇa everything is placed within a conceptual scheme of twenty-five fundamental categories or principles of reality (*tattva*). These principles (that is, the entire Sāṃkhya analysis of reality including the evolutes of *prakṛti* and the *puruṣa*) are what constitutes reality. On an individual level, the categories correspond to the entirety of one's experience. The Sāṃkhya analysis is based upon essentially pragmatic considerations, in order to understand something one first creates simplifying categories. Initially there was some variation as to the precise number of categories, but in the *Sāṃkhya Kārikā* we find a scheme of twenty-five fundamental principles (see Figure 2).

From a cosmological perspective the scheme of *tattvas* provides an explanation of the evolution of the universe. However, from an individual and soteriological perspective the scheme provides an individual blueprint or map of the personal experience of each individual *puruṣa* and the means of liberating oneself from the material world. There have been a variety of attempts to render the Sāṃkhya position amenable to one interpretation or the other (see Parrott, 1986), but such attempts tend to homogenise the long history of Sāṃkhya philosophical speculation and also dichotomise the two hermeneutical strands as if they are always incommensurable. Indeed, the Vedic recognition of homologies (*bandhu*) between microcosm and macrocosm renders such a dichotomy problematic. Nevertheless, in the post-Vedic period when Sāṃkhya flourished as a school with a number of divergent traditions (*saṃpradāya*), there were a variety of interpretations on this question. The *Yuktidīpikā,* for instance, cites and rejects the view of one such school which suggested that there is a separate *prakṛti* for each individual *puruṣa*. This is clearly one extreme version of the individualistic interpretation and suggests that the question of the import of the Sāṃkhya account was subject to considerable contestation and debate with regard to the question of individualistic vs cosmological interpretations of the Sāṃkhya philosophy. It is likely, therefore, that these two hermeneutical strands coexisted, particularly in the peak period of Sāṃkhya history (c. 200–1000 CE). In later Sāṃkhya (for example in the *Sāṃkhya Pravācana Sūtra* and Vijñānabhikṣu's commentary upon it) the orientation of the school became increasingly cosmological in outlook. In many respects this could be seen

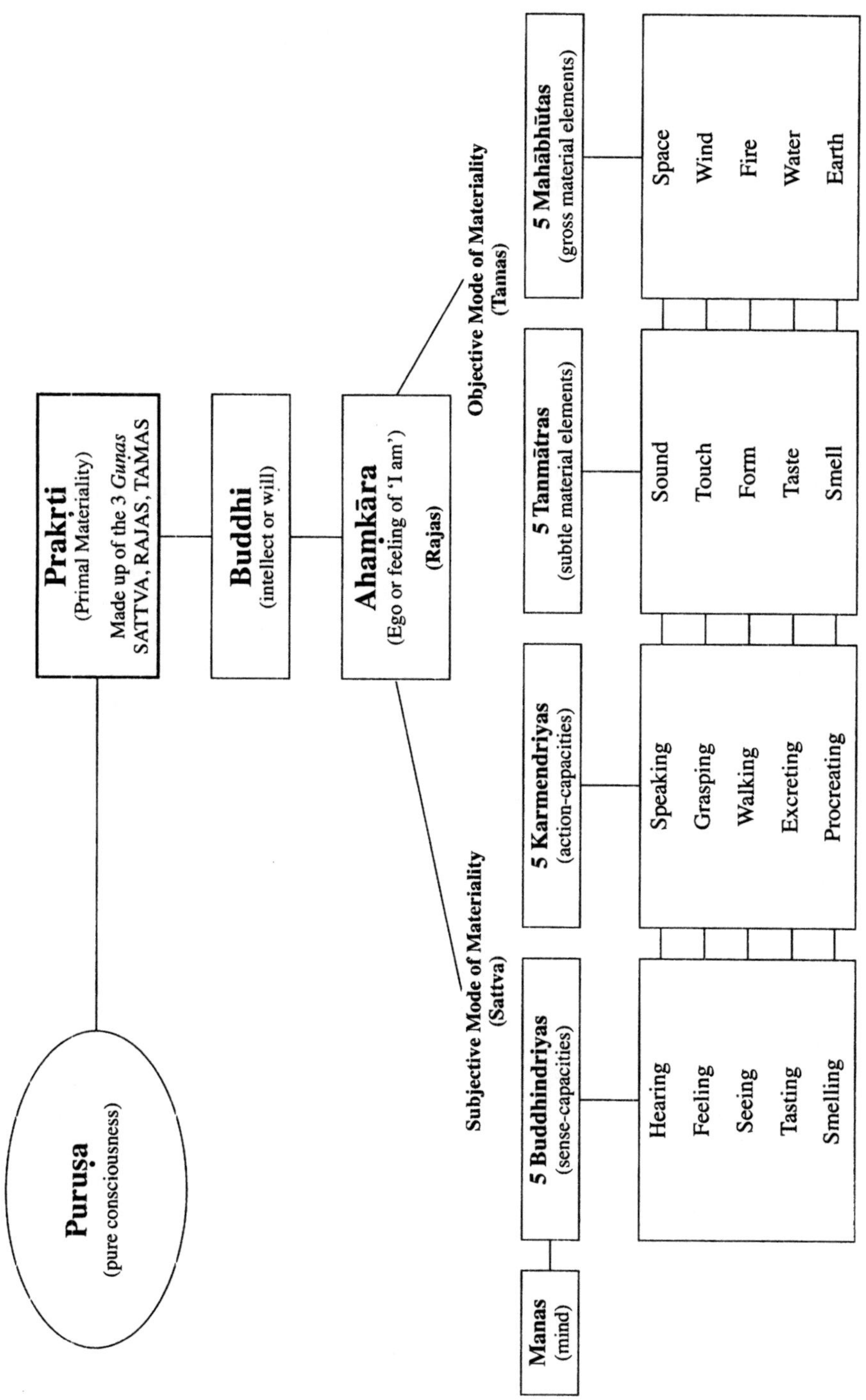

Figure 2: The Evolutionary Scheme of twenty-five Principles (*tattva*) according to the Sāmkhya School

as a return to the earliest speculations within the school, but such a move also reflects contact with the Advaita Vedānta tradition which increasingly influenced interpretations of Sāṃkhya thought in later centuries.

By examining the scheme of twenty-five *tattvas* expounded in the *Sāṃkhya Kārikā* we can gain some insight into the creation of the world (either as a cosmogony or as an analysis of the emergence of our experience as embodied individuals). *Puruṣa* first stirs up *prakṛti*, disturbing the equilibrium of the *guṇas*, and intellect or *buddhi* is the immediate result. The relationship between *puruṣa* and *buddhi* – the first evolute – became an important issue, bound up as it was with the broader question of the nature of the interaction between consciousness and matter. Intellect is characterised by ascertainment or cognition (*adhyavāsaya*). *Buddhi* then constitutes the closest approximation to pure consciousness (*puruṣa*) that can be found within our experience. In many respects it is reminiscent of the Plotinean *Nous* – the first emanation of the One in the Neoplatonic system of thought. *Buddhi* is of course constituted by subtle matter, being an evolute of *prakṛti*. More specifically *buddhi* is pure *sattva*, denoting the most subtle and transparent strand of matter. It represents the mediating point of intersection between consciousness and matter (k. 36).

In later Sāṃkhya thought Vācaspati Miśra (yes, he of Nyāya and Advaita fame), put forward what is known as the reflection theory (*pratibimba-vāda*) to explain how the *buddhi* takes on the appearance of sentience. *Buddhi* acts as a mirror which reflects the *puruṣa*'s own nature as pure consciousness like the moon reflecting the light of the sun. The *puruṣa*, rather like the Greek character Narcissus, becomes besotted with its own reflection in the *buddhi* and forgets that it is in fact separate from *prakṛti* – which is now dancing seductively for the *puruṣa*'s entertainment.

At this point the *puruṣa* becomes mesmerised by the activities of the emerging evolutes of *prakṛti*. Nevertheless, at this stage, there is still no notion of an individual ego. Intellect (*buddhi*) is not an aspect of the individual mind since it precedes the emergence of a sense of ego and the activities of a mind (*manas*). This occurs at the next stage with the development of *ahaṃkāra*, or 'the feeling of I am'. *Ahaṃkāra* is the sense of ego individuality, but precedes the emergence of mental activity in this system of thought. Thus, even when I am not thinking I still have a sense of my own individual existence.

With the emergence of the *ahaṃkāra*, creation branches off into two directions (k. 24). The *sattva* strand of *prakṛti* leads to the development of the subjective aspect of experience or the constructed self (*vaikṛta*). This is itself constituted by eleven factors: the mind (*manas*), the five sense organs (*buddhīndriyas*) and the five organs of action (*karmendriyas*). The second aspect of creation arising from *ahaṃkāra* is the development of the five subtle elements (*tanmatra*). This subtle level of matter then leads to the emergence of the five gross elements which make up the empirical world of material objects and bodies.[3] This aspect of creation is composed of the *tamas guṇa*, making the world dense and gross in nature, and constitutes the objective aspect of our experience.

The construction of the subjective and objective correlates of material reality is activated by *taijasa*, a bright and fiery energy. This is the *rajas guṇa*, denoting movement, activity and energy in motion. Without *rajas* as the dynamic strand within the material substrate, creation could not have occurred. On a cosmological level *rajas* can be identified with the activity, energy and heat of creation (*tapas*). On a psychological level *rajas* denotes the passion or desire of creative and sexual reproduction.

The Sāṃkhya system propounds a causal theory known as the doctrine of the (pre-) existence of the effect in its cause (*satkāryavāda*, see k. 8–11 and Chapter 9). This is a basic presupposition of the school since it necessitates the existence of some primeval first cause behind all effects – in this case (*mūla*)-*prakṛti*, the primordial nature. There is no possibility of a creation out of nothing in the Sāṃkhya system, only a progressive manifestation of already existing but as yet 'unmanifested' products. The Sāṃkhya school upholds a particular version of this causal theory, known as the theory of real-transformation (*pariṇāma-vāda*). Creation is the manifestation (*pariṇāma*) of what already exists *in potentia*. The relationship between cause and effect is one of identity in the sense that the effect is the transformation of its cause into a new form, like the transformation of milk into butter. Likewise, the unmanifested *prakṛti* evolves into the world as we know it.

Prakṛti, however, is one, eternal and all-pervasive. How then is the primordial unity of matter to be reconciled with the transient and pluriform nature of the universe? Why is it that this world is so varied in its manifestations? How can the one become many? This is where the *guṇa* theory comes into its own. According to the Sāṃkhya school, the diversity of the universe can be explained in terms of the relative preponderance of the three 'strands' of *sattva*, *rajas* and *tamas* in the manifold objects that constitute it. This is a common feature of archaic world-views. In ancient Greece similar attempts were made by the Pre-Socratic philosophers to reduce the number of basic entities to a definitive and irreducible number. For the Greeks this resulted in the postulation of four primary elements: fire, earth, water and air. In India similar procedures resulted in a scheme of five basic elements (*mahābhūta*, see Chapter 4). In the *Upaniṣads* we find a theory of five primal elements, and also a scheme of three. It is in such a context that the development of the Sāṃkhya theory of the *guṇas* should be located, though it should be made clear that the *guṇas* are not to be confused with the idea of primal atomic elements – these are gross manifestations of nature and are therefore predominantly tamasic. The difference between the theory of atomic elements and the *guṇas* can be seen if we observe the wider application of the *guṇa* theory in Sāṃkhya thought.

We have already noted that there is a divergence within Sāṃkhya circles as to whether the school's fundamental message is cosmological, individual or some combination of the two. It was pointed out earlier that, at least in the formative period of Sāṃkhya ideas – that is, in the late Vedic and Upaniṣadic period (c. 800 BCE–200 CE) – the microcosm and the macrocosm were identified on a number of levels using an elaborate scheme of homologies or correspondences (*bandhutā*) between the cosmic and the individual. This can be found throughout the brahmanical literature of this period, but is perhaps most strikingly illustrated in the *Puruṣa Sūkta*, or Hymn to the Cosmic Man. In such a context a sharp dichotomy between cosmological and individualist interpretations of Sāṃkhya ideas would have been inappropriate. Similarly, in the *Sāṃkhya Kārikā* the three *guṇas* operate on both levels.

We have already seen that the *tri-guṇa* theory was used by Sāṃkhya to explain the internal diversity of *prakṛti* that allowed for the evolutionary diversity of the manifold universe. Like the *yin–yang* scheme in China, the three *guṇas* are complementary and dynamic principles that interact, mutually dominate and rely upon each other (k. 12). On an individual level *sattva*, *rajas* and *tamas* also correspond to various psycho-physiological states and personality types. *Sattva* corresponds to clarity of thought and purity of mind, *rajas* denotes passionate, excitable and aggressive states of mind, and *tamas* denotes indifference, confusion, stability and depression. Moreover, just as external objects affect the mind of the individual, one brings one's own predispositions and disturbed state of mind to the objects that one perceives. In his commentary on the text Gauḍapāda gives the example of a beautiful and virtuous woman. Such a woman exhibits the qualities of *sattva* and is said to be a delight for all. However, she may also be a source of pain for her fellow wives and a source of delusion for those consumed by passion. Similarly, a king exhibits rajasic qualities but will produce pleasure and contentment (sattvic qualities) in his subjects and pain and delusion (tamasic qualities) in the wicked (*Gauḍapāda Bhāṣya* on k. 12). These examples reflect not only the ways in which each of the *guṇas* produce each other but also the way in which our perception of the world and of other beings is conditioned by our own psycho-physiological make-up.

Thus, the *tri-guṇa* theory functions as a classification scheme for psychological and physiological types. It is easy to see how such a scheme could have originated or at least gained greater recognition in the context of the development of Indian medical traditions (*Āyurveda*). Nevertheless, the *guṇas* also correspond to the basic ontological components or strands of matter itself. Here we find the cosmological focus again, for the *guṇas* denote the primary threads out of which all material objects are made.

Prakṛti, however, is only the material cause of creation (*upādāna-kāraṇa*) – it is only the primal material out of which the world is made and does not initiate the causal process. *Prakṛti* is insentient and so cannot provide the motivating force for creation to occur. It is not the creator but rather that out of which the created world is moulded. This is why the Sāṃkhya tradition posits another primal category, that of the *puruṣa*, or pure consciousness. It is due to the motivating force or purpose of the *puruṣa* (*puruṣārtha*) that the world comes into being.

The situation in which the *puruṣa* finds itself highlights the ambivalent status of *prakṛti*. Creation is for the sake of the *puruṣa*; however, at the same time the *puruṣa's* aim is to be isolated from creation. The purpose of creation, therefore, seems to be to enable the *puruṣa* to become liberated from it (see end of k. 17).[4] Again, *puruṣa* as pure consciousness can only perceive or witness, it therefore requires the help of nature in order to be liberated from nature. *Prakṛti* at the same time bonds and liberates.

> The conjunction (*saṃyoga*) of the two, like that between a blind man and a lame man, is for the purpose of seeing the primordial nature (*pradhāna*) and for the purpose of the isolation (*kaivalya*) of the *puruṣa*. From this [conjunction] creation proceeds.
>
> *Sāṃkhya Kārikā* 21

For Īśvarakṛṣṇa the relationship between *puruṣa* and *prakṛti* is like that between a lame man and a blind man. *Puruṣa* can see but cannot act, while *prakṛti* can act but cannot see. To achieve their goal the two must work together. It is because of the proximity of the two that the unconscious (*prakṛti*) appears as conscious (*puruṣa*).

> Again, just as these two, the blind and the lame man, will separate from each other when their purpose is served, when they have reached the desired destination, in this manner, the Nature [*prakṛti*] also will cease to act after having secured the liberation of the Spirit [*puruṣa*] and the Spirit also will reach liberation and abstraction after contemplating the Nature. There will be the separation of the two, when they have gained their object. Further, the creation is the result of that ... Just as from the union of a man and a woman a son is born, so from the union of the Nature and the Spirit is the creation produced.
>
> *Gauḍapāda Bhāṣya* on k. 21, trans in Mainkar, 1972: 102

One can, of course, question the appropriateness of this analogy. *Prakṛti* is insentient matter and can hardly be compared to a blind man in this regard. Similarly, the analogy implies a consonance of aims between two sentient beings, but *prakṛti* is insentient and acts only for the sake of *puruṣa*. Gauḍapāda's passing reference to the reproductive union between man and woman is also highly significant since it would seem that the Sāṃkhya notion of creation as the consequence of the interaction of two primeval principles has its roots in the ancient reproductive cosmogonies of the Vedas and early *Upaniṣads*.

The gender imagery used in the *Sāṃkhya Kārikā* and earlier dualistic cosmogonies is also highly significant. '*Puruṣa*' is a masculine noun; spirit or pure consciousness is implicitly, if not quite literally (given the doctrine of multiple sexed-embodiments), male. In contrast, the insentient but dynamic primordial matter is female – the matrix of the universe! We should be wary, however, of reading too much into this distinction, since all beings experience male and female embodiments during their cycle of rebirths and the equation of the two fundamental principles with specific gender types is never made in the *Kārikā* itself. Nevertheless, the association of the female with the material and the male with consciousness or spirit is one that has become widespread within Hindu culture through the influence of Śaktism and Tantrism. In contemporary India '*Puruṣatva*' has come to denote the 'essence of masculinity' and as K. M. Ganguli notes 'Women in almost all dialects of India derived from Sanskrit are commonly called *Prakṛti* or symbols of *Prakṛti*, thus illustrating the extraordinary popularity of the philosophical doctrine about *Prakṛti* and *Puruṣa*.'[5]

Although the point can be over-emphasised (Jacobsen, 1996), gender-specific roles are evident in *Sāṃkhya Kārikā* 59 and 61 where *prakṛti* is compared to a dancing girl (*nartakī*):

> As a dancer stops the dance once she has been observed by the audience so does *prakṛti* stop, having displayed herself to *puruṣa*.
> Nothing, in my view, is more shy than *prakṛti*. Once aware that 'I have been seen' she does not reveal herself again to the *puruṣa*.

There is much more that could be said about Īśvarakṛṣṇa's conception of gender roles. The feminised *prakṛti* is here described as modest and generous in that she devotes herself to the aims of the *puruṣa* (k. 58). Clearly, we are close here to the model of the good and submissive wife acting only according to the wishes of her man. At this juncture, however, I wish to draw the reader's attention to the Indian identification of the female principle as active and dynamic, and the male principle as a passive and detached observer. In western culture it is usually the female who has been represented as passive and the male as dynamic. This is clearly not the case in India where gods are often seen as impotent without their female consorts. Much of Hindu culture attributes the fundamentally creative (and destructive) aspect of the universe to be a manifestation of the goddess as *śakti* – the power of the universe. Of course, the association of the female with action and pleasure (*kāma*) in traditional Indian society perpetuated a strong sense of gender-differentiation within an overwhelmingly patriarchal social system. Although it is true to say that the female is revered within Hindu culture, as the Sāṃkhya example illustrates rather well it is the male qualities of detachment and reflection or sentience that have been most highly valued in Indian culture as a whole. After all, in the Sāṃkhya school we are all ultimately *puruṣas* (token males?) and should learn to dis-associate ourselves from the activities of *prakṛti* – the seductive, female dancer.

During British rule in India, however, Indian conceptions of the female as active and male as passive witness clashed with the prevailing Victorian notion of the female as passive. The cultural clash between these (patriarchal) systems of gender-differentiation seems to have contributed to the development amongst British rulers of the myth that the Hindu male was idle and effeminate, precisely because he was seen to exhibit qualities that the British identified as quintessentially feminine attributes. Although such stereotyping probably says more about the projection of British presuppositions about the inherent inferiority of the Indian male than about the activities of Hindu men themselves, these characteristics ironically represent the qualities traditionally associated with masculinity (*puruṣatva*) within traditional Brahmanical circles. As Ashis Nandy notes,

> The Brāhmaṇ in his cerebral, self-denying asceticism was the traditional masculine counterpoint to the more violent, 'virile', active Kṣatriya, the latter representing – however odd this may seem to the modern consciousness – the feminine principle in the cosmos.
>
> Nandy, 1983:10

The relationship between British and Indian notions of gender and sexuality and the mutual imbrication of these in the power-dynamics of patriarchy and colonialism are beyond the scope of this current study (see M. Sinha, 1995). However, it is worth noting the ease with which western feminist rhetoric about the patriarchal nature of Indian society can become implicated in a neo-colonial acceptance of the cultural superiority of the west. 'Holier than thou' attitudes do not become the western aggressor and it is important to remember the patriarchal dimensions of western cultures as well. Moreover, an appreciation of the differences between western and traditional Indian constructions of gender are vitally important if we are to gain some understanding of the complex nature of gender-differentiation within diverse cultures and provide a way forward for feminism in a cross-cultural and post-colonial context. In this regard, Nandy draws our attention to the ways in which Gandhi developed his own model of non-violent activism based upon traditional Hindu notions of the feminine (*nārītva*) as active, maternal and powerful:

> [T]he concept of *nārītva*, so repeatedly stressed by Gandhi nearly fifty years before the woman's liberation movement began, represented more than the dominant Western definition of womanhood. It included some traditional meanings of womanhood in India, such as the belief in a closer conjunction between power, activism and femininity than between power, activism and masculinity. It also implied the belief that the feminine principle is a more powerful, dangerous and uncontrollable principle in the cosmos than the male principle. But even more central to this concept of womanhood was the traditional Indian belief in the primacy of maternity over conjugality in feminine identity. This belief specified that woman as an object and source of sexuality was inferior to woman as source of motherliness and *caritas*.
>
> Nandy, 1983: 53–4

To return to our discussion of Sāṃkhya philosophy, the world comes into being as a result of the conjunction of the male *puruṣa* with the female *prakṛti*. *Puruṣa* constitutes the motivating principle that initiates the evolution of the world and is the witness of all that occurs. Everything that one perceives (including the activities of one's own mind – i.e. mental processes) are the product of *prakṛti* – the material cause of everything. One is tempted to describe *prakṛti* as the mother (matrix) of the universe but this would be somewhat misleading from a Sāṃkhya point of view since nature is devoid of any sentience. Although the created realm is the product of this primordial interaction between spirit or pure consciousness and matter, the final truth for the Sāṃkhya school is that

> [The *puruṣa*] is neither bound, nor liberated, equally, it does not transmigrate. Only *prakṛti* in its various forms transmigrates, is bound and is liberated.
>
> *Sāṃkhya Kārikā* 62

This realisation is the fundamental aim of the Sāṃkhya school. Our true nature is to be eternally in a state of isolation (*kaivalya*). The creation of the world then is based upon *puruṣa's* mis-association of itself with *prakṛti*. *Puruṣa* 'thinks' that it is part of *prakṛti* whereas in actual fact it is eternally and forever in isolation. This is an important point about the Sāṃkhya position that is often missed – the *puruṣa* is not a soul entrapped in matter, it only thinks that it is! This highlights a particular problem for the Sāṃkhya position. How does one integrate the voluntarism of aspiring to liberation with a rigid metaphysical dualism which does not allow for a legitimate association of spirit and matter, consciousness and activity? If the *puruṣa* is already and always isolated from *prakṛti* (as verse 62 states), what is it that is bound and liberated? The answer, of course, is that it is *prakṛti* itself which takes part in the transmigration process. More specifically, what undergoes rebirth is the individualised self (*jīva* or *liṅga*) – an entity composed of subtle matter, which transmigrates from one gross body to another.[6] However, if *puruṣa* is not a part of *prakṛti* and never really was, then what does it matter what happens to this subtle transmigrating entity? After all, it is not the real you! The consequences of the rigid and unbreachable dichotomy of consciousness and matter in Sāṃkhya philosophy is that the world and the activities of the empirical self, however real they might be, do not really concern the essential self in *kaivalya*. Why concern oneself with the liberation of the empirical self in this context? This is a point noted by Gauḍapāda, for whom the objection that the *puruṣa* is not an agent presents problems for the establishment of a foundation for moral action (*dharma*):

> It may be asked: if the Spirit [*puruṣa*] is a non-agent, how does it exercise volition – 'I shall practise virtue, I will not practise vice.' Then it would be the agent; but it is not the agent; in this way both the positions would be faulty.
>
> *Gauḍapāda Bhāṣya* on k. 20, Mainkar, 1972: 99

One possible response to this problem, of course, is to shift attention towards the *puruṣa* as the source of consciousness and the true self. The very fact that the empirical self continues to become enmeshed in the world of rebirth demonstrates that the *puruṣa* remains deluded with regard to its true nature. However, such a response is curtailed by those who wish to insist that the *puruṣa* is a purely transcendental consciousness, always characterisable as in isolation (*kaivalya*). Gauḍapāda, for instance, taking his lead from k. 62, argues that the relationship between the *puruṣa* and the empirical self is like that between a hot fire or cold water and a clay pot:

> [T]he Liṅga [transmigrating self] ... appears as if intelligent through its relation (*saṃyoga*) with the Spirit (*puruṣa*). Just as in life a jar when in contact with coolness is cold, and when in contact with heat is hot ... hence, the volition is exercised by the Attributes (*guṇas*) and not by the Spirit.
>
> *Gauḍapāda Bhāṣya* on k. 20, Mainkar, 1972: 99

The jar is affected by heat, but not vice versa. The *puruṣa* may be the witness of experiences and in that sense, an enjoyer (*bhoktṛ*), but it is also said to be detached (*mādhyasthya*) and isolated (*kevalin*) from the activities of the three *guṇas* (k. 19) and so is 'free from any interruption due to its character of being in isolation' (*Yuktidīpikā* on k. 17). A similar position is, of course, outlined in the *Bhagavad Gītā* where the absolute immutability of the essential self (*ātman*) is used by Kṛṣṇa to justify Arjuna's involvement in a righteous war on the grounds that the real selves of Arjuna's enemies will not die, only their material bodies will perish (*Gītā* 2.14, 18–22, 30–1). We shall return to the problem of identifying a point of intersection between the activities of prakṛtic embodiment (the empirical agent) and a transcendent immaterial self when we come to examine the Yoga school of Patañjali. In the *Yuktidīpikā* (on k. 1 and 6) it is the connection (*abhisambandha*) between the internal organ (*antaḥkaraṇa*) and the power of consciousness (*cetanāśakti*) which allows for the experience of pleasure and pain. The *puruṣa* itself does not really become enmeshed in material processes. If one imagines the *puruṣa* to be like a torch, it is the power of that torch – the beam of light if you like, that instigates the process, the torch itself remains transcendent and unaffected. However, Īśvarakṛṣṇa implies in *kārikā* 55 that the *puruṣa* directly experiences pleasure and pain and is affected by the actions of the empirical self:

> The *puruṣa*, which is consciousness, experiences suffering arising from decay and death, until deliverance with regard to the subtle body.[7] Suffering (*duḥkha*), therefore, is of the nature of things.

That suffering (*duḥkha*) is the fundamental problem to overcome has already been established from the very outset by Īśvarakṛṣṇa. To overcome suffering (*duḥkha*) and the perpetuation of re-embodiment (*saṃsāra*), it is imperative that the *puruṣa* learns to detach itself from the activities of material existence. The fact that the empirical self continues to suffer demonstrates that isolation (*kaivalya*) has not yet been achieved. Later Sāṃkhya commentators, such as the Vedāntin Vijñānabhikṣu (c. 1500–1600 CE), extended Vācaspati Miśra's theory of reflection (*pratibimba-vāda*), which was originally used to explain the manner in which the *buddhi* became endowed with sentience by the *puruṣa*, and postulated the notion of mutual reflection (*anyonya-pratibimba*). Vijñānabhikṣu argued that although the *puruṣa* is not an agent of any kind, this does not mean that it cannot be acted upon. In fact, the experiences occurring in the *buddhi* cast a reflection (*chāyā*) upon the *puruṣa*, which is, of course, the source of the *buddhi*'s apparent sentience. The light of pure consciousness (*puruṣa*) is reflected in the intellect (*buddhi*) and the experiences of satisfaction and pain are in turn reflected back from the *buddhi* onto the *puruṣa* in the form of limiting adjuncts (*upādhi*). Both *puruṣa* and *buddhi*, therefore, act as mirrors in relation to each other. The former shining the light of sentience onto the *buddhi* and the latter shining the resultant experiences back onto the *puruṣa*.

For the Sāṃkhya school liberation is the realisation that 'I am not a part of the material world (*prakṛti*)'. My true nature as *puruṣa* is totally separate from the mind and body that I usually associate with my 'self' (in *kaivalya*).[8] The idea then is to discriminate (*viveka*) the twenty-five *tattvas* or principles of reality, in order to reverse step by step the creation process ('I am not this', 'this is not me') in a manner reminiscent of the Buddha's analysis of experience into the five bundles (*skandhas*).

> Thus, from an analysis of the principles (*tattva),* knowledge arises that 'I am not, nor does it belong to me, nor do I exist'. This [knowledge] is free from error, pure and abstract (literally, 'isolated' *kevala*).
>
> *Sāṃkhya Kārikā* 64

In the various Buddhist schools such introspective analysis leads to the realisation that there is no underlying subject or witness to experience – merely the fluctuating experiences themselves. For the Sāṃkhya school, however, discriminative knowledge (*viveka-jñāna*) allows one to focus one's attention upon the real source of consciousness (*puruṣa*) – the detached witness that is continually observing the world but ultimately remains distinct from it.

A further problem for the Sāṃkhya school is the question of how one differentiates between the many *puruṣas* if they are all characterised as pure consciousness with no spatio-temporal boundaries or limitations. If a sense of individuality (*ahaṃkāra*) only develops after the emergence of the intellect (*buddhi*), in what sense can the *puruṣa* be described as an individual? Presumably, the Sāṃkhya point is that notions of an empirical ego require not only some objective correlate (*prakṛti*) with which to contrast oneself but also other beings. In its natural state the *puruṣa* is isolated and so has nothing with which to contrast itself. No ego-consciousness, therefore, can occur in *kaivalya*. Īśvarakṛṣṇa, however, does not speculate with regard to the relationship between the innumerable *puruṣas* in the state of isolation (*kaivalya*). Are they all individually isolated from each other as well as from *prakṛti*? If a *puruṣa* has no ego-awareness, what distinguishes one *puruṣa* from another?

These kinds of reservations led Śaṅkara and the Advaita Vedānta tradition to argue that it makes more sense to speak of a single self (*ātman*) or *puruṣa* becoming involved in the world. For Śaṅkara there are a variety of empirical selves (*jīvātman*), but they are all ultimately a product of ignorance – there is in reality only the non-dual *ātman*. Indeed, such a view would integrate the cosmological and individualistic interpretations of Sāṃkhya thought at a stroke. Īśvarakṛṣṇa, however, is keen to hold onto the common-sense distinction between a plurality of sentient beings, particularly in so far as this accounts for the differences between the karmic experiences of individual selves (*jīva*). Solipsism is not an option for the classical Sāṃkhya system. Indeed, if there were only one *puruṣa*, only one pure consciousness tied to *saṃsāra*, the first liberated person would stop the world from evolving. Since this has not happened it seems sensible to accept that there are as many *puruṣa*s as there are conscious beings. Note that within Indian culture this includes not only humans, but also the animal and divine realms. For the Jainas, everything (including the plant and mineral realms) is inhabited by sentient beings (*jīva*) requiring a lifestyle of non-violence (*ahiṁsā*) to avoid undue harm to a universe that is positively brimming with diverse lifeforms. Similarly, in the *Sāṃkhya Kārikā* there are fourteen levels of embodiment, ranging 'from Brahmā to a blade of grass' (k. 53, 54).

However, in so far as Īśvarakṛṣṇa emphasises the individualistic and soteriological strand of Sāṃkhya thought in his work, he leaves unresolved the question of how to make sense of the older cosmological interpretation of the relationship between *puruṣa* and *prakṛti*. The reason for this difficulty seems to stem from the fact that the earlier, pre-classical formulations of Sāṃkhya generally accepted a unifying principle, or a single *puruṣa*, whether that be *brahman*, as in the *Upaniṣads*, or Kṛṣṇa, as in the *Bhagavad Gītā*. Īśvarakṛṣṇa seems to have been unable to shrug off this earlier tradition and develops his own dualistic position in the shadow of these earlier formulations.

Īśvarakṛṣṇa's Sāṃkhya philosophy is an uncompromising dualism. One of the most striking features of this philosophy is the dichotomy between spirit or consciousness on the one hand and material nature on the other. Unlike Cartesian dualism which involves a distinction between mind and body, mind in the Sāṃkhya system, as in many other systems of Indian thought, is a subtle form of matter. Although the distinction between mind and body is regularly made within Indian culture, there is no sharp distinction between the two as they are usually conceived as inter-related and existing on a continuum rather than as wholly separate realities. This is as true in Hindu philosophy as it is in Buddhist thought. For Hindu schools like Sāṃkhya, however, in sharp contrast to the Buddhists with their doctrine of no-abiding-self (*anātman*), consciousness is separate from the mind and is the transcendent and animating principle of beings which imbues the mind (constituted, remember, by subtle matter) with the quality of sentience.

The mind, as we noted in the previous chapter, is the sixth sense-organ in many Indian schools and this is certainly the case in the Sāṃkhya tradition. Mental events such as thoughts, ideas and volitions are simply subtle forms of matter. The Sāṃkhya school propounds an image-theory (*sākāra-vāda*) of perception. What we perceive are mental modifications (*vṛtti*) – that is, an image (made, of course, of subtle matter) – imprinted with the form of the external object being perceived. In perception the internal organ or *antaḥkaraṇa* (constituted by the intellect (*buddhi*), the 'feeling of I am' (*ahaṃkāra*) and the mind (*manas*) and corresponding to the mental or subjective dimension of experience) goes out and takes on the form of the external object. It remains, however, like the object that it grasps, a material product (if a subtle one). Both gross and subtle matter are evolutes of *prakṛti*. The transmigrating self and the dream self – usually conceived as non-material in western culture – are composed of subtle material elements (the *tanmatras*) and so are to be distinguished from the principle of sentience – the true self (*puruṣa*). It is important to remember, nevertheless, that Sāṃkhya is a realist school of thought – the material world really does exist and its existence is independent of our perception of it. Fundamentally, however, it is not us! Sāṃkhya dualism, therefore, represents a middle position between idealism (where the world is a product of consciousness) and materialism (where consciousness is simply an emergent product of matter).

The current situation that we are experiencing now – the intermingling of consciousness and matter – is the result of the *puruṣa*, the pure consciousness, becoming besotted by *prakṛti*, primordial materiality. As I suggested earlier, this is rather like watching a play or a film and becoming absorbed in the storyline. The various *puruṣas* become intrigued by the activities of matter (the dance of *prakṛti*) which they themselves have initiated and consequently forget their true natures as transcendental 'bubbles' of consciousness. This results in the emergence of a subtle, transmigrating entity (*liṅga*) which performs on behalf of the *puruṣa* as an actor takes on a number of roles (*Kārikā* 42). The Sāṃkhya tradition, therefore, sees the highest ideal of human existence to be self-reflexivity – analysis and reflection upon one's own subjectivity, summed up in the question: 'what am I?'

The self, however, is not to be found within the material realm. The body is not the real you because it is possible to say 'this is my body' – making a distinction between possessor and possessed. We inhabit or possess bodies if you like, but they are not us. Moreover, the Sāṃkhya argues, if the body was the self it would also obey our command at all times. It is inconceivable, argues the Sāṃkhya tradition, that one could not be in control of one's own essential self – in cases of complete identity the issue of control cannot arise. On this view, the only time one can say 'I cannot control this' is when there is a dualism or a separation between the controller and the controlled. Since one can say 'I cannot control my body' this suggests that I am not my body. Of course, we all have some degree of control over our bodies – but this control is not complete. That is enough, so the Sāṃkhya tradition believed, to make their point.

The mind is also not the self for similar reasons. If I am my mind, then I am constantly changing and becoming something else, as the Buddhists suggest. The Sāṃkhya school, of course, did not want to deny that there is a person having an experience – the Buddhist view of *anātman*. One cannot deny the validity of one's experience of subjectivity. We are all aware of being subjects, of having experiences of this and that. For Sāṃkhya, therefore, the true self is the principle of pure consciousness (*puruṣa*). Each living being in the universe has its own witness-consciousness which thereby constitutes the subjective ground of all experiences.

For the Sāṃkhya school, of course, the mind is simply an evolute of materiality and appears sentient because of the proximity of the *puruṣa*. Moreover, it would make no sense to say 'My mind is playing tricks on me' unless there is a distinction to be made between the self (the possessor or 'owner' of the mind) and the possessed (the mind itself). Similarly, we are perhaps in even less control of our minds than we are of our bodies. The Buddha is believed to have remarked that those who associate the self with the body (the Cārvākas perhaps) were at least on firmer ground than those who associated their selves with their minds since the body at least appears to have a degree of stability and duration over time. Consequently, in Buddhism the mind is compared to a monkey – constantly swinging from one tree to another and refusing to settle down and remain stable. Our minds in fact are constantly disobeying us and drifting off. How many times, for instance, has your attention drifted whilst reading this chapter? Surely this is a result of your untrained mind and not my exciting prose style! When beginning to practice yoga one of the first things that usually strikes the novice is how quickly the mind changes and moves onto something else. The question of stabilising the activities of the mind becomes the central concern of the Yoga tradition to which we shall shortly turn.

Sāṃkhya philosophy has an importance and influence that extends well beyond its own literary output. It remains an important source for all major Hindu thought, not necessarily as a philosophical school (*darśana*) but as a metaphysical canvas or background that has pervaded Indian culture in general. The cosmology of great Hindu Epics such as the Mahābhārata and the Pūranic and Tantric literature are infused by Sāṃkhya philosophical concepts and themes. The Hindu idea of *śakti* (the female dynamic power behind creation) is intimately connected with the Sāṃkhya notion of *prakṛti*. The gods Śiva and Viṣṇu are powerless without the goddess, their consort and at the same time their creative power. Even in the Hellenistic and Judaeo-Christian traditions we find the idea that the *Logos* or *Sophia* is needed to bridge the gap between the Godhead (God in himself) and the creation of the world (see, for instance, the prologue to John's Gospel). Classical Sāṃkhya in many respects represents a systematisation of ideas already present in existing Indian mythology.

– THE YOGA SYSTEM OF PATAÑJALI –

The *Yoga Sūtra* of Patañjali is the classic Hindu handbook on yoga and is something of a compendium, including wide-ranging material and practices, not all of which are necessary (or perhaps even compatible). Its importance resides in the fact that it constitutes the primary textual authority and paradigm for the practice of yoga within most Hindu traditions. The *Sūtra* is older than the *Sāṃkhya Kārikā* of Īśvarakṛṣṇa and so one should be wary of seeing the text as a direct attempt to 'iron out' some of the ambiguities and problems encountered in the *Kārikā*, though it may be, as A. B. Keith argued, that the final compilation of the *Sūtra* was precipitated by the appearance of Īśvarakṛṣṇa's work (Larson and Bhattacharya, 1987: 166). The Yoga system is a school of thought in its own right but clearly has a close relationship with the Sāṃkhya tradition, sharing many of its basic presuppositions. The extent to which Patañjali adhered to a rigid dualistic metaphysics, however, remains a contentious issue with scholars such as Feuerstein (1979, 1980) and Whicher (1998) arguing that there are significant differences between the two schools.

The metaphysics of the *Yoga Sūtra* is closely related to the position of the Sāṃkhya school in that the goal is the disassociation (*kaivalya*) of pure consciousness (*puruṣa*, the essential self) from the mind–body complex which is a product of primordial matter (*prakṛti*). Through the practice of yogic techniques and the cultivation of an attitude of detachment one eventually achieves an isolation of one's subjective centre of awareness from the material body and the changing states of mind that we normally associate (erroneously) with ourselves. Until this disassociation is achieved one continues through a succession of lives experiencing suffering (*duḥkha*) as a result of the reality gap – that is, the gap between what we really are (centres of pure consciousness) and what we believe we are (individual mind–body complexes with a finite life-span).

What follows is a brief overview of the Yoga system based upon the early verses of the *Yoga Sūtra* itself. The *Sūtra* begins with a definition of yoga as the 'cessation of the fluctuations of consciousness' (*citta vṛtti nirodhāḥ,* YS 1.2).[9] The goal of the Yoga system then is to bring an end to the false identification or conjunction (*saṃyoga*) of *puruṣa* – the seer (*draṣṭā*) and *prakṛti* – the seen (*dṛśya*). The fluctuations of the mind are, of course, constituted by subtle matter and are mistakenly identified with the witness-consciousness. James Haughton Woods (1914) translates *citta-vṛtti* as 'the fluctuations of mind-stuff' to convey the fact that Yoga is not merely about the restriction of the fluctuations of the mind, but also of the fluctuations of the mental object of experience. Yoga is what is going to affect the passage from the mobility of thought to the immobility of the knowing agent, the *puruṣa*. Yoga then is the progressive control of the mind and its experienced objects, and a heightening of the awareness of its various processes and forms.

When all fluctuations of consciousness have stopped 'the seer [i.e. the *puruṣa*] dwells in its own form' (1.3). However, for as long as the fluctuations persist, the seer takes on the form of those fluctuations (1.4). The mental fluctuations themselves are fivefold. Some are hindered by defilements (2.3) and present obstacles to the yoga practitioner whilst others are undefiled (1.5) and are steps on the path to liberation. The hindered fluctuations are the field for the accumulation of *karma*, that is, they lead to the production of further karmic seeds or residual impressions which reside within the consciousness of the individual. The unhindered (*akliṣṭa*) fluctuations have discriminative awareness (*viveka-khyāti*) as their object and they function to hinder the incessant activities of the three *guṇas*. These unhindered fluctuations also produce residual impressions but in a more positive sense. It is through the cultivation of these that the wheel of fluctuations unceasingly rolls on until the highest concentration (*samādhi*) is attained. This is interesting because it means that for the *Yoga Sūtra* liberation from the fluctuations of mind is dependent upon the cultivation of wholesome habits and techniques which themselves are nothing more than fluctuations of consciousness. We found a similar ambivalence in the Sāṃkhya system too, since it was *prakṛti* which was the source of both bondage and liberation. In the Yoga school, however, this ambivalence is expressed in terms of the relationship between defiled and pure consciousness. So, even the practices which lead the yogin to eventual liberation are ultimately obstacles in his path since they are also fluctuations of the mind, being (at first at least) unstable and temporary.

The fluctuations of the mind can be classified into five categories. They are: valid knowledge (*pramāṇa*), misconception (*viparyāya*), conceptualisation (*vikalpa*), sleep (*nidra*) and memory (*smṛti*) (1.6). For the Yoga school there are three valid independent means of knowledge (*pramāṇa*) – perception, inference and tradition (*āgama*, 1.7). Misconception is erroneous knowledge that does not correspond to the form of things (1.8). Conceptualisation (*vikalpa*) denotes knowledge that is merely verbal in nature and has no corresponding object. *Vikalpa* is a very important term in Indian philosophy used in both Hindu and Buddhist contexts and as we have seen in chapter six this concept is central to Indian debates about the nature of perception. As a product of the imagination, *vikalpa* always denotes a conceptualised knowledge of something. Consequently, it is said to be derived from a knowledge of words and their meanings. As a result of this, *vikalpa* is said to be devoid of an object. Its field of reference is purely conceptual or imaginary, being based upon linguistic considerations. With the exception of arch-realists such as the Nyāya-Vaiśeṣika and Mīmāṃsā schools, *vikalpa* is often viewed in Indian philosophy as a distorting means of knowledge since it requires the mediation of words. What the yogin is interested in achieving is a meditative state which is devoid of all words and concepts, a direct yogic perception (*yogī-pratyakṣa*) of the way thing truly are. This type of knowledge is intuitive and non-conceptual. The aim then, is to grasp reality before it becomes distorted by concepts and distinctions, which are products of the fluctuating mind.

Sleep is a fluctuation of the mind characterised by an absence of experience (1.10). Finally, memory (*smṛti*) denotes that mental activity which does not add to what has already been experienced (1.11). All five fluctuations of consciousness, however, can be inhibited through practice (*abhyāsa*) and the cultivation of detachment (*vairāgya*, literally 'passionlessness', 1.12). Practice basically involves a sustained attempt to establish stability of mind and must be carried out in an uninterrupted, correct and systematic fashion over an extended period of time to furnish results (1.13–14). Detachment, meanwhile, is knowledge that one has mastered the desire for the objects one experiences (1.15). The culmination of this process is when the *puruṣa* achieves detachment with regard to the activities of the *guṇas* (1.16).

The experiential goal of the Yoga tradition is the attainment of *samādhi*. This is a difficult concept to translate denoting the idea of being 'collected together' or concentrative union. So far I have rendered the term in English as 'meditative concentration'. Mircea Eliade (1969) has suggested 'enstasy' as a translation of *samādhi*, thus providing a technical term denoting the opposite of ecstasy (literally 'standing outside oneself'). In everyday experience (in Yoga terms the *vṛtti* states) consciousness adverts towards the world. It is extrovertive and projects outward towards sensory objects. Enstasy, in contrast, denotes an introverted and reflexive flow of consciousness (YS I.29). The yogin's awareness turns back upon itself and reflects upon its own nature. Enstasy is also a useful term because it contrasts with the feelings of excitement associated with being 'in ecstasy'. *Samādhi* is an experience of mental pacification and results eventually in the cessation of the fluctuations of consciousness (*citta-vṛtti-nirodhāḥ*, YS I.2). *Samādhi*, however, should not be confused with a trance or hypnotic state where there is a loss of volitional control and awareness. The cessation of the fluctuations of consciousness does not lead to the attainment of a blank state of mind, but instead results in a reflexive and stable awareness of the witness-consciousness in its own form. Moreover, *samādhi* is not merely a mental state, since it affects the entire mind–body complex of the yogin. This is even more clearly the case in the Haṭha Yoga tradition where the body is a vehicle for liberation and is transformed in the process.

Nevertheless, we should bear in mind that there are a number of types of *samādhi* and not all conform strictly to Eliade's notion of 'enstasy' (Whicher, 1997: 33). Some *samādhi* states involve the process of conceptualisation and are oriented towards objects (*saṃprajñāta-samādhi*). These are of varying intensity ranging from states involving an analysis of gross material objects (*vitarka*) to more refined states involving reflection upon subtle objects (*vicāra*), that is, internal or private 'objects' such as sensations, ideas, images, emotions and the subtle forms of matter (*tanmatra*) which provide the basis for gross (that is, visible, tactile etc.) manifestation.[10] Such states can also involve an experience of bliss (*ānanda*) or a reflexive examination of one's own ego-identity (*asmitā*, 1.17) and so cannot be unproblematically described as 'enstatic'.

The various stages of meditative attainment are part of a hierarchy of experience which includes our everyday states of mind as well. Vyāsa, for instance, outlines five levels at which consciousness functions (*Yoga Sūtra Bhāṣya* 1.1):

1. Unsteady (*kṣipta*)
2. Confused (*mūḍha*)
3. Distracted (*vikṣipta*)
4. One-pointed (*ekāgra*)
5. Restricted (*niruddha*)

The first three states of mind are what one might call 'everyday consciousness', whilst the final two are said by Vyāsa to be cultivated through the practice of yoga. Meditative states then are essentially a specific category of experience, having a superior position for the yogin in relation to the so-called 'normative' experiences of everyday life. Surendranath Dasgupta has argued that *(sa-)vitarka samādhi* – the analysis of gross objects – 'does not differ from ordinary conceptual states ... the mind has not become steady and is not as yet beyond the range of our ordinary consciousness' (Dasgupta, 1924: 151), but it is not clear that this is the case (Feuerstein 1971: 39), since *sa-vitarka samādhi* involves a direct perception (*sākṣātkāra*) of the gross form of an object in all its past, present and future states (Vijñānabhikṣu, *Yoga Sāra Saṃgraha*, chapter 1) and is characterised by 'an appeased flowing of the mind' (*citta prasanta vahita*).

Who indeed is to say where the boundary between different states of consciousness can be drawn? We flip in and out of a variety of states of mind all of the time and so many people may well have experienced what the *Yoga Sūtra* calls *sa-vitarka samādhi* at some time in their lives, particularly during moments of intense concentration. Nevertheless, this does not necessarily make it a 'normal' state of mind. Who is to say what is or is not a 'normal' state of consciousness? Indeed, according to Vyāsa, *samādhi* 'is a quality of the mind-stuff (*citta*) which belongs to all stages' (Woods, 1914: 3), being the quality of stability (*sthiti*) within all mental states. Yoga then, involves the cultivation of what is already present within consciousness. We can see this as the Yoga school's experiential rendering of the Sāṃkhya causal theory of *satkāryavāda* – the effect (in this case the restriction of mental fluctuations in meditative concentration or *samādhi*) preexists within its cause (i.e. within earlier states of consciousness).

Although *saṃprajñāta-samādhi* clearly denotes a series of advanced states of meditative concentration, they are ultimately only preliminaries to the achievement of *asaṃprajñāta-samādhi*. The attainment of this level constitutes a new order of conscious experience. In this state of concentration, there is no longer any dependence upon external objects; it is a totally interiorised experience. The basis for this state of consciousness is the subliminal impressions (*saṃskāra*) deposited by past experiences (1.18). It is therefore a seedless (*nirbīja*) concentration since it does not lead to the implantation of further 'seeds' or *saṃskāras* which perpetuate the fluctuations of consciousness (1.46). It is also a state of great insight *(prajñā)* and is truth bearing (1.48). Indeed, the significance of *asaṃprajñāta-samādhi* is that it produces subliminal activators (*saṃskāra*) that inhibit the production of further subliminal activators (1.50).

Thus, according to the *Yoga Sūtra*, there are two basic types of *samādhi*. The first focuses itself upon an object and involves concepts (*vikalpa*), while the second is an objectless concentration devoid of conceptualisation (*nirvikalpa*) focusing instead upon the source of consciousness itself (namely, the *puruṣa*). This latter state is perpetuated by subliminal impressions (*saṃskāras*) which were produced by previous meditative practice. This shows again the necessity of constant practice (*abhyāsa*). By practising yoga regularly and intensely training the mind, one produces wholesome traces (*vāsanā*), making it easier and easier to attain higher and higher states of deep concentration. In the highest stage of attainment reality is experienced from the point of view of the isolated *puruṣa* and no longer from the point of view of the psycho-physical entity known as the aspiring yogin. From the point of view of the *puruṣa* it no longer makes the mistake of identifying with the mind–body complex of the yogin. From the point of view of the psycho-physical entity which we know as the yogin, his or her *buddhi* has been purified and has become completely sattvic and transparent to pure consciousness. The yogin's experience having become truly transparent, the *puruṣa* detaches itself from the activities of the material world (*prakṛti*) and dwells in its own form (I.3). This realisation is also described as *Dharma-megha-samādhi* – 'the meditative-concentration of the Rain-cloud', perhaps referring to the fact that at this stage the *puruṣa* has attained isolation from *prakṛti*.[11] As such, *prakṛti*, the primal matter, retires from view resembling a rain-cloud blowing away in the wind.

There are a number of differences between the Sāṃkhya and Yoga philosophies that can be discerned from a comparison between the *Sāṃkhya Kārikā* and the *Yoga Sūtra*. One of these is the interest the Yoga tradition displays in the nature and operations of consciousness. '*Citta*' or consciousness is a crucial technical term for Patañjali, occurring twenty-two times in the *Sūtra* and functioning as an umbrella term for the mental apparatus in general. As such, it encompasses the 'internal organ' (*antaḥkaraṇa*) of the Sāṃkhya tradition, representing the attributes of the *buddhi*, *ahaṃkāra* and *manas* in a single concept. Consciousness is both the cause of bondage and the means of escaping from it, being that which is coloured by the seer (i.e. *puruṣa*) and the seen (*prakṛti*) – that is the point of intersection between consciousness and materiality (YS 4.23).

> The stream of consciousness (*citta-nādī*) flows in both directions. It flows to the good and it flows to the bad. The one beginning with knowledge and ending with isolation flows to the good. The one beginning with ignorance and ending in rebirth (*saṃsāra*) flows to the bad.
>
> *Yoga Sūtra Bhāṣya* 1.12

Consciousness, however, is suffused and structured by subliminal activators (*saṃskāra*), which form sub-conscious traces (*vāsanā*) within the mind (4.24). It is these which feed the fluctuations or revolutions (*vṛtti*) of the mind. It is worth noting the relationship between these two concepts. *Vāsanā* is the trail left by mental actions. The notion is based upon the analogy of the unseen and intangible trace of aroma left in a room by someone wearing perfume. These karmic 'perfume traces' of previous mental activities are constituted by subconscious activators or *saṃskāra*. There are clear links with the Buddhist use of this term to denote one of the five bundles (*skandha*) which constitute the fluctuating mind–body complex and as one link in the twelve-fold scheme of inter-dependent-origination and also with the Mahāyāna Buddhist notion of a store-consciousness (*ālaya-vijñāna*), a concept adopted by the Yogācāra school to provide a 'psychological' account of the operations of karma.

The *Yoga Sūtra* also introduces a new concept – the notion of 'I-am-ness' (*asmitā*). Consciousness is said to arise from 'I-am-ness' alone (*asmitā-mātra*, 4.4). Thus, it is the notion that we are a cognising subject, a self undergoing various experiences, which causes consciousness to arise in the first place. It is the notion of an ego, therefore, which requires eradication if one is to attain liberation. 'I-am-ness' (*asmitā*) denotes the perpetual error of associating oneself with the body and the activities and contents of the mind. Nothing within our experience corresponds to our true self since everything that we experience is transitory and fluctuating (*vṛtti*). Clearly this notion bears some resemblance to the Sāṃkhya notion of *ahaṃkāra* – the feeling of 'I am'. In the *Yoga Sūtra*, however, *asmitā* is unambiguously classified as one of the five defilements (*kleśa*): 'Ignorance, the notion of "I-am-ness", passion, aversion and clinging to existence are the five defilements' (YS 2.3). Indeed, all of these defilements exist within ignorance which is the field (*kṣetra*) of their activity (YS 2.4).

> The notion of 'I am-ness' occurs when the power of the seer (*puruṣa*) and the power of seeing (i.e. the mind and the sense-organs) [appear] as if one self.
>
> *Yoga Sūtra* 2.6

Within Īśvarakṛṣṇa's Sāṃkhya system it was never clear at what point defilement occurred. If *buddhi* is defiled, for instance, what hope can there be of attaining liberation? On the other hand, if *buddhi* is pure how does it become defiled in the first place? Patañjali's Yoga system gives a name to the point where *puruṣa* and *prakṛti* become confused – it is when the notion of 'I-am-ness' (*asmitā*) arises.

The *Yoga Sūtra* of Patañjali and the *Bhāṣya* of Vyāsa display similarities with the thought of the Sāṃkhya philosopher Vindhyavāsin (c. 300–400 CE, see Larson and Bhattacharya, 1987: 141–6, 165–6) and suggests that the school may be influenced by or even be a development of his philosophical tradition (*saṃpradāya*). The all-embracing notion of consciousness (*citta*), for instance, dispenses with the need for a subtle material body (the *liṅga-śarīra* in Īśvarakṛṣṇa's system) to explain transmigration from one life to the next. This is a position adopted by Vindhyavāsin. The other significant difference between the Sāṃkhya and Yoga schools is the acceptance in the case of the latter of the notion of a divine being at least as a useful construct for contemplation and probably also as a metaphysical reality in its own right (see Chapter 9). The question still remains as to whether the Yoga system of Patañjali succeeds in avoiding the conflict between voluntarism and dualism that results from the Sāṃkhya adherence to a rigid and unbreachable dichotomy between *puruṣa* and *prakṛti*. Stephen Phillips (1985) argues that the tension between a voluntaristic acceptance of yogic practice and a rigid metaphysical dualism remains unresolved, whereas scholars such as Feuerstein (1980) and Whicher (1995: 52) argue that the Yoga system does indeed move beyond a rigid dualism of the Sāṃkhya variety.

> For Patañjali this puzzle is no puzzle at all, but an eminently practical issue. As long as the 'correlation (*saṃyoga*) between Self and world obtains, there is also suffering (*duḥkha*). Since the root of this correlation, or rather phantom correlation, between Self and non-self is nescience (*avidyā*), it is this which must be terminated.
>
> Feuerstein, 1980: 20

The Sāṃkhya and Yoga traditions, despite their differences, both focus attention upon the self as a 'transcendent consciousness'. The result is a philosophy which attempts to disentangle the principle of awareness from the vicissitudes of the mind–body complex that it is 'observing'. We have forgotten what we really are. In contrast, the Buddhist traditions question such approaches arguing that an analysis of awareness demonstrates its radically fluctuating and processual nature. There is no transcendent observer-self only a series of conditioned psycho-material processes. In both cases, however, our everyday conception of the self as a permanent and autonomous agent is an illusion, but for quite different reasons.

– NOTES –

1. Such an attempt to integrate the Āyurvedic scheme of the three dimensions of health/disease (*tri-dhātu/tri-doṣa*) with the *guṇas* occurs, for instance, in Ḍalhaṇa's commentary on the *Suśruta Saṃhitā*.
2. Note that the *Gauḍapāda Bhāṣya* differs in minor respects from Vātsyāyana's account, though Paramārtha follows the Nyāya tradition more closely in his analysis of the threefold nature of inference.
3. Note that the subtle elements (*tanmatra*) are not mentioned in the *Gītā* account of Sāṃkhya, instead we find the five gross elements followed by five sense objects.
4. Here we see the Sāṃkhya school's own version of the Brahmanical system of the four goals of man. These are righteousness and duty (*dharma*), wealth (*artha*), pleasure (*kāma*) and liberation from rebirth (*mokṣa*). Although the fourth goal was added later and exists in tension with the other three 'worldly' goals, this was obviated in the Brahmanical system by the association of different goals with the different stages of life (*āśrama*). The tension between worldly goals and other-worldly transcendence is represented here by the ambivalence of *prakṛti*.
5. K. M. Ganguli (Pratap Chandra Roy), The *Mahabharata of Krishna-Dwaipayana Vyasa*, Calcutta, Oriental Publishing Co., 1883–96), vol. 9: 97, cited in Jacobsen, 1996: 69–70.
6. What we know as the subjective self is composed of thirteen elements according to the Sāṃkhya school: *buddhi*, *ahaṃkāra*, and *manas* (i.e. the *antaḥkaraṇa*), the five sense-organs and the five organs or 'capacities' for action. These thirteen elements, in combination with the five subtle elements (*tanmatra*), make up the eighteen elements which

constitute the transmigrating subtle body (*liṅga-śarīra*). Bodily functions are regulated through the five vital breaths (*pañcavāyu*): *prāṇa*, *apāna*, *udāna*, *samāna* and *vyāna*. These relate to such life-maintaining activities as breathing, swallowing, digestion, excretion, sexual activity and the circulation of bodily fluids.

7. Crucial here is the phrase '*liṅgasyā'vinivṛtteḥ*', which I have translated as 'deliverance with regard to the subtle body' to preserve the ambiguity in the Sanskrit. Mainkar (1972: 181) renders this phrase as an ablative – 'deliverance from the subtle body', implying that the deliverance discussed refers to a change in the status of the *puruṣa*. Larson (1979: 272), however, translates the phrase as a genitive – 'deliverance of the subtle body', implying that what is in fact liberated is the subtle body itself. On this rendering it is possible to present the *puruṣa* as unaffected by the fate of the subtle entity with regard to isolation. The *puruṣa* is eternally in isolation and never really took part in the transmigratory process (k. 62).
8. For this reason we should perhaps be wary of interpreting Sāṃkhya thought according to modern western ideas of the 'individual' since it is clear that the ego-entity in Sāṃkhya terms is in fact a 'dividual' – a separable entity, constituted by an erroneous conjunction of consciousness and material processes. The goal of the Sāṃkhya system, therefore is precisely to undermine any notion of personal (i.e. ahaṃkāric) individuality and replace it with a model of the individual as an impersonal and transcendent witness-consciousness.
9. In his commentary Vyāsa provides an alternate definition of yoga in terms of its experiential goal – meditative concentration (*samādhi*).
10. Vācaspati Miśra draws an analogy between the yogin and an archer to explain the relationship between *vitarka* and *vicāra* forms of *samādhi*. Just as an archer begins by aiming at a larger target and then proceeds to smaller ones, the yogin, focuses upon increasingly more refined objects of experience and proceeds from gross objects to subtle objects (*Tattva-Vaiśāradī* on YS 1.17, see Woods, 1914: 41).
11. There is no doubt some connection here with the Mahāyāna Buddhist scheme of the ten stages of the *bodhisattva*. The final stage is described as the 'rain-cloud'. Who influenced whom in this regard, however, is an open question.

CHAPTER 9

Creation and Causality: Where do we come from?

– MYTH AND HISTORY –

It has often been said that traditional Indian culture lacks a developed sense of history. The problem here, as with the case of philosophy, turns on what one means by 'history'. Here again we find a modern incarnation of the *mythos–logos* distinction in the establishment of a rigid distinction between 'myth' and 'history' (see Chapter 1). The polarisation of 'myth' and 'history' is a characteristic feature of western modernity. It seems to have derived from the Judaeo-Christian sense of the importance of the 'historical truth' of God's covenant with humanity and an understanding of history as the linear unfolding of God's plan in the light of this. Thus the early Christians explicitly contrasted what they saw as the 'historical truth' of the life of Jesus Christ with the 'mythological' accounts of gods adhered to by the pagans. Modern notions of history, however, also reflect the secular distinction between 'facts' (and science) and 'fiction' (and literature) that increasingly predominated in Europe from the seventeenth century.

Clearly the factors that have resulted in 'the modern historical consciousness' were not present in traditional India. Romila Thapar, a contemporary Indian historian, argues that much of traditional Indian history has in fact been 'embedded' within cultural forms such as myths, that is, in 'forms in which historical consciousness has to be prised out' (Thapar, 1993: 137–8). Nevertheless, she argues, in the later epics (*itihāsa purāṇa*) we find 'the germs of a more conscious and less embedded historical tradition' (Thapar, 1993: 147) culminating in a much greater interest in a representation of chronological order in the post-Gupta period of the first millennium of the Common Era.

The view that Indian culture lacks a developed sense of history is usually associated with the representation of India as profoundly other-worldly in nature and with the Indian notion of time as cyclic, encompassing an endless repetition of events (and of rebirths) rather than linear and progressive in nature. As such 'the cyclic theory of time' has often been used by westerners as a powerful Orientalist trope for classifying, criticising and, ultimately, ruling India. In the nineteenth century Colonel Francis Whitford for instance argued that 'With regard to history, the Hindus really have nothing but romances, from which some truths occasionally may be extracted as well as from their geographical tracts' (Viyagappa, 1980: 237). It was left, therefore, to British scholars such as James Mill to provide the history that the Indians were deemed incapable of writing for themselves (Inden, 1990: 45–6). Indeed, as Johannes Fabian (1983) has argued, the denial of a historical consciousness and the location of 'Third World' cultures in a non-progressive past is a standard feature of western discourses of 'the Other', allowing for a separation of 'First' and 'Third Worlds' and an avoidance of responsibility in the continuing oppression of the latter by the former.

It is true that Indian culture has generally conceived of the creation and dissolution of the universe as cyclic in nature. Note, for instance, the Hindu brahmanical scheme of the four 'ages' (*yuga*). This begins with an age of perfection (*satya* or *kṛta yuga*) where the *Dharma* reigns supreme before proceeding through successive ages of decline, finally culminating in the current age of *kali yuga* where cosmic, social and moral 'entropy' undermines the orderliness of earlier periods. In most Indian systems of thought the cycle of the creation and destruction of the universe is recurrent. Every thousand cycles of creation and dissolution of the universe are known as a *kalpa* and this constitutes nothing more than a 'day of Brahmā'. Brahmā is often seen as the creator God, though often in a rather secondary role (rather like the Platonic *demiurge*) when compared to gods such as Viṣṇu and Śiva. Overall there are 1,000 cycles of creation and destruction of the universe for each day and night for the god Brahmā. After a hundred Brahmā years, the creator too is re-absorbed into the Absolute before emerging again and starting the process anew. Consequently, Indian cosmology tends to be of gargantuan proportions.

The polarisation of Indian and western conceptions of time, however, has been over-emphasised and has frequently been used as the justification for a whole host of stereotypical images about India and its 'otherness'. In the colonial period the British often criticised what they saw as the 'primitive' and 'indolent' nature of the Indian, failing to appreciate the 'oddity' of the 'protestant work ethic' that characterises much of Northern Euro-American culture and lifestyle. Moreover, it was in Britain and Northern Europe that the Industrial Revolution first took shape (established as it was on the plundering of resources from India and the other colonies). The modernisation process that this initiated transformed the traditional agricultural lifestyle of hard labour punctuated by periods of relative inactivity into the routinised regime of urban industrial production. Given the prevalence of the doctrine of rebirth in India, it is hardly surprising that many Hindus, particularly those living and working in a traditional village context rather than in urban centres like Bombay and Delhi, have a more 'long-term' conception of the time-scale in which their lives will unfold. Of course, in drawing this distinction I am not attempting to establish some kind of essentialised dichotomy between Indians and westerners. Indeed, in this respect as in many others the difference between the rich in Bombay and the rich in London may be less significant than those between different class-groupings within 'the same' city (Gupta and Ferguson, 1992: 20).

Furthermore, Indian notions of time as cyclic are not unusual even in a western context. Ancient Greek notions of time (if this counts as western) were also predicated on a similar scheme of progressive decline and in the case of movements like Orphism, Pythagoreanism and Platonism, were also explicitly associated with a doctrine of rebirth. Moreover, even in modern western culture the tropes of circular time are constantly invoked in the 'boom and bust' language of economics, in the routinisation of the work-place (the eternal recurrence of the 'nine-to-five' job), in the cyclic patterns of the seasons, the biological rhythms of the body and the 24-hour clock, and so on. What is strikingly *different* about modern western conceptions, however, is the rigidity of the distinction that is made between *beings* and *things,* which, as Akhil Gupta notes, allows for a constant recycling of ideas, commodities, fashion and even garbage, but does not allow for the possibility of the rebirth of beings:

> The idea that persons can be reborn in a manner analogous to commodities appears deeply threatening in the West precisely because it attacks the entire ideological edifice of capitalism. For if persons were not unique, individual, and singular in some primal sense, what would it mean for them to make promises, have wills, and enter contracts? The whole ideology of democratic capitalism, of participation in an economy and in a polity, is predicated upon the maintenance of this sharp and irrevocable distinction between persons and things.
>
> Gupta, 1992: 205

It would seem more prudent then, to note that, while there are of course differences *between* Indian and western conceptions of time, there are also differences *within* them. In the Nyāya and Vaiśeṣika systems time is an all-pervasive, infinite and partless substance, providing the basis for all movement and change. For the Vaibhāṣika Buddhists past, present and future all exist (hence the school's other name – '*sarvāstivāda*' – the doctrine that everything exists). In contrast, the Sautrāntikas conceived of time as a succession of moments (*kṣaṇa*) that cease as soon as their manifestation has ended. Nāgārjuna and the Madhyamaka school rejected the independent reality of time (along, of course, with everything else) seeing it as a nothing more than a dependent set of relations between phenomena (MMK ch. 19). For the Sāṃkhya school, time is also conceived of as a relation between events rather than as a substance, but remains a real manifestation of *prakṛti* – the primordial materiality. According to Vyāsa, the Yoga school posits the moment (*kṣaṇa*) as the smallest dimension of time (as the atom is the smallest dimension of matter) and believes that only the present moment really exists (*YS Bhāsya* 3.52). In contrast, for the Advaita Vedānta school time itself is, in the final analysis, an illusion (*māyā*) since only *brahman* – the unchanging absolute – is ultimately real. For Bhartṛhari the grammarian, time is not only real but establishes the nature of existence itself, being an important factor in the creation of the universe by *śabda-brahman* (see Chapter 3). Not only are these conceptions of time quite different from each other, not all of them are easily assimilated to a cyclic conception of time.

– ANCIENT INDIAN COSMOGONIES –

Cosmogony or the question of the origins of the universe has always been of interest to Indian philosophers. The creation of the universe is a particular preoccupation of the hymns in Book ten of the *Ṛg Veda*. These materials probably date from the tenth to the eighth centuries BCE and are diverse in the accounts they offer. In a manner reminiscent of the Hebrew Genesis narrative, some of these early Vedic hymns conceive of creation as the result of the word (Vāc) and as the establishment of a rhythmic order (*ṛta*) to the universe. The structure of reality resembles and in fact is in many respects bound up with the syntactical and grammatical structures of language. Just as we express our ideas through words (which are often imperfect expressions of our thoughts, feelings and experiences), the world is created through the expressive power of the word. For this reason the Vedas are also known as *śruti* – that which is heard; they are an aural revelation. The wise seers (*ṛṣi*) do not so much compose the Vedic hymns as 'tune into' the natural rhythms of the cosmos. The various brahmin officiants pay homage to the revelations that they have received through constant recitation in a highly ritualised and sacrificial context.

Ṛg Veda X.129 offers an example of very early philosophical speculation on the nature of reality before the creation of the universe. The hymn declares that there was neither being (*sat*) nor non-being (*asat*) before creation. Indeed

> There was neither death nor immortality then. There was no distinguishing sign of night nor of day. That one breathed windless [i.e. without breath], by its own impulse. Other than that there was nothing beyond.
>
> *Ṛg Veda* X.129.2, translation in O'Flaherty, 1981: 25

This undivided oneness is described as darkness and water, but is energised by the power of heat (*tapas*, v. 3). '*Tapas*' is a term with a variety of shades of symbolic meaning, denoting the cosmic heat of creation, the procreative heat of sexual desire, the ritual heat of the sacrificial fire and the psycho-physiological heat induced by the practice of yogic austerities. The hymn, however, ends on a sceptical note

> Who really knows? Who will here proclaim it? Whence was it produced? Whence is this creation? The gods came afterwards, with the creation of the universe. Who then knows whence it has arisen?
> Whence has this creation arisen – perhaps it formed itself, or perhaps it did not – the one who looks down on it in the highest heaven, only he knows, or perhaps he does not know.
>
> *Ṛg Veda* X. 129.6–7, O'Flaherty, 1981: 25–6

These verses seem to imply that there is a supreme being beyond the gods but that even he may not know the secret of creation. This hymn is clearly also a record of some of the *brahman*-riddles (*brahmodya*) endlessly disputed by brahmanical officiants of the sacrificial rites. As we saw in Chapter 3, such debating contexts between Vedic scholars constituted one of the earliest sources for the later development of a formal structure for Indian philosophical debate.

There are a variety of other cosmogonic accounts to be found in the tenth book of the *Ṛg Veda*. Notable in particular is X.121 which speaks of a 'golden embryo' (*hiraṇyagarbha*) out of which the universe emerges and X.90 – the *Puruṣa Sūkta* – which conceives of creation as the sacrificial dismemberment of a cosmic person. As we saw in Chapter 8, this hymn provided a justification of the classification of Indian society into four class-groupings (*varṇa*) through the identification of each *varṇa* with a different part of the Cosmic Man's body.

– CREATION AND CAUSALITY IN BUDDHISM –

In contrast to the Vedic brahmanical traditions, the Buddhist tradition is often represented as being unconcerned with the question of the origin of the universe. There are a number of occasions in the early Buddhist texts, for instance, where the Buddha refuses to give a definitive answer to certain questions. These became known as the ten 'unanswered' (Sanskrit: *avyākṛta*, Pāli: *avyākata*) questions and are as follows:

> Is the world eternal? Is the world not eternal? Is the world finite? Is the world infinite? Is the self (*ātman*) identical with the body? Is the self different from the body? Does an enlightened being (*buddha*) continue to exist after death? Does a *buddha* cease to exist after death? Does a *buddha* both exist and not exist after death? Does a *buddha* neither exist nor not exist after death?

In a 'short discourse to Māluṅkya' the Buddha explains that these matters are not his concern, being obstacles to the alleviation of suffering *(duḥkha)*:

> It is as if there were a man struck by an arrow that was smeared thickly with poison; his friends and companions, his family and relatives would summon a doctor to see to the arrow. And the man might say 'I will not draw out this arrow as long as I do not know whether the man by whom I was struck was a brahmin, a kṣatriya, a vaiśya, or a śūdra ... as long as I do not know his name and his family ... whether he was tall, short or of medium height ...' That man would not discover these things, but that man would die.
>
> *Cūla-Māluṅkya Sutta*, *Majjhima Nikāya* i, 429, translation in Gethin, 1998: 66

On another occasion the Buddha remained silent when asked similar questions by his disciple Vacchagotta regarding the existence or non-existence of the self (*ātman*). Later, when asked by Ānanda to explain his silence, the Buddha declared that both questions ('does the self exist?' and 'does the self not exist?') already presuppose extreme views. Questions such as 'does the self exist?' and 'is the self identical or different from the body?' imply that there is an abiding-presence or persisting self – the extreme of eternalism (*śāśvata-vāda*). On the other hand, to ask 'does the self not exist?' implies the opposite position that there is nothing at all, or that the self has ceased to exist (but existed before). This is the extreme of annihilationism (*uccheda-vāda*). Similarly, questions concerning the future ontological status of an enlightened being are based upon a dichotomy between 'existence' and 'non-existence'. In contrast, the Buddhist view is that there is no abiding-self or substance persisting through each stream of experience, merely the dynamic processes of the five *skandhas* themselves (see Chapter 4). In this sense the questions themselves must be questioned. If the Buddha had given a verbal response to Vacchagotta's enquiries he would have misled the questioner. Better to remain silent and let Vacchagotta reflect upon the problematic status of the questions themselves. Similarly, if one asks 'did Gautama like Coca Cola?' one cannot expect a definitive yes or no answer because the question itself is inherently problematic due to its radically anachronistic nature.

Despite the existence of a philosophical strand, culminating in the Madhyamaka school of Nāgārjuna, which rejected cosmogonic and metaphysical speculation as fruitless, there are Buddhist texts which do appear to offer an account of the creation of the universe. Most notable in this regard is the *Aggañña sutta* or 'Discourse on What is Primary'. In this text the Buddha pokes fun at the brahmanical priests for believing that they originate from the mouth of the god Brahmā (a later version of the *Puruṣa Sūkta* cosmogony discussed above). Do they not realise, Gautama mockingly asks, that they are born from their mothers' wombs? The second half of the *sutta* is devoted to a rival account of creation, this time based upon Buddhist values and principles. Beings were originally immaterial in nature but became enmeshed in the material world once they tasted of its pleasures. This, however, is the source of craving and as beings became more attached and selfish, crime and social divisions arose. Eventually the people appoint one of their own as a king to legislate in disputes and maintain law and order.

Clearly, one of the functions of this cosmogony is to provide an account of the origins of the four *varṇa* which does not privilege the brahmanical priestly class as the authentic 'mouthpiece' of society. In the *Aggañña sutta* the *varṇa* system of social stratification is no longer seen as 'natural' in the sense of reflecting the nature of the deity but is instead a consequence of human greed, attachment and craving. Brahmins arose not because they derive from the mouth of Brahmā, but because of social divisions constructed by humans themselves.

The *Aggañña sutta*, along with countless others, demonstrates the rather limited status of gods (*devas*) within the Buddhist tradition. It is sometimes said that Buddhism is an atheistic religion, but again this rather depends upon what one means by 'atheism'. Certainly there is no all-powerful creator god 'outside the system', but Buddhist texts and cultures readily accept the existence of a whole host of divine beings. Gods from the Buddhist perspective are superhuman beings – powerful and long-lived entities, born as such due to previous karmic attainments. Indeed, the boundaries between the various stations in life (god, human, animal, hungry ghost and inhabitant of a hellish realm) are fluid within the Buddhist worldview. All beings, including the most powerful gods, remain part of the cycle of rebirth and experience lives in a variety of forms. It should be no surprise to learn then that the popular board game of snakes and ladders originated in India as a game about rebirth. Even the great Brahmā is liable to slide down a snake and have to begin all over again. *Saṃsāra*, however, is not a game, nor is it a race! Although the lifespan of a god is said to be long and relatively luxurious, the Buddhist tradition generally views such heavenly existences as obstacles to the attainment of *nirvāṇa*. The point after all is to get off the board and not to stay on it!

An enlightened being (*buddha*) like Gautama, therefore, is considered superior in authority to the most powerful deity. This can be seen from the early Buddhist attitude to the god Brahmā, the divine archetype of the Hindu brahmins on earth. In the *Kevaddha Sutta* Brahmā is represented as an arrogant and flawed god, unable to answer certain questions about the nature of reality but unwilling to admit his ignorance to others. Elsewhere, Brahmā is seen to be deluded about his status as the creator of the universe. It turns out that he is nothing more than the first being to be born after the dissolution (*mahāpralaya*) of the previous universe. Brahmā becomes lonely and desires companionship. Eventually, other beings come into existence as determined by the *karma* of their previous lives. Brahmā mistakenly thinks that he has created them. Again, this story is a Buddhist re-telling of a familiar Brahmanical account of creation that occurs throughout the *Upaniṣads*. Thus,

> In the beginning this world was just a single body (*ātman*) shaped like a man. He looked around and saw nothing but himself. The first thing he said was, 'Here I am!' and from that the name 'I' came into being ... He wanted to have a companion ... So he split (*pat*) his body into two, giving rise to husband (*pati*) and wife (*patnī*) ... He copulated with her, and from their union human beings were born ... It then occurred to him: 'I alone am the creation, for I created all this.'
>
> *Bṛhadāraṇyaka Upaniṣad* 1.4.1–5, trans. in Olivelle, 1996: 13–14

It is clear, however, that for the early Buddhist traditions, not only does 'Brahmā' denote a category or an office with a variety of levels of attainment rather than a single being, but the universe itself comprises of an incalculable number of world spheres (*cakra-vāda*), each with their own Brahmā deities.

> Clusters of a thousand 'world spheres' may be ruled over by yet higher gods called Great Brahmās, but it would be wrong to conclude that there is any one or final overarching Great Brahmā – God the Creator. It may be that beings come to take a particular Great Brahmā as creator of the world, and a Great Brahmā may himself even form the idea that he is creator, but this is just the result of delusion on the part of both parties. In fact the universe recedes ever upwards with one class of great Brahmā being surpassed by a further, higher class of Great Brahmā.
>
> Gethin, 1998: 114

In the *Tevijja Sutta*, the Buddha is asked by some young brahmins how one might attain union with the god Brahmā. Gautama proceeds to criticise the brahmins and their teachers for debating the nature of something that they have not themselves experienced. However, instead of rejecting the question, the Buddha astounds the brahmins by stating that he has experienced such a state and is able to teach them the way to attain it. What then follows is an outline of a set of meditative practices known as the four 'divine dwellings' (*brahma-vihāra*). These involve the cultivation of loving-kindness (*maitrī/mettā*), compassion (*karuṇā*), sympathetic-joy (*muditā*) and impartiality (*upekṣā/upekkhā*). In a stroke the brahmanical goal of abiding in a heavenly realm with the god Brahmā is reinterpreted in Buddhist terms. 'Dwelling with Brahmā' no longer denotes an other-worldly and heavenly realm, but is transformed into a set of meditative practices and a moral code of conduct for acting towards others.

The Buddhist rejection of the existence of an all-powerful creator is reflected in the Budddhist theory of inter-dependent-origination (*pratītya-sam-utpāda*). In Chapter 4 it was noted that this scheme provided an account of the causal process, and of the cycle of rebirths in particular, establishing causal continuity without personal identity. What we have here is a series of mutually reinforcing processes and not permanent or abiding substances. The scheme (usually represented as a wheel) has no first cause. It is also used by Buddhists, therefore, to account for causation without requiring a prime mover. *Saṃsāra* is beginningless, at least in the sense that the beginning of the series of rebirths is impossible for us to conceive. Our destiny then is in our hands.

In the Abhidharma schools the doctrine of momentariness (*kṣaṇa-vāda*) led to the adoption of a causal theory known as *asat-kārya-vāda* or 'the doctrine that the effect does not exist (in its cause)'. Causal processes involve the creation of new entities and are not to be characterised in terms of the transformation of abiding-substances. This theory of causation, in a slightly different form, is also adopted by the Nyāya and Vaiśeṣika schools, as we shall see. In the Mahāyāna schools of Buddhism, however, the Buddhist concept of inter-dependent-origination was interpreted to mean that everything lacked independent existence (*svabhāva-śūnya*). As we have seen, this is what Nāgārjuna means by the term emptiness (*śūnyatā*). The realisation that there are no substantial entities, however, led Nāgārjuna to argue that inter-dependent-origination (*pratītyasamutpāda*) really meant no origination at all (*an-utpāda*). In other words, the insubstantiality and relativity of everything requires us to give up the idea that there are any substances undergoing change. All causal theories attempt to explain the relationship between a cause and its effect. However, in so far as one takes the cause and the effect to be independently established entities, such accounts are doomed to failure. It is only once one realises that everything is empty of independent existence, or, to put this another way, that nothing is an ultimate and independently established entity, that one can make sense of change at all. Mutual interdependency, therefore, leads to the realisation that from the ultimate point of view nothing really changes at all, since there are no 'things' to change.

Such a radical rejection of change was unlikely to gain many supporters from the other schools of Indian philosophy. Sometimes the Madhyamaka view is compared to the absolutism of the non-dualistic school of Vedānta. According to this tradition, change is also an illusion (*māyā*) and nothing has ever really come into existence (*ajātivāda*). This view is first put forward in a systematic fashion in the *Gauḍapādīya Kārikā* (sixth century CE), the earliest *śāstra* of the Advaita school. Although the work has clearly been influenced by Mahāyāna Buddhist ideas (King, 1995), the nature of the doctrine is quite different. Whereas Nāgārjuna argues that nothing originates because there are no real substances or ultimate entities at all, the Advaita school understands non-origination to mean that there is an unoriginated or unborn reality – *brahman* – the absolute. The Madhyamaka Buddhist school is a radically non-theistic philosophy, grounded in the impossibility of a first cause. In stark contrast, the Advaita Vedānta school is a broadly theistic tradition, grounded in the immutability of the first cause (see below).

– God and Causality in Nyāya-Vaiśeṣika –

> Tell me, Yājñavalkya – how many gods are there? ... Three hundred and three and three thousand and three ... Thirty-three ... Six ... Three ... Two ... One and a half ... One.
>
> *Bṛhadāraṇyaka Upaniṣad* 3.9.1, Olivelle, 1996: 46

Within the various schools of Hindu philosophy there are a number of different attitudes towards and conceptions of the divine. This itself reflects the rich pluralism of Indian culture which contains polytheistic, henotheistic, monotheistic, non-theistic and atheistic traditions. The *Nyāya* and *Vaiśeṣika sūtras*, for instance, are somewhat reticent on the question of a divine being. It is Uddyotakara (sixth century CE) who is primarily responsible for first representing Nyāya as an unequivocally monotheistic school (Matilal, 1977: 91). The divine being is the efficient cause of the world (*nimitta-kāraṇa*), that is, the initiator of the creation of the universe. The creator is also the being who dispenses the fruits of *karma* to the various beings inhabiting the universe.

In the Vaiśeṣika system atoms are inert and require an external force to create motion. In the original *Vaiśeṣika Sūtra* little mention is made of a divine being as a cause of the created world, though there is an obscure reference to 'That' (*tat*) from which the Vedas derive their authority (VS 1.1.3) and brief mention of *karma* as an unseen force (*adṛṣṭa*, VS 10.2.8). Again it was later thinkers, beginning with Praśastapāda, who interpreted the early *sūtras* in a theistic manner, arguing that God (*īśvara*) is the principle of intelligence and the architect of the universe, creating the world out of the eternal substances (atoms and individual selves). The god conceived by the Nyāya-Vaiśeṣika is limited in his power by the *karma* of each individual self that is carried over from previous universes. Later Udayana (eleventh century CE) developed a number of arguments for the existence of God (see Chemparathy, 1972).

The introduction of a divine creator no doubt reflects shifts in the religious map of India between the time of the composition of the Nyāya and Vaiśeṣika *sūtras* and later commentators. Nevertheless, it also seems that the notion of a creator was introduced to address certain issues arising from the Nyāya-Vaiśeṣika theory of causality. This position is known as 'the doctrine that the effect does not exist in the cause' (*asat-kārya-vāda*) or alternatively as 'the doctrine of new production' (*ārambha-vāda*). For the Nyāya-Vaiśeṣika systems causation involves a combination of causal factors (*kāraṇa sāmagrī*) of three distinct types:

1. Inherent cause (*samavāyi kāraṇa*). This category represents the basic constituents in which an entity or whole inheres, that is, that out of which it is made. Ordinarily, this would be the same as the material cause (*upādāna-kāraṇa*), but since the Nyāya-Vaiśeṣika accept non-material substances such as *ātman* and space, these too can function as causal substrates for certain effects (see Matilal, 1985: 286). The inherent cause of a cloth, therefore, is the threads that make it what it is. The important point for this tradition, however, is that the entity (in this case the cloth) is a newly created entity (hence the designation of this theory as 'the doctrine of new production'). Thus, whilst the parts (the threads) inhere in the whole, the whole is a new entity created by the coming together of the various parts (the threads). The cloth resides within the parts in a relation of inherence (*samavāya*). Of course, one of the problems with this account is that it leads the Nyāya-Vaiseṣika to the counter-intuitive assertion that the cloth (the whole) and the threads (its parts) coexist in the same space but remain different (see Chapter 5, note 5).
2. Non-inherent cause (*asamavāyi kāraṇa*). This category refers to those properties that belong to the inherent cause but have a mediated relationship with the effect. Thus, the threads may be blue in colour. The colour blue does not function as a direct cause of the cloth, but it is an inherent attribute of the thread which is the direct (inherent) cause of the cloth.
3. Efficient cause (*nimitta-kāraṇa*). This category refers to the agency that produces the effect from the first two causes. In the cloth example the weaver and the loom would be seen as the efficient causes. For the Nyāya-Vaiśeṣika the creation of the universe requires an efficient cause – an agency producing it. This is God (*īśvara*).

– CAUSAL THEORY IN SĀṂKHYA AND YOGA –

The theory of causation adopted by the Sāṃkhya, Yoga and the Vedānta schools is based on a causal theory known as *satkāryavāda*, or 'the doctrine that the effect exists within its cause' (SK 9/BS 2.1.7). According to this view creation is the transformation (*pariṇāma*) of a cause into its effect and does not, as the Nyāya-Vaiśeṣika system suggests, result in the production of a new entity. The roots of this debate are ancient and go back to the earliest speculations in the Vedic hymns as to whether the world emerged from a pre-creative condition of non-existence (*asat*) or existence (*sat*). The classic scriptural source for the *sat-kārya* view that the effect preexists in its cause is found in the *Chāndogya Upaniṣad*:

> It is like this, son. By means of just one lump of clay one would perceive everything made of clay – the transformation is a verbal handle, a name – while the reality is just this: 'It's clay.'
>
> *Chāndogya Upaniṣad* 6.1.4, trans. in Olivelle, 1996: 148

Based upon this position, there can be no creation out of nothing in the Sāṃkhya, Yoga and Vedānta schools. Creation is a transformation or change (*pariṇāma*) in the state of what is already there. For the Sāṃkhya school, primordial materiality (*prakṛti)* literally becomes the world, which in that sense can be said to exist in potential within the unmanifested *prakṛti* (*pradhāna*) before creation. So, for Sāṃkhya, creation is the making manifest of what is already there but in an unmanifested state. According to the *sat-kārya* theory no amount of effort could bring a non-existent effect into existence. Milk cannot produce oil and, as the saying goes, you cannot get blood out of a stone. Moreover, there must be some kind of invariable relation (*samavāya*) between a cause and its effect. For such a relationship to exist, however, implies that the effect already exists in some sense within the cause, otherwise what is the relationship between? (see *Sāṃkhya Kārikā* v. 9).

Although early Sāṃkhya thought is difficult to distinguish clearly from Vedāntic philosophy and therefore tends to be decidedly theistic in nature, the most famous exponent of the Sāṃkhya philosophy as a definitive philosophical school (*darśana*) – Īśvarakṛṣṇa – expounds a view that is remarkably similar to the Buddhist position. The *Sāṃkhya Kārikā* states that the elemental or gross material creation (*bhautika sarga*) of *prakṛti* results in fourteen levels of embodiment. Eight of these are divine realms, one is the human realm and there are five realms below the human.

> There is predominance of Sattva in the world above; below the creation is full of Darkness. In the middle Rajas predominates. *This is so from Brahmā down to a blade of grass.*
>
> *Sāṃkhya Kārikā* verse 54, trans. in Mainkar, 1972: 179 [my italics]

All realms, including existence as the highest deity, are a manifestation of primordial materiality and in that sense are, if you like, part of the snakes and ladders board – the cycle of rebirths (*saṃsāra*). The final goal in the

Sāṃkhya school, of course, is to disassociate one's pure consciousness (*puruṣa*) from the agency of the dancing *prakṛti*. We have taken the game too seriously and identified ourselves, our hopes and our desires with a moving counter on a board.

Later interpretations of Sāṃkhya tended to incorporate a theistic element into the tradition, though this is clearly incompatible with Īśvarakṛṣṇa's dualistic metaphysics which leaves no room for a creator god. This shift reflects the gradual introduction of theism to the various Hindu schools of philosophy, particularly with the rise of monotheistic devotionalism (*bhakti*) in India and the increasing influence of the Vedānta traditions. Thus, according to Vijñānabhikṣu (1550–1600 CE), the non-theistic stance of the Sāṃkhya system is 'a mere hyperbolic assertion' (*prauḍhivādamātram*) or a 'concession to current views' (*abhyupagamavāda*).[1] Such an interpretation, of course, is only possible because as Vijñānabhikṣu himself notes, by this time

> The Sāṃkhya doctrine has been devoured by the sun of time and only a tiny crescent of the moon of knowledge is still visible.[2]
>
> *Sāṃkhya Pravācana Bhāṣya* v. 5, trans. in Hulin, 1978: 157

Nevertheless, one can find much earlier evidence of an attempt to incorporate theism into a dualistic metaphysics in the *Yoga Sūtra* of Patañjali. Here contemplation of the deity (*īśvara-praṇidhāna*) is mentioned alongside the practice of austerities (*tapas*) and the cultivation of self-analysis (*svādhyāya*) as the yoga of action (*kriyā yoga*, YS 2.1). It is also included as part of a regime of self-discipline (*niyama*), the second limb of the eight-limbed yoga that is usually associated with Patañjali. Indeed the inclusion of the notion of a deity is one of the distinguishing features of the Yoga school. How though is the notion of a divine being to be reconciled with Patañjali's metaphysical dualistic system which explains the creation of the universe in terms of the mis-identification of the principle of pure consciousness (*puruṣa*) with the fluctuating activities of the mind (*citta vṛtti*)? In this scheme, as in the Sāṃkhya school, there is no need to posit a divine creator to bring the universe into existence, the notions of *puruṣa* and *prakṛti* are sufficient in themselves (YS 2.17). According to Patañjali, therefore, the distinctive feature of the deity is that

> The Lord is a special [kind of] *puruṣa*, untouched by hindrances, *karma*, its fruition, and latent-deposits [of karmic actions].
>
> *Yoga Sūtra* 1.24

The uniqueness of the Lord, therefore, lies in the fact that he remains forever untouched by the activities of *prakṛti*. Of course, as the *Sāṃkhya Kārikā* points out, in a very real sense the *puruṣa* also never really becomes entangled in materiality and the cycle of rebirths (SK 62). The difference, however, is that the Lord never makes the mistake of identifying himself with materiality, whereas the individual *puruṣas* evidently do. The deity, therefore, remains forever aware of his status as transcendent to the world, unaffected by *karma* and its consequences. This is a highly unusual conception of the divine. The Lord is not the creator of the universe. Nevertheless, he is supreme in his omniscience (YS 1.25),[3] and has been a teacher (*guru*) from the very beginning, being unbound by time (YS 1.26). The symbol for contemplating the deity is the sacred syllable Om (YS 1.27).

The Yoga conception of God, however, raises a number of questions. Is a god who never creates and never becomes involved in the world a god at all? Why would such a being be worth considering? Why is contemplation of the Lord mentioned if such a being has no part to play in the life of the practitioner? We should note that the *Yoga Sūtra* is in many ways a compendium of a variety of yogic practices. Since contemplation of the deity is an important yogic practice for many Hindu traditions perhaps Patañjali included it in an attempt to be comprehensive. He does note, after all, that meditative-concentration (*samādhi*) can be attained by concentration on an object of one's choice (YS 1.39). Thus, Ninian Smart (1968: 30) argues that 'Yoga has borrowed a concept from popular religion and put it to a special use', though scholars such as Eliade (1973: 75) and Feuerstein (1980: 3) have argued that *īśvara* is included by Patañjali precisely because it is an experiential datum encountered during yogic practice. This in all probability involved some degree of visualisation of the Lord's form. Such a practice would eventually lead to a revelation, sometimes visionary sometimes not, of the Lord's true form. The experience of the Lord, then, was an experienced reality for the yogin, and so must be included in any comprehensive review of the practice. Although one can question whether Patañjali himself practised a form of theistic yoga he certainly endorsed it in some form. Indeed, had this not been the case it is unlikely that the *Yoga Sūtra* would have been so influential in Hindu circles.

In what sense, however, can a fully transcendent deity like *īśvara* act as a teacher? Patañjali seems to view the Lord (this special untouched self) as a kind of archetypal figure, that is, as an example of someone who has already reached the end point of the yogic path. Sometimes this Lord is identified with the god Śiva who is (amongst other things) said to be the god of all yogins. There is no evidence of specific sectarian allegiances within the *Yoga Sūtra*, however, *īśvara* being little more than the name for a special kind of eternally liberated *puruṣa*. Nevertheless, as the archetypal yogin, *īśvara* is a representative of the first yogin to attain liberation (although he in fact has never made the mistake of becoming involved in the world).

> If one excludes the possibility of *īśvara* actively entering into a teaching situation by mysteriously phenomenalising himself, there remains only one logical alternative, and this is that his role as a teacher is entirely passive ... In other words, *īśvara* is the archetypal *yogin* who 'instructs' by his sheer being. Pressing this metaphor still further, one could say that 'communication' between him and the aspiring *yogin* is possible by reason of the ontic co-essentiality of god and the inmost nucleus of man, *viz*. the Self (*puruṣa*).
>
> Feuerstein, 1980: 11–12

Contemplation of a supreme being, therefore, is another way in which one can investigate the nature of the self for the Lord represents the goal to be achieved by the yogin. Yoga then is the means whereby one becomes like the Lord (in that one returns to one's original and primeval condition – the isolation (*kaivalya*) of pure untouched consciousness). In some brahmanical traditions the goal of yoga is to attain some form of ontological union with the divine being rather than to become like him in attaining a state of freedom from *karma* and rebirth. In Patañjali's Yoga system, like the Sāṃkhya system of Īśvarakṛṣṇa, there appear to be many *puruṣas* (YS 2.22), though this well-established interpretation (found, for instance, in the standard commentaries of Vyāsa and Vācaspati Miśra) has been disputed by some (for example, Feuerstein, 1980: 22–4).

– THE EARLY VEDĀNTA OF THE BRAHMA SŪTRA –

The *Brahma Sūtra* (c. 250 BCE–450 CE) is attributed to Bādarāyaṇa and constitutes an early attempt to systematise the philosophy of the *Upaniṣads*. *Brahman* is the absolute divinity within the Vedānta traditions. Although *brahman* is the creator of the universe (*kartṛ*, BS 1.4.6), it is not a personal deity or being (*puruṣa*), being essentially without organs (*karaṇa*, 2.1.31). In that sense it is not to be confused with our earlier discussion of the god Brahmā or with a cosmic person as in the ancient Vedic hymn the *Puruṣa Sūkta*. *Brahman* is an impersonal (or perhaps supra-personal) absolute and as such is the ground of all being. It is limitless (*ayama*), omnipresent (*sarvagata*, 3.2.37), eternal (*ananta*, 3.2.26), without parts (*niravayava*, 2.1.26) and devoid of form (*arūpavad*, 3.2.13). The essence of *brahman* is bliss (*ānanda*, 3.3.11), being the source of all happiness (1.1.14; alluded to in 1.2.15).

All Vedānta traditions, with the exception of the dualistic school of Madhva, see *brahman* as that which creates the world (that is, its efficient cause or *nimitta-kāraṇa*) as well as that out of which the world is created (its material cause or *upādāna-kāraṇa*, BS 1.4.23; 2.1.19–20).[4] It is 'that from which the origin, subsistence and dissolution of [the universe occurs.]'

(1.1.2). *Brahman* is the womb (*yoni*) out of which the universe is born (1.4.27).

According to the *Brahma Sūtra* the creation of the universe involves a real transformation of *brahman* itself (*brahma-pariṇāma-vāda*, see BS 1.4.26). No separate factor such as the primordial matter (*prakṛti*) of the Sāṃkhya school is required to explain the manifestation of the universe. *Brahman* is the principle of intelligence in the universe (*prājña or jña*, I.1.5; 1.1.9; 1.1.10; 3.2.16). This view is clearly expounded in response to the dualism of the Sāṃkhya school where the material cause of the world is said to be primordial, insentient matter. Indeed much of the *Brahma Sūtra* appears to have been composed in order to refute the position of the Sāṃkhya school (Nakamura, 1985: 472). This suggests that the historical and philosophical roots of early Vedānta were closely associated with the development of Sāṃkhya thought. Evidence of this can be found, for instance, in the Sāṃkhya-cum-Vedānta doctrines to be found in the *Bhagavad Gītā* and chapter XII of the *Mahābhārata* and from Buddhist and Jain accounts of Vedānta before the advent of Śaṅkara in the eighth century CE.[5]

– ŚAṄKARA AND THE PHILOSOPHY OF NON-DUALISM (ADVAITA VEDĀNTA) –

According to the *Brahma Sūtra*, the universe is a product of the dynamic creativity of *brahman*. However, an objection is raised in BS 2.1.26 that the *brahma-pariṇāma* theory cannot be maintained without relinquishing the immutability of *brahman*. Thus, the opponent suggests

1. If the whole of *brahman* transforms, it becomes another, rendering *brahman* non-existent, and yet,
2. If only a part of *brahman* is transformed, this contradicts the unity and partlessness of *brahman*.

The objector suggests that if *brahman* is immutable and without parts and yet transforms itself into the world, then 1. *brahman* must be ultimately responsible for what happens in that world, and since the world has much unhappiness in it, *brahman* cannot be free from that unhappiness, and 2. *brahman* cannot remain immutable at the same time as transforming itself into the universe. The text's response to the objection is to avoid it. The student of the Vedānta must accept the views of the scriptures regardless of logical problems and apparent philosophical inconsistencies (2.1.27).

Problems in maintaining the immutability of the absolute alongside its status as the efficient and material cause of the universe precipitated the development of the radical non-dualistic (*advaita*) stance of Śaṅkara (eighth century CE). In his commentary on *Brahma Sūtra* 2.1.26 Śaṅkara replies to the objection that *brahman* either changes (and becomes something else) or does not and therefore cannot be the material cause of the world. Śaṅkara's response is to suggest that the appearance of a world of multiplicity is in fact a result of ignorance (*avidyā*). *Brahman* remains immutable and does not undergo any real change in manifesting as the universe.

> For a thing does not become multiformed just because aspects are imagined on it through ignorance. Not that the moon, perceived to be many by a man with blurred vision ... becomes really so ... In Its real aspect *brahman* remains unchanged and beyond all phenomenal actions.
>
> *Brahma Sūtra Bhāṣya* 2.1. 27, Gambhirananda, 1977: 356

Brahman may appear to have become the universe, but this is merely the way things appear from an unenlightened perspective. *Brahman* remains forever an immutable, unchanging and unified ultimate reality. The non-dualistic (*advaita*) strand of Vedānta is based upon the idea that there are two levels of truth – empirical and ultimate – a doctrine first developed by the Buddhists. The *Brahma Sūtra* argues that *brahman* is incapable of being affected by anything, but maintains also that *brahman* is still capable of transforming itself into the universe. In this sense, the text never really deals with this anomaly within its own perspective. However, once one adopts the idea of levels of truth, it becomes clear that ultimately Brahman is changeless (as the *Brahma Sūtra* asserts), and the created world must therefore be somehow *less real* than *brahman*. This is the position adopted by Śaṅkara.

Today Śaṅkara is probably the most famous of all Hindu thinkers, though evidence suggests that this was not so during his lifetime nor in the immediate centuries after his death. It is also safe to say that for at least a century, Śaṅkara's commentary on the *Brahma Sūtra* has been the most famous and widely influential philosophical text in India. It is worthwhile spending some time exploring the import of this work, not only for its own sake, but also as an introduction to themes that have preoccupied many Hindu thinkers over the last hundred years.

Śaṅkara's philosophy is known as *advaita-vāda* – the doctrine of non-dualism. On this view reality is literally 'not-two', that is, the appearance of a multiplicity of separate things is an illusion (*māyā*). Only *brahman* is real. The monistic philosophy of Advaita Vedānta provides the philosophical basis for much in the way of modern Hindu theology, influencing a variety of figures from Śrī Aurobindo, Swāmi Vivekānanda, Sarvepalli Radhakrishnan, to Mahātma Gandhi. In the modern era Śaṅkara's philosophy has become a powerful cultural icon in India and a focal point in the development of modern conceptions of Hinduism and Hindu theology (King, 1999: Chapter 6).

Ramana Maharishi (1879–1950), a modern Neo-Vedantic sage, explains the Advaita position rather succinctly. He suggests that Śaṅkara makes three major statements:

1. *Brahman* is real.
2. The universe is unreal.
3. The universe is *brahman*.

The third statement is meant to explain the significance of the first two. This world is unreal *as such*, that is, as the world, but is real in so far as it is seen as non-different from *brahman* – the ground of existence. Clearly Śaṅkara does not wish to imply that the world is *absolutely* unreal in the sense of being without any basis in reality. As he states in his famous commentary on the *Brahma Sūtra,*

> As the space within pots or jars are non-different from the cosmic space or as water in a mirage is non-different from a (sandy) desert ... even so it is to be understood that this diverse phenomenal world of experiences, things experienced, and so on, has *no existence apart from Brahman*.
>
> BS Bh 2.1.14, Gambhirananda, 1977: 327–8 [my italics]

The world cannot be completely unreal then since it is a manifestation of *brahman*. However, at the same time the world is not real in the same sense as *brahman*, that is, from the level of ultimate truth (*paramārtha-satya*), because it is subject to change. Only *brahman* is real in this ultimate sense. Implicitly then, one can talk of three levels: the unreal or delusory (*pratibhāsika*), that which is real on a practical or empirical level (*vyavahārika-sat*) and ultimate reality (*paramārtha-sat*). Delusions, as in seeing a snake where there is really only a rope, are not real. Śaṅkara is adamant that hallucinations and dreams do not correspond to a real world, whereas waking perceptions do. Empirical truth is the validating criterion for deciding if a given experience is a delusion or is truthful. Thus, one shines a light and sees that the snake is in fact a piece of rope, or one wakes up and realises that 'it was all a dream'. We realise that such experiences are false because they are not shared by others and are contradicted by a whole host of later experiences which confirm their delusory status. This is a realisation of what Śaṅkara calls empirical truth (*vyavahārika-satya*). Acceptance of the validity of empirical truth is necessary if one wishes to function effectively in the world and for as long as one conceives of oneself as an ontologically discrete individual self. For Śaṅkara this also requires us to accept the authority of Vedic injunctions:

> So long as the oneness of the true Self is not realized, nobody entertains the idea of the unreality when dealing with the means of knowledge, objects of knowledge and the results; rather, as a matter of fact, all creatures discard their natural one-

> ness with Brahman to accept through ignorance the modifications themselves as 'I and mine' – that is to say, as one's Self or as belonging to oneself. Hence all common human dealings or Vedic observances are logical (and valid) prior to the realization of the identity of the Self and Brahman.
>
> BS Bh 2.1.14, Gambhirananda, 1977: 330

In the Mahāyāna Buddhist traditions empirical or practical truth is known as conventional truth (*saṃvṛti-satya*), being the network of truths established by common consent and mental imputation. Such a characterisation, however, would have been unacceptable to Śaṅkara because it implies that empirical truth is subject to human conventions alone. As a Vedāntin, Śaṅkara took it for granted that the structure of the empirical world was established by *brahman* in its role as the 'Lord' (*īśvara*) or creator of the universe and not by human convention. Theism is not a 'take-it-or-leave-it' option for Śaṅkara. As long as one conceives of oneself as an individual creature one must accept the reality of *īśvara*.

Finally, we have ultimate truth (*paramārtha-satya*). This is reality as it really is, that is, the universe from the perspective of *brahman* – the absolute. Here the world is seen to have no independent reality of its own. Only *brahman* is. According to Śaṅkara it is through our experience of *brahman* and from the words of the Vedas (notably the *Upaniṣads*) that we realise that *brahman* is the sole reality.

The distinction between empirical and ultimate levels of truth allows Śaṅkara to make a distinction between two ways of apprehending *brahman*. As long as one is operating on the level of practical realities (*vyavahārika-satya*) and therefore conceives of oneself as a created and contingent being, one must accept, Śaṅkara maintains, that the world is created by God (*īśvara*). Indeed, from this perspective *brahman* appears to possess various personal qualities (*saguṇa brahman*) and can be approached and appealed to by a devotee (*bhakta*). These qualities (*guṇa)* are not to be confused with the Sāṃkhya notion of the three 'strands' of primordial materiality. For Śaṅkara the qualities denote limiting adjuncts (*upādhi*) that are superimposed onto *brahman* as a result of ignorance. These adjuncts appears to limit or qualify *brahman* but do not actually affect it. Although one might have a limited conception of *brahman* as a personal deity this does not limit *brahman* in itself. Thus, *brahman*, from the point of view of the unenlightened, is a personal Lord, but from the ultimate point of view (*brahman*'s point of view, if you like), *brahman* is beyond all qualification, being ineffable and devoid of any and all limiting qualities (*nirguṇa brahman*).

– CAUSAL THEORY IN ADVAITA –

As we have seen, the *Brahma Sūtra*, like the Sāṃkhya and Yoga schools, upholds a theory of causation known as *satkāryavāda* – the doctrine that the effect pre-exists in the cause, see BS 2.1.7). This provides the basis for its view that the universe is a real manifestation or transformation (*pariṇāma*) of the cause into its effect. Thus, the world exists *in potentia* within its material cause prior to the creative act (BS 2.1.16). Śaṅkara cleverly reworks the view that the effect pre-exists in the cause into a declaration of the sole reality of the cause (*sat-kāraṇa-vāda*). Since the world emerges out of *brahman,* then *brahman* as cause and the world as effect are non-different (*ananya*, BS 2.1.14). In other words, if the effect exists before its manifestation as the cause, it cannot be essentially different from that cause.

Śaṅkara uses a number of analogies to illustrate his interpretation. The relationship between *brahman* and the world is like that between clay and a clay pot, or between gold and a gold earring, or again between space and the space enclosed within a jar. Clay may take on the form of a pot, but it never ceases to be what it always was, namely clay. *Brahman* remains essentially unchanged while it appears as the world just as the clay remains unchanged in its intrinsic nature despite taking on the form of a pot. Moreover, just as the clay pot never ceases to be clay, in the same way the individual self and the empirical world never cease to be *brahman* – it merely appears as if they do.

As we have seen, the scriptural basis of this view can be found at *Chāndogya Upaniṣad* 6.1.4. A clay pot involves the imposition of name and form upon the clay and is merely 'the result of the activity of speech', i.e., is the product of linguistic or conceptual convention. Language creates a web which masks reality as it is. Śaṅkara explains this text in the following manner,

> When a lump of clay is known as nothing but clay in reality, all things made of clay, for instance, pot, plate, jar, etc., become known, since they are non-different as clay, because of which fact it is said 'A modification has speech as its origins and exists only in name' ... But speaking from the standpoint of the basic substance, no modification exists as such (apart from the clay). It has existence only in name and is unreal. As clay alone is it real.
>
> *BS Bh* 2.1.14, Gambhirananda, 1977: 327

The clay pot may break up, that is, the name and form which characterise its status as a pot may end, but the 'clayness' of the pot will always remain. Likewise, birth, decay and death continue, the universe may even cease to exist, but the essential '*brahman*-ness' of the universe will never cease to be. Similarly, the individual self (*jīvātman*) appears to have various limitations like the confined space in a jar. However, if one breaks the jar one realises that the confined space is not separate from space in general and that this indeed has always been the case. Again, the universe is like the foam on top of a wave, though appearing distinct it is in actual fact identical with the seawater all along (BS Bh 2.1.13).

The purpose of these analogies is to suggest that the apparent disparity between the plurality of the universe and the unity of *brahman* is itself a misunderstanding of the (non-different) relationship between appearance and reality. The world is an appearance of *brahman* but has no reality apart from *brahman*. For Śaṅkara and the Advaita Vedānta school there is really no duality whatsoever, the empirical world just happens to be the way that *brahman* appears to an unenlightened individual.

Śaṅkara's *nirguṇa* brahman is often portrayed in rather abstract and dry terms as a static and formless Absolute, devoid of any activity, mutability or indeed any predicable qualities whatsoever. Śaṅkara makes it clear, however, that *brahman* is described as formless (*avikāra*) precisely because it is the cause of all forms (*Taittirīya Upaniṣad Bhāṣya* 2.7). Śaṅkara thereby establishes a dialectical tension between a dynamic and creative personal deity (*saguṇa brahman*/*īśvara*) on the one hand, and an unchanging and ineffable ground of being (*nirguṇa brahman*) on the other, resulting in a fertile and dynamic form of 'dialectical theism' grounded in the conception of two levels of truth.

Śaṅkara's adherence to the non-difference of the effect from its cause and its attendant analogies (gold and gold earring, clay and clay-pot, foam and seawater, space and space-in-jar) avoids the problem of reconciling *nirguṇa brahman* (that is, *brahman* as it is in itself – without qualifying attributes) and *saguṇa brahman* (*brahman* as it appears from the empirical or creaturely perspective – with attributes). This stance allows the Advaitin to argue that monotheistic devotionalism (*bhakti*) is an appropriate manner in which to approach *brahman*. This is a remarkable feat in theological synthesis. This end is achieved by arguing that *brahman* appears to the world as a supreme creator with personal qualities (*īśvara*). *Brahman*, if you like, is like a diamond with a number of facets. *Īśvara* is simply one facet of that diamond, the one turned towards us in so far as we conceive of ourselves as involved in a Creator–creature relationship. Despite the fact that *brahman* in itself is beyond the limitations of 'having qualities', it is not incorrect to see *brahman* as such for this is how *brahman* will appear from the perspective of a creature (empirical self, *jīva*). Devotion (*bhakti*), however, always remains secondary to knowledge (*jñāna*) within Śaṅkara's system, though for later Advaitins such as Madhusūdana Sarasvati (1540–1647), it is the key element in the path to the realisation of the essential unity of *ātman* and *brahman*.

After Śaṅkara there was considerable speculation about the precise ontological status of the universe. The term which came to the fore in this context was *māyā*, usually translated as 'illusion'. The Advaita school argues that *māyā*, the world of many things that we experience, is *anirvacanīya* – inexplicable in terms of existence (*sat*) and non-existence (*asat*). The world is not a complete delusion, because delusions are imagined by the mind, and the world is not the product of the delusions of a single mind (solipsism). Nevertheless, the world is also not an ultimate reality because it is subject to change. Only *brahman* is not subject to change and is thus an ultimate reality.

There has undoubtedly been a Buddhist contribution to the Advaita doctrine of *māyā*, and the term is used to denote the illusory nature of the world in the early Mahāyāna Perfection of Wisdom *sūtras*. The notion, however, is also found much earlier in the *Ṛg Veda* where it denotes the creative 'magic' or power of the gods. When the term is not applied to a Vedic god, *māyā* often denotes one who is cunning and ingenious. *Māyā* is the power or capacity to transform the universe. It is the means whereby the gods transform themselves into various forms, and also into the created universe itself. The important Vedic gods Indra and Agni are described as having many forms, and as such are said to be *māyin* – sorcerers or magicians. Indra in particular is said to be born through *māyā*:

> Of every form and every being, the likeness he has assumed; every form seeks to reveal him. His steeds are yoked, all ten hundred; Indra by his wizardry (*māyā*) travels in many forms.
>
> *Ṛg Veda* VI.47, Olivelle, 1996: 33

It is through the magical or miraculous power of the divinity that the world is created. In Vedānta circles this also became associated with the notion of divine play (*līlā*, see Śaṅkara's commentary on *Brahma Sūtra* 2.1.33). The universe is created through the sportive impulse of *brahman*. Implicitly then, *māyā* is that which 'pulls the wool over our eyes', seeing the universe but failing to see that it is *brahman* at play. Thus, the *Īśa Upaniṣad* states that 'the face of truth is covered with a golden dish' (verse 15). *Brahman* is hidden behind the sun. It has been suggested that the term '*māyā*' derives from the root '*mā*' – to measure (Shastri, 1911: 29). In this sense *māyā* denotes the construction of boundaries and conceptual distinctions (*vikalpa*) in that which has none (*nirvikalpa*). It is a measuring (*mā*) of the immeasurable (*amātra*).

In the Buddhist-influenced *Gauḍapādīya Kārikā* (sixth century CE), a major influence upon Śaṅkara's own thought, *māyā* clearly denotes the illusory nature of the manifold universe:

> Just like a dream, an illusion (*māya*) or a castle in the air,
> is this universe seen by those well-versed in the Vedānta.
>
> *Gauḍapādīya Kārikā* 2.31

Nevertheless, even within this early Advaita text one finds traces of Vedic theism in references to *māyā* as the divine power of *ātman* (2.12; 2.19; 3.10; 3.24). Yet, the world is not real because it is 'merely *māyā*' (1.17; 3.27). The self (*ātman*) deludes itself through *māyā* (2.12). In this sense *māyā* at least has more ontological status than the 'son of a barren woman' (3.28) which cannot even appear. For Gauḍapāda it is through *māyā* that the mind vibrates into the duality of a perceiver and a perceived (3.29). The frequent juxtaposition of *māyā* and 'dream' also alludes to the 'dream-like status of the world' (2.31; 3.10; 4.68–9). Origination can only occur in the conventional world, that is, in the realm of *māyā*, not in reality. However, *māyā* itself does not really exist. Those who see origination are seeing a 'footprint in the sky' (4.28).

The idea that *brahman* is the material cause of creation remained central to later Advaita theorists but was rendered problematic because of the view that *brahman* only *appears* to transform itself into the world. As Gauḍapāda had stressed so firmly before Śaṅkara, creation is only apparent. *Brahman* is immutable and so nothing ever really comes into existence (*ajātivāda*). What then is *brahman* the material cause of? For Śaṅkara only *brahman* (the cause) is truly real. The world is *brahman* as it appears or manifests itself to those conditioned by ignorance. For later Advaita thinkers this was taken to mean that the world could no longer be seen as a real transformation (*pariṇāma*) of *brahman*, but should instead be described as an illusory transformation (*vivarta*). *Brahman* only appears as it does because of the individual's ignorance of the unity of existence.

In making this philosophical move a quite substantial paradigm shift occurred within the Vedānta traditions. In the *Brahma Sūtra*, and some might argue even within Śaṅkara's own account, *brahman* is essentially a dynamic and transformative reality. *Brahman* is that which expands (*bṛh*) to create the universe. As Paul Hacker (1953) has argued, the technical usage of '*vivarta*' to denote an 'illusory transformation' does not occur in Śaṅkara's clearly authenticated works.[6] Subsequent thinkers in the Advaita tradition, however, have used the term in this sense, placing it in direct opposition to the idea of '*pariṇāma*' or 'real transformation'. '*Vi-varta*' then comes to imply a false 'dis-tortion' of Brahman. The world appears as if it is real, but it is really nothing but a distortion, a false apprehension of the undifferentiated unity of *brahman*, like a rope mistaken for a snake. In the works of the later followers of Advaita Vedānta it is clear then that *brahman* is a static and unchanging Absolute. The concept of *māyā*, used by Śaṅkara but sparingly so, was soon pressed into service by later thinkers to establish the connection between *brahman* and an unreal world. In this context *māyā* became not only an inexplicable (*anirvacanīya*) material cause that neither exists nor does not exist but also took on the role of a cosmic power (*śakti*). Similarly, later followers of Śaṅkara, even his immediate disciple Sureśvara, describe ignorance (*avidyā*) as the material cause (*upādāna-kāraṇa*) of the universe.[7] This is clearly not Śaṅkara's view (Rao, 1996). *Brahman* constitutes the basic essence (*svabhāva*) of the universe (BS Bh 3.2.21) and as such the universe cannot be thought of as distinct from it (BS Bh 2.1.14). Similarly, for Śaṅkara ignorance (*avidyā*) is a psychic defilement (*kleśa*) associated with the superimposition of qualities onto *brahman*.

It is clear that the earliest usage of the term '*vivarta*' implied the 'rolling out' or 'unfolding' of creation. Bhartṛhari (fifth century CE) uses the term but does not imply by this that the world is an illusory manifestation of *śabda-brahman*. It does not appear to have implied the illusory nature of the causal process as it does in later Advaita, nor does Bhartṛhari explicitly contrast it with the idea of a 'real transformation' (*pariṇāma*, see Chapter 3). Metaphorically, one might imagine '*vivarta*' as *brahman* 'twirling' or 'twisting' itself around, thereby creating the cyclic whirlpool of *saṃsāra* – the wheel of rebirth – without thereby affecting *brahman*'s own essentially unchangeable nature. The notion of 'unfoldment', of course, does not imply any *essential* change in the thing that is being unfolded (in this case the unfolding of *brahman* at creation). When one unrolls a rug, the rug remains unchanged – it is simply being presented in a different way, that is, flat instead of rolled up. This conforms to Śaṅkara's metaphysical realism and his use of the language of real transformation (*pariṇāma*), grounded as it is in his own distinctive rendering of the *satkāryavāda* theory of causality. Creation is apparent and involves *brahman* manifesting what is essentially already there. Where Śaṅkara's view differs from the realism of the *Brahma Sūtra*, of course, is in his refusal to accept the reality of an effect when viewed as something separate from its cause. The world is real, but only in so far as its existence is seen as totally dependent upon *brahman*.

– RĀMĀNUJA AND NON-DUALISM OF THE QUALIFIED (VIŚIṢṬĀDVAITA VEDĀNTA) –

The *Brahma Sūtra* expounds a position known as 'the doctrine of difference-cum-non-difference' (*bhedābheda-vāda*) in order to explain the relationship between an individual self and *brahman* – the absolute. Each self is non-different (*abheda*) from its cause, being a part (*aṃśa*) of *brahman* (BS 2.3.43). However, the self is not a world-creator (BS 1.1.16) and *brahman* is not subject to suffering or impurity (BS 1.2.8; 2.1.13; 2.3.46). The two therefore remain in some sense distinct (*bheda*). We have already seen that for the *Brahma Sūtra brahman* is essentially partless (BS 2.1.26). How then are we to make sense of the relationship between the part (the individual self) and its apparently partless whole (*brahman*)? The *Sūtra* seems to propound a type of holism reminiscent in some respects of the Nyāya-Vaiśeṣika view that a whole (*avayavin*) is a separate reality over and above its constituent parts (see Chapter 5). *Brahman* is the plenitude (*bhūman*) which transcends the sum of its parts and yet fully inheres within them (3.2.20). As an intelligent, formless principle, it is not subject to spatio-temporal limitations (1.3.10; 3.2.26; 3.2.37; 3.3.33) and cannot, therefore, be literally divided into parts.

A modern analogy might help to explain the *Brahma Sūtra* conception of 'difference-cum-non-difference'. Imagine that *brahman* is a giant cosmic hologram. One feature of a holographic image is its radically 'gestalt' nature. Smash the glass on which the hologram is projected (that is, analyse *brahman* in terms of individual selves) and each fragment will be found to contain the entire holographic image within it. A hologram, like *brahman*, is a seamless whole that cannot be reduced into smaller parts. *Brahman* inheres fully within each individual self, being the receptacle (*āyatana*, 1.3.1) or totality that dwells within and yet transcends the sum of its parts. Just because *brahman* as a partless whole dwells within individual selves (3.2.20) does not mean that the individual self is absolutely identical with *brahman*. This would be like taking a fragment of a plate of glass and saying that it is identical in every way to the larger plate of glass on which the hologram was originally projected. The analogy is not perfect, but it does, I think, illustrate the point.

Śaṅkara's philosophy of non-dualism (*advaita*) involves the radical claim that the individual self is (ultimately) non-different (*bheda*) from *brahman* – the absolute. This requires him to stress that the *Brahma Sūtra* notion of the self as a part of *brahman* is purely metaphorical (BS Bh 2.3.43). The Advaita philosophy, however, came under stringent criticism from Rāmānuja (c. 1056–1137 CE), the central figure in a Vedānta tradition which has since become known as *Viśiṣṭādvaita* or 'Non-dualism of the Qualified'.

Rāmānuja was a Tamil Brahmin initiate of the South Indian Śrī Vaiṣṇava tradition (*saṃpradāya*), that is, the order of priests devoted to the worship of the god Viṣṇu and his consort (*Śrī*). He is said to have been the general manager (*śrīkāryam*) of a Vaiṣṇava temple in Śrīrangam. Rāmānuja was the first great *bhakti* theologian, that is, the first thinker to incorporate devotionalism into mainstream Vedāntic theology. The Śrī Vaiṣṇava tradition was founded by Nāthamuni (traditional dates: 824–924 CE) and is based upon the devotional hymns of the Āḷvārs, a group of twelve Tamil saints devoted to Viṣṇu, living in South India between the sixth and tenth centuries of the Common Era. It is also heavily influenced by the tantric theology and temple ritual of the Pañcarātra, providing a ritual life structured around the idea of the immanent presence of the divine (Viṣṇu) in the icon.

Rāmānuja is said to have been the disciple of Yamunācārya, the grandson of Nāthamuni and a philosopher of the Śrī Vaiṣṇava tradition in his own right. Rāmānuja's philosophical system involved the integration of three key elements: popular devotionalism (*bhakti*) and folklore, the Pañcarātra and what became known as the three foundations (*prasthānatraya*) of the Vedānta traditions, namely the *Upaniṣads*, the *Brahma Sutra* and the *Bhagavad Gītā*.

In the Advaita Vedānta of Śaṅkara knowledge (*jñāna*) is emphasised as the means to achieving liberation. Devotional approaches (*bhakti*) were acceptable but only at a lower level. Not surprisingly, Rāmānuja reacted strongly against this view. Devotionalism represented a strong movement in the South of India and to a certain extent called into question the rigidity of traditional caste divisions. *Bhakti* denotes a deep emotional longing for God and such movements generally stress devotion to God above all else regardless of one's social status. Rāmānuja is an important figure in the process of Sanskritisation or 'Vedānticisation' of these non-Vedic *bhakti* movements, that is, their incorporation into the culture and language of Brahmanical thought. More specifically this involved the articulation and practice of non-Vedic ideas in the language and philosophical categories of the Vedānta traditions. In this regard Rāmānuja attempted to reconcile such devotionalism with the various Vedāntic texts, a task made considerably easier by the inclusion of the *Bhagavad Gītā* as an authoritative Vedāntic text. The *Gītā* had already begun this process of synthesis and emphasised the devotional path (*bhakti-yoga*) as the best means of achieving liberation. We should note, however, that the *Gītā's* conception of *bhakti* is rather different from the emotional longing of the Tamil poets since it involves the cultivation of an attitude of detachment (*niṣkāma*).

Rāmānuja's approach, however, is quite conservative. In the process of Vedānticisation *bhakti* no longer emphasised the casting off of all social inequalities, but required the performance of the various social and religious obligations that are appropriate to one's station in life (*sva-dharma*). For Rāmānuja it was only male members of the twice-born castes who could attain liberation. Others must wait for a suitable rebirth for such an opportunity to arise. The way of *bhakti* then became the path of a select few within society, despite its originally egalitarian aspects. In this manner Rāmānuja made *bhakti* an orthodox Vedāntic approach to religion. This was partially achieved through a monotheistic interpretation of the *Upaniṣads*, providing an ancient basis for *bhakti* and allowing Rāmānuja to identify the god of the devotee (*bhakta*) with *brahman* the supreme principle of the *Upaniṣads*. In this sense, devotional contemplation of Lord Viṣṇu thereby became equivalent to the *Upaniṣadic* notion of liberation (*mokṣa*).

The paths of knowledge (*jñāna*) and action (*karma*) are integrated in Rāmānuja's system in terms of the path of devotion (*bhakti*). In this regard he already has a precedent in the earlier synthesis of these paths in the *Bhagavad Gītā*. The three are not viewed as antithetical approaches in the final analysis and Rāmānuja, in his concern to represent *bhakti* as authentically Vedāntic, describes knowledge of the divine in terms of the experience of devotional contemplation (*upāsana*, *Gītā Bhāṣya* 18.65). In the Pañcarātra context of Rāmānuja's Śrī Vaiṣṇava tradition this denotes the practice of concentrating upon an iconic representation or divine form (*divya rūpa*), understood in this tradition to be an incarnation (*avatāra*) of the divine. Rāmānuja clearly saw such practices as leading to the kind of theophany described in chapter 11 of the *Bhagavad Gītā*.

Liberation, then, depends to a significant degree upon the grace of God, rather than the individual attainment of knowledge, or through ritual performance and the practice of meritorious and selfless deeds. These are, however, important prerequisites on the path and should not be forsaken in the quest for liberation. Rāmānuja regarded self-surrender (*prapatti*) to Viṣṇu to be the first step in *bhakti*. Subsequently, two strands of interpretation developed within the Viśiṣṭādvaita Vedānta tradition after Rāmānuja regarding the nature of the path towards liberation. The southern school (Tenkalai) emphasises the self-surrender aspect to such a degree that liberation was seen as totally dependent upon the grace of Viṣṇu. Aspirants can do nothing except devote themselves totally to the Lord and have faith that they will be liberated by the Supreme Being. The northern school (Vaḍakalai) argues that liberation depended not just on the grace of the deity but also on the performance of meritorious acts. These two schools are often known in terms of the two analogies they use to illustrate their basic point. The southern school expounds the cat-hold theory (*mārjāra-nyāya*). Viṣṇu lifts up beings as a cat picks up a new-born kitten in its mouth and carries it off to safety. Liberation then amounts to a complete self-surrender of oneself to the deity. The northern school upholds the monkey theory (*markaṭa-nyāya*). Viṣṇu carries the devotee but like a baby monkey clinging to its mother, this requires co-operative effort on the part of the aspirant if liberation is to be achieved.

Rāmānuja criticised the doctrines of Advaita Vedānta, in particular the school's philosophy of absolute non-dualism, that is, the view that there is complete identity between the individual self and *brahman* – the absolute. Rāmānuja's position has come to be known as Viśiṣṭādvaita – 'Non-dualism of the Qualified'. The emphasis here is crucial. It is not that non-dualism as such is qualified, as one often finds in accounts of Rāmānuja's thought. In a very real sense Rāmānuja is a non-dualist, but of a specific (*viśeṣa*) kind! As Dasgupta notes (1988, vol. 3: 194) '"Difference" as such has no reality according to Rāmānuja, but only modifies and determines the character of the identical subject to which it refers.' Individual souls and the material world then are distinct forms but are not ontologically separate from *brahman*. Rāmānuja's view, however, is that the reality that is non-dual is qualified by personal characteristics. Consequently, he rejects Śaṅkara's notion of *nirguṇa brahman* – that the absolute lacks qualities or attributes. For Rāmānuja the absolute is a personal creator endowed with superlative attributes (*saguṇa brahman*). Moreover, he rejects the Advaita claim that truth is grasped by the attainment of a non-conceptual awareness (*nirvikalpa jñāna*) of reality. Knowledge is always determinate (*savikalpaka*) in nature.

> Rāmānuja's Vedānta is called the philosophy of the Non-dualism of the Qualified Brahman (Viśiṣṭādvaita). Some writers call it simply Qualified Non-dualism. The term does not mean non-dualism with a proviso, but that Brahman is non-dual and is yet qualified or characterized by the world and the individual spirits, both of which form its body (*śarīra*).
>
> Raju, 1985: 442

Let us explore this view further. For Rāmānuja the difference-non-difference (*bhedābheda*) position, which he associates with Bhāskara (c. eighth century CE), but in actual fact seems to be the position outlined in the *Brahma Sūtra* itself, is inadequate because it implies that an unqualified *brahman* can undergo modification. *Brahman* is the Lord (*īśvara*), a deity endowed with personal qualities. It is this *saguṇa brahman* that undergoes a real transformation (*pariṇāma*) in the creation of individual selves (*jīvātman*) and an insentient world (*jagat*). The creator then is not-different from his creation, but is not an impersonal Absolute as the Advaita tradition contends. How then are we to understand the relationship between *brahman* and the created realm?

The relationship between the individual self (*jīva*) and *brahman* is one of non-difference but not one of *unqualified* identity. There are many individual selves, but only one *brahman* or supreme self (*paramātman*). Likewise, individual selves are not identical to the world (*jagat*), nor is that world identical to *brahman*. Nevertheless, *brahman* really does transform itself into the universe and the multitude of individual selves. Thus, there are three distinct modes (*prakāra*) of existence for Rāmānuja: the plurality of individual selves, the inanimate world in which they are continually reborn and the Supreme Lord of that realm. The relationship between the individual selves and the Supreme Lord is further elaborated by Rāmānuja in terms of the analogy of the relationship of the 'body-embodied relationship' (*śarīra-śarīri-bhāva*).

Rāmānuja's use of the analogy of the body probably reflects the influence of the Pañcarātra upon his thought as much as Vedāntic sources such as the *Puruṣa Sūkta* and the *Bhagavad Gītā*. Infused as Pañcarātra theology and ritual is with the sense of the presence of the divine within the temple icon, Rāmānuja's conception of *brahman* reflects this emphasis upon embodiment. In Vaiṣṇava theology, Viṣṇu has incarnated a number of times, the most famous incarnations (*avatāra*) being Rāma (the hero of the *Rāmāyana*) and Kṛṣṇa (the central figure in the *Bhagavad Gītā*). For Rāmānuja, then, the relationship between *brahman* and the individual selves is the same as the relationship between the individual *ātman* and the body it inhabits. *Brahman* ensouls the universe, and is its inner controller (*antaryāmin*). *Brahman* remains the sole reality, the principle of existence itself, and the individual selves are 'modes' (*prakāra*) of *brahman*, that is, *brahman* in a certain state of being (*avasthā*). In this sense then the self is indeed not-different from *brahman*.

It would be a mistake, however, contends Rāmānuja, to equate the individual self with *brahman* in an unqualified manner as the Advaita school does, because the individual self is only an aspect or a mode of *brahman*. It would be like identifying oneself with a particular part of one's body. In some sense that bodily part is you but it would wrong to see this relationship in terms of unqualified identity. I am not my arm, though my arm can be said to be part of what constitutes me. Together all of the individual selves constitute the subtle body of *brahman*, while after creation, these same selves inhabit gross bodies which together make up the universe, that is, the gross physical body of *brahman*. Everything is *brahman* but there is a distinction nevertheless between 'me' as a molecule of *brahman*'s body, and *brahman* as pure being itself. Similarly, Rāmānuja explains that the relationship between *brahman* and individual selves is akin to that between a substance and its various qualities (for example, *Śrī Bhāṣya* on BS 3.2.28).

The inanimate world (*jagat*) into which beings reincarnate is also a product of the creative act of *brahman*. The creation of the inanimate universe is simply the acquiring of name and form (*nāma–rūpa*). This could not have occurred if the individual selves had not been 'ensouled' by *brahman*. The universe then is the body of *brahman*. In this way, Rāmānuja brilliantly integrates the notion of a personal creator with ancient Vedic myths such the Hymn to the Cosmic Man (*Puruṣa Sūkta*, *Ṛg Veda* X.90), where the universe originates from and derives its specific qualities from the Cosmic Person.

Creation for Rāmānuja, then, is seen as the transformation (*pariṇāma*) of *brahman*'s body from the subtle (*sūkṣma*) to the gross (*sthūla*) level of manifestation. This does not thereby affect *brahman* in its own intrinsic form (*svarūpa*). When *brahman* and its body exists in a subtle form it is known as in 'the causal state' (*kāraṇāvasthā*). The creation of the universe, however, involves *brahman* transforming itself into a manifested form, known as 'the effect state' (*kāryāvasthā*). All of this, however, essentially remains *brahman*. As Dasgupta notes,

> [Rāmānuja] is no doubt a *sat-kārya-vādin*, but his *sat-kārya-vāda* is more on the Sāṃkhya line than on that of the Vedānta as interpreted by Śaṅkara. The effect is only a changed state of the cause, and so the manifested world of matter and souls forming the body of God is regarded as effect only because previous to such a manifestation of these as effect they existed in a subtler and finer form. But the differentiation of the parts of God as matter and soul always existed, and there is no part of Him which is truer or more ultimate than this.
>
> Dasgupta, 1988, vol. 3: 200

Not surprisingly, Rāmānuja criticises the illusionism (*māyā-vāda*) that he sees as characteristic of the Śaṅkarite Advaita school. This position is rejected on a number of grounds. Firstly, Rāmānuja suggests that the Advaitin is a crypto-Buddhist (*pracchana bauddha*) in his use of the notion of *māyā* and the doctrine of two truths to deny the reality of the world. In contrast, Rāmānuja notes, one should understand *māyā* in its more positive (and earlier) Vedic usage as that which denotes the wonderful effects and manifestation of *prakṛti* (*Śrī Bhāṣya* 1.1.1). Moreover, if the appearance of the world is the result of ignorance (*avidyā*), where is this to be located? *Brahman* cannot be deluded, but neither can the empirical self (*jīva*) because on Advaita grounds such a being does not really exist. Rāmānuja was also suspicious of the paradoxes that seemed to result from the Advaitic doctrine that the world is indeterminable (*anirvacanīya*) as either existent of non-existent. Either the world is real or it is not. Again, Rāmānuja rejects Śaṅkara's absolutist view that only the cause really exists (*satkāraṇavāda*). The effect may be impermanent (*anitya*), but this does not mean that it does not really exist as Śaṅkara contends. The doctrine of levels of truth, on this view, is little more than an expedient device for having one's cake and eating it.

For Rāmānuja the individual selves are real 'modes' (*prakāra*) of *brahman* and are affected by their own actions, intentions and desires and are reincarnated accordingly. *Brahman*, however, remains essentially partless and is unaffected by *karma* and impurities. In this regard Rāmānuja is merely following the position outlined in the *Brahma Sūtra*. *Brahman* abides (*sthiti*) within the created world and assimilates experiences (*adanāmyām*: literally 'eats', BS 1.3.7). The apparent imperfections and injustices (*vaiṣamya*) of the world, however, are not attributable to *brahman* since they are dependent upon the actions (*prayatna*) of individual selves (2.1.34; 2.3.42). Karmic residues caused by actions performed by individual selves (*jīvātman*) in previous creations provide the structural basis for the creation of the universe, which is envisaged in the *Brahma Sūtra* as a process for the working out of each individual's karmic residue. The objection that the individual selves cannot be responsible for their conditions since they did not exist before creation is dismissed by the *Sūtra* on the grounds that *saṃsāra* is beginningless (BS 2.1.35–6).

As to the reason behind the creative act, this is also already explained in the *Brahma Sūtra* as an expression of *brahman*'s playfulness (BS 2.1.33). *Brahman* has all of its desires fulfilled (BS 2.1.22) and so creates for the fun of it. The notion of play (*līlā*) is an important theological theme and has been particularly emphasised in the Vaiṣṇava traditions. Most notably in those traditions which focus upon Kṛṣṇa as a child, the notion of god as a playful being is expounded to full effect. Śaṅkara, like Rāmānuja, accepted the *līlā* motif as a way of explaining the rationale behind the act of creation. *Brahman* has all of its desires fulfilled. In a very real sense, then, there is no reason or motivation behind the creation of the universe (BS 2.1.32). The universe is *brahman* at play! The real question, however, is 'how real is the game?'

– NOTES –

1. See Vijñānabhikṣu's *Sāṃkhya Pravacana Bhāṣya* V.12, cited in Hulin, 1978: 157 and Larson and Bhattacharya (eds), 1987: 378.
2. Note, however, that Gerald Larson (1979: 278) reports the existence of a modern school of Sāṃkhya in Madhupur (Bihar).
3. It has been suggested that Patañjali is here providing an argument for the existence of God (e.g. Hiriyanna, 1996: 125), similar in some respects to the 'argument from perfection' put forward by Descartes (1596–1650). It is more likely, however, that reference to the omniscience of the deity is a veiled rebuke of the Buddhist claim that the Buddha is an omniscient being. Omniscience can only be a quality belonging to the supreme Lord, and if the Buddha is omniscient he cannot really be the Buddha, but must be the Supreme Lord. This would have been unacceptable to the Buddhist, for whom the notion of a supreme deity is inappropriate.
4. Madhva (thirteenth century CE) as a monotheistic proponent of the dualist philosophy (Dvaita Vedānta) agrees that *brahman* is the creator (efficient cause) of the universe, but rejects the idea that *brahman* is also that out of which the universe is made (the material cause). Individual selves are different from each other and from the material world (*jagat*) which is a manifestation of insentient primordial matter (*prakṛti*).

5. Buddhist and Jain texts suggest that the early Vedānta traditions resembled the Sāṃkhya school in a number of significant respects, using the term '*puruṣa*' to denote the self and utilising a theory of three *guṇas* (Nakamura, 1985: 146; 154).
6. Śaṅkara uses the term '*vivartate*' and related compounds only twice in his commentary on the *Brahma Sūtra* (BS Bh 1.3.39; 2.2.1, though the latter is a disputed reading) and once in his commentary on *Taittirīya Upaniṣad* 1.6. Each time the term is used to imply this sense of 'unfolding' or 'rolling out' and it does not have a particularly illusionistic connotation. See also Mayeda, 1973: 40.
7. Maṇḍana Miśra conceives of ignorance in terms of two aspects: occluding (*ācchādika*) and projective (*vikṣepika*). The former denotes ignorance as a result of non-apprehension, whilst the latter denotes false apprehension. Occluding ignorance (not-knowing) provides the causal basis for projective ignorance (false apprehension). For Maṇḍana the question of 'whose ignorance is it?' is answered firmly in favour of the empirical self (*jīva*). Brahman cannot possess ignorance but the individual self can.

CHAPTER 10

Philosophy in a Post-Colonial World

– POSTMODERNISM, ETHNOCENTRICITY AND WESTERN PHILOSOPHY –

There is an apocryphal story about a Philosophy department in the USA, which, in an attempt to improve its status within the academic institution, decided to re-name itself the Department of Conceptual Engineering. One aspect of contemporary western culture which this story reflects is the relative disparity between the level of authority invested in the respective spheres of philosophy and scientific technology in the modern west. Semantic ploys notwithstanding, there have been an increasing number of thinkers who have suggested that philosophy needs reconstructing or 'revisioning' in the contemporary context. Strikingly, much of the critique of contemporary philosophy has focused upon the attempt to model philosophical investigation on the natural sciences. Some of the most important work in this area has been carried out by feminist and post-structuralist thinkers who have reflected upon the epistemological foundations of contemporary western perspectives and approaches. With regard to the question of the future of philosophy as a substantive discipline, there have been a number of variant and discordant voices ranging from a complacent rejection of the need for such reappraisal on the one hand, to pessimistic indictments of the future of the subject on the other.

Modern western conceptions of philosophy have often been characterised as a series of attempts to define the discipline of philosophy in terms of the natural science paradigm furnished by Enlightenment scientific rationalism. Contemporary post-structuralists such as Hans Georg Gadamer and Michel Foucault have questioned the foundationalism of the Enlightenment orientation which emphasises objectivity and absolute truth as the only worthwhile goals in the pursuit of knowledge. One contemporary philosopher who remains particularly critical of this aspect of Enlightenment thought is the neo-pragmatist Richard Rorty. Rorty provides a diagnosis of the contemporary malaise in western philosophy in his book *Philosophy and the Mirror of Nature* (1979). The central thesis of this work is that western philosophy, at least since the seventeenth century, has been seduced by the metaphor of the mind which 'mirrors' the world. This has led philosophers to conceive of themselves as an elite for whom there is a direct correspondence between the philosophical theories which they expound and reality as it actually is. Consequently, philosophers have become infatuated with the search for absolute truth, a search which Rorty suggests is ultimately futile.

Rorty himself propounds a thoroughgoing pragmatism, which he aligns with the American pragmatism of John Dewey and William James. He argues that philosophers should repudiate all attempts to discern the nature of 'Truth' and come to terms with the implications of historicism, namely that the views and attitudes which one holds are conditioned by the socio-historical and cultural environment in which one lives. Rorty proposes an end to philosophy as it has been practised in the past. In the post-philosophical culture which Rorty endorses, philosophers would relinquish their goal of attaining an accurate representation of 'the way things are' in favour of "edifying discourse". Thus, it is not so much that Rorty provides new answers to the traditional questions of philosophy but rather that he wants to ask new questions. When critics of Rorty ask him what he thinks truth is from his pragmatist perspective, Rorty's response has usually been to suggest that the nature of the question itself is part of the problem and that it would be more fruitful to change the subject. This tactic is seen as evasive by Rorty's opponents but it is consistent with his own position which is that, given the impossibility of attaining an absolute foundation for one's own beliefs, one should judge philosophical views on purely pragmatic grounds.

In his later works, Rorty has further elaborated upon this position. Everyone, he points out, has a "final vocabulary", that is, 'a set of words which they employ to justify their actions, their beliefs and their lives.' (Rorty, 1989a: 73f) These are a reflection of our most deeply seated beliefs and prejudices, to which no recourse to noncircular argumentation can be made. This, ultimately then, is where we stand. However, given the realisation of the contingency of culture, history and belief-systems, Rorty argues that one can only be ironical about such "final vocabularies". Ironists, according to Rorty, have radical doubts about the appropriateness of their own final vocabularies, are impressed by the vocabularies of others and realise that their own vocabularies are no closer to reality than any other. Consequently, 'The ironist spends her time worrying about the possibility that she has been initiated into the wrong tribe, taught to play the wrong language games'

(Rorty, 1989a: 75). Rorty does not believe that this situation should be interpreted in negativistic and nihilistic terms, and in one sense the ironist's insight is liberative precisely because it enables the philosopher to dismiss the old epistemological and ontological questions which have 'dogged' philosophy for centuries in favour of becoming an "informed dilettante". In such a situation it is not so much that philosophy ceases to be a meaningful pursuit as it is to be pursued for the purposes of edification rather than foundational knowledge. Rorty's "edifying philosophers" are thinkers such as James and Dewey, Heidegger, Gadamer, Derrida and Foucault, all of whom repudiate, in their own individual manners, the search for absolute truth. Philosophy as a discipline, then, can continue in this new environment but the purpose of debate is no longer the establishment of foundational and universal truths, but rather merely to keep the conversation going! (Rorty, 1979: 373)[1]

Despite this postmodernist emphasis upon the displacement of the values, hierarchies and dichotomies of Enlightenment thought, and the replacement of monopolies with a heterogeneity of local discourses, there is an ethnocentric narrowness to postmodernist narratives which stems from their origins within the élite intellectual circles of modern, western capitalist democracies. Feminists have also criticised postmodernism as a movement for its blindness to issues of gender and sexual inequality, but the debate as it has ensued is also decidedly Eurocentric in scope (a criticism which extends to much in the way of contemporary feminist thought). In other words, in so far as postmodernist and feminist critiques are constructed in agreement with or in dialectical opposition to the prevailing Enlightenment, modernist or patriarchal paradigms, they remain fundamentally bound to the object of their intended attack, whether that be the 'modernity project', patriarchy or western culture in general. One might very well ask, for instance, what the debate between 'Enlightenment' and 'Counter-Enlightenment' perspectives has to say to the cultures of the non-western world. What does postmodernism, for instance, have to offer other than a rejection of the possibility of meta-narratives at precisely the point in history when the non-western world is attempting to construct its own legitimating meta-discourses in response to the hegemony imposed by western colonialism? This is a point which is often made by feminist writers such as Nancy Hartsock, who argues that women, like colonised people, have been marginalised by patriarchal discourses and that postmodernist narratives, in their denial of foundational knowledge, subvert any attempt by the marginalised to establish 'a vision of the world in which we are at the center rather than at the periphery' (Hartsock, 1987: 201). Thus, Rorty's notion of a post-philosophical culture that participates in philosophical discussion merely to 'keep the conversation going' will simply not suffice as a basis for the establishment of a marginalised perspective.

What is needed, therefore, is an approach which takes into account the postmodernist critique of Enlightenment and the colonial discourses perpetuated by it, whilst at the same time constructing a cultural space based upon indigenous insights and orientations from the non-western world which is not easily assimilable by western culture, in either its modernist or postmodernist incarnations. Thus, what I am suggesting is that the Enlightenment and postmodernism be neither wholly embraced nor wholly repudiated, but that something akin to "postwesternism" be developed, that is, an approach which takes into account the changing formation of international politics, globalisation and inter-cultural dialogue, and which is overtly motivated towards facilitating a postcolonial 'inter-culturalism' with the goal of an end to the political, economic and philosophical hegemony of the western world. In a Foucauldian sense one could conceive of this as the construction of new *epistēmēs* in the silent spaces or gaps to be found in the hegemonic discourses of the present. In such a situation one could be said to be motivated by a vision of the twenty-first century as an era which would be globally 'postwestern' rather than Eurocentrically 'postmodern'. Examining and engaging with Indian cultural traditions is one of many important elements within such a process.

Richard Rorty, in rejecting an absolute, foundational or universal principle of rationality, argues that an individual can (and in fact must) appeal to the foundations provided by a common history, culture and tradition. This has been widely condemned by a number of critics as implicitly ethnocentric.[2] Rorty points to the historically conditioned nature of philosophy in the west, arguing that it is the result of particular social and political preoccupations in the west and the culturally specific nature of the departmental structure of western universities. Consequently, to attempt to compare Indian thought with western philosophy is to distort the former by attempting to fit it into a conceptual framework based upon criteria deriving from the particularity of the latter. Thus, Rorty says,

> It is perfectly reasonable to ask, without condescension and in honest bewilderment … 'Is There Philosophy in Asia?' For this is not the question 'Is Asia intellectually mature?' but the question 'have Asians had any of the needs which have led Western universities to teach Seneca, Ockham, Hume, and Husserl in the same department?'
>
> Rorty, 1989b: 333

This way of framing the question, however, already presupposes that 'philosophy' is confined to the corridors of academia. Such a narrowly conceived notion of 'philosophy' of course is hardly likely to find any evidence of its existence further afield. We might just as well define lunch as eating a Big Mac and then point out that this activity does not occur amongst vegetarian brahmins! Perhaps in time, given the influence of large multinational corporations, even this will change!

Nevertheless, Rorty goes on to suggest that the notion of a rigorous discipline called "comparative philosophy" is also dubious because of the impossibility of finding a neutral, cultural space in which such an activity could take place. 'There is no skyhook,' Rorty argues, 'which will lift us out of this parochialism' (Rorty, 1989b: 334). However, as we noted in Chapter 2, the distinction between a variety of cognitive disciplines has also been made in the Indian context (indeed, it pre-dates the European creation of academic departments of philosophy which does not seem to go back further than the twelfth century CE). Whilst Rorty is correct to point out that there is no neutral cultural ground upon which a cross-cultural philosophical debate could proceed, this in itself should not prevent us from attempting to engage with the thought processes of another culture. Indeed, given that the Indian context provides us with cognitive distinctions of its own, one could equally well conceive of an approach which presupposed Indian categories and looked for the existence of *ānvīkṣikī* in western culture, rather than attempting to search for European-style philosophy in the east.

John Clayton (1992: 26) has suggested that the Indian *vāda*-tradition might serve as a useful model for contemporary philosophical debate since it combines 'public contestability and respect for particularity and difference' within a decidedly pluralistic context. One of the more interesting features of the *vāda*-tradition of Indian philosophical debate was that it provided a public forum for the exploration of divergent views based upon contestability and a recognition of the positionality of its participants. As Clayton has suggested, this provides a model for interaction and philosophical debate amongst divergent groups that is not limited by some spurious search for neutrality. Furthermore, the end-product of such *vāda* debates was not to achieve some kind of consensus or universal agreement amongst its participants. Rarely would either side have expected to convince the other of the truth of their own position. One of the central aims of the *vāda* debates was to articulate, in a philosophically precise manner, the reasons why a position was held. Crucially, this usually included tradition-specific reasons as well as more widely accepted considerations. Debate, therefore, was not grounded in unanimity or neutrality but on the clarification of differences between the various *darśanas* based upon the principle of contestability and philosophical accountability. In this sense, Clayton suggests, such debates demonstrate the sense in which rationality is always constructed within particular contexts and traditions whilst acknowledging that through mutual interaction and contestation, such traditions become answerable to a broader constitutive-rationality.

> Philosophical contests were thus tradition-*constituting*. By means of debate rationality constructed itself. But the conduct of public debates was also tradition-*constituted*, in the sense that reasons could be given for one's own school, even when they were not also reasons for members of the opponent's school.
>
> Clayton, 1992: 29

The problems of understanding the other in discussing philosophy in a cross-cultural context are, of course, much greater than those encountered by the interaction of Indian *darśanas* in ancient India. As scholars such as Gadamer remind us, all interpretations of Indian thought will inevitably involve an assimilation or submission of those materials to the 'host' culture of the interpreter (a point noted, without its political consequences, by the philosopher Donald Davidson).[3] However, to repudiate 'comparative philosophy' because one cannot reach the absolutist heights of neutrality, or, in a Foucauldian sense, because one cannot disentangle one's analysis from 'discourses of power', is to remain deeply conservative and implicated in the existing power structures of predominating discourses, interpretations and approaches.

Raimundo Panikkar (1988) has described an approach which takes these limitations into account as *imparative* rather than comparative, since it involves a dialogical openness to other world-views, an acceptance of the provisional nature of one's own position and a willingness to be transformed by the encounter. Most importantly, such an approach accepts that there is no 'objective, neutral and transcendent vantage point' from which to compare philosophies, without accepting that this entails the rejection of the cross-cultural enterprise as flawed from its inception.

Another problem for Rorty's isolationist position is that there is no homogeneous 'western culture' nor any universally accepted definition of philosophy even amongst western philosophers. Indeed, the heterogeneity and unfinished nature of western culture is a point which has been made by Rorty himself (see above). Thus, it is as problematic to cite Seneca, Hume and Heidegger as examples of philosophers as it would be to include Nāgārjuna and Śaṅkara (Mohanty, 1992: 237). The lack of a culturally neutral ground for philosophical discussion to proceed is an issue which is equally applicable to the interpretation of Western thought by other westerners and has not prevented Professor Rorty from discussing the philosophical merits of ancient and modern western philosophers, despite their widely disparate languages, world-views, orientations, cultural presuppositions and perspectives. Accepting Gadamer's insight that all interpretation involves prejudices and imaginative recontextualisation, as Rorty does, suggests that issues related to interpretation within one's own cultural tradition and those related to interpretation between cultures are differences of degree and not of kind.

Rorty's ethnocentric isolationism stems from a failure to appreciate the hermeneutical openness which is implied by the realisation that neither the individual nor the particular culture to which she belongs has any fixed self-identity or essence (a 'postmodernist' position which Rorty endorses). The unfinished, ungrounded and hence the interactive potential of Rorty's 'ironism' is expressed well by postmodern theologian Don Cupitt who describes the ironist position in the following terms,

> There are many vocabularies, and some of them seem to work as well as mine. I don't see any truly independent criteria by which to judge that mine is the best one, or the truth. Anyway I have found that my own final vocabulary develops as my life goes by. My beliefs and I are fluid, changing things. I don't have a fixed position or a fixed identity. I am an ironist in that I am both firmly committed to my own final vocabulary, for in it I define my very self, and yet at the same time I am also uncommitted, because my final vocabulary and I are always open to revision and change.
>
> Cupitt, 1990: 14–15

Interestingly, Cupitt's rejection of a fixed position reflects the influence of the Buddhist thinker Nāgārjuna upon his thought rather than American neo-pragmatism, but it is certainly the case that Rorty's ironism, when combined with his rejection of the unity of western culture and his claim that "the western project" remains unfinished, suggests a position which does not sit easily with an isolationist position.

– THE POLITICS OF TRANSLATION –

Much of the debate about the viability of cross-cultural comparison has focused upon what has often been called 'the problem of cultural relativism'. The fear of relativism, however, is rooted in a robust conception of knowledge modelled on the scientist as a detached and neutral observer in possession of a universally applicable, trans-cultural and objective truth. This has become a central theme of post-Enlightenment epistemological thought. By ignoring, or at least under-emphasising, the 'historical situatedness' of knowledge and rationality and the iniquitous power-relations that undergird western claims to a universal rationality, it has become possible in the modern era to describe the possessor of such knowledge in the language of neutrality, universality and objectivity. Equally, through the exaltation of the autonomy of the individual in modern, liberal society, the role of tradition and culture in formulating a person's beliefs, attitudes and actions has become obscured.

> Implicit in the well-advertised fear of 'relativism' is the extraordinary thought that the cultural life of human beings is the product of conscious criticism and objective choice. It is extraordinary because, although arguments are clearly important in different social situations, the reasons for a person's attachment to a given way of life, or conversion to another, cannot be reduced to an idealized model of scientific theory building.
>
> Asad, 1993: 235

The furore over relativism has continued unabated in the academic fields of philosophy and anthropology in particular and has recently been renewed with the advent of 'postmodernist' thought. However, the issue of cultural relativism is – in my view – something of a red herring. Cultures do in fact interact, even if one accepts the specificity of their historical contexts. Indeed, it is because of the intrinsic involvement of cultures in the web of historical change that they are constantly undergoing transformation through internal differentiation and cross-cultural interaction.

> [T]he supposed 'indeterminacy of translation' need not usher in claims of relativism or nihilism. Cross-cultural studies ... do not have to choose between such polarities ... meaningful and truthful information can cross cultural boundaries even if that information is necessarily limited, not comprehensive and not the Truth.
>
> Shaner, 1989: 41

In any case, as Talal Asad has suggested, a far more interesting question is how this process of interaction and cultural translation operates. In particular, what needs to be addressed is the issue of 'how power enters into the process of cultural translation' (Asad, 1993: 198). Thus, as Richard Burghart points out,

> The different commitments of translators raise questions about what is translatable in a text and what texts are untranslatable. Such controversies underscore the fact that – despite one's intentions – a translation is not a neutral activity. Consensus arises only where there is prior agreement on the purpose of translation. The translations carried out by spokesmen for Hinduism may be rather different from those of observers of Hinduism.
>
> Burghart, 1989: 217

Perhaps the greatest obstacle to the translation of Indian thought into western vernacular languages is what Asad has described as the inequality of languages:

> To put it crudely, because the languages of third world societies, ... are seen as weaker in relation to Western languages (and today, especially to English), they

> are more likely to submit to forcible transformation in the translation process than the other way around.
>
> Asad, 1993: 190

Thus, when a western academic translates classical Indian texts into western cultural idioms and languages, the text is transformed not only linguistically but also in terms of the interests, rules and modes of life of the translator and her audience. The audience 'is waiting to read about another mode of life and to manipulate the text it reads according to established rules, not to learn to live a new way of life' (Asad, 1993:193). Asad remains critical of the western expert who, in a manner reminiscent of the relationship between analysts and analysand, creates and authorises meanings for the subject, claiming that they are implicit or unrecognised by that subject. The claim to be able to discern the 'real intentions' or meanings of a foreign text, person or event, is an attempt to privilege the academic discourse above all others. Often, however, the 'insights' which the expert puts forward do not sit easily with the explanations given by the people he or she is claiming to examine. In particular, what Asad has in mind here is 'the sociologism according to which religious ideologies are said to get their real meaning from the political or economic structure' (Asad, 1993: 199).

As a general methodological principle of translation Asad suggests that the interpreter should seek to convey the nature and structure of an alien discourse within the translation. Thus, interpretations or translations which are too anglicised (for example), tend to obscure and subordinate differences. This is an important point to bear in mind in the light of our previous discussion. Gadamer reminds us that all interpretation involves prejudices. In this sense, all western translations of India thought will inevitably involve some degree of westernisation, if only because of the nature of the interpretive act and because of the absence of any neutral cultural or linguistic space upon which such a translation could be objectively grounded. However, this does not prevent us from attempting to minimise the consequences of this, firstly by bringing one's own prejudices to the fore as much as is possible, and secondly by 'yielding' to the horizons of the text as much as possible. In this sense we should allow the text to retain what Asad calls 'a discomforting – even scandalous – presence within the received language' (Asad, 1993: 199). Thus, translation should attempt to expand and transform the received language by retaining some of the 'discomforting' foreignness of the original. The result, of course, is a sense of rupture and discontinuity in the translated western product, but this is necessary if one is to minimise the westernising impact that results from the disparity of power between Indian and western languages and cultures.

– STUCK BETWEEN A ROCK AND A HARD PLACE: ENTERING THE WESTERN PHILOSOPHICAL ARENA –

Modern western cultural presuppositions and interests clearly exhibit a hegemonic status in the contemporary world. In contrast, Indian approaches are largely marginalised in the 'global' arena. There are, however, clearly a number of other factors which militate against the interaction of western and Indian thought. One problem is the ongoing tendency to dichotomise and reify the distinction between 'East' and 'West' (what Edward Said describes as 'the Orientalist mind-set'). The essentialist attachment to these notions restricts the possibilities of interaction. Moreover, labels such as "Indian philosophy" actually contribute to the marginalisation process by defining a diverse group of philosophical traditions in terms of a contemporary geo-political category. India is not a 'first world' nation, it is not, to use a sporting metaphor, in the "Premier League" of international politics. However, because of this it is all too easy to assume that Indian culture is also an unimportant and relatively minor enclave in the history of philosophy.

A second problem is Specialisation-itis. This is an affliction that the modern western academic is particularly susceptible to. It manifests itself in the tendency to view "Indian philosophy" as an obscure sub-discipline or minor chapter in the history of philosophy (if at all). Thus, even in Philosophy departments where courses on Indian thought are offered the subject remains marginalised by the degree of emphasis placed upon the cultural and geographical specificity, that is, the peculiar "Indianness" of 'Indian philosophy'. The outline of a typical curriculum might contain courses in epistemology, philosophy of science, philosophy of religion and Indian philosophy. However, placing Indian thought within a philosophy curriculum as an isolated and self-contained subject perpetuates the marginalisation of the subject matter in a new form, implying as it does that Indian philosophical works do not contain insights that are relevant to the various sub-disciplines of western philosophy. This is perhaps inevitable to some extent within the university structure given the increasing specialisation of academic research. However, as Robert Bernasconi argues,

> One cannot understand why there has never been a serious debate about the origin of philosophy, unless one understands what is at stake in the question ... [Even] if the history of the discipline and the conception of the discipline that history supports was not racist in design, the question must still be addressed as to whether it has not become racist in its effects. Whole peoples experience themselves as excluded, in part because of the systematic diminishment of the achievements of their group. Philosophers almost everywhere are implicated. The

> problem must be addressed not just in research, but also at the institutional level in each and every department.
>
> Bernasconi, 1997: 224–5

James Ogilvy has also suggested that professional philosophers, in accepting their modern role within the secular institution, have abdicated the responsibility to discuss the fundamental questions about the meaning of life. This is clearly not just a reflection of contemporary scepticism about such issues but reflects changes in the structure of higher education in the western world, where the professional benefits of specialisation are greatly emphasised.

> Academic deans are responsible for awarding promotions, but they are not usually students of philosophy. Because they need clear proof of incremental progress in an assistant professor's chosen field, there are far more rewards for finite steps than for valiant attempts to grapple with the infinite and ineffable. Better to build a career by figuring out how adverbs work than by seeking something so elusive as wisdom.
>
> Ogilvy, 1992: xv

A further problem in attempts to open up philosophical debate to a cross-cultural context is what I would call 'gatecrasher's syndrome' or the problem of 'going to the party uninvited'. Some liberal-minded western philosophers might take the view that non-western thought should not be excluded from philosophy and that Indian materials (for example) ought to be included in contemporary debates. However, joining the debate means entering a philosophical arena that has already been established according to the hegemonic presuppositions and preoccupations of modern western philosophy. However, one might legitimately ask who is the real "gatecrasher" in this context? Is it the philosopher of "Indian thought" looking for a way into philosophical debates or is it the westerner who has exported, through a history of colonialism, violence and political hegemony, a discourse which claims to be universal but in fact is suspiciously European in its presuppositions and orientation? In any case, in the process whereby 'westernisation' becomes indistinguishable from 'modernisation', it would appear that the Indian philosopher's invitation to the party has been lost in the post!

This brings up a crucial question for those interested in the thought processes of marginalised cultures. Should the "colonised" (in this case Indian thought) attend the party if they are only to be treated as servants to a dominant Eurocentric agenda? Should the Indian philosopher (or the African or the Chinese philosopher for that matter) join the party if they are to be left carrying the drinks tray rather than being welcomed as equal participants in the merry-making? This is the question with which all those involved in the study of non-European modes of thought must wrestle. Should one allow the marginalised to remain as such, or should one endeavour to facilitate an awareness of non-western thought amongst western philosophers?

The answer, I suspect, is that despite the inherent dangers one must eventually take the plunge. The problems facing positive engagement between western and non-western modes of thought, however, are many. Some of these, one might argue, are endemic to the powerful institutional structures of the university system which, in the distinctions that they make, reinforce old Eurocentric prejudices and stereotypes. Let us consider some of these problems.

If one is going to be fair and balanced in approaching Indian philosophical ideas it is important that they are understood in context. It is far too easy to abstract specific arguments and to treat them as if they are statements by a contemporary western philosopher engaged in the same debate as oneself. Thus, a proper engagement with Indian philosophical ideas requires some understanding and knowledge of the cultural forms and context of that world-view. This, of course, militates against the involvement of academics for a number of professional reasons. Firstly, there is the increasing pressure upon academics to produce qualitatively and quantitatively substantial research publications. Particularly in these days of budget-watching and belt-tightening and the gradual (and sometimes not so gradual) superimposition of a consumerist model of education onto university institutional structures (resulting in a commodification of knowledge), there is a limit on the amount of time available to produce quality research. In a situation of increasing academic specialisation, who is going to have the time to immerse herself in the culture of another <u>and</u> engage with her own?

That is not all. Once attempts are made to understand and then engage with the thought forms of another culture one is immediately confronted by the methodological and hermeneutical problems of cross-cultural analysis. However, confronting these issues is inevitable if one is ever to transcend the limiting confines of Eurocentric discourse. *Prima facie* this would seem to be of major concern to the philosophical 'lover of wisdom', particularly in an increasingly multi-cultural environment. Indeed, it is precisely the discipline of philosophy, often portrayed as the pursuit of knowledge for its own sake, which should be at the forefront of attempts to extend the frontiers of conceptual thought to their utmost limit.

A further problem for the professional academic philosopher is one of peer disapproval. All human beings (even philosophers) are subject to social, institutional and professional pressures. "Indian philosophy" is not fashionable in western academic circles (one reason for this being the overwhelmingly secular orientation of western academia since the Enlightenment). Consequently, displaying an interest in such 'arcane' areas is likely to lead to accusations of "strangeness" and subtle (if not more explicit) forms of ostracism. Such interests are also less likely to gain a high degree of financial, moral and institutional support, though this is a predicament that the modern professional philosopher already knows quite well.

Nevertheless, one should not despair! Professional constraints such as these may deter the majority of academic philosophers from a systematic engagement with non-European modes of thought, but this does not prevent specialisation in these areas by individual philosophers. Outside the university, of course, there is no shortage of groups already engaging, synthesising and interacting with "eastern philosophy", though the results often lacks intellectual rigour, methodological sophistication and a proper consideration for the integrity of such ideas and practices in their original context. In the institution of the university, however, one is frequently confronted by a number of professional obstacles to attempts to engage in cross-cultural philosophy. The real issue here is the refusal of the majority of philosophy departments in western universities to validate such specialisations both in the work of current professional philosophers and in the appointment of new staff. At some level this may stem from a fear that such work threatens the 'integrity' of the discipline. Certainly, such cross-cultural work, if taken seriously, will undermine the post-Enlightenment claim to universalism. As Raimundo Panikkar has argued,

> [C]rosscultural studies do not mean to study other cultures, but to let other cultures impregnate the very study of the problem which by this very fact has already been transformed. In this sense a crosscultural Philosophy does not study other philosophies but changes the very perception of what philosophy is.
>
> Panikkar, 1992: 236

Whilst it is clear that overcoming the pitfalls of cultural isolationism and facilitating a proper engagement with non-western thought involves a redrawing of disciplinary boundaries and a 'revisioning' of philosophy, the question of what is to be jettisoned in this process of course is still up for grabs. Fears that such approaches will undermine "the Enlightenment project" mistakenly fall into the trap of postulating an essentialist and homogeneous trajectory to western philosophy which only functions to suppress the heterogeneity of human expression. Accepting the historicity of all cultural patterns of thought need not lead to the much feared anarchy of relativism if one accepts one's historical situatedness as a starting point for interaction between cultures.

– CONCLUSION –

The exclusion of non-European modes of thought from "philosophy" reflects a Eurocentric conception of the category. However, the famous line from Rudyard Kipling's *Ballad of the East and West* that 'East is East and West is West and never the twain shall meet' has been comprehensively overturned by events since the nineteenth century. As we move into the twenty-first century the old binary division between 'East' and 'West' is proving less and less appropriate as a description of the way things are. It is no longer acceptable to hide behind Kipling's remark and suggest that 'this is our cultural tradition and we don't have time to consider yours' as suggested, for instance, by Richard Rorty who is at least one of the few contemporary philosophers to have considered the issue of the relevance of non-western thought, however cursory his analysis. The cultural isolationism prevalent in the work of most western philosophers not only reifies the concept of "culture" (as if "European" and "Indian" cultures are static entities that do not change, develop or interact with one another), but also masks the implicit ethnocentricity of such approaches, viz. the view that non-western "philosophies" are inferior and tangential to the concerns of the modern western philosopher. Indeed, if we place Kipling's famous phrase in context, we should note that he too is hopeful of a way beyond the impasse.

> Oh, East is East and West is West,
> and never the Twain shall meet,
> Till Earth and Sky stand presently
> at God's great Judgement Seat;
> But there is neither East nor West,
> Border nor Breed, nor Birth,
> When two strong men stand face to face, tho'
> they come from the ends of the earth!

The irony of this verse is that the cultures of East and West, here portrayed as strong men, do not stand face to face on an equal footing as Kipling proposes. This is precisely the point that I have been trying to make. It is precisely because of the political disparity between western and non-western nations in the modern era that western philosophers must develop a much greater awareness of the ideological and ethnocentric dimensions of their own thought processes. Karl Marx's epitaph famously attacks philosophers for describing the world rather than attempting to change it. It is my contention that the practice of philosophy should be one which endeavours to transform political circumstances. If one believes, as I do, that an attempt should be made to overturn the colonial parochialism and hegemonic domination of one culture, nation or movement over another, then engagement with the theoretical perspectives of the non-western world is an absolute necessity if philosophy as a discipline is to cease to be the handmaiden of western colonialism.

Such an approach not only makes a contribution to the pushing back of colonial frontiers and ideologies but also participates in the expansion of philosophical debate into a wider cultural arena. In effect, I suppose I am arguing that western philosophers must come to terms with the fact that they are no longer living in the nineteenth century where the belief in the cultural supremacy of Europe was enthusiastically derived from its apparent political and technological superiority.[4] Such hubris is no longer appropriate in a post-colonial world. To hold onto such beliefs is to participate in a neo-colonial agenda which further contributes to the marginalisation of non-European culture. It is often said that we live today in a globalised, pluralistic and multi-cultural society. Shouldn't the way we practice philosophy reflect that?

– NOTES –

1. Rorty's critics have focused upon the ethical and political relativism of his position, suggesting that the final implication of such a thoroughgoing rejection of foundational principles is fascism. Rorty, of course, repudiates such interpretations of his work, arguing that, on pragmatic grounds, modern, liberal democracies are to be favoured over totalitarian regimes. In his later work (for example, Rorty, 1989a), Rorty suggests that recourse can be made to ideals of group solidarity as a way of safeguarding liberalism.
2. In a recent article Richard Rorty (1992b) outlines what he considers to be three meanings of the terms 'rationality' and 'culture' which are often confused. Rationality$_1$ refers to an organism's ability to cope with its environment and survive (which Rorty describes as "technical reason"); rationality$_2$ is the name given to a specifically human ability to establish an evaluative hierarchy rather than merely to fulfil the requirements for basic survival, and rationality$_3$ denotes tolerance, that is 'a reliance upon persuasion rather than force, an inclination to talk things over rather than to fight' (Rorty, 1992b: 581). With regard to 'culture', culture$_1$ denotes the shared values, habits and perspectives of a specific community, culture$_2$ refers to the specific virtues of "high culture" (*belles lettres*), i.e. the abstract reflections and highly literate expressions of an intellectual elite. Finally, culture$_3$ is that which is to be contrasted with nature and is thus claimed to be a specific result of the human possession of rationality$_2$. Rorty suggests that ethnocentrism occurs whenever there is an equation of culture$_1$ (the values and world-views of a specific community) with culture$_3$ (the exercise of rationality$_2$ and the successful overcoming of the natural world). As a pragmatist Rorty wishes to repudiate the notion of rationality$_2$. However, he maintains that a specific example of culture$_1$, namely the perspectives and approaches of the western world, can be said to exhibit a greater degree of rationality$_1$ (the ability to adapt and survive) and rationality$_3$ (tolerance) and in so far as this claim is made Rorty's position can be criticised for being explicitly ethnocentric. Rorty maintains that western culture has proved itself to be technologically superior (and thus presumably superior in

its use of rationality$_1$), and also superior in the degree of tolerance which it exhibits (rationality$_3$). The latter, Rorty suggests, is a consequence of the secularism of modern western culture. However, the claim that secular rationality leads to a greater tolerance of perspectives requires a more detailed and sensitive analysis of diverse cultures than Rorty has been prepared to venture.

3. Donald Davidson (1977: 244–54) argues that our general method of interpretation makes it impossible to discover if others have radically different conceptual schemes to our own since we can only refer to our own scheme. For Davidson, 'those who can understand one another's speech must share a view of the world, whether or not that view is correct.' However, he continues, 'Successful communication proves the existence of a shared, and largely true, view of the world.' The version of the paper which I am referring to is reprinted in Baynes, Bohman and McCarthy (eds, 1987: 167–8).
4. Though even the commonly held thesis that European culture was technologically superior to Indian and Chinese culture can be seriously questioned. Claude Alvares (1991) has suggested, for instance, that the technological supremacy of Europe from the sixteenth century onwards involved the appropriation and/or suppression of indigenous technological advancements in both India and China.

Bibliography of Cited Works

Ahearne, Jeremy (1995), *Michel de Certeau. Interpretation and its Other*, Cambridge: Polity Press.

Alvares, Claude (1991), *Decolonizing History. Technology and Culture in India, China and the West 1492 to the present day*, Goa, India: The Other India Press, and New York: Apex Press.

Anacker, Stefan (1975), 'The Abhidharma-piṭaka', in Charles S. Prebish (ed.), *Buddhism. A Modern Perspective*, University Park and London: Pennsylvania University Press, pp. 59–64.

Asad, Talal (1993), *Genealogies of Religion*, London: Johns Hopkins University Press.

Babb, Lawrence (1981), 'Glancing: visual interaction in Hinduism', *Journal of Anthropological Research* 37: 387–401.

Barlingay, S. S. (1975), *A Modern Introduction to Indian Logic*, Delhi: National.

Bernal, Martin (1987), *Black Athena. The Afroasiatic Roots of Classical Civilisation*, London: Free Association Books.

Bernasconi, Robert (1997), 'Philosophy's Paradoxical Parochialism: The Reinvention of Philosophy as Greek', in Keith Ansell-Pearson, Benita Parry and Judith Squires (eds), *Cultural Readings of Imperialism. Edward Said and the Gravity of History*, London: Lawrence and Wishart, pp. 212–26.

Bhattacharya, K., E. H. Johnston and A. Kunst (1990), *The Dialectical Method of Nāgārjuna. Vigrahavyāvartanī*, Delhi: Motilal Banarsidass, third edition.

Burghart, Richard (1989), 'Something Lost, Something Gained: Translations of Hinduism', in G. D. Sontheimer and H. Kulku (eds), *Hinduism Reconsidered*, Delhi: Manohar.

Chakrabarty, Dipesh (1992), 'Postcoloniality and the artifice of history: who speaks for Indian pasts?' in *Representations* 37: 1–26.

Chattopadhyaya, D. (1968), *Lokāyata: A Study in Ancient Indian Materialism*, New Delhi: People's Publishing House, first published in 1959.

Chemparathy, George (1972), *An Indian Rational Theology. Introduction to Udayana's Nyāyakusumāñjali*, Leiden: E. J. Brill; Vienna: Gerold and Co.; Delhi: Motilal Banarsidass.

Chennakesavan, Sarasvati (1980), *The Concept of Mind in Indian Philosophy*, Delhi: Motilal Banarsidass.

Clayton, John (1992), *Thomas Jefferson and the Study of Religion*, inaugural lecture delivered at the University of Lancaster, England on Wednesday, 18 November 1992.

Collins, Steven (1982), *Selfless Persons. Imagery and Thought in Theravāda Buddhism*, Cambridge and New York: Cambridge University Press.

Conze, Edward (1962), *Buddhist Thought in India: Three Phases of Buddhist Philosophy*, London: Allen and Unwin.

Conze, Edward (1978), *The Prajñāpāramitā Literature*, Tokyo: The Reiyukai, second edition.

Coward, Harold and K. K. Raja (1990), *The Philosophy of the Grammarians*, Encyclopaedia of Indian Philosophies, vol. V, Princeton: Princeton University Press.

Cupitt, Don (1990), *Creation Out of Nothing*, London: SCM Press.

Dasgupta, Surendranath (1924), *Yoga as Philosophy and Religion*, Calcutta: University of Calcutta.

Dasgupta, Surendranath (1988), *A History of Indian Philosophy*, vol. 1–5, Delhi: Motilal Banarsidass. Originally published in 1922, first Indian edition 1975.

Davidson, Donald (1977), 'The Method of Truth in Metaphysics', in *Midwest Studies in Philosophy II*, pp. 244–54, reprinted in K. Baynes, J. Bohman and T. McCarthy (eds) (1987), *After Philosophy. End or Transformation?* Cambridge, Mass. and London: Massachusetts Institute of Technology.

Deleuze, Gilles and Félix Guattari (1994), *What is Philosophy?* translated by Graham Burchell and Hugh Tomlinson, London: Verso.

Dowling, Thomas (1976), *Vasubandhu on the Avijñapti-Rūpa: A Study in Fifth-Century Abhidharma Buddhism* (unpublished Ph.D. thesis, Columbia University).

Dreyfus, George (1997), *Recognising Reality. Dharmakīrti's Philosophy and its Tibetan Interpretations*, Albany NY: State University of New York Press.

Eliade, Mircea (1973), *Yoga. Immortality and Freedom*, Princeton, Princeton University Press.

Fabian, Johannes (1983), *Time and the Other: How Anthropology Makes its Object*, New York: Columbia University Press.

Feuerstein, Georg (1971), 'The Essence of Yoga' in Feuerstein and Miller (eds), *A Reappraisal of Yoga. Essays in Indian Philosophy*, London: Rider and Company: 1–47.

Feuerstein, Georg (1979), *The Yoga Sūtras of Patañjali. A New Translation and Commentary*, Kent: Dawson and Sons Ltd.

Feuerstein, Georg (1980), *The Philosophy of Classical Yoga*, Manchester: Manchester University Press.

Flew, Anthony (1971), *An Introduction to Western Philosophy*, London: Thames and Hudson.

Franco, Eli (1983), 'Studies in the *Tattvopaplavasiṁha* I: the criterion of truth', *Journal of Indian Philosophy* 11: 147–66.
Frauwallner, Erich (1973), *History of Indian Philosophy Vol. I and II*, reprinted 1993, Delhi: Motilal Banarsidass.
Gambhirananda, Swami (1977), *The Brahma Sūtra Bhāṣya of Śrī Śaṅkarācārya* (English translation), Calcutta: Advaita Ashrama.
Ganeri, Jonardon (1996), 'The Hindu Syllogism: 19th Century Perceptions of Indian Logical Thought', *Philosophy East and West* 46.1: 1–16.
Gangopadhyaya, Mrinalkanti (1976), *Nyāya Philosophy. A Literal Translation of Gautama's* Nyāya-Sūtra *and Vātsyāyana's* Bhāṣya*, along with a free and abridged translation of the Elucidation by Mahāmahopādhyāya Phaṇibhūṣaṇa Tarkavāgīśa*, 5 vols, Calcutta: Indian Studies Past and Present, R. K. Maitra.
Gautama (Gotama), *The Nyāya Sūtras*, translated by S. C. Vidyabhusan, Sacred Books of the Hindus, Allahabad, 1930. Reprinted in 1990, Delhi: Motilal Banarsidass.
Gethin, Rupert (1998), *The Foundations of Buddhism*, Oxford and New York: Oxford University Press.
Granoff, Phyllis (1978), *Philosophy and Argument in Late Vedānta* (containing a partial translation of Śrīharṣa's *Khaṇḍanakhaṇḍakhādya*), Dordrecht: D. Reidel.
Griffiths, Paul (1986), *On Being Mindless. Buddhist Meditation and the Mind–Body Problem*, La Salle, Illinois: Open Court.
Gupta, Akhil (1992), 'The reincarnation of souls and the rebirth of commodities: representations of time in "East" and "West", *Cultural Critique* 22: 187–211.
Gupta, Akhil and James Ferguson (1992), 'Beyond "culture": space, identity, and the politics of difference', in *Cultural Anthropology* 17.1: 6–23.
Gupta, Bina (1991), *Perceiving in Advaita Vedānta*, London and Toronto: Associated University Press.
Habermas, Jurgen (1970), *Towards a Rational Society*, Boston: Beacon Press.
Hacker, Paul (1953), *Vivarta. Studien zur Geschichte der illusionistischen Kosmologie und Erkenntnistheorie der Inder*, Mainz: Verlag der Akademie der Wissenschaften und der Literatur.
Hacker, Paul (1958), 'Ānvīkṣikī', *Wiener Zeitschrift für die Kunde Süd-und Ostasiens* 2: 54–83.
Hacker, Paul (1964), 'On Śaṅkara and Advaitism', in Wilhelm Halbfass (1995, ed.), *Philosophy and Confrontation. Paul Hacker on Traditional and Modern Vedānta*, Albany: State University of New York Press, pp. 27–32.
Halbfass, Wilhelm (1988), *India and Europe. An Essay In Understanding*, Albany: State University of New York Press.
Halbfass, Wilhelm (1992), *On Being and What There Is. Classical Vaiśeṣika and the History of Indian Ontology*, Albany: State University of New York Press.
Halbfass, Wilhelm (1995, ed.), *Philosophy and Confrontation. Paul Hacker on Traditional and Modern Vedānta,* Albany: State University of New York Press.
Harris, Ian (1991), *The Continuity of Madhyamaka and Yogācāra in Indian Mahāyāna Buddhism*, Leiden: E. J. Brill.

Hartsock, Nancy (1987), 'Re-thinking modernism: minority vs. majority theories', *Cultural Critique* 7.

Hatab, Lawrence J. (1990), *Myth and Philosophy. A Contest of Truths*, La Salle, Illinois: Open Court.

Hattori, Masaaki (1968), *Dignāga, On Perception*, Cambridge, Mass.: Harvard University Press.

Heesterman, J. C. (1968–9), 'On the origin of the Nāstika', *Wiener Zeitschrift für die Kunde Süd-und Ostasiens* 12/13: 171–85.

Heidegger, Martin (1956), *What is Philosophy?*, London: Vision Press.

Hicks, R. D. (1972), *Lives of Eminent Philosophers by Diogenes Laertius*, vol. 1, Cambridge, Mass.: Harvard University Press.

Hiriyanna, M. (1996), *Essentials of Indian Philosophy*, London: Diamond Books, originally published in 1949 by George Allen and Unwin.

Howard, Don (1996), 'The History That We Are: Philosophy as Discipline and the Multiculturalism Debate', in Anindita Balslev (ed.), *Cross-Cultural Conversation (Initiation)*, American Academy of Religion, Atlanta: Scholars Press, pp. 43–76.

Hulin, Michel (1978), *Sāṃkhya Literature*. A History of Indian Literature, vol. VI, Fasc. 3, Wiesbaden: Otto Harrassowitz.

Huntington, C. W. (1989), *The Emptiness of Emptiness. An Introduction to Early Indian Mādhyamika*, Honolulu: University of Hawaii Press.

Husserl, Edmund (1970), *The Crisis of European Sciences and Transcendental Phenomenology,* The Vienna Lectures of 1935, translated by David Carr, Evanston, Ill.: North-Western University Press.

Inden, Ronald (1990), *Imagining India*, Oxford: Basil Blackwell.

Ingalls, Daniel (1952), *Materials for the Study of Navya-Nyāya Logic*, Harvard Oriental Series, Cambridge, Mass.: Harvard University Press.

Iyer, Subramania K. A. (1965), The *Vākyapadīya of Bhartṛhari and its Vṛtti*, Poona: Deccan College Monograph.

Iyer, Subramania K. A. (1969), *Bhartṛhari: A Study of the Vākyapadīya*, Poona: Deccan College Monograph 68.

Jackson, David P. (1987), *The Entrance Gate for the Wise (Section III). Sa-Skya Paṇḍita On Indian and Tibetan traditions of Pramāṇa and Philosophical Debate*, vol. 1, Wien: Universität Wien.

Jacobi, H. (1911), 'Zur Frühgeschichte der indischen Philosophie', reprinted in L. Schmithausen (1978, ed.), *Kleine Schriften* II, Glasenapp-Stiftung 15: 547–58.

Jacobsen, Knut A. (1996), 'The Female Pole of the Godhead in Tantrism and the *Prakṛti* of Sāṃkhya', *Numen* 43: 56–81.

Johnston, William (1994), *The Bhagavad Gītā*, Oxford: Oxford University Press.

Kaplan, Stephen (1987), *Hermeneutics, Holography and Indian Idealism*, Delhi: Motilal Banarsidass.

Keenan, John P. (1989), *The Meaning of Christ. A Mahayana Theology*, Mary Knoll, NY: Orbis Books.

King, Richard (1994), 'Early Yogācāra and its relationship with the Madhyamaka School', *Philosophy East and West* 44, No. 4: 659–86.

King, Richard (1995), *Early Advaita Vedānta and Buddhism*, Albany: State University of New York Press.

King, Richard (1998), '*Vijñaptimātratā* and the Abhidharma Context of Early Yogācāra', *Asian Philosophy* 8.1: 5–17.

King, Richard (1999), *Orientalism and Religion. Post-Colonial Theory, India and "the Mystic East"*, London and New York: Routledge.

Kochumottum, Thomas (1982), *A Buddhist Philosophy of Experience: A New Translation and Interpretation of the Works of Vasubandhu the Yogācārin*, Delhi: Motilal Banarsidass.

Krishna, Daya (1991), *Indian Philosophy: A Counter Perspective*, Delhi, Oxford and New York: Oxford University Press.

Lang, Karen (1986), *Āryadeva's Catuḥśataka: On the Bodhisattva's Cultivation of Merit and Knowledge*, Indiste Studier 7, Copenhagen: Akademisk Forlag.

Larson, Gerald (1979), *Classical Sāṃkhya. An Interpretation of Its History and Meaning*, Santa Barbara: Ross/Erikson, second edition.

Larson, Gerald (1993), 'Āyurveda and the Hindu philosophical systems', in Kasulis, Ames and Dissanayake (eds), *Self as Body in Asian Theory and Practice*, Albany: State University of New York Press, pp. 103–21.

Larson, Gerald and Ram Shankar Bhattacharya (1987, eds), *Encyclopaedia of Indian Philosophies Volume IV: Sāṃkhya. A Dualist Tradition in Indian Philosophy*, Delhi: Motilal Banarsidass.

Lindtner, Christian (1982), *Nāgārjuniana*, Delhi: Motilal Banarsidass.

Long, Elizabeth (1992), 'Textual Interpretation as Collective Action', in Jonathan Boyarin (ed.), *The Ethnography of Reading*, Berkeley: University of California Press.

Mādhava, Acharya (1996), *Sarvadarśanasaṃgraha*, translation by E. B. Cowell and A. E. Gough, Delhi: Motilal Banarsidass.

Mainkar, T. G. (1972), *Sāṃkhya Kārikā of Īśvarakṛṣṇa with Gauḍapāda Bhāṣya*, Poona: Oriental Book Agency, second revised and enlarged edition.

Matilal, Bimal Krishna (1968), *The Navya-Nyāya Doctrine of Negation*, Harvard Oriental Series, Cambridge, Mass.: Harvard University Press.

Matilal, Bimal Krishna (1971), *Epistemology, Logic and Grammar in Indian Philosophical Analysis*, The Hague and Paris: Mouton.

Matilal, Bimal Krishna (1977), *Nyāya-Vaiśeṣika*. A History of Indian Literature, vol. VI, Wiesbaden: Otto Harrassowitz.

Matilal, Bimal Krishna (1985), *Logic, Language and Reality. An Introduction to Indian Philosophical Studies*, Delhi: Motilal Banarsidass.

Matilal, Bimal Krishna (1986), *Perception. An Essay on Classical Indian Theories of Knowledge*, Oxford and New York: Oxford University Press.

Mayeda, Sengaku (1973), *Śaṅkara's Upadeśasāhasrī*, Tokyo: Hokuseido Press.

Mayeda, Sengaku (1992), *A Thousand Teachings. The Upadeśasāhasrī of Śaṅkara*, Albany: State University of New York Press. Originally published in 1979,

Tokyo: University of Tokyo Press.

Mohanty, J. N. (1992), *Reason and Tradition in Indian Thought. An Essay on the Nature of Indian Philosophical Thinking*, Oxford: Clarendon Press.

Murti, T. R. V. (1955), *The Central Philosophy of Buddhism: A Study of the Mādhyamika System*, London: Allen and Unwin.

Nagao, Gadjin (1989), *The Foundational Standpoint of Mādhyamika Philosophy*. Translated by John P. Keenan, Albany: State University of New York Press.

Nakamura, Hajime (1985), *A History of Early Vedānta Philosophy, Vol. I*, Delhi: Motilal Banarsidass.

Nakamura, Hajime (1989), 'The Meaning of the Terms "Philosophy" and "Religion" in Various Traditions', in Gerald Larson and Eliot Deutsch (eds), *Interpreting Across Boundaries: New Essays in Comparative Philosophy*, Delhi: Motilal Banarsidass, pp. 137–51.

Nandy, Ashis (1983), *The Intimate Enemy. Loss and Recovery of Self under Colonialism*, Delhi: Oxford University Press.

Nightingale, Andrea Wilson (1995), *Genres in Dialogue. Plato and the Construct of Philosophy*, Cambridge: Cambridge University Press.

Nye, Andrea (1990), *Words of Power. A Feminist Reading of the History of Logic*, London and New York: Routledge.

O'Flaherty, Wendy Doniger (1981), *The Rig Veda*, Harmondsworth: Penguin Classic.

Ogilvy, James (1992), 'The Need For Revisioning Philosophy', in James Ogilvy (ed.), *Revisioning Philosophy*, Albany: State University of New York Press.

Olivelle, Patrick (1996), *The Upaniṣads*, Oxford: Oxford University Press.

Ong, Walter (1982), *Orality and Literacy: The Technologizing of the Word*, London and New York: Methuen.

Panikkar, Raimundo (1988), 'What is Comparative Philosophy Comparing?', in Larson and Deutsch (eds), *Interpreting Across Boundaries. New Essays in Comparative Philosophy*, Delhi: Motilal Banarsidass, pp. 116–36.

Panikkar, Raimundo (1992), 'A Nonary of Priorities', in James Ogilvy (ed.), *Revisioning Philosophy*, Albany: State University of New York.

Parrott, Rodney J. (1986), 'The problem of the Sāṃkhya tattvas as both cosmic and psychological phenomena', *Journal of Indian Philosophy* 14: 55–77.

Pesala, Bhikkhu (1991), *The Debate of King Milinda. An Abridgement of the Milindapañha*, Delhi: Motilal Banarsidass.

Phillips, Stephen H., (1985), 'The conflict of voluntarism and dualism in the *Yoga Sūtra*', *Journal of Indian Philosophy* 13: 399–414.

Potter, Karl H. (1957), *Translation and Commentary on Raghunātha's* Padārthatattvanirūpana, Cambridge: Harvard-Yenching.

Potter, Karl H. (1963), *Presuppositions of India's Philosophies*, Englewood Cliffs, N.J.: Prentice Hall, Inc. Indian Edition, 1991, Delhi: Motilal Banarsidass.

Potter, Karl H. (1977, ed.), *Indian Metaphysics and Epistemology: The Tradition of Nyāya-Vaiśeṣika up to Gaṅgeśa*, Princeton: Princeton University Press. Indian Edition, Delhi: Motilal Banarsidass.

Potter, Karl H. (1981, ed.), *Advaita Vedānta up to Śaṃkara and His Pupils*. Encyclopaedia of Indian Philosophies, vol. III, Delhi: Motilal Banarsidass.

Puligandla, Ramakrishna (1997), *Fundamentals of Indian Philosophy*, New Delhi: D. K. Printword (P) Ltd. Originally published in 1975.

Qvarnström, Olle (1989), *Hindu Philosophy in Buddhist Perspective. The Vedāntatattvaviniścaya Chapter of Bhavya's* Madhyamakahṛdayakārikā, Lund: Plus Ultra.

Radhakrishnan, S. and C. Moore (1957), *A Sourcebook in Indian Philosophy*, Princeton: Princeton University Press.

Raju, P. T. (1985), *Structural Depths of Indian Thought*, New Delhi: South Asian Publishers.

Ram-Prasad, C. (1993), 'Knowledge and the "Real World": Śrī Harṣa and the *Pramāṇas*', *Journal of Indian Philosophy* 21: 169–203.

Rao, Srinivasa (1996), 'Two "myths" in Advaita', *Journal of Indian Philosophy* 24: 265–79.

Robinson, Richard H. (1967), *Early Mādhyamika in India and China*, Delhi: Motilal Banarsidass.

Rorty, Richard (1979), *Philosophy and the Mirror of Nature*, Princeton: Princeton University Press.

Rorty, Richard (1984), 'The historiography of philosophy: four genres', in Rorty, Schneewind and Skinner (eds), *Philosophy in History*, Cambridge: Cambridge University Press.

Rorty, Richard (1989a), *Contingency, Irony and Solidarity*, Cambridge: Cambridge University Press.

Rorty, Richard (1989b), 'Review of Gerald J. Larson and Eliot Deutsch (1988), *Interpreting Across Boundaries: New Essays in Comparative Philosophy*', in *Philosophy East and West* 39.

Rorty, Richard (1992a), 'Philosophers, Novelists and Intercultural Comparisons: Heidegger, Kundera, and Dickens', in Eliot Deutsch (ed.), *Culture and Modernity: East–West Perspectives*, Honolulu: University of Hawaii Press.

Rorty, Richard (1992b), 'A pragmatist view of rationality and cultural difference', *Philosophy East and West* 42, No. 4.

Ruegg, David Seyfort (1981), *The Literature of the Madhyamaka School of Philosophy in India*. A History of Indian Literature, vol. VII, Wiesbaden: Otto Harrassowitz.

Ruegg, David Seyfort (1986), 'Does the Mādhyamika have a Thesis and Philosophical Position?' in Matilal and Evans (eds), *Buddhist Logic and Epistemology*, Dordrecht: Reidel.

Russell, Bertrand (1940), *An Inquiry into Meaning and Truth*, London: Allen and Unwin, reprinted 1962, Harmondsworth: Pelican Books.

Russell, Bertrand (1982), *The Problems of Philosophy*, Oxford: Oxford University Press, first published in 1912.

Said, Edward (1978), *Orientalism. Western Conceptions of the Orient*, London: Routledge and Kegan Paul.

Sastri, Gaurinath (1959), *The Philosophy of Word and Meaning*, Calcutta: Calcutta Sanskrit College Research Series.

Serequeberhan, Tsenay (1991), 'African Philosophy: The Point in Question', in Serequeberhan (ed.), *African Philosophy. The Essential Readings*, New York: Paragon.

Shaner, David Edward (1989), 'Science and Comparative Philosophy', in D. Shaner, S. Nagatomo and Y. Yasuo (eds), *Science and Comparative Philosophy. Introducing Yuasa Yasuo*, Leiden: E. J. Brill.

Shastri, Dharmendra Nath (1964), *Critique of Indian Realism: A Study of the Conflict between the Nyāya-Vaiśeṣika and the Buddhist Dignāga School*, Agra: Agra University. Reprinted in 1976 as *The Philosophy of Nyāya-Vaiśeṣika and its Conflict with the Buddhist Dignāga School*, Delhi: Bharatiya Vidya Prakashan.

Shastri, Prabhu Dutt (1911), *The Doctrine of Māyā*, London: Luzacs and Co.

Shils, E. (1961), *The Intellectual between Tradition and Modernity: The Indian Situation*, The Hague: Mouton and Co.

Siderits, Mark (1989), 'Thinking on Empty: Madhyamaka Anti-Realism and Canons of Rationality', in S. Biderman and B. Scharfstein (eds), *Rationality in Question. On Eastern and Western Views of Rationality*, Leiden and New York: E. J. Brill, pp. 231–49.

Siderits, Mark (1997), 'Matilal on Nāgārjuna', in P. Bilimoria and J. N. Mohanty (eds), *Relativism, Suffering and Beyond. Essays in Honour of Bimal K. Matilal*, Delhi: Oxford University Press, pp. 69–92.

Singer, Milton (1971), 'Beyond Tradition and Modernity in Madras', in *Comparative Studies in Society and History* 13.

Sinha, Jadunath (1958, 1961, 1969), *Indian Psychology*, 3 vols, Delhi: Motilal Banarsidass.

Sinha, M. (1995), *Colonial Masculinity. The 'manly Englishman' and the 'effeminate Bengali' in the late nineteenth century*, Manchester: Manchester University Press.

Smart, Ninian (1968), *The Yogi and the Devotee*, London: George Allen and Unwin.

Solomon, Esther (1976–8), *Indian Dialectics: Methods of Philosophical Discussion*, 2 vols, Ahmedabad: Institute of Learning and Research, Gujarat Vidya Sabha.

Streng, Frederick (1967), *Emptiness. A Study in Religious Meaning*, Nashville: Abingdon Press.

Sutton, F. G. (1991), *Existence and Enlightenment in the Laṅkāvatāra Sūtra*, Albany: State University of New York Press.

Takeuchi, Shoko (1977), 'Phenomena and Reality in Vijñaptimātra Thought (I)', in Leslie Kawamura and Keith Scott (eds), *Buddhist Thought and Asian Civilisation. Essays in Honour of Herbert V. Guenther on his sixtieth birthday*, Emeryville, California: Dharma Publishing, pp. 254–67.

Tatya, Tookaram (1972), *The Haṭha Yoga Pradīpikā of Svātmārāma*, translation by Srinivasa Iyangar, Adyar: The Adyar Library and Research Centre.

Temple, Sir William (1970), *Essays on Ancient and Modern Learning and On*

Poetry, edited by J. E. Spingarn, Oxford: Oxford University Press. Originally published in 1690.

Thapar, Romila (1993), *Interpreting Early India*, Oxford: Oxford University Press Paperbacks.

Thrasher, Allen Wright (1993), *The Advaita Vedānta of the Brahma Siddhi*, Delhi: Motilal Banarsidass.

Udayana (1950), *Nyāyakusumāñjali*. Edited with various commentaries by Padmaprasadopadhyaya, Benares: Kashi Sanskrit Series.

Ueda, Yoshifumi (1967), 'Two main streams of thought in Yogacara philosophy', *Philosophy East and West* 17: 155–65.

Viyagappa, Ignatius (1980), *G. W. F. Hegel's Concept of Indian Philosophy*, Rome: Universitá Gregoriana.

Warder, A. K. (1973), 'Was Nāgārjuna a Mahayanist?' in M. Sprung (ed.), *The Problem of Two Truths In Buddhism and Vedānta*, Dordrecht: Reidel.

Wayman, Alex (1965), 'Review of *The Yogācāra Idealism*', *Philosophy East and West* 15 (1): 65–73.

Wezler, A. (1974), 'Some Observations on the *Yuktidīpikā*', *Wiener Zeitschrift Deutscher Morgenlandischen Gesellschaft,* Supplement II: 434–55.

Whicher, Ian (1995), 'Cessation and integration in classical Yoga', *Asian Philosophy* 5 (1): 47–58.

Whicher, Ian (1997), 'Nirodha, Yoga Praxis and the Transformation of the Mind', *Journal of Indian Philosophy* 25: 1–67.

Whicher, Ian (1998), *The Integrity of the Yoga Darśana. A Reconsideration of Classical Yoga,* Albany: State University of New York Press.

Woods, James Haughton (1914), *The Yoga-System of Patañjali*, Cambridge: Harvard Oriental Series. Reprinted 1983, Delhi: Motilal Banarsidass.

Index and Glossary of Important Sanskrit Terms

CPSIA information can be obtained at www.ICGtesting.com
Printed in the USA
BVOW031056190613

323722BV00002B/685/A

9 780878 407569